A CULTURAL HISTORY OF WORK

Volume 3

A Cultural History of Work (6 vols.)

Winner of the 2020 PROSE Award for Multivolume Reference/Humanities

A Cultural History of Work
General Editors: Deborah Simonton and Anne Montenach

Volume 1
A Cultural History of Work in Antiquity
Edited by Ephraim Lytle

Volume 2
A Cultural History of Work in the Medieval Age
Edited by Valerie L. Garver

Volume 3
A Cultural History of Work in the Early Modern Age
Edited by Bert De Munck and Thomas Max Safley

Volume 4
A Cultural History of Work in the Age of Enlightenment
Edited by Deborah Simonton and Anne Montenach

Volume 5
A Cultural History of Work in the Age of Empire
Edited by Victoria E. Thompson

Volume 6
A Cultural History of Work in the Modern Age
Edited by Daniel J. Walkowitz

A CULTURAL HISTORY OF WORK

IN THE EARLY MODERN AGE

Edited by Bert De Munck and Thomas Max Safley

BLOOMSBURY ACADEMIC
LONDON • NEW YORK • OXFORD • NEW DELHI • SYDNEY

BLOOMSBURY ACADEMIC
Bloomsbury Publishing Plc
50 Bedford Square, London, WC1B 3DP, UK
1385 Broadway, New York, NY 10018, USA
29 Earlsfort Terrace, Dublin 2, Ireland

BLOOMSBURY and the Diana logo are trademarks of Bloomsbury Publishing Plc

First published in Great Britain 2018
This edition published in Great Britain, 2021

Copyright © Bloomsbury Publishing, 2018

Bert De Munck and Thomas Max Safley has asserted their right under the Copyright, Designs and Patents Act, 1988, to be identified as Editor of this work.

Cover image © MCLA Collection / Alamy Stock Photo

All rights reserved. No part of this publication may be reproduced or transmitted in any form or by any means, electronic or mechanical, including photocopying, recording, or any information storage or retrieval system, without prior permission in writing from the publishers.

A catalogue record for this book is available from the British Library.

A catalog record for this book is available from the Library of Congress.

ISBN:	HB:	978-1-4742-4487-9
	PB:	978-1-3502-7883-7
	Set:	978-1-4742-4503-6

Series: The Cultural Histories Series

Typeset by Integra Software Services Pvt. Ltd.
Printed and bound in Great Britain

To find out more about our authors and books visit www.bloomsbury.com and sign up for our newsletters.

CONTENTS

LIST OF FIGURES — vi
GENERAL EDITORS' PREFACE — x
CONTRIBUTORS — xii

Introduction — 1
Bert De Munck and Thomas Max Safley

1 The Economy of Work — 17
  Thomas Max Safley

2 Picturing Work — 33
  Ilja Veldman

3 Work and Workplaces — 67
  Josef Ehmer

4 Workplace Cultures — 89
  Anna Bellavitis

5 Work, Skill, and Technology — 101
  Karel Davids

6 Work and Mobility — 113
  Jason P. Coy

7 Work and Society — 129
  Catharina Lis and Hugo Soly

8 The Political Culture of Work — 145
  Bert De Munck and Jan Dumolyn

9 Work and Leisure — 159
  Alessandro Arcangeli

NOTES — 174
FURTHER READINGS — 199
INDEX — 211

LIST OF FIGURES

CHAPTER TWO

2.1 Simon Bening, *The Month of August*, painted miniature, 1515. The Morgan Library & Art Museum, New York. — 34

2.2 Pieter van der Heyden after Pieter Bruegel the Elder, *Summer*, engraving, c. 1570. Rijksmuseum, Amsterdam. — 35

2.3 Hieronymus Wierix, *Man Born to Toil*, engraving, 1579. Museum Boijmans van Beuningen, Rotterdam. — 36

2.4 Raphael Sadeler after Maarten de Vos, *Labor or Adult Age Dedicated to Work*, engraving, 1591. Rijksmuseum, Amsterdam. — 38

2.5 Raphael Sadeler after Maarten de Vos, *Honor or Mature Age Receiving Riches and Respect*, engraving, 1591. Rijksmuseum, Amsterdam. — 38

2.6 Balaam Master, *St. Eloy in his Workshop* (1440–60), engraving, Rijksmuseum, Amsterdam. — 39

2.7 Jost Amman, *The Hat Maker*, from *Panoplia,* 1568. British Museum, London. Photo: Trustees of the British Museum. — 41

2.8 Studio of Philips Galle after Johannes Stradanus, *The Preparation of Guayaco for Treating Syphilis*, engraving, c. 1591. Rijksmuseum, Amsterdam. — 42

2.9 Studio of Philips Galle after Johannes Stradanus, *The Production of Refined Sugar from Sugarcane*, engraving, c. 1591. Rijksmuseum, Amsterdam. — 42

2.10 Johannes Stradanus, *The Heating of the Silk Worm Eggs and the Reeling of Silk*, engraving, c. 1595. Rijksmuseum, Amsterdam. — 43

2.11 Anonymous, *Two Tanners*, oil on panel, c. 1580. Museum Gouda, Gouda. © Museum Gouda. — 44

2.12 *Glass blowing*, woodcut in *De re metallica*, 1556. Wellcome Library, London. Wellcome Images images@well. — 46

2.13 Isaac Claesz van Swanenburg, *The Spinning, Warping and Weaving of Wool*, 1594–6. Museum De Lakenhal, Leiden. © Museum De Lakenhal, Leiden. — 47

LIST OF FIGURES vii

2.14 Petrus Christus, *A Portrait of a Goldsmith Visited by a Wealthy Couple*, oil on panel, 1449. Robert Lehman Collection, Metropolitan Museum of Art, New York. 48

2.15 Circle of Marinus van Reymerswale, *The Tax Collector*, 1545. Fine Arts Museum, Bilbao. 49

2.16 Adriaen Collaert, *The Fraudulent Sale Agreement*, engraving, c. 1595. Rijksmuseum, Amsterdam. 50

2.17 Georg Pencz, *The Children of the Moon*, woodcut, 1531. Rijksmuseum, Amsterdam. 52

2.18 Herman Jansz. Muller after Maarten van Heemskerck, *The Children of Mercury*, engraving, c. 1568. Rijksmuseum, Amsterdam. 53

2.19 Jan Saenredam after Hendrick Goltzius, *The Children of Jupiter*, engraving, 1596. Rijksmuseum, Amsterdam. 54

2.20 Pieter de Jode after Maarten de Vos, *A Soldier and Camp Follower as the Choleric Temperament*, engraving, c. 1600. Rijksmuseum, Amsterdam. 55

2.21 Nicolaes Jansz Clock, *A Blacksmith as the Element Fire*, engraving, 1597. Rijksmuseum, Amsterdam. 56

2.22 Crispijn de Passe after Maarten de Vos, *Fish Mongers as the Element Water*, engraving, c. 1600. Rijksmuseum, Amsterdam. 57

2.23 Joachim Beuckelaer, *Fish mongers at the Market*, 1568. Metropolitan Museum, New York. Lila Acheson Wallace gift and Bequest of George Blumenthal. 58

2.24 Joachim Beuckelaer, *Kitchen Scene*, oil on panel, 1565–70. Museum voor Schone Kunsten / MAS, Antwerp. 58

2.25 Diego Velázquez, *Kitchen Maid with Christ in the House of Martha and Mary*, c. 1618. National Gallery, London. 59

2.26 Dirck Volkertsz Coornhert after Maarten van Heemskerck, *The Virtuous House wife Selling her Wares to a Pedlar*, engraving, 1555. Rijksmuseum, Amsterdam. 60

2.27 Crispijn de Passe the Elder after Maarten de Vos, *The Wise Virgins at Work*, engraving, c. 1600. Rijksmuseum, Amsterdam. 61

2.28 Pieter Pietersz, *Temptation to Idleness*, oil on panel, c. 1570. Rijksmuseum, Amsterdam. 62

2.29 Contemporary copy after Dirck van Baburen's, *A Procuress, a Prostitute and a Client*, oil on panel, 1622–30. Rijksmuseum, Amsterdam. 64

2.30 Jan Vermeyen, *Spanish Prostitutes*, etching, 1545. Rijksmuseum, Amsterdam. 65

CHAPTER THREE

3.1	Anonymous, *The Polder Het Grootslag*, 1595. © City of Enkhuizen.	72
3.2	Jost Amman, Tailors' workshop, *Book of Trades*, 1568. Public domain.	75
3.3	Jost Amman, Tanners working in the water workshop, *Book of Trades*, 1568. Public domain.	76
3.4	Jan Collaert after Jan van der Straet (Johannes Stradanus), Printers at work, *Impressio librorum*, c. 1590. Metropolitan Museum of Art, New York. Public domain.	78
3.5	Georgius Agricola, Miners working in three shafts, *De re metallica*, 1556. Public domain.	80
3.6	Georgius Agricola, Women shaking the sieve, *De re metallica*, 1556. Public domain.	81
3.7	Jacopo de Barbari, The Venice arsenal, *Veduta di Venezia*, 1500. Detail: Arsenale, Museo Correr, Venice.	82

CHAPTER FOUR

4.1	Dirck Volkertsz Coornhert after Maarten van Heemskerck, *The Virtuous House wife Serving a Meal to her Family*, engraving, 1555. Rijksmuseum, Amsterdam.	94
4.2	Brunswijkse Monogrammist, *Brothel Scene with a Brawl*, oil on panel, 1537. Gemälde Galerie, Berlin.	100

CHAPTER FIVE

5.1	*The Anatomy Lesson of Doctor Willem van der Meer in Delft*, oil on canvas, 1617. Municipal Hospital, Delft, the Netherlands. Image courtesy of Getty Images.	106
5.2	Crispijn van de Passe, possibly, *Instructie van zeevaarders*, (II), 1652. Image courtesy of Rijksmuseum, Amsterdam. Public domain.	108

CHAPTER SIX

6.1	Pieter Bruegel the Younger, *The Harvester's Meal*, 1565. Private Collection. Image courtesy of Getty Images.	116
6.2	Pieter Bruegel the Elder, *The Parable of the Blind*, 1568. H. Armstrong / ClassicStock. Image courtesy of Getty Images.	120
6.3	The slave trade and a slave ship, eighteenth century. DEA / M. Seemuller. Image courtesy of Getty Images.	126

LIST OF FIGURES ix

CHAPTER SEVEN

7.1 Hans Holbein, *Portrait of the Merchant Georg Gisze* (1532), oil on panel, Gemäldegalerie, Berlin.   132

7.2 Michiel Claesz, *The Predella of the Altarpiece of the Carpenter's Guild for the Church of St. Jan in Gouda*, oil on panel, c. 1560–5. Museum Gouda, Gouda. © Museum Gouda.   136

CHAPTER EIGHT

8.1 Johan Meyer, *Procession of the Guild of Butchers in Zurich*, seventeenth century. Cabinet des Éstampes et des Dessins, De Agostini / DEA / M. Seemuller. Image courtesy of Getty Images.   153

8.2 Signboard of the Guild of Cooperage, Italy, seventeenth century. De Agostini / DEA / A Dagli Orti. Image courtesy of Getty Images.   157

CHAPTER NINE

9.1 Jacob Esselens, *Coast Scene*, 1626–87. Metropolitan Museum of Art, New York. Public domain.   163

9.2 Pieter Bruegel the Younger, *The Return from the Kermis*, 1564–1637/8. Phillips, London.   168

GENERAL EDITORS' PREFACE

Issues around work and the workplace seem to be having a renaissance and are no longer embedded solely in the discourses around Marxism and labour movements. Similarly, new and fresh research has been taking place around guilds, skill, control and gender issues. *A Cultural History of Work* takes an approach that focuses on culture in order to explore the subtleties of the character and dynamics of work and the people and relationships involved in working and the workplace in a theoretically holistic way to bring together disparate historical traditions and historiographical approaches. The aim and scope of *A Cultural History of Work* is to offer a comprehensive survey of the social and cultural construction of work across six historical periods. This approach that focuses on the *cultural* history of work provides an opportunity to explore the dynamics of work and the people and relationships involved in working and the workplace, helping to rethink boundaries and the issues of work. This is not an "economic" history of work, but a cultural one. Of course, we talk about economics, but the fundamental concept is to explain the ways in which work was situated in and influenced cultural dynamics of the western world. It is a key contribution to the process of rethinking boundaries and issues of work.

A Cultural History of Work draws on "the western world." Contributors approached their chapters with a great deal of freedom, drawing on their specific expertise in national and regional histories, but throughout the thirty-six chapters that make up the series, they have tried to embrace the "West." The series does not intend to "cover" all of western culture, or even all of Europe and North America. Authors instead have aimed at *representing* the broad trends and nuances of the culture of work from antiquity to the present. Thus *A Cultural History of Work* concentrates on the central themes in western work, with some sensitivity to areas we know less about.

This is a work of scholarly reference designed to provide scholars and students with a detailed, nuanced overview. Each contribution has been written as an original chapter presenting an *overview* of a theme in a period, but each also includes a wide range of case material and has a particular thrust or point of view (or points of view) informing the organization of the piece. The series is structured into six time periods—though historians will always quibble about what these periods mean and will blur the edges. That is part of the process of understanding the past. And time does not have the same meaning across regions, much less countries or continents. Each volume covers a long period of time and a broad geography that can and will introduce a range of variables. Each volume uses the same chapter titles so that readers can read on a theme across volumes, or read through a period exploring the range of themes and nuances that each volume presents. There are also overlaps within volumes and across them that enrich the discussion.

The editorial decision to study work rather than labour is suggestive of a broader, more encompassing field of study that lends itself more readily to different periods. For example, in particular it is more appropriate to use *work* for periods such as the Antiquity and the Middle Ages because labour looks in one sense as an eighteenth/nineteenth-century concept. English is rather unusual in having two words whose meanings overlap considerably, but are not identical. For example, there is only one word in French, *travail*, like *Arbeit* in German, arbejde in Danish/Swedish/Norwegian, *lavoro* in Italian. Some other languages tend to have one primary word also, for example, *trabajo* in Spanish, though there are other usable words. From a definitional point of view we can argue that *labour* means the use of mental or physical capacities/faculties, so it implies suffering and difficulty, whereas *work* has to do with the simple act or fact of doing something/the activity/the action in progress. From the point of view of the political economy, *labour* seems to refer to the Marxist discourse; work is more pragmatic and less laden with cultural overtones. So, work describes the parameters of this project while *labour* is one aspect of it, which is more important in the nineteenth and twentieth centuries, and to a lesser extent in the eighteenth. Thus we argue *work* seems more neutral and general and therefore more applicable across six centuries.

Moving from the world of antiquity and into the twenty-first century, the culture of work has shifted considerably as technologies, organisation and locations have changed. Workplace relations have also undergone transformations from small scale and familial settings to large-scale and potentially less personal environments. And yet, the world of work remains complex with great variations between national cultures, political and economic approaches to managing the fields of work, and especially in the ways that people have negotiated their own spaces and places within them. Work retains many meanings from the simple need to survive to senses of deep satisfaction for the character of the job and the creativity one can achieve. It may be valued for the income or wealth it can generate; conversely, some choose to work less and on their own terms. Part-time, job-sharing, self-employment and the IT revolution have offered different routes for some people. Workers can, however, remain tied to an employer and though nominally slavery does not exist in the West, there are those, like sweated immigrant workshops, and live-in domestic workers, who may feel that little has changed. *The Cultural History of Work* traces and explores many of these routes and their implications for people and their cultural experience of work.

CONTRIBUTORS

Alessandro Arcangeli is Associate Professor of Early Modern History at the University of Verona, Italy. He is a cultural historian with particular research interests in leisure and dance (both in Europe and in cultural encounters), as well as in the body, passions, and medical thought. He is the author and editor of various academic publications in these fields. He has also worked on cultural history methodologically and historiographically, both with reference to Italy and in a wider perspective (see his reference book *Cultural History: A Concise Introduction*, 2012). From 2013 to 2017 he served as Chair of the International Society for Cultural History.

Anna Bellavitis is Professor of Early Modern History and director of the *Groupe de Recherche d'Histoire* at the University of Rouen-Normandie, France. She is a senior member of the Institut Universitaire de France and her most recent publications include *Il lavoro delle donne nelle città dell'Europa moderna*, Rome, Viella, 2016; *Garzoni. Apprendistato e formazione tra Venezia e l'Europa in età moderna* (ed. with Martina Frank and Valentina Sapienza), Mantova, University Studiorum, 2017; "Patterns of Transmission and Urban Experience: When Gender Matters," in Deborah Simonton, ed., *The Routledge History Handbook of Gender and the Urban Experience* (2017).

Jason P. Coy is Professor of History at the College of Charleston, SC, USA, and received his doctorate at the University of California, Los Angeles, CA, USA, in 2001. He is the author of *Strangers and Misfits: Banishment, Social Control, and Authority in Early Modern Germany* (2008) and coeditor of *The Holy Roman Empire, Reconsidered* (2010), *Kinship, Community, and Self: Essays in Honor of David Warren Sabean* (2014), and *Migrations in the German Lands, 1500–2000* (2016). He is currently working on a manuscript on divination in early modern Germany.

Karel Davids is Professor of Economic and Social History at the Vrije Universiteit Amsterdam, the Netherlands. He has published widely on the history of knowledge, the history of technology, and maritime history. His books include *Religion, Technology, and the Great and Little Divergences: China and Europe Compared, c.700–1800* (2013) and (coedited with Bert De Munck) *Innovation and Creativity in Late Medieval and Early Modern European Cities* (2014).

Bert De Munck is Professor in the History Department at the University of Antwerp, Belgium, teaching "Early Modern History," "Theory of Historical Knowledge," and "Heritage and Public History." He is a member of the Centre for Urban History, Antwerp, and the Director of the interdisciplinary Urban Studies Institute and the international Scientific Research Community (WOG) "Urban Agency: The Historical Fabrication of the City as an Object of Study." His research concentrates on early modern cities, in particular craft guilds, civil society and urban governance, labor and technical knowledge, and the "repertoires of evaluation" regarding skills and products. Relevant publications include "Artisans, Products and Gifts: Rethinking the History of Material Culture in Early Modern Europe," *Past and Present* 224, no. 1 (August 2014): 39–74; "Disassembling the City: A Historical and an Epistemological View on the Agency of Cities," *Journal of Urban History* 43, no. 5 (2017): 811–29; with Karel Davids, eds., *Innovation and Creativity in Late Medieval and Early Modern European Cities* (2014); and with Dries Lyna, eds., *Concepts of Value in Material Culture, 1500–1900* (2015).

Jan Dumolyn is Senior Lecturer in the Department of History, Ghent University, Belgium. He is a specialist in the social and political history of the later medieval Low Countries. His research interests include the urban history of the Low Countries, medieval collective action, social groups and prosopography, discourse-analysis and medieval ideologies, and social theory and historical sociology.

Josef Ehmer was Professor of Modern History at the University of Salzburg, Austria, and Professor of Social and Economic History at the University of Vienna, Austria, where he retired in 2015. Currently, he is an Associate Fellow at the International Research Centre, *Work and Human Life Cycle in Global History*, at Humboldt-University Berlin, Germany. His research fields encompass a broad spectrum of comparative European social history from the early modern period to the present day. He is particularly interested in labor history and the history of work, artisans and guilds, migrations, family and the life course, aging and old age, and historical demography.

Catharina Lis is Professor Emeritus at the Free University of Brussels, Belgium, and Guest Professor at the University of Antwerp, Belgium. She is interested in processes of social change in preindustrial Europe. She has published books on poverty and social policy, the political economy of craft guilds, industrialization and entrepreneurship, forms of "deviant behaviour," and perceptions of work and workers, including (with Josef Ehmer) *The Idea of Work in Europe from Antiquity to Modern Times* (2009) and (with Hugo Soly) *Worthy Efforts: Attitudes to Work and Workers in Pre-Industrial Europe* (2012).

Thomas Max Safley is Professor of Early Modern European History at the University of Pennsylvania, USA. A specialist in the economic and social history of early modern Europe, roughly 1450–1750, he has published extensively on the histories of marriage and the family, poverty and charity, and labor and business.

Hugo Soly is Professor Emeritus at the Free University of Brussels, Belgium, and Guest Professor at the University of Antwerp, Belgium. He is interested in processes of socio-economic change in preindustrial Europe. He has published books on commercial capitalism and urban development, poverty and social policy, the political economy of craft guilds, industrialization and entrepreneurship, forms of "deviant behaviour" and perceptions of work and workers, including (with Catharina Lis) *Worthy Efforts: Attitudes to Work and Workers in Pre-Industrial Europe* (2012).

Ilja Veldman was Assistant Professor at the University of Amsterdam, the Netherlands (1969–84) and Professor in the History of Art at the Vrije Universiteit of Amsterdam, the Netherlands (1984–2006). Her main field of research is Dutch art, 1400–1700, with an emphasis on meaning, function, prints, and drawings. Among her publications are *Maarten van Heemskerck and Dutch Humanism in the Sixteenth Century* (1977),

Crispijn de Passe and His Progeny: A Century of Print Production (2001), *Profit and Pleasure: Print Books by Crispijn de Passe de Oude* (2001), *Images for the Eye and Soul: Function and Meaning in Netherlandish Prints (1450–1650)* (2006), and (with Y. Bleyerveld) *Netherlandish 16th-Century Drawings in Teylers Museum Haarlem* (2016).

Introduction

BERT DE MUNCK AND THOMAS MAX SAFLEY

A Cultural History of Work in the Early Modern Age (1450–1650) requires a bit of explanation—if not justification—by way of introduction. Neither the topic nor the period is self-evident. Quotidian understandings of work as an effort undertaken to achieve a purpose or result or as an activity to earn a living do not usually extend to matters of culture. So, why create a volume on the culture of work rather than, simply, on work? Historians do not unanimously associate the early modern age with dramatic transformations in the performance of purpose efforts or remunerative activities. So, why create a volume that examines change from 1450 to 1650? This introduction will attempt to respond to both these questions. Then it will address some of the larger, structural transformations that make the culture of work in the early modern age worthy of study.

Let us start with the first question: Why the culture of work? Work seems to be connected to the hard facts of life, such as subsistence, earning a living, creating wealth, and, in its modern guise, competition and efficiency. Moreover, it is preeminently a set of *practices*, even in a very literal sense. It is doing, crafting, constructing, assembling, toiling, manipulating raw materials with material devices such as tools, instruments, and machines. This is even more the case in the late medieval and early modern periods, in which the largest part of the active population was engaged in either agriculture or manufacturing and, hence, in hand-making material products rather than providing services. Although our book will also focus on merchants and shopkeepers, doctors and surgeons, and lawyers and clerks and the like, the stress will inevitably be on material processes. In contrast, the concept of culture invokes systems of meaning, symbols, signs, and language, perceptions, and representations, in combination perhaps with rituals and ceremonies, or customs and habits. The term culture invokes the immaterial rather than the material stuff of life.

Nevertheless, the aim of this book is not to address only the perceptions and representations of work. While these are important aspects, they are fundamentally entangled with work as an economic activity and a daily practice. Both culture and the economy are to be understood here in the broadest possible sense, with culture being predicated upon daily, material practices and with the economy being fundamentally embedded in cultural systems of ritual and meaning. Admittedly, this is still not unproblematic from a historical perspective. After all, the dominant tradition in history and historical sociology has been to see the economy as gradually becoming a separate sphere and an autonomous force in society. Whether this history was addressed from a Marxist or a "Smithian" perspective, it was written as the gradual triumph of market forces. One might genuinely ask, therefore, whether we are not at risk of eclipsing the very history of modernity by focusing on the culture of work?

A great many of the grand debates of the last half-century have actually been concerned with the history of capitalism in general and the history of proletarianization in particular. What was at stake in both the so-called Brenner-debate and the debate on protoindustrialization was the question to what extent the economic actors, particularly the workers, lost ownership of the means of production—whether it was land, machines, tools, or materials. The debate over the so-called industrious revolution revolved around the question to what extent work—especially female work—became commodified. Whatever the oppositions and differences of opinion about it, agreement emerged about the long-term trend, which was one of commodification—whether it was seen as a good thing or not. Even culture eventually started to commodify in the early modern period, as historians of consumer preferences and material culture have learned.[1]

So, work was seen mostly as being subject to long-term processes of commodification in the late medieval and early modern periods, but this was a very paradoxical history. In the history of economic thinking a shift occurred from a mercantilist set of ideas in which trade was the source of wealth (because it resulted in the inflow of silver and gold) to a focus on productivity. For some, notably the so-called Physiocrats, the source of productivity was land, to be made fruitful by agriculture. Increasingly, however, the ultimate source of wealth was considered to be work. At least from about the mid-seventeenth century onwards, work was progressively considered the source of the "wealth of nations," to refer to Adam Smith's famous book, which was an important step in this history. Work was thereby reduced, however, to its economic value and to a factor of production. It was all, in Marx's terminology, about abstract labor, obtaining a value in a labor market and an exchange context. In the process, labor was made measurable and countable. In other words, it was stripped of culture.

All too often, historians and historical sociologists who have tried to understand the long-term history of capitalism, proletarianization, and commodification have created teleological views, in which the free market unfolded naturally as soon as barriers were removed and the invisible hand could freely do its work. One of the most interesting attempts to make sense of it in the twentieth century comes from Karl Polanyi, who, in his pivotal work *The Great Transformation* (1944), argued that the economic system progressively became entirely disembedded, with market forces gradually not only replacing the traditional focus on reciprocity and redistribution, but also transforming human mentalities—culture. What emerged in the long run was a new human "nature," one in which human choices are based upon utility-maximizing impulses. However, given that this so-called "nature" is created by political institutions, one could just as well see the market as being over-determined—the more so if we also take into account the role of discourses and systems of meaning, including the views of political economists, which have helped to fabricate the market as we know it today.

Recent trends in history and the social sciences no longer consider the emergence of the market or capitalism as a natural and self-evident process. The market is not something which unfolded inherently as soon as barriers such as guild regulations and commercial tolls were lifted, hence the renewed focus on institutions by social and economic historians. The problem here is that especially economic historians still focus rather exclusively on the question of efficiency, thus retaining a teleological framework. Historians studying the guilds have debated whether they should be understood as economic institutions that helped to lower transaction costs or as social and political organizations in the hands of rent-seeking actors.[2] Likewise, the history of the commons has often been framed as a question of how to manage it efficiently and in a sustainable way.[3] While to a point, this adds to our understanding of local mechanisms of governance, it is nevertheless symptomatic of the fact that access to and the management of common resources are seen more as a technical rather than political—let alone ideological,—issue in which the connection between communal resources and work is made explicit.

This book will rather present a view in which the very connection between economic mechanisms and the social, political, and cultural context takes center stage—although without prioritizing the one or the other dimension, and without implying the inevitable victory of economic forces. Instead, we will reveal historical contingency and the profound ambivalence of the rise of market forces—which was more a process of fabrication than it was a natural one.

The focus on the early modern period, 1450–1650, will help to do so, which brings us to the second question to be addressed here: Why a book on work in the early modern period? At least the most visible transformations in the history of work are situated either before or after the period addressed in this volume. The medieval period witnessed the urban and commercial revolutions, the loosening of feudal ties, and the expansion of trade and industry based upon free labor. Most of the major technological innovations that accompanied this were also invented and introduced long, even ages, before the fifteenth century—think about the horizontal loom and water and wind mills. Machines such as the spinning wheel were vastly improved in the fifteenth and sixteenth centuries (think about the introduction of the flyer), but these were mostly incremental improvements rather than revolutionary inventions or discoveries. Alternatively, during the so-called Industrial Revolution major organizational and technological breakthroughs occurred—which jointly enabled the economy to expand considerably in scale after the mid-eighteenth century. One could easily claim that at least for large sections of the urban population not a single dimension of life was untouched by the Industrial Revolution and the accompanying technological transformations. For the period covered in this book, this is clearly less evident.

Nevertheless, the rationale of a focus on the period 1540–1650 is obvious in the context of recent trends in the history of work. Up to the 1970s, labor history focused mostly on the Industrial Revolution and, by implication, on technological and organizational transformations. Work was understood to have been transformed only as a result of processes of mechanization and reorganization, that is, the rise of factories, as a result of which an increasingly intensive division of labor materialized. In addition to the emergence of a working-class consciousness and the labor movement, this was interpreted as having resulted in a process of deskilling and the reduction of workers to robot-like providers of work power. This was in turn connected to new disciplinary techniques, such as the introduction of foremen and line production.[4] But, what has become clear in recent research, is that all this was prepared for in the fifteenth, sixteenth, and seventeenth centuries. It is, moreover, thanks to a focus on culture that the early modern period has gained importance.

Owing to the influence of symbolic anthropology and post-structuralism, that is, strands in anthropology and the social sciences in which cultural systems of meaning take center stage, scholars since the 1980s no longer understand culture as an effect of class or material conditions, but rather as a relatively autonomous force, embedding and structuring practices, including economic practices. One of the first to acknowledge this was Edward P. Thompson, who, in his classic *The Making of the English Working Class*, wrote the history of the emergence of a working-class consciousness in England, concentrating on the agency and the life experiences of the workers themselves. In so doing, he paved the way for a labor history in which the cultural discourses, practices, and expressions of workers had causal force. In his wake, social historians, such as Gareth

Stedman-Jones, William Sewell, and Patrick Joyce, severely criticized the concept of class, as it was used in "structuralist" social history, as the basis of a cultural and political "superstructure." They shifted the historical attention to issues of continuity. Analyzing the discourses of nineteenth-century artisans, both William Sewell (1980) and William Reddy (1984) showed that the artisans themselves harked back to the preindustrial period when arguing in defense of the honorable value of their artisanal skills.

Even for the nineteenth century, work cannot be understood properly when looking at the factory or economic conditions alone. Patrick Joyce, in his book *Work, Society, and Politics* (1980), argued that neither class relations nor ideas and discourses alone can explain the emergence of the modern labor movement. He considered it key also to examine personal experiences and communal identities starting from the daily realities on the factory floor. While he acknowledged that life was deeply marked by the social régime of the factory, factory life was in turn deeply embedded in the broader social context of family and community, explaining the importance of paternalistic social relations and feelings of subordination and deference. In line with this, cultural systems of meaning are to be seen as forces in history that themselves can shape and embed labor relations and the perception of skills. This is illustrated in work on the discourses and views of intellectuals (Stedman-Jones) and artisans (Sewell) and the impact thereof on the articulation of class interests and the emergence of the nineteenth-century labor movement.

Catharina Lis and Hugo Soly, while being steeped in Marxist social history, have written in the wake of this scholarly development a long-term history of the perceptions of work in the preindustrial period, in which the focus is on views, attitudes, and discourse related to work of intellectual and other elites.[5] Their work also critically addresses teleological views in which the origins of modern capitalism are to be sought in the early modern period. While starting from a thorough knowledge of long-term continuities, they emphasize the importance of understanding the complex and hybrid character of each historical period in its own right. This is also William Sewell's point in his brilliant theoretical book *Logics of History* (especially chap. 6): A proper understanding of diachronic transformations and transitions inevitably has to start from a deep insight into the layered synchrony of a specific historical period and context.

In summary, recent theoretical and historiographical shifts have opened new horizons for labor history. Specifically, they have created an opportunity to reopen the debates about the connection between perceptions, ideas, and systems of meaning regarding work on the one hand and economic developments on the other. Such debates can now be tackled without invoking either the Industrial Revolution or the broader horizon of capitalism. We can now concentrate on historical contingency and on the fundamental entanglement of economic, social, and cultural practices. Nor is this inevitably to result in a sterile and unengaged type of history-writing. Patrick Joyce and others have abundantly argued that their critical attitude is simply based on a different conception of power. While Marxist social historians reduced power to the agency of capital, which materialized in either the opinions and action of economic elites or in hegemonic political institutions (or else in material conditions like the city), present-day social historians are more likely to assume Foucauldian notions of power, in which power is more distributed and relational and emerges from social practices and discourses.

It is here that the opportunities for a book on the early modern period emerge. In older strands of research, this was the period in which the modern age was born, in which humanist's individualism and critical inquisitive attitude emerged. It would have been the cradle of rationalism, even if this first emerged only as a more rational version of Christianity.

All this has long since been debunked by critical scholars as largely mythmaking, or at least a type of history-writing that is subject to modernity narratives and Eurocentric thinking. But, this should not lead us to deny the profound changes occurring in this period, most of which must have had an impact on the cultural history of work. In the following section, we will briefly touch upon some of these transformations and reflect on their potential impact of the perceptions, experiences, and practices of work.

REFORMATION AND COUNTER-REFORMATION

The religious conflicts and schisms of the sixteenth and seventeenth centuries had limited effect on work or work culture. None of the major reformers of the period were critics of work as purposeful or remunerative activity, though all condemned those forms that involved exploitation of the poor. Martin Luther, to offer a single, famous example, excoriated usurers and merchants for practices that increased the cost and suffering of consumers.[6] John Calvin defended all forms of work, including mercantile and financial engagements that provoked criticism from others, provided they were carried out in the spirit of Christian charity (here understood in the sense of *caritas* or brotherly love) and sobriety.[7] God called all people to their employments and, insofar as their employments were God-given, they were to be performed in a God-fearing manner.

Max Weber made much of this connection between one's work and Calvin's notion of a calling. Relying on the writings of Puritan divines, especially the sermons of Richard Baxter, he concluded that the followers of Calvin's doctrines developed what he called a "Protestant ethic." According to this ethos, the faithful could achieve some assurance of their own spiritual sanctification by diligently practicing a worldly vocation—some form of divinely specified work—and observing an ascetic lifestyle. Weber believed this ethos transformed ancient economic practices that were oriented more towards short-term consumption and display into modern capitalism. The religious impulses and orientations of Calvinist teachings faded over time, and the pursuit of profit emerged as an end in itself, conducted in a rational, disciplined manner that now serves less as a means to control sin than to accumulate capital.

Historians, too, often misread or misused Weber, looking for—and not finding—specific evidence of a link between reformed religion and modern capitalism. Much evidence exists for the rational pursuit of profit for purposes of accumulation long before the Reformation, just as much evidence exists for irrational acquisition and consumption among modern capitalists. While taken up and reconsidered by scholars from Amitore Fanfani to Richard H. Tawney and, most recently, Brad Gregory, the Weber Thesis remains one of the most notorious and controversial links between the Reformation of religion, the modern economy, and the culture of work.[8] Nor is it usual to discuss Weber's thesis about economic modernization in the context of workers, of the working poor or of a cultural history of work. *Die protestantische Ethik und der Geist des Kapitalismus* (1904/5) took as its topic, above all, the economic values and behaviors of mercantile elites, especially their emancipation from "traditionalism."[9] Weber captured the essence of traditionalism in that Dutch sea captain, who "would sail through hell for profit, even if his sails were singed."[10] His enterprise was a speculative adventure to amass fortune rather than a rational effort to accumulate capital, when one considered the spirit that moved the captain, determined his lifestyle, and guided his business.[11] Weber understood traditionalism, at least as it applied to entrepreneurs, as an ethos, an attitude to life, and an approach to management that resisted change.

Yet the theory remains unclear. Weber's distinction between economic traditionalism and modern capitalism is difficult to establish.[12] At least two problems beset the effort. First, it is difficult to identify what is traditional and what is modern in economic activities. Weber limits his discussion to wages, that is, responsiveness to economic incentives. Economic conduct is subject to many influences, however, not simply economic, but social and political, as well as ideological and moral. Second, it is difficult to determine the rationality or irrationality of economic behavior. Resistance to incentives and a preference for leisure may result from imperatives other than a simple desire to live as one is accustomed to live.

Since the 1980s, some have followed the lead of George Ovitt, Jr., to argue a variant of Weberian traditionalism.[13] They have assumed that purposeful or remunerative work lacked social or cultural status in the Middle Ages, based on the biblical story of the Fall from Grace, according to which leisure characterized paradise and work was the result of sin. They noted as well such ideal-typical notions as the so-called "three orders," according to which society was organized into three groups of people: those who pray, those who fight, and those who work. Lynn White, Jr., has countered that the *regula* of certain monastic orders, especially the Benedictines and Cistercians, placed work close to the center of their spiritual lives, and that their monasteries became in consequence centers for technological innovation and economic development.[14] Jeroen Deploige has recently expanded the point, arguing that

> ever since the eleventh century, and since the beginning of the urbanization of western society, there has been a succession of voices, even if contingent, especially on the fringes of the Church, who considered it plausible and even salutary for lay and semi-religious people (craftsmen, Tertiaries ...) to aim for a life in which labour was seen as perfectly compatible with some sort of calling.[15]

Other scholars build rather on the older ideas of Jacques Le Goff and continue to advocate the social and cultural stigma of work before the sixteenth century.[16] Without generalizing about medieval attitudes towards work, they argue that the Reformation, particularly Calvin's doctrines of predestination and calling, encouraged a more positive attitude towards work and its essential place in a faithful Christian life.

None of this scholarship takes up the voices of working men and women. As with Weber, the debate inspired by his thesis rests solidly on a foundation of prescriptive, elite sources, such as sermons and tracts that argued how one ought to view work and workers, rather than how workers viewed themselves or their activities. The appeals and petitions of working men and women, recorded in negotiation with the state, permit a reconsideration of economic traditionalism and set it in a different light. They suggest three aspects of the economic conduct of the working poor that call Weber's concept into question. The result is a somewhat different, broadly shared, understanding of economic activity that has been elsewhere termed the "patrimony of poverty."[17] First, the working poor supplemented property with an insistence upon entitlements, among which were access to poor relief and participation in a craft. Second, they exploited what Bronislaw Geremek has described as an elasticity of the margin, an economic flexibility or opportunism that made use of existing institutions but turned them to their own account.[18] Third, they demonstrated an awareness of labor and commodity markets, an aversion to risk, and an ability to assess costs and benefits that were all oriented towards advantage. Far removed from Weber's notion of traditionalism as some sort of reactionary resistance to progress, the calculated pursuit of advantage within a framework of traditional institutions enabled working men and women to negotiate their interests and pursue their utility.

The so-called "patrimony of poverty," evokes another respect in which the Reformation influenced the cultural history of work. It influenced the development of new social responses to poverty, many of which depended on work or work-related relief. Martin Luther advocated the duty of a Christian magistracy to assume responsibility of religious and social programs. As reform progressed, cities and territories that declared themselves evangelical, usually undertook programs of secularization, a poor term, given the religious motives and purposes that guided—and, in many instances, still guide—these actions. Broadly speaking, traditionally ecclesiastical functions, such as church administration, general education, and poor relief were placed under government supervision. Yet it must be said that the Reformation did not invent this initiative. As Brian Pullan and others have conclusively demonstrated, lay oversight of religious foundations was not new in the sixteenth century. Nor did the inspiration for such changes come from reforming theologians. Rolf Kießling has pointed to the financial motivations and lay interests that led to secular involvement in social programs long before the Reformation and the intellectual efforts of humanists, especially Juan Luis Vives (of whom more below), shifted the emphasis away from *beneficia*-based charity towards work-based relief. Henceforth, even in Catholic communities, poor relief would increasingly distinguish between the deserving and the undeserving poor, between those who could not and those who would not work. Such policies certainly strengthened an already present disregard for unproductive poverty and the idle poor; that they might also have improved the cultural value of work remains largely unstudied.

HUMANISM AND SCIENTIFIC REVOLUTION

Traditionally, humanist ideas about work have likewise been described in a rather pessimistic manner. Social historians have linked them with disciplining efforts as they materialized in bans on begging and the foundation of workhouses. All this was in turn connected to processes of proletarianization and the attempts of economic elites to preserve social order and force uprooted poor people to work at low wages and in poor working conditions. This would have been accompanied by the justifying and rationalizing discourses of humanists, such as Juan Luis Vives, who in his *De subventione pauperum* (1525) stressed the importance of working and learning for the needy and, hence, argued in favor of bans on begging, forced apprenticeship, the foundation of work-schools, and the restriction of poor relief to those who were unable to work. In a way, work was certainly presented as uplifting here, because it prevented vagrancy, misery, and debauchery, but it was nevertheless far removed from work as a spiritual activity.[19]

A more optimistic perspective comes from historians of science and art, who have argued recently that the so-called mechanical arts gained prestige, especially in the fifteenth and sixteenth centuries. Artisans and artists would have gradually become better at imitating nature, which was of crucial importance in an era when nature was believed to mirror the perfection of God.[20] Recent research has even suggested that artisans through their specific approach to knowledge and truth (called their "artisanal epistemology" by some scholars) played a major part in the emergence of the experimental sciences in the seventeenth century. While the "new sciences" were based upon experimenting with matter and the observation of nature, this is exactly what artisans and artists were good at, as has been argued by Pamela Smith and Pamela Long among others. To a certain extent, this was already acknowledged during the early modern period itself. Smith has drawn attention to the correspondence between, on the one hand, the practices of some artists and artisans and, on the other, the ideas of the sixteenth-century philosopher and physician Paracelsus, who argued that knowledge (*scientia*) did not reside in the mind of the observing scientist, but was rather inherent in things, because God was immanent in them.[21] Artisans, whose basic activity was handling raw materials, could thus be seen as having access to knowledge, that is, to God's wisdom and truth. Around the turn of the fifteenth century, some humanist scholars in the circle of Jacques Lefèvre d'Étaples opined that so-called *idiota*, or "untutored minds," could have privileged—that is, an unmediated and more direct—access to truth simply by crafting.[22] So up to the first half of the seventeenth century at least, crafting was often seen as an epistemic model of sorts, if only because it was akin to dealing with proportion and measurement and, hence, helped to understand the perfection of Nature.[23]

To be sure, such ideas did not survive the seventeenth century and were always laden with a degree of ambivalence. As early as the sixteenth century, learned scholars and their rhetoric were considered indispensable at least for the communication and "translation" of the naïve and cunning knowledge of artisans, their epistemic importance notwithstanding.[24] Moreover, a certain mathematization of knowledge was underway, with mathematics gradually replacing language as the place where knowledge is located.[25] Nor was the impact thereof limited to scientific discourses and practices. While mathematics emerged from the practices of such actors as architects and engineers, it had a profound bearing on economic practices as well. Hélène Vérin has coined the concept of "réduction en art" to refer to a process in which large-scale entrepreneurs were capable of integrating several artisans in their production networks because they could mentally picture the production process in a more abstract way. Following Vérin the routines of artisans were progressively replaced in the sixteenth century by the abstraction and systematization of engineers, architects, and entrepreneurs.[26] Clearly, this was a partial and uneven process at best, and one which must have provoked resistance on the part of artisans defending the value of their tacit and embodied skills. But the early modern period nevertheless heralded processes of deskilling that were not caused by technological innovation and the emergence of factories, but by cultural and epistemological transformations.

In the period covered here, artists increasingly distanced themselves from the mechanical arts, aligning themselves with the liberal arts, claiming that for art (*conste*) one needs to have intellectual capacities and be acquainted with a learned culture. Hence a division emerged within the world of the artisans, with some acquiring ancient languages and learned knowledge, while others were gradually denied ingenuity and creativity.[27] While incipient already in the fifteenth century, this process resulted in the emergence of art academies in the seventeenth and eighteenth centuries. In these new institutions painters, sculptors, and architects gathered to form a group of artists distanced from guilds and handicrafts. As is well known, artisans from construction and other trades too eventually frequented art academies and drawing schools, which is testimony of the growing importance of drawing skills.[28] This must have been connected in turn, to changes in consumer preferences. This was a context in which designing products became more important—as historians of material culture have shown. However, it simultaneously signals transformations related to the perception and conception of skills and talents. As art historians have shown, "disegno" referred to both drawing and invention and it was seen as the visible manifestation of genius ("ingegno").[29]

All this is not to say, of course, that hands-on skills grew less important; in all likelihood, the reverse was true. But the representations, perceptions, and conceptions of hands-on skills progressively disfavored the artisans' intuitive ways of knowing and working, in part perhaps because knowledge was increasingly stored in books, plans, and schemes, thus undergoing a process of codification and abstraction. In this context, drawing held the promise of emancipation, but simultaneously it must have highlighted the fact that, in some trades, crafting was no longer sufficient in itself.

STATE FORMATION, BUREAUCRATIZATION, AND OLIGARCHIZATION

All this can in turn be connected to the observation that guilds of manufacturing artisans experienced difficulties in being accepted as legitimate organizations when it came to representing the interests of the artisans themselves. This history is most visible in the period after the mid-seventeenth century, but, again, the seeds are to be sought in much earlier periods. Guilds are traditionally associated with community feelings and a struggle for self-rule and autonomy on the urban level. Artisans organized into guilds had fought for economic and political independence—literally so during the urban revolts from the thirteenth to the fifteenth century.[30] From at least the fifteenth century onwards, however, their power was systematically curtailed in many places. Processes of oligarchization and state formation combined to limit the power of the guilds or incorporate them into increasingly bureaucratized territorial state administrations.[31] This is not to say that guilds became less powerful per se. In the Holy Roman Empire, there are many instances of territorial princes creating and promoting guilds as a counter-weight to the economic might and political independence of cities. The point is rather that manufacturing artisans, which had often gained political clout through their guilds, were on the defensive.

In England and France, guilds were used by mercantile and state elites to control product quality, regulate labor, and discipline the workforce. In regions where cities were more autonomous and independent, guilds, too, were often more powerful. In some regions, the southern Netherlands among them, manufacturing masters were moreover likely to have a large say in them. But here, too, the political autonomy and power of manufacturing masters was waning in the long run. The struggles between territorial princes and cities were often entangled with the struggle between political elites and guilds, which was of course also a struggle for taxes and surplus-extraction.[32] The gradual erosion of the guilds' regulations as well as the eventual abolition of the guilds in a period long after the mid-seventeenth century came down to abolishing local monopolies based on a new "raison d'état" and mercantilist and, later, laissez-faire ideas concentrated on the wealth of the state rather than of local corporations. Victors of this process, next to political administrators, were mercantile elites, whose interest most often chimed with those working in the service of the state.

Of course, artisans and guilds were not simply passive actors. On the one hand, inequality among artisans within the same trade was clearly on the rise before the sixteenth century. Evidence comes even from the so-called strong guilds, that is, guilds in which manufacturing masters were in charge (and in which these manufacturing masters often had a great deal of political influence). While in theory masters would be more or less equal in such guilds, limits to workshop size were often significantly lifted or simply ignored, which speaks to concentration trends already underway.[33] Perhaps related to concentration, processes of oligarchization within the guilds also occurred, most visibly in England, where the fifteenth century witnessed the emergence of a formal distinction between "yeomen" and "liverymen." The latter not only had the exclusive right to wear the livery, but also had a privileged access to guild governance. Elsewhere, too, ever smaller elites of freemen monopolized the leadership of guilds, often with the help of systems of co-optation as has been recorded for Rome among other cities.[34] And this is not to mention guilds, cities, and regions in which manufacturing masters did not have any political agency at all, because merchants controlled the guilds and the municipalities—as was the case in the northern Netherlands and most cities in Italy.

All this suggests that the communal character of the guilds drastically transformed in this period. Among others, James R. Farr has notoriously described the artisanal world as one of order, solidarity, and community feeling—attaching a great deal of importance to the rituals and symbols with which insiders were distinguished from outsiders. From the outset, internal coherence and solidarity may have been more typical for small cities—while Farr has worked on Dijon, similar arguments have been raised by Walker in his work on the so-called home towns.[35] But the overall picture may nevertheless have changed drastically in the period focused on here. Indeed, scholars have long since recognized that guilds in cities large and small were rife with conflict among masters, between masters and merchant-entrepreneurs and between masters and journeymen. The claims of order, solidarity, and community were prescriptive rather than descriptive. The guilds' collective activities also came under severe pressure in this period, as can be deduced from the fact that guild ordinances increasingly mention fines for masters who failed to attend processions, masses, the burials of fellow members, and so on.[36] Guild records likewise record with great frequency the penalties assessed against masters who refused to observe production guidelines and journeymen who refused to submit to the masters' authority. In part, this may have been due to Reformation ideas, which included a great suspicion towards the forms of communal worship which involved patron saints, special liturgies, and dedicated chapels, that helped to underwrite guild solidarity. Guilds, like other brotherhoods, surely fell victim to such disrupting actions as the removal of altar tables and the melting of religious silver.[37] Yet evangelical ideals were not alien to the guild-based masters themselves. A strong case has been made for the argument that artisans in some trades were often at the vanguard of the Reformation movement, perhaps because what was at stake was often the definition of the urban community.[38] Nor was this a process limited to guilds in northwestern Europe. Processes of oligarchization and the erosion of communal values have also been recorded for the often large and powerful Italian confraternities after 1500.[39]

The history of the guilds is obviously relevant for the political culture of work, but the guilds' political actions have seldom been connected to the history of work or to social history in recent decades. Scanning the literature on popular protest, it is striking how seldom rebellion and revolt are connected to issues of work in a structural way. While scholars such as Charles Tilly held to a "grand" historical sociology, with its focus on the effects of capital and coercion,[40] the attention has shifted to forms and expressions of popular politics. Not only did the formation of coalitions often fail to fit in a class-based conception of early modern society, but protest was often geared towards customs and performed in a ritual or ceremonial way. William Beik, for instance, studied urban protest primarily from a cultural point of view, looking for repetitive forms of behavior in the tactics, gestures, slogans, or beliefs of crowds wanting to punish and humiliate their enemies while communicating their views of how the community should be governed. Beik saw artisans and wage workers often at the forefront of urban protest, as catalysts of the struggle, but labor disputes were seen in his work as stimulating broader political movements rather than as determinants as such.⁴¹ This appears to be even more the case in research on early modern England, which has focused far less on economic issues or the roles of guilds and artisans. Perez Zagorin's recent overview of sixteenth- and seventeenth-century rebellion hardly gives any attention to the relationship between revolt and work or its cultural values.⁴² It may be time, therefore, again to appreciate that work played a constitutive role in the formation of political identities and positions, however varied they were, when looking at skilled artisanal labor, specialized husbandry, and unskilled industrial or rural labor as well as at different periods and regions.

POPULATION GROWTH AND GLOBALIZATION

All this is not to deny, of course, the importance of transformations in the economic and, perhaps especially, the demographic spheres. Probably beginning in the mid-fifteenth century, the population of Europe began its slow, secular recovery from the effects of the pandemic diseases that swept across the continent in the mid-fourteenth century. Valid generalizations prove elusive, because not all regions of Europe suffered similar levels of mortality, and not all regions recovered at the same rate. It seems true, however, that most of those places that had lost the greatest numbers to starvation and disease, especially the manufacturing centers of northern Italy and the Low Countries, began to display indications of population growth by the beginning of the sixteenth century. While this recovery lasted until roughly the mid-seventeenth century, it had severe consequences for the world of work.

For one thing, population growth was accompanied by geographic mobility: People took to the road in the sixteenth century. Contemporary accounts testify to huge rates of migration. Demographic expansion put pressure on the land; constraints on land tenure, whether under systems of partible inheritance or primogeniture, forced rural workers to seek employment elsewhere; large population shifts took place from rural to urban, from the countryside to towns, from small towns to large. This had consequences for the agricultural workforce, reducing it in some regions to such an extent that those areas became net importers of foodstuffs, a process that contributed to the specialization and integration of European commodity markets. It also had consequences for the cost of living, driving up the price of foodstuffs and, as is well noted, driving down real wages.

One especially noteworthy consequence of migration was urbanization, the growth in size, number, and importance of large cities. Medieval and early modern cities suffered notoriously high levels of mortality and low natality; they expanded only through immigration. As a result of migration during the sixteenth century, the proportion of truly large cities, those with populations above 100,000 increased relative to the number of smaller-sized cities. The large cities drew from the countryside, of course, but they appear to have done most of their growing at the expense of regional towns. Cities traditionally attracted people to markets for raw and finished goods, but in the early modern period they increasingly drew people to what might be called an early form of futures markets. Immigrants tended to be younger: They came in search of work; they came in search of spouses; they came in search of charity. Early modern records testify to the varied impact of immigration: Competition with resident workers; pressure on real wages; fissures in work organizations, especially guilds; and limits on poor relief. Population growth and mobility thus altered nearly every aspect of the material and cultural history of work in the early modern period.

Another consequence of population growth, at least in certain areas, was protoindustrialization. On the one hand, population growth brought with it higher levels of consumption that raised prices for a wide range of finished goods and acted as a spur to increased production. On the other, it also created a larger, manufacturing workforce, especially in rural areas. The limitations imposed by land tenure forced ever larger numbers of people to adopt wage labor, either in agriculture or manufacturing. This enabled merchants and merchant-entrepreneurs to rely on homeworkers in rural districts, especially in the textile sector. To meet demand in those markets, merchants not only had to produce goods to export but also had to produce them efficiently and in bulk. To accomplish these ends, they organized production networks. The putting-out system was a familiar form, but other kinds of domestic industry emerged and flourished. Franklin Mendels named this phase of intense industrial development "protoindustrialization" both to mark the expansion of manufacturing into rural households, where it involved increasing numbers of women and children in wage relations, and to signal its contribution to modern industrialization of which it was thought to be the beginning. The term has been often challenged by such scholars as D. C. Coleman, Martin Daunton, and Sheilagh Ogilvie for its failure to include urban and workshop manufacturing. It did not occur across Europe, nor did it lead to the Industrial Revolution proper.

What is clear is that it was not favorable for labor relations. Available hands provided capacity that encouraged an expansion of productivity and a search for new products and new markets. Innovations in production techniques and organization broadened the array of finished products and increased the efficiency of their manufacture. But workers often became entrapped in wage and credit relations, with merchants providing cash advances at interest or raw materials on consignment and paying for work by the piece, both of which rendered producers increasingly dependent. Reliance on production networks created patterns of debt dependency that robbed workers of their independent status and income. Whether producers received cash from or owed money to merchants, they became more subordinate to the dictates of commerce, more open to new methods and products as stipulated by merchants who were familiar with conditions on foreign markets.

The increasing power of merchants and the related turn to the countryside in turn had multiple origins. One is certainly the declining power of the guilds of manufacturing artisans to defend their urban privileges, which often included the prohibition to produce their products in the countryside. Movement of production into the countryside created competition between local and foreign, guilded and nonguilded, workers. Another, related factor is the increasing importance of overseas expansion. Beginning in the fifteenth century, European workers found themselves increasingly caught up in global markets. A degree of global engagement was by no means new at the time. Western textile manufacturers had long produced luxury woollens for sale in the Middle and Far East. They had likewise depended on non-European producers for various industrial commodities, including raw cotton, alum, and dyestuffs. Yet that degree of engagement and dependence increased greatly with the search for direct overseas trade routes to Asian markets.

Fustian manufacturing around Augsburg, Germany, provides an example of this development and some of its consequences. Fustian is a mixed textile with linen warp and cotton weft. Known since the second century and commonly produced in Italy since the twelfth, it emerged as a mass produced, export commodity in the second half of the thirteenth century that combined local flax production in the region and foreign cotton importation from Syria via Venice. Wholesale merchants organized the supply of local linen and foreign cotton. An increasing number of Augsburg weavers produced an increasing amount of cloth that Augsburg merchants carried to export markets in Frankfurt, Cologne, Krakow, Prague, and Vienna. By the fifteenth century, production had expanded to such an extent that capital began to seek more producers, drawing upon weavers in neighboring towns and villages. It utilized a putting-out system, a kind of production network that relied on an extensive division of labor. Merchants purchased the raw materials, which they put out on consignment to artisans in their homes or workshops. When one step in the production process was completed, the merchant delivered the partially finished materials to workers who completed the next step and so on until the finished product was ready for market. Workers provided only their tools and labor for which they were paid a piece rate, usually upon completion of their task. The Weavers' Guild in Augsburg attempted repeatedly to prohibit the resort to production networks that relied on rural weavers. That repetition suggests that their efforts bore little fruit and that their influence was already waning.

In short, organized to meet the needs of export markets in a rapidly globalizing economy, domestic industry employed surplus labor, thus expanding the workforce. It led to specialization that encouraged economic integration and favored reciprocal trade and economies of scale. It provided essential management experience in such aspects of industry as material logistics, production coordination, and work discipline, all of which affected the experience of work. It increased the incomes—and therewith the consumption—of working families. Jan de Vries has notoriously connected this process to the consumer revolution, suggesting that the driving force was not solely increased productivity and its associated processes of worker marginalization and immiseration, but rather people's motivation to engage in consumption by working and earning more. Again, it is far from clear how widespread this "industrious revolution" may have been, but it clearly affected workers in a range of industries. Increased consumption, whatever its causes, may be the most under-estimated and under-studied aspect of any history of work. Overseas and colonial goods, such as coffee, tea, and sugar, altered consumer preferences even among common workers from the seventeenth century onwards. The same applies to a range of "populuxe goods," the availability of which transformed workers' lives. Richard Goldthwaite and other historians have suggested that such changing sensitivities towards material goods are visible throughout the period 1450–1650.[43] Research has further suggested that the shift from intrinsic to extrinsic value, that is, from the value of the raw material to the cultural or sign value based upon criteria such as design and novelty, as the determining factor in the quality and price of a product has contributed significantly to the historic marginalization of work as an occupation and workers as members of industrial society.[44] The valorization of consumer goods as "cheap" may have influenced the association between working classes and political subordination.[45] This is yet another reason to study work in the early modern period.

A CHANGING ECONOMIC AND GEOPOLITICAL ENVIRONMENT

Perhaps the most important transformation of all was a change in political–economic relations that raised transaction costs along established trade routes and further encouraged the search for alternatives. The expansion of the Ottoman Empire into the Eastern Mediterranean basin reached a dramatic high point with the siege and sack of Constantinople in 1453. Although the Ottomans had been an expanding power in central and western Asia for some centuries, having established themselves on the shores of the Black Sea and on the European side of the Bosporus and penetrated the Balkans by the late fourteenth century, the fall of this ancient bastion of Christianity caught the immediate attention of the West. Moreover, the Ottomans defeated Persia and conquered Egypt under Selim I (1470–1520). His successor, Suleiman (1494–1566), known among Europeans as "the Magnificent," would extend Ottoman suzerainty along the northern coast of Africa, seize Mesopotamia and its access to the Persian Gulf from the Persians, and partition the Caucasus with them. This placed established routes and entrepôts between East and West in the hands of a power that was perceived to be less welcoming to European merchants than its predecessor. The fear of increased political instability in the region and of increased economic costs of its trade prompted European commercial interests to seek new routes to the East.

This is not to say that trade through the Mediterranean basin ceased. There were too many established overland and overseas trade routes from Asia to Europe that transited Ottoman territories for this to be the case. The trade in spices with South and Southeast Asia passed into the Persian Gulf and Red Sea, from whose ports it made its way via caravan to Cairo and Alexandria, to be purchased there by European merchants. Aleppo and Bursa were the termini for overland trade routes with Persia and points further east, from which European merchants acquired raw silk. They exchanged not only luxury woollen goods but other commodities much desired in the East, such as mirrors and clocks. To preserve this trade and its revenues, the Ottomans offered privileges to European merchants, especially those from countries with whom they enjoyed friendly relations. As a result, German, Dutch, and Iberian merchants suffered commercial disadvantages, while French, English, and Italian merchants could trade more freely in Ottoman ports and markets.

Though international trade persisted in the Mediterranean, its relative importance and value began to change in the fifteenth century as European princes and merchants sought direct connections to trading partners in Asia. The narrative of that search for alternatives need not be rehearsed here, neither the slow, consequent exploration of the African coast and southeastern Atlantic by the Portuguese that resulted in Vasco da Gama's successful landing on the Malabar coast of India in 1498, nor the daring Spanish attempt at a direct route west that brought Christopher Columbus to the New World in 1492. The opening of direct, overseas trade with Asia and the beginning of intense economic exploitation in the Americas had immediate consequences for the economy of Europe and the history of work, however. It generated trade in a seemingly ever increasing volume and variety of industrial and consumer goods. It stimulated both production and consumption. It expanded the reliance on industrial forms of production, such as slave-operated plantations and waged production networks. It quickened the accumulation of capital. And that capital, in turn, necessitated investment that increased production and consumption.

Among these effects is what scholars refer to as the "little divergence," the postulated differential economic growth in Europe during the period 1300–1800 that resulted in the emergence of England and the Low Countries as the most dynamic regions of the continent at the expense of the Mediterranean. It takes its name from the "great divergence," which attempts to explain how Europe forged ahead of East Asia in economic power, arguing instead that not all of Europe but a little corner of it diverged onto a path of rapid development. The developing importance of northwestern Europe is not a new supposition, having been posited decades ago by Ralph Davis, whose "rise of the Atlantic economies" argued that the economic takeoff of northwestern Europe resulted from geographical advantages linked to the shift in overseas trade routes away from the

Mediterranean. The current discussion departs from Davies' earlier theory in the breadth and depth of its data, which extends beyond wages to include indicators of productivity and consumption. These studies seem to show that northwestern Europe experienced near uninterrupted growth from the fourteenth to the eighteenth century, in contrast to other parts of Europe where comparable indices stagnated or declined. Causes are thought to be institutional changes, especially the growing strength both of representative political institutions and of private property protections or the shrinking effectiveness of corporate, that is guild, regulations.

The "little divergence" remains the subject of considerable controversy, especially in its implications for work. As will become clear, wages are not an ideal measure of the economy or culture of work, especially before the Industrial Revolution. Moreover, such modern measures as gross domestic product, which summarizes the value of all goods and services or consumer spending and reduces consumption to a function of income and accumulated wealth, apply poorly to premodern economies where data is available only for certain communities or industries, if at all. Nor, finally, do theories of northwestern dominance square well with close studies of other regions, such as south Germany in the sixteenth century, which argue for considerable growth in production and consumption outside the privileged northwest. Grand theories gloss over regional or industrial differentials that were telling in the period 1450–1650, and obscure even more the experience of work as an economic, social, or cultural phenomenon.

That said, the "little divergence" points to facts that are the object of historical consensus. European workers, especially those in the Low Countries and England, though one might include parts of France and Germany, increasingly labored for wages and produced for export. Again, neither development is new in 1450, as the fustian manufactory of Augsburg and Swabia make clear, but both intensified as a result of overseas expansion. They are not common to all industries, but limited largely to those producing high-volume goods for foreign markets. The accumulation of capital that resulted from long-distance trade changed the terms and organization of production from the fourteenth century onwards. With knowledge of supply and demand in foreign markets, merchant-entrepreneurs employed their capital, both financial and intellectual, to underwrite the production of new goods for export.

CONCLUSION

The period 1450–1650 witnessed important structural transformations with a potential impact on the culture of work. Most of these transformations—religious and cultural transitions; institutional and political developments; population growth, consumer preferences and globalization; and so on—have already engendered important debates among labor historians and others. Most of these debates have remained inconclusive, not seldom because the historical record resists being fitted with in a teleological modernity narrative or reduced to a mono-causal explanatory framework.

The challenge of the present volume, then, is to examine the period 1450–1650 in all its complexity in its own right—without, of course, losing sight of longer-term developments. This is what all authors in this volume have done: While briefly touching upon the specific historiographic debates in their own subfield, they present a careful synthesis of what is typically a very complex and contingent set of processes. And, while refusing to frame this in a long-term narrative of modernity, they nevertheless present building blocks for an informative long-term cultural history of work.

CHAPTER ONE

The Economy of Work

THOMAS MAX SAFLEY

An "economy of work" in the early modern age must immediately acknowledge and confront a series of terminological and methodological problems. What exactly does the title promise?

The *Oxford English Dictionary* defines an "economy" as "the organization or condition of a community or nation with respect to economic factors, esp. the production and consumption of goods and services and the supply of money."[1] Put somewhat more broadly, it is that system of human activities related to the production, distribution, exchange, and consumption of goods and services. Accordingly, the study of an economy, past or present, should extend beyond the workings of markets, the purview of economics in the narrow, classical sense, to include the influences of technology, history, society, geography, and ecology, among many others. So broad—almost imperial—an approach renders any "economy of work" nearly inseparable from topics treated elsewhere in this volume: "workplace cultures"; "work, skill, and technology"; "work and society"; "work and mobility"; "work and leisure." To avoid poaching and preempting other contributions and discussions, this chapter is rigorously limited to considerations of the supply of workers and the demand for their work as statistical abstractions, excluding any structural, organizational, institutional, or cultural features, an odd prospect at best. Furthermore, an "economy of work" suggests that "work" exists as a good or a service, as a commodity for consumption or as a factor of production, in a single economy. In the period between 1450 and 1650, however, the European economy did not exist as an integrated unit in its own right, nor was it part of a densely knit, intensely functioning global economy, though aspects of both were beginning to develop. The degrees of regional, even local, fragmentation, variation, and isolation render difficult any attempt to generalize about the topic at hand.

"Work" poses no less intractable difficulties. Economics and economic history insist quite uniformly on the term "labor," examining laborers and labor economics, rather than workers and work economics. Yet the *Oxford English Dictionary* defines work as synonymous with labor. Generally understood, work is an "action, labour, activity; an instance of this," or, put in more economic terms, an "action or activity involving physical or mental effort and undertaken in order to achieve a result, esp. as a means of making one's living or earning money; labour; (one's) regular occupation or employment."[2] This seems clear enough, but the anglophone world makes certain, informal distinctions. Leaving aside orthographic variations, labour as opposed to labour, this term has become associated with modern economic and political developments—slave labor, factory labor, organized labor, labor movements, labor parties—despite Marx's call for "workers" of the world to unite. The name Marx evokes in turn the emphasis placed by scholars on workshop and factory labor at the expense of intellectual or artistic employments in a study, studio, or office. Labor may also connote suffering and struggle, though people continue to "work themselves to death." Moreover, as the dictionary definition makes clear, both terms, but especially labor, suggest an exchange relationship in which a task is performed for the purpose of "making one's living or earning money," though many forms of work contribute to economic life with little or no economic reward.

These terminological nuances point to specific methodological challenges. Insofar as the early modern European economy experienced limited integration, uniform archival data on the "economy of work" do not exist, even within individual, economic sectors. Where primary sources, whether qualitative or quantitative, can be found, they seldom support reliable translocal or transregional comparison. Moreover, they seldom provide strictly economic information of the sort described above. Most economic histories of early modern work are "economic" only in that broader sense: they take up political, social, or cultural aspects of the organization and performance of work.

To address—or avoid—these difficulties, this chapter takes up the history of wage studies for the period 1450–1650. Scholars have constructed wage series that have shown remarkable traction in studies of the medieval and early modern "economy of work." They have argued that wages may reflect the market value of labor, but they have also recognized that wages reflect the organization and condition of that market, including barriers to entry, asymmetries of information, constraints on action, and so forth. The existence of these and other market imperfections, so-called, indicates the workings of factors beyond supply and demand, such as community and custom. Encounters with the limitations of wages in the early modern age have increased scholarly awareness of the political, social, and cultural contexts of work and its economy. This chapter will review the limitations of wage studies. It will also consider the implications of revisions to this approach, touching upon such macrohistorical developments as the spread of production networks, the resort to bound labor, and the intervention of political entities. Finally, it will pose the question whether labor markets *stricto sensu* existed in the early modern age and return to the fundamental problem of an "economy of work."

THE EARLY HISTORY OF WAGE STUDIES

In the two centuries between 1450 and 1650 the "economy of work" changed profoundly in Europe. This is not to say that all parts of Europe and all forms of work experienced change in the same manner or to the same degree. Indeed, debates concerning economic continuity and change in this period are so familiar as to need no rehearsal. Scholars intent on explaining the long-term causes of European industrialization—the emergence of a so-called modern, industrial economy—tend to view the period in terms of restructuring and takeoff, one in which a variety of forces promoted the emergence of professional organizations, efficient institutions, and integrated markets, the result of which was an accumulation of capital and a globalization of exchange that yielded a modern economic system. These modernity narratives often assumed an expansion of wage labor, at least in the most advanced regions of northwestern Europe. This perspective has profoundly shaped the resort to wages as a lens through which to study the economy of work. Their opponents, often engaged in the close examination of local or regional economies, cannot help but notice the persistence of premodern practices, organizations, and institutions, a noteworthy example being the persistence of artisanal and merchant guilds. Their studies have resulted in many useful correctives, deepening an appreciation for the complexities—even ambiguities—of wages in relationship to work.

Modernists and medievalists might incline to orient the period in opposing directions, but none would deny the extraordinary forces that influenced the economy of work between 1450 and 1650. Following the demographic crisis of the fourteenth century, the European population reached a low point around 1450 and began its slow recovery in the mid-sixteenth century, altering the supply of workers and consumers and, therewith, shifting the value of work and the cost of living. Wages for many parts of Europe stood at a historic high point only to collapse to a no less historic low. The creation of direct, overseas routes from Europe to East Asia and to the New World, resulted in accumulated capital, industrial commodities, and consumer goods that profoundly transformed how workers worked, what they produced, and how much they were paid. These two forces, population recovery and overseas commerce, contributed to a period of inflation during the sixteenth century, a price revolution that undoubtedly altered the terms of trade within which workers worked, even if scholars continue to argue the relative weights of the likely causes. Neither of these developments were felt uniformly across the peninsula of Europe. Both nonetheless altered wages to varying degrees in various places between 1450 and 1650.

Attempts to measure these changes began in the late nineteenth century, when economists and economic historians began to create wage and price series, gathering and collating data, preserved in such sources as tariff lists and account books. The pioneers in this field, for example, A. L. Bowley in Britain, Émile Levasseur in France, and Gustav von Schmoller in Germany, were not interested in the early modern "economy of work," but rather sought in the first instance comparisons to the cost and standard of living of workers under the influence of industrialization. By the mid-twentieth century, an International Scientific Committee on Price History had formed to coordinate the construction of long-term wage and price series. It encouraged the publication of national studies that continue to shape quantitative work on wages and prices to this day: William Beveridge on England; Moritz Elsas on Germany; Earl Hamilton on Spain; Henri Hauser on France; Nicolaas Posthumus on Holland; and Alfred F. Pribram on Austria. The committee eventually ceased activity, the result of philosophical and methodological differences among its members, but its achievement provided the statistical foundation for the work of E. H. Phelps Brown and Sheila V. Hopkins, upon which so much of contemporary scholarship rests.

In a series that covered seven centuries, from 1264 to 1954, Phelps Brown and Hopkins tracked nominal wages, that is, wages measured in current values, among building workers in England.[3] They came to four observations that have engaged economic historians ever since. First, they noted the "extraordinary absence of falls," that is, that nominal wages rose without interruption of any sort over the entire period of study. Second, they found that "wages did not vary from year to year with the price of provisions," the so-called "stickiness" of preindustrial nominal wages. Third, they observed a "remarkable stability" in the difference between wages paid to skilled and unskilled workers. Fourth, and for the purposes of this volume most important, they documented the extraordinary rise in nominal wages that began in the early-sixteenth century and persists to the present day. These findings set the agenda for the modern study of real wages and living standards.

In the years that followed the appearance of their first essay, Phelps Brown and Hopkins refined and expanded their initial findings. Moving from nominal to real wages, that is, wages measured in terms of their purchasing power against the price of a representative basket of goods, they again arrived at observations that became a point of reference for the field of economic history.[4] The period 1450–1650 opens with "a time of much greater prosperity" that ends abruptly in the first decade of the sixteenth century. A "Tudor inflation," which was marked by a steep rise in the price of consumer goods, resulted in an "impoverishment of the [English] wage-earner" that was itself an event of enormous historical consequence. Between the early-sixteenth and the mid-seventeenth centuries, the purchasing power of construction workers sank to roughly 40 percent of what it had been at the close of the fifteenth century. Nor was this pattern limited to England.[5] Borrowing from the work of peninsular scholars, they "found that the purchasing power of builders' wage-rates fell at much the same time and to much the same extent in France and Alsace." They could not resist a dramatic conclusion: "From the Rhine to the Thames, the standard of living of one section of the working population was brought down progressively for more than a century." Relying on historical statistics gathered by Elsas, Hamilton, Pribram, and others, they found the same patterns of stagnant nominal wages, rising consumer prices, and falling real wages in the cities of Augsburg, Münster, Valencia, and Vienna, from the early sixteenth to the mid-seventeenth century.[6] "The outstanding finding is that in all four places the basketful a day's pay would buy shrank drastically during the sixteenth century, just as it did in the three regions we studied before." The timing of the collapse demonstrates striking similarities across the peninsula. They concluded that the same cause affected real wages in the same way in each place: "This movement in the terms of trade … is the second salient feature of our findings." The growth of population, especially in urban areas, drove up the price of food.

Phelps Brown and Hopkins concluded that the demography of work shaped the economy of work. They took their cue from Thomas Malthus and reasoned, without direct reference to demographic data, that population pressure, more than American silver, industrial scale, business organization, or economic mentality, drove consumer prices upward and, accordingly, real wages downward. Here they parted company with that earlier generation of scholars, whose work they had mined. Earl Hamilton had argued that the immiseration of working men and women had monetarist roots, that is, that the flood of specie from the New World worked to raise prices in the Old. Thorold Rogers had insisted that ruthless exploitation and oppression constituted the "perfectly intelligible causes." Earlier still, von Schmoller had also seized upon oppression: the loss of "traditional, social institutions."[7] Phelps Brown and Hopkins reasoned instead that the increased supply of labor, itself a consequence of the demographic recovery that becomes visible in the sixteenth century, could not be absorbed by rural society, because agricultural production had reached its maximum, barring technological or organizational changes. The surplus population was forced off the land into cities, where it sought other work. Increased demand bid up the cost of consumer goods, especially food, at a time when nominal wages rose slowly, if at all.

Viewed from the perspective of wages, therefore, the economy of work between 1450 and 1650 changed strictly as a function of supply and demand. From the mid-fifteenth century until the early sixteenth century, the supply of labor remained scarce, relative to demand, which kept nominal wages in a stable state. That real wages showed greater volatility, falling sharply from the early years of the sixteenth century until the mid-seventeenth century, resulted from the increased supply of labor, relative to demand, itself a reflection of demographic recovery and growth. It is a deceptively simple explanation that, as noted, has proven remarkably durable.

THE PROBLEM WITH WAGE STUDIES

Economic historians have long relied on the real wage index of Phelps Brown and Hopkins as a benchmark for the "economy of work" in the medieval and early modern ages. Herman van Der Wee incorporated it into his wage-price comparison between England and Belgium. Peter Scholliers used it to illustrate the historical movement of wages over time in his contribution to *The Oxford Encyclopedia of Economic History*. Karl Gunnar Persson's recent survey, *An Economic History of Europe: Knowledge, Institutions and Growth, 600 to the Present*, makes reference to the pattern without citing the essay.

Yet students of economic change and development have long recognized the problems that attend the study of real wages and living standards in the past. Adam Smith doubted that they could be analyzed in any consistent, rational manner: "The price of labour, it must be observed, cannot be ascertained very accurately anywhere, different prices being often paid at the same place and for the same sort of labour, not only according to the different abilities of the workmen, but according to the easiness or hardness of the masters."[8] Wages were not set by abstract market forces, but were the result of individual negotiations between masters and men, a product less of supply and demand than of personality and circumstance. Smith believed that economists and historians might at best learn "what [wages] are the most usual," but that the usual would bear little resemblance to the actual. It might be quantified in the form of sums and averages that change over time, much as Phelps Brown and Hopkins had done, but those figures and their historical movements would not reveal what was paid, much less how or why.

Donald Woodward expressed precisely the heart of the matter: "English society during the sixteenth and early-seventeenth centuries had not yet become a predominantly wage-earning society."[9] Many of the workers whose wages made up the series constructed by Phelps Brown and Hopkins were not wage-earners in the modern sense, but rather self-employed craftsmen who exercised some control over the work they performed. They could earn wages, but could also work independently, subcontract other laborers and bear the costs of tools and materials. That these workers might be self-employed raised issues not only about the purpose, but also about the meaning of their wages. Beyond measuring the accepted value of their work, wages reflected their status as independent artisans, practitioners of a craft, masters of skill. Many of these workers could, and often did, pursue by-employments of various kinds. Different groups of workers earned in different ways and at different rates: agricultural laborers, to take up a single example among many possible ones, endured seasonal changes in their earnings; certain workers customarily received payment at least partly in kind; female and child workers earned differently—usually less—than did male adults. If "using formal wages as a proxy for 'labour income' may be quite misleading," as Joel Mokyr argued for the nineteenth century,[10] it is much more so in the period 1450–1650, when market integration and information symmetry were even less advanced, when the forms and implications of wages were much more various and when the rhythms and techniques of work were likewise further from uniform.

Wages mirror work, but darkly. As Donald Woodward asserted, "there can be little doubt that the chief influence on the level of wage rates in early-modern England was the interaction between the supply of labour and the demand for it."[11] Yet, "custom—in part the product of the interplay of economic forces, but also the product of perceptions of social hierarchy—also played a role in determining the level and movement of nominal wages."[12] They provide thus entrée into the "economy of work" in all its complexity.

Aggregate studies tend to obscure the messiness, the interplay of wage form, social hierarchy, seasonal variation, work organization, and state regulation that shape wage rates no less than supply and demand. Close studies of individual industries, individual worksites, make it clearer, however. Consider, by way of example, the mercury mine and refinery at Idrija, Slovenia, part of the Archduchy of Austria in the early modern age. The mine operated without notable interruption from its discovery around 1495 until its closure in 1995. A single wage account from 1537 indicates that employment rose annually from 94 workers in 1527 to an all-time maximum of 180 in 1532 before declining to 60 in 1536.[13] They received for their various labors a weekly cash wage that ranged from three *Gulden* for a highly skilled smelter to one *Gulden* thirty *Kreuzer* for his assistant.[14] Less-skilled workers, such as a water-lifter, that is, a worker charged with draining water from the mines, earned one *Gulden* eight *Kreuzer* for a week of backbreaking effort. Relatively high remuneration reflects not only the difficulty but also the importance of keeping the mines free of water. The carpenters who built the pumps, flumes and lifts and shored the mines with timbers earned one *Gulden* per week. Miners, by contrast, earned a base wage of fifty-one *Kreuzer* two *Pfennigs* per week, plus a premium that varied with the amount and quality of ore they dug. Thus, they appear to have been paid both a time and a piece rate. Common workers, the jacks-of-all-trades around the mine, earned forty-five *Kreuzer* per week. These were not necessarily starvation wages, but they did not necessarily guarantee a livelihood either. By way of comparison, the city of Augsburg, where many of the mine operators and some of the mine workers originated, set a net worth of fifty *Gulden* yearly as its poverty line. Persons unable to certify that minimum of capital or income were not permitted to become citizens or even to marry in the city, because they were understood to be unable to support themselves or their families. Only the least important workers at Idrija would have failed to meet this standard.

Real wages at Idrija have proven impossible to calculate. Workers did not purchase the necessities of life on local markets, because the isolated location of the mine rendered transportation inefficient. A substantial part of a worker's earnings was paid in the form of foodstuffs, lighting, equipment, and clothing, in a system that became known as *Pfennwert*, for which the account offers no monetary value. Workers thus received their remuneration not only in cash, but also in kind. They were dependent upon their employers' arbitrary policies in supplying essentials, because food and other supplies were scarce and had to be imported in large quantities from nearby villages. The mine operators clearly understood that trading in foodstuffs and other useful goods represented a further source of earnings deriving from mining, a source that might become even more important in hard times. Accordingly, the operators might indirectly squeeze wages by raising the prices of these goods. Speculation on foodstuffs and the sale of poor-quality products at high prices were the order of the day.

Austrian mining ordinances, from 1427 until the state law on mines, attempted to regulate *Pfennwert* and to maintain fair prices. Unfortunately, all these prohibitions, injunctions, and controls were short-lived and ineffective. Until the restoration of the Austrian state mining industry in 1871, when all salaries were paid in cash, payment in kind remained a permanent source of bitter controversy. In consequence, miners in central Europe often stopped work or abandoned one mine for another, aware of their importance as specialized and highly sought-after laborers. Surviving records contain no indication of any work stoppage, but much evidence of regular, bitter complaints at Idrija during the sixteenth and seventeenth centuries.

According to this 1537 account, wage modality and form were mixed at Idrija; time and piece rates, cash and in kind, all were paid at the same time. It does not permit a calculation of wage change; it does reveal employment change. These wages indicate a somewhat different relationship to time. Historical studies have made much of work time, the seasonality and periodicity of preindustrial labor, emphasizing how the study of wages must account for the rhythms of work. The Idrija record indicates different kinds of cadences that affected both the work and the economy of work underground. One of these was the cadence of the market. The numbers of workers rose and fell dramatically over the course of a single decade, a fact utterly obscured by long-term wage indices. Given that the mine continued in operation, it appears that the supply of its products—mercury and cinnabar—exceeded demand. In short, the mine overproduced, and mine workers were periodically laid off. In consequence, wages at Idrija reflect not only the work, but also the productivity of that work and the sales of its product.

A marginal note in the wage account of 1537 refers to the protestation of workers against lay-offs that seemed arbitrary or lacked due process. This suggests further the possibility that a negotiated degree of job security may have been part of the miners' culture, perhaps part of their wage. Another of these cadences concerned the weather. Mining is not considered seasonal work in the same manner as agriculture, but weather could hinder work underground as well as above and reduce wages accordingly. The hazard and expense caused by flooding was a constant challenge at Idrija. The mine lies above the Idrica River in narrow, low-lying calcareous mountains, consisting of soft, porous limestone. Given its location and bedrock, it is particularly subject to drainage problems. Seasons of rain make the flooding worse, as the wage account reflects, rendering some of the mine shafts unproductive. They required, in 1537, the animal power of seven horses, down from eleven at the beginning, as well as twenty-seven assorted workers at a cost of seventy-nine *Gulden* per week, just to pump the water out. The authoritative texts of Georg Agricola and others show clearly that the problems posed by draining and venting deep mines prompted some of the greatest technological advances of the early modern age. Animal- or wind-powered vacuum pumps of considerable sophistication aided the men in their work. Therefore, both the problem and its solution affected work and wages.

The necessity of draining and venting mine shafts and galleries to enable the work of extraction to proceed, raises yet another wage-related element of the "economy of work." Productivity at Idrija required able producers, not only skilled, but also healthy. No less than water, fumes in the mine endangered workers and slowed production, as the 1537 wage account makes again clear. As the miners dug deeper and farther, these dangers intensified. Poisonous fumes were a constant hazard that worsened over time, especially in mercury mines. Their amelioration required ventilators—giant animal-, wind-, or water-driven fans or bellows—or special constructions to permit cross-currents of air in the mines. Failure to invest in such devices had costs of its own, however. Employees and employers alike feared the effects of mercury poisoning with good reason. The presence of toxic fumes at Idrija were such that, according to the operators, the mine could be worked no more than eighteen work-weeks out of the year, and a miner could not work underground for more than fourteen days, but had regularly to be shifted from one form of labor to another. This created problems in the work process itself, because the mining could not cease, just because miners had to work outside the mine. Shifts had to be created and coordinated so that the work continued apace with adequate personnel. The deeper the mines went, the shorter the work period a miner could tolerate. The difficulties extended well beyond coordinating the work process; early industrial hazards engendered early health-care costs. The account mentioned no fewer than twenty disabled laborers, whom the mine supported with regular payments. Moreover, the fear of mercury poisoning complicated the recruitment of healthy workers.

These few examples suffice to confirm what other studies have found in other industries.[15] Wages are not a simple metric for the value of work. At Idrija, they were affected by work times and patterns unique to the physical and environmental specificities of a single workplace. They took a variety of forms, reflected hierarchies among workers and their work, and were subject to work processes and organizations that were themselves subject to change over time and space. Such a realization by no means refutes the value of their quantitative studies, but wage series alone, shorn of their cultural, social, political, and ecological contexts, separated from close consideration of wage form and modality, obscure as much as they reveal. Wages express, therefore, not only the economy but also the political economy of work.

THE REVISION OF WAGE STUDIES

In light of such scruples, it comes as no surprise that the most striking conclusions drawn from Phelps Brown and Hopkins' wage series—the "stickiness" of wages, their absence of declines, their long periods of fixity, their stable differentials—have been subject to criticism and revision. The objection arose almost immediately that wages exist within a matrix of factors other than those of the market, that they expressed also custom, power, and identity. Eric Hobsbawm, for example, recognized early that workers understood wages to be governed by certain "rules of the game."[16] The supposedly simple factor of supply proved suddenly complex; it comprised not all those willing and able to perform a certain kind of work, but rather only those permitted or privileged to do so by virtue of familial relationship, guild membership, or urban citizenship. Hobsbawm's interest centered on labor negotiations in the mid-nineteenth century, and he spared little thought for earlier centuries. The implication seemed broader, however. His "rules" encouraged what Peter Scholliers and Leonard Schwarz aptly termed a "social approach to the wage."[17] This broader, more complex interest in wages shifted the ends towards which they were studied. Scholars questioned the basic assumptions that inform wage indices: that all workers were wage-earners; that wages represented only payment for work; that wages captured, if not a worker's total earnings, then at least the rate at which those earnings changed over time; that calculated real wages represented a worker's standard of living. Among historians of work a methodological debate also began. Wage series, calculated on the basis of a measure of central tendency, obscure the dispersion of data around the mode, those rapid fluctuations in wages that de Vries, Boulton, and many others have noted. Many economic historians argued that these changes more accurately reflect not only the true volatility of wages, but the working lives of preindustrial wage-earners.[18] Whereas the issue had once been the living standards among preindustrial and industrial workers, the goal became what might be called the lived experience of preindustrial and industrial workers.

One aspect of this lived experience was certainly the differences in wages earned by workers in a single industry. Phelps Brown and Hopkins had anticipated potential wage differentials between skilled and unskilled construction workers. By contrast, they did not consider the possibility of different forms and systems of wages, as Woodward, Mokyr, and many others quickly realized.

It has, in fact, long been clear to economic historians that preindustrial workers received their earnings in kind as well as in cash. Von Schmoller argued that non-monetary payments continued to be an important form of compensation well into the period of industrialization, making their long-term persistence a means to compensate for falling real wages and their eventual disappearance a cause for conflict between employee and employer. He suggests, in fact, that the long-term stability of wage forms contributed to the long-term stagnation of wage levels. This certainly proved true for mine workers at Idrija, and it was generally true in all European crafts. Wage forms and differentials persisted for centuries. Examining French trades in the eighteenth century, Michael Sonenscher observed that "custom" among preindustrial workers might include different wage levels paid to workers of different status in a trade. It might also include a wide range of nonmonetary payments and perquisites, including kind and credit, room and board. Different workers, sorted by craft or status, might enjoy different privileges and entitlements that could range from the right to work to access to materials, tools, and so on, all of which could render monetary wages a very incomplete index of earnings. Multiple wage forms existed and even coexisted particularly in times or places when the specie necessary to pay cash wages was scarce, making payment in kind or perquisite as well as resort to by-employments and makeshifts particularly important. Hence, non-cash payments resulted not only from custom, but also and equally from necessity.

The variety of wage forms and supplements begs the question of wage systems. If workers were paid in different media, were they also paid in different ways? Being paid by the piece or by the hour might have made no difference in earlier centuries, as John Rule has famously argued, when "workmen produced an accepted output for an accepted remuneration from an accepted working week."[19] Yet, by the early modern age, employers in protoindustrial or domestic-industrial organizations often preferred piece-rates because they believed them to increase the level of productivity and decrease the need for supervision. Over time, as Reinhold Reith documents clearly for early modern Germany, piece-rates replaced time rates in more and more crafts, suggesting a direct relationship between wage systems and industrial productivity. Much of the shop floor experience of industrialization, as Leonard Rosenband has argued, can be understood in terms of a conflict between the workers' customary determination of wages and their employers' revolutionary instrumentalization of them. It has become clear to a new generation of economic historians that wages—not merely their amount, but broadly their form and system as well—stand in intimate relationship to the process and productivity of work.

Beyond measuring living standards and life quality, wages gauge a struggle for power that characterizes much of the changing economy of Europe in the period 1450–1650. Questions of how much would be paid in what form and for which kinds of work had pitted hands against masters since the Middle Ages, if not since the dawn of history. With the passage of time, certainly in the early modern age, new forces entered this contest with increasing frequency. As states developed the means to marshal their resources and articulate their authority more effectively, they sponsored and protected industrial enterprises, and created and enforced regulatory statutes, both of which were intended to increase their economic and political power. These developments often established new levels of privilege that favored workers in those favored industries or worksites, shielding them from competition, paying them prize wages, or easing their access to factors of production. At the same time, they dictated what goods these privileged workers would produce and how that work would be compensated. State sponsorship usually relied on the skills of capitalists, contributing thus to the historical process of capital accumulation and spurring its intervention in work processes.

Where capital took the initiative to establish what products would be produced, what production methods would be employed, and at what costs, wage form and modality frequently shifted. Many scholars speak of a process of early proletarianization, evoking the anachronism of a mobile, industrial workforce before centralized, industrial production, but a growing marginalization of workers seems apparent in many manufacturing sectors of the early modern age, consistent with the low wages of Phelps Brown and Hopkins. These historical processes altered negotiations and conflicts that had long been presumed to be two-sided. They came to involve more parties. Catharina Lis and Hugo Soly have pointed to conflicts among merchant-entrepreneurs, improving masters, and small masters over questions of workshop relations and regulations in the cities of the Southern Low Countries. Similarly, mine workers at Idrija appealed to the state against the mine operators and implicated capital in the question of their earnings. It came to involve more interests: wages and profits expressed not only economic relations between employees and employers, but also the political ambitions of the state and the commercial intelligence of capital. It came to influence more outcomes: the material survival of workers and employers became embedded in questions of evolving power relations and global markets. The level of their productivity depended upon supplies of raw materials or demand for finished goods in distant markets, access to which too often depended upon commercial capital or political accommodation. The "economy of work" had likely never been a simple function of the supply of fit workers or the demand for their efforts. There had likely always been what economists since A. O. Hirschmann refer to, perhaps too narrowly, as "nonmarket forces," that is, those forces acting from outside the market system, including social networks, cultural values, and so on, that help the market and the economy to function.[20] A case can be made, however, that the early modern age witnessed an ever more frequent and conscious integration of the links that bound the "economy of work" to the advantage of emergent nations and global trade.

Wage conflict usually masked a related but quite separate element in the "economy of work," production. Employers, investors, and regulators might take an interest in wages as a factor in the cost of production and in the margin of profit, but they worried more about the quality and quantity of goods that would eventually find their way to market. Even workers seldom considered their wages as a thing apart from their skill, the ways they produced what they produced. Phelps Brown and Hopkins considered productivity to be extraneous to wages, but most economic historians understand a fundamental link between the two. They theorize that rising aggregate demand, which is the product of population size and per capita income, will trigger specialization in work, a division of labor that becomes an engine for technological advances. The result is Smithian gain: rising productivity accompanied by rising real wages.

This appears to have been the general case in Europe until 1450. From the mid-fifteenth until the early sixteenth century, real wages and work productivity stood at historically high levels. From the early sixteenth century until the mid-seventeenth century, real wages collapsed in most parts of Europe—Castile appearing to be a noteworthy exception. At this point, a puzzle emerges: from the mid-sixteenth to the mid-seventeenth century, even as real wages fell, work productivity rose. Economists insist this should not be the case, given that real wages were falling; historians have yet to explain why it might have been, even in light of rising numbers of workers.

Obviously, the statistical data necessary to measure productivity exactly does not exist for preindustrial economies. Historians have struggled to overcome this lack by reasoning with such information as exists and seems reliable: secular trends in population, prices, and wages. They assume that if population, prices, and wages all increase, then productivity must be increasing. They assume as well that land and capital per laborer remain essentially stable before the Industrial Revolution, meaning that any increase in total productivity rests upon an increase in labor productivity. They note that not all regions or localities experienced growth equally. Remote, less well integrated areas tended to stagnate: wages and prices lagged; growth was slower. Even within well integrated, better developed regions, growth patterns might differ, certain areas might lag.

The reality of regional differences notwithstanding, historical studies have achieved a momentary consensus with regard to the productivity of preindustrial work. Rising population and rising wages yielded rising aggregate demand, which supposedly, theoretically prompted in turn higher productivity from the mid-seventeenth century onwards. But what about the century or more between the great prosperity and the great productivity of workers?

This conundrum may be more apparent than real. The lack of economic integration, as often noted, makes it difficult to generalize about Europe. The existence of different wage systems—piece as opposed to time rates—may offer a partial explanation. Changes in the organization of work—the expanded reliance on networks of waged labor and on forms of coerced labor—may do so as well. These also influenced wages and wage-earners in ways that wage series alone cannot account. The impact of changing organization on the "economy of work," to say nothing of the political economy of work, was significant between 1450 and 1650. Because production networks and coerced labor existed mostly, though not exclusively, to produce inexpensive goods for export, they linked the "economy of work" and wages as a measure of that economy to the globalizing market for goods and services. Earnings were no longer, if they ever were, as Smith had understood them, strictly a function of the "easiness or hardness of masters" in single negotiation with individual workers. They involved more directly the interests of the state and the requirements of capital. They call attention to the changing context of wages.

BEYOND THE WAGE

Wages reveal much about the "economy of work." They provide information not only about the supply of and demand for work, but also about the earnings and living standards of workers. They shed light on the nature of work relations, the role of customs and community, the shifting balance of power between workers and their employers, as well as the influence exercised with ever greater force and immediacy by capital and the state. They provide a metric for the productivity of labor as well, changing in level, configuration, and modality with the introduction of new technologies and organizations.

Yet, wages remain an imperfect lens through which to observe the "economy of work." They obscure the noted lack of integration in the European economy during the early modern age. Barriers to entry and exit and asymmetries of information, all of which hindered the movement of workers and segregated the value of work, were consequences of this lack of integration, functions of local and regional autarchy. The workings of local custom and community fostered these technical problems compromised the development of a labor market, except on the local level. They had a direct impact on the ability of workers to find employment and earn compensation.

Wage historians have tended to treat the object of their study as a simple transaction. *The Oxford Encyclopedia of Economic History* defines wage as the compensation of "labour performed by a free person" and noted that it "may take the form of goods, privilege and money or a mixture of these," though over time "there was an evolution toward the generalization of money wages according to the pace by which economies became more market oriented."[21] Even allowing for different forms, the term itself still constrains the inquiry. It entered the English language in the course of the fourteenth century and was understood to refer widely to any "payment to a person for service rendered, e.g. for the salary or fee paid to persons of official or professional status."[22] Over time, its meaning became more restricted: "The amount paid periodically, esp. by the day or week or month, for the labour or service of an employee, worker, or servant." Wage appears to signify, thus, a particular work relationship. The anachronism becomes clear when one considers the variety of terms, for example salary, stipend, diet, and so on, used to describe different kinds of compensation for different kinds of work in the early modern age. It obscures the fact that the compensation for the performance or completion of a given task might vary considerably according to the status of the person to whom it was offered. And, it applies ambiguously to the economy of intellectual work, domestic work, professional services, or forced labor, none of which were new, but all of which were growing in importance between 1450 and 1650.

As Woodward, Mokyr, and others have made clear, many premodern workers remain excluded from consideration, because they earned no wage in the strict sense. The early modern age experienced an increase in the resort to unfree labor, whether in the form of indenture, serfdom, or slavery. In the later Middle Ages serfdom began to disappear in western Europe, even as it spread to the East. In the West, changes in the economy, population and tenancy made the labor of serfs less attractive to the landowners. At about the same time that it disappeared in the West, serfdom became dominant in the East. There, high land-to-labor ratios gave landlords an incentive to bind peasants to their holdings. With increased demand for agricultural produce in western Europe, the result of the population growth, urban expansion, and capital dependence that had led to the abolition of it in the first place, serfdom remained in force throughout eastern Europe into the modern age so that landed estates could produce agricultural products for export to the West. Wages had little or no relevance for agricultural workers caught in the system of serfdom, but that system's agricultural production helped moderate food prices and support real wages in cities and towns.

While serfdom expanded in the East, slavery began to expand in the colonies. The trade in African slaves to the Americas between 1500 and 1870 is easily the greatest, best documented, long-distance traffic in enslaved peoples in history. It played an integral part in European expansionism throughout the early modern age and contributed essentially to the colonization of the Americas and the exploitation of its natural resources. At the center of this process stood sugar, which Europeans transplanted from the Atlantic islands off Europe and Africa to Brazil and later to the West Indies. The labor needs of sugar plantations dictated the scale of the slave trade, especially after the collapse of native populations. The use of African slaves to cultivate and produce sugar was by no means new; European capital had set them to this work in Mediterranean and Atlantic islands since the Middle Ages. In the New World, the scale of slave labor took on entirely new proportions. From 1530 to 1650, the number of slaves leaving Africa for the Americas varied between five thousand and ten thousand per year. The expansion of sugar production in the Caribbean from the 1640s onwards greatly increased the volume of slave shipments in the following century and a half. Nearly all of these slaves were traded by western European, especially Portuguese, merchants, an activity in some ways analogous to the use of serfs by eastern European landlords. Like serfs, the effects of slaves on wages and work are important but indirect. In terms of wages and production, they help to explain how one could fall and the other rise between 1550 and 1650. In terms of real wages, their production might lower the price of a basketful of goods, but the profits from their labor might spur inflation. That they earned no wages to speak of strengthens the argument that wage studies are an imperfect means for understanding the complexities of the "economy of work" in the early modern age.

Phelps Brown and Hopkins built wage differentials into their initial index. By so doing, they made some allowance for the variation in earnings between skilled and unskilled workers. They did not, however, extend their analysis to age or, above all, gender. Natalie Davis's observation that "women suffered for their powerlessness ... as female guilds dwindled, as the female role in middle-level commerce and farm direction contracted, and as the differential between male and female wages increased,"[23] inspired a generation of women's historians to revisit the material realities that female workers confronted in the early modern age. They found that women were systematically excluded from most incorporated trades and that their wages lagged behind those of men. In this, they confirmed the findings of turn-of-the-century pioneer Alice Clark, and added substance to the charge that discrimination was institutional as well as cultural. It was, in part, a function of patriarchal ideology and received notions of a woman's "proper place." It was also a function of economic competition and widespread fear of a woman's power to displace. They also helped to refine the analysis of work and compensation, not only for women, but for all workers. In a review essay, John Hatcher argued that one must attend carefully to the system of payment, piece rates tending to vary less than time rates according to skill, age, or gender. His point was quite simple: "Differentiation between workers and their wage, based on perceived variations in productivity and skill, has been a commonplace in casual labour markets throughout history."[24] Employers paid more to employees they thought more productive. Accordingly, women tended to earn less than men when paid time rates for work, because their employers were convinced that they produced less than men in a given period of time; paid by the piece, which connected earnings directly to productivity, women earned at the same rate as men. One must, therefore, distinguish wage discrimination from wage differentiation.

Hatcher noted as well that the household duties of working women, which are seldom reflected in account books, may have contributed to their lower productivity in paid labor. An analogous point can be made for other members of the household, the very young and the very old. By virtue of youth or infirmity, they would have been less productive. Yet, their payment, however marginal, would have contributed to the overall earnings of the household and, so, increased its real wage level. They also were far more likely to work without compensation of any sort, reckoned simply a part of the laboring family. The same can be said for apprentices and servants as well, who often worked for no more compensation than room and board as they learned their trade, but whose labors contributed nonetheless to the economic unit of the household in which they lived—while relieving the burden in terms of food and lodging for their household of origin. Considering the effects of modern industrialization on living standards, Sara Horrell and Jane Humphries argued in 1992 that wage studies must extend beyond the occupational payment of men to the real income of the family, including the earnings of women and children. Family real income might draw not only upon the wages earned by multiple members of a family or household, but also upon the contributions of by-employments, payments in kind, and various perquisites, all of which make it a better index not only for living standards but also for the "economy of work." Considering the multiplicity of wage forms and systems, as well as the multiplicity of workers and earners, family real income may indeed have risen even as individual real incomes fell in the period 1500–1650. It is, however, much harder to calculate, because so many of its component parts are obscure.

The centuries from 1450 to 1650 experienced an expansion of part-time labor, especially on the parts of women and children laboring in households, in consequence of an increasing resort to domestic industry. Known under a variety of names, including protoindustry and cottage industry, it refers to a production network in which goods are manufactured in the homes of workers for export to distant markets. This kind of organization keeps costs low: it requires no fixed capital for factories; it relies on hand tools owned by the workers; it utilizes small batches of raw materials; it retains the merchant-industrialist's immediate ownership of raw materials and finished products. Workers receive piece-rate wages as a rule. In some instances, work is uncompensated, especially when it involves traditional skills that were learned as needed in the domestic setting. The increased resort to domestic industry as a modality of work in the early modern age may have resulted in reduced wages for wage-earners, despite expanded productivity, because they were paid by the piece, rather than for a period of time, and because batch production prevented the payment of wages during periods of idleness. Domestic industry could thus also help explain how rising population and productivity might be accompanied by stagnant real wages.[25]

Serfs, slaves, and subalterns all appear in greater numbers among the working population of Europe. Many of them were unwaged or underwaged. Many of them worked outside the geographical boundaries of Europe. All participated in organizations of production, systems of labor, that were, if not new in 1450, then expanding in importance during the centuries that followed. All influenced productivity and wages in Europe, to say nothing of the development of its economy. On the economic value of convict labor, very little has been written. A recently edited volume by John Donoghue and Evelyn Jennings explores the relationship between state recruitment of unfree labor and capitalist and imperial development, showing western European states as agents of capitalist expansion, imposing diverse forms of bondage on workers for infrastructural, plantation, and military labor. Its argument is, not unexpectedly, political and cultural rather than strictly economic. Since the mid-twentieth century, scholars have argued the economic quality and value of such labor—whether or not coerced labor was profitable and rational—and its influence on development—whether or not industrialization depended on unfree workers. This second issue has inspired in turn a related and no less spirited discussion among American scholars concerning the role of unfree workers in the rise of industrial capitalism. A consensus seems to have arisen among scholars that slavery helped to finance the Industrial Revolution, but debate continues as to the extent and form of the contribution. Most of this discussion concerns the period after 1650 and focuses, not surprisingly, on North America and Great Britain, but its implications for the global economy in previous centuries are clear and striking. Similar, if less contentious arguments have been made for serfdom and the economic specialization and integration of Europe in the seventeenth and eighteenth centuries. Following the arguments of Maurice Dobbs and Robert Brenner, economic historians now recognize that the emergence of a modern industrial economy, based on free, wage labor, began with a transformation of rural society, driven by a desire to increase productivity and lower costs in order to sell surplus to an expanding population. To achieve these ends, landowners innovated agricultural techniques and altered land tenures, according to R. H. Hilton, turning rural peasants into urban workers and consumers. Eric Hobsbawm connected the resort to unfree labor, especially but not exclusively slaves, to this development, the necessity of serving this growing population of urban, manufacturing, and industrial workers. In course, according to James Oakes, an "ancient system of labour transformed into a highly rationalized system of production."[26] It seems clear that the competitive pressures of unfree and subordinate workers should have affected the earning opportunities of free and wage-earning workers in global labor markets, just as the flood of inexpensive goods they created would have impacted real earnings, but scholars have yet to attempt this complex comparison.

The divergence between real wages and work productivity in the early modern age remains a problem that requires a solution. The period before early industrialization has often been described as one of increasing population and prosperity. Certainly, the argument has been made that the economic lives of workers at the outset of the seventeenth century could not have gotten much worse. Living standards, measured in terms of real wages to individual workers, had reached a truly historic low in most parts of the peninsula. Yet, the economic model of expanding population and rising incomes leading to increased aggregate demand and economic growth does not describe the lived reality of many parts of Europe between 1450 and 1650. Much of the data and findings that have been published remain contested or limited. Much work remains to be done on the early modern "economy of work."

CONCLUSION

The study of wages has provided a durable, albeit crude, outline of the "economy of work" in the early modern age. Scholars generally agree that the earnings of workers and the quality of their lives stood at historic high points by the middle of the fifteenth century. This generalization applies particularly in those parts of Europe that enjoyed the highest levels of economic integration and urban development, usually understood as a broad swathe that ran from the Low Countries south and east to northern Italy. Those parts of Europe that were more rural or isolated tended to lag behind. By the early-sixteenth century, this prosperity began to erode. Even if wages remained stable, their purchasing power contracted for reasons that remain open to debate. Again, the geographic extent of this contraction seems to have varied according to many factors that have to do with the level of economic development and integration. Not all parts of Europe suffered alike. Interestingly, the radical decline in earnings among workers did not signal a loss of productivity. Though the evidence remains partial, local studies suggest that workers produced more, even as they earned less, a complex interplay that has yet to be fully understood. By the early-seventeenth century, earnings appear to have begun to rise slowly but steadily.

Nor do wages alone provide a full sense of the complexities of the "economy of work" in the early modern age. Nominal wages indicate the market value of work, it is true, but they also reflect "the abilities of the workmen" and the "easiness or hardness of the masters," to recite Smith. Real wages give a sense of the living standards of preindustrial working men and women, how those lives became better or worse over time, but they obscure the effects of different wage forms and systems, whether payments in kind or perquisite or the contributions of by-employments. Indeed, scholars are only beginning to appreciate the complex ways in which wages were linked to organizations of production and levels of productivity. Wage levels reflect, but do not reveal, the workings of custom and power in work relations, workers' sense of their own worth, their mastery of skill, their economic independence, and their membership of a community of work and workers. In this regard, custom seems to have outweighed other "institutions" in this period. Nor do they account for the economic value of under-compensated or uncompensated work, whether that of women, children, servants, serfs, or slaves.

This, perhaps, is the most striking and puzzling aspect of the "economy of work" between 1450 and 1650. The increasing influence of global commerce prompted an increased reliance on precisely these forms of under-compensated and uncompensated work and workers that appear marginal from the perspective of wages. This was not new in 1450. Women and children, whether waged or not, had always worked at a variety of tasks in the household, workshop, and garden. The efforts of convicts, serfs, and slaves had long expanded the productivity of estates and enterprises. A case can be made, however, that resort to the work of these groups began to grow after 1450 and continued to expand throughout the period of study. Agricultural estates in eastern Europe used serfs to produce foodstuffs for export to the West. Domestic industry depended on the work of women and children to manufacture finished goods for export overseas. Overseas colonies exploited the work of convicts and slaves to produce industrial and agricultural commodities for export to Europe. The labors of these socially and politically marginal groups may help to explain how productivity could expand while wages did not in the mainstream.

It seems indisputable that the "economy of work" grew between 1450 and 1650 under the influence of globalization. This growth may have had more to do with the size of the workforce and the organization of work than with new techniques or technologies. It may also have changed as a result of local and regional specialization. Again, this was not new in 1450, but appears to have accelerated over the period of study. Scholars speak of the expansion of serfdom in the East and of manufacturing in the West. They speak as well of the "rise of the Atlantic economies" as northern Europe developed the commercial and manufacturing basis to trade with a wider world. These divisions East–West and North–South created short-term regional differences in work performed and regional differentials in wages earned. Ironically, they also contributed to long-term, economic integration that would eventually mobilize the workforce and reduce the differentials.

Wages return hence not only to the market for work, but to a society of work: one based on simple relations of supply and demand; one comprised of the myriad relations among employers and employees that are simultaneously common and specific; one emergent in the early modern age; one established since time immemorial. They reveal, finally, the intricacy of any "economy of work" in the first stages of globalization, but before industrialization.

CHAPTER TWO

Picturing Work

ILJA VELDMAN

This chapter is an attempt to gain some insight into the overwhelming number of visual examples depicting work in the early modern period. It was a dynamic period. Technical innovations, explorations, and changes in religious and social life deeply influenced the visual arts and other cultural expressions. The invention of book printing and the graphic arts contributed highly to the possibilities of educating large sections of the population. Whereas in Italy fresco and panel painting were always important pictorial media, panel painting came to full bloom in northern painting after 1450. The period is also characterized by urbanization and the rise of the middle class. In the north, especially after the Reformation, it was the middle class that became the new consumers of art. While the aristocracy had always played a modest role, private and civic patronage increasingly complemented and even replaced ecclesiastical commissions. The function and meaning of art are dependent on the intended consumers, with the result that it was the new public of middle-class customers that imposed their norms and values on cultural expressions. Artists started to produce paintings for the art market which meant a commercialization of art and a different choice of subjects. Numerous iconographic innovations that had an impact on later eras were created during the sixteenth century in Flemish towns. For a while the art of the southern Netherlands dominated visual culture throughout Europe, thanks also to the graphic arts that were dispersed all over and functioned as an important means of communication and instruction. The sixteenth century occupies the center stage in this chapter, because it represents a very interesting period of transition in visual imagery from medieval iconography to seventeenth-century genre paintings.

Northern art showed a particular interest in the depiction of daily life. That is another reason why it is such a valuable source for the visualization of work.[1] Consequently the visual arts of the Low Countries will take the main place in my overview, with a few excursions to Germany, France, Italy, Spain, and England. Despite the predilection for daily life and the seemingly realistic depictions, the realism is only relative.[2] Many so-called genre pieces turn out to be the outcome of an earlier allegorical or pictorial tradition.

THE "WORKS OF THE MONTHS" AND THE FARMER AS THE PROTOTYPE OF THE WORKER

During the Middle Ages, the "Works of the Twelve Months" were a common theme in the sculpture of churches, wall paintings, and calendar illustrations, in books of hours and other manuscripts commissioned by the nobility and high clergy. In Flemish manuscripts, this tradition continued until far into the sixteenth century, particularly in the work of the miniaturists of the Ghent–Bruges school, with Simon Bening as their main representative. The "Works of the Months" were often executed as full-page miniatures depicting peasants working in the fields or engaged in other activities appropriate to the time of the year. The traditional cycle is a pictorial convention, with some variation as to climatic differences. We see the planting of young vines in March, milking in April, hunting in May, haymaking in June, sheep-shearing in July, harvesting in August (Figure 2.1), grape-picking, harrowing, or sowing in September and October, and the slaughter of livestock in November.

Scenes of people cutting wood for the fire, warming themselves by a fireplace, and sitting around a covered table are traditionally reserved for the winter months. But only a selection of work is represented in these cycles that present human life as a continuous cycle governed by the seasons. The peasants obediently working on the fields suggest thus a reassuring image of order and regularity in the world that perfectly suited the religious context.[3] The social reality and the kind of work that had to be done were naturally quite different. Also, the iconography of the "Works of the Months" on the walls of Italian Palazzi appear to be different, due to the noble patrons who ordered them. Francesco Cossa's murals in de Salone dei Mesi (1470) in the Palazzo Schifanoia in Ferrara depict an astrological and calendrical cycle with little attention for real scenes of work or common people. They are a continuation of the tradition of wall paintings as seen in the Castello del Buonconsiglio in Trento (c. 1400) and rather an expression of self-representation and prestige.

It was Pieter Bruegel who transmitted the theme of the months to panel paintings and the civic domain. His six large paintings of the "Months" (1565) decorated a single room in the country villa of the prominent Antwerp merchant Nicolaes Jongelinck in Ter Beecken—five of them survive. They still represent an idealized image of country

FIGURE 2.1 Simon Bening, *The Month of August*, painted miniature, 1515. The Morgan Library & Art Museum, New York.

life, seen through the eyes of an urban citizen. In the graphic arts of the Netherlands, the "Works of the Twelve Months" remained a popular subject until far into the seventeenth century, although the accent shifted from the depiction of seasonal activities to different kinds of landscapes according to the change in fashion and taste. A "condensed" variation of the theme appeared in the form of the four seasons. The Antwerp print publisher Hieronymus Cock published two compositions of Bruegel and two by Hans Bol as a series of "Four Seasons" around 1570. In the foreground of Bruegel's *Summer* (Figure 2.2) a peasant drinks greedily from a jug. Other peasants are reaping and gleaning corn; sheaves of corn are carried away and fruit is picked from trees.[4]

Bruegel's peasants are rendered with a sense of humor, but also with respect for their indispensable role in society. There also existed a very different iconographical tradition: the peasant as an example of foolishness and uncivilized manners. That tradition started at the end of the fifteenth century in German satirical prints and continued until far into the seventeenth century in genre paintings of the Low Countries.[5] Peasants are not shown working, but attending fairs, drinking, openly cuddling, and fighting. This tradition remains an important theme in Dutch seventeenth-century art which is probably due to the assumption that more civilized city dwellers, who could afford to buy such paintings and hang them on their walls, would have been amused by the uncouthness of the farmers, while at the same time the scenes confirmed them of their own moral superiority.

A different depiction of peasants and other laborers is seen in France around 1640. In a country that preferred more elevated subjects from religion and mythology, the

FIGURE 2.2 Pieter van der Heyden after Pieter Bruegel the Elder, *Summer*, engraving, c. 1570. Rijksmuseum, Amsterdam.

paintings of "low subjects" by Louis Le Nain were a rare genre, influenced by his Netherlandish colleagues. However, Le Nain's peaceful scenes like *A Family of Peasants* (1542) and *The Forge* (c. 1542/43; Louvre, Paris) are very different from their northern counterparts. His compositions of workers are not amusing or grotesque but harmonious and even solemn, according to French seventeenth-century art theory, and they foreshadowed the social realism of the nineteenth century. Other examples, like Diego Velázquez's representation of a blacksmith's forge in his painting *The Forge of Vulcan* (1630; Prado, Madrid) should been seen in the light of the pictorial tradition of this mythological subject in Italy that became quite popular at the time.

WORK AS A DUTY FOR EVERYBODY: FROM HEAVENLY BLISS TO EARTHLY HONOR

As seen in the "Works of the Month" and according to the tripartite medieval system, the farmer provided the food for the other groups in society. The prototype of the farmer was Adam, who was condemned to work after the Fall (Gen. 3:17–19). A nearly full-page woodcut of Adam and Eve after the Fall is one of the first woodcuts in the *Nuremberger Chronicle* (1493) by Hartmann Schedel, lavishly illustrated by Michael Wolgemut and Wilhelm Pleydenwurff. Adam is depicted digging the rocky

FIGURE 2.3 Hieronymus Wierix, *Man Born to toil*, engraving, 1579. Museum Boijmans van Beuningen, Rotterdam.

earth with a pickaxe, while Eve is suckling her children. The motif of an Adam performing agriculture and an Eve tending small children and often holding a distaff at the same time was derived from illustrations in the *Speculum humanae salvationis* and continued in Netherlandish prints until the beginning of the seventeenth century. The notion that God imposed physical labor on mortals as a heavy task and obligation (see also Job 5:7, "Man is born to work") was the basis for more complex allegories, like a series of engravings by Philips Galle after Maarten van Heemskerck, *The Reward of Labour and Diligence* (1572). The main figures are the personification of Labor, shown as a peasant with a spade and with flints of steel on top of his hat, and Diligence, a woman with a whip, spurs, and an hourglass. They are joined in matrimony by the personification of Fear of the Lord with Hope as their witness. Their industrious work provides them with food and clothing, but the greatest reward will come after death, in Paradise, as the last print demonstrates.[6]

In the sixteenth century, the duty to work applied not only to the traditional farmer, but also to other members of the third estate.[7] In the visual arts, this conviction is depicted explicitly only in the second half of the century, when the representation of a laborious Adam and Eve after the Fall is transformed in a more general exhortation to perform work. A print by Hieronymus Wierix (1579; Figure 2.3) refers to Adam and Eve but shows the work of a more modern couple.

The man is surrounded by tools not only belonging to physical work but also by attributes of intellectual professions, like a celestial globe and a rod of justice. At the woman's side are a washing basket, cradle, porridge bowl, spindle, basket, and broom. The original motif of the small Cain or Abel has been transformed into a child blowing bubbles, the *Homo Bulla*, that alludes to the transitory nature of earthly existence. In a print series after Maarten de Vos, *The Divine Charge to the Three Estates* (c. 1585), the representation of the third state is more suitable to the reality of urban life. A man in burgher's clothes is seated next to the personifications of Obedience and Patience; the ox and horse (called "Labor" and "Perseverance") are laden with farmer's tools but also carpenter's tools and a painter's palette and brushes. The fourth and concluding print, however, still embodies the traditional Christian view that the reward for dutifully performing the task allotted by God is a seat in Heaven.[8]

This traditional Christian view in art was eclipsed by humanist ideas arriving from Italy. Whereas there had been no link between manual work and status or honor, work became more and more a means of acquiring not only prosperity and self-confidence but also esteem and respect in society. Besides, work should not be done in order to attain heavenly bliss but for material ends, and everybody should work in order to avoid shameful poverty and want. These ideas are expressed in elaborate allegorical print series, like *The Use and Abuse of Time* (c. 1570) by Gerard de Jode, and another one with the same title by Crispijn de Passe after de Vos (c. 1600). The iconography of the theme of the traditional "ages of man" also reflects the changing attitude towards work and accentuates that work is an essential and necessary stage in human existence. In the *Four Ages* (1591) by Raphael Sadeler after de Vos, the man in the prime of life is titled "Labor" (Figure 2.4) and is surrounded by attributes of both physical work (farmer's, carpenter's, and smith's tools) and intellectual activity (a book, palette, brushes, and instruments for geometry and astronomy). One

FIGURE 2.4 Raphael Sadeler after Maarten de Vos, *Labor or Adult Age Dedicated to Work*, engraving, 1591. Rijksmuseum, Amsterdam.

FIGURE 2.5 Raphael Sadeler after Maarten de Vos, *Honor or Mature Age Receiving Riches and Respect*, engraving, 1591. Rijksmuseum, Amsterdam.

notes that Pallas Athene, the goddess of science, is showing him the right direction. The next print reveals that his works lead to honor—the title of the print—and material reward (Figure 2.5). Other prints demonstrate that idleness is a great sin and that time should be properly used—for time also meant money in urban society. An instructive example is Philips Galle's print series *The Idler's Punishment*, in which the idler is chased away and becomes an outcast; several other allegorical engravings depict the theme "Time Rewarding Diligence and Punishing Indolence."[9]

REPRESENTATIONS OF PROFESSIONS IN BOOKS AND PRINTS

Urban life and work performed in towns became more and more a subject of depiction in the sixteenth century. A traditional genre was the representation of patron saints, and when this patron saint had been a craftsman it was customary to represent him in his workshop. A very early representation of *St. Eloy*, the patron of gold- and silversmiths, is a print of around 1450 attributed to the German or Burgundian French Balaam Master (Figure 2.6). It displays a metalworker's shop filled with all kind of implements. The saint is chasing a metal cup, an assistant at the left is drawing wire through the die he is standing on, and to the right an assistant seems to add detail to a crude chasing with a punch, while the female assistant next to him is hammering a sheet of metal. The presence of a female assistant or pupil is seldom revealed in images of work and, therefore, remarkable; it suggests, perhaps, that women, whether members of the family or employees of the workshop, might sometimes have been entrusted with the more refined handiwork. The various animals seem a fancy of the artist, but the rack with the assortment of all kind of instruments used in metalwork seems realistic. It includes the

FIGURE 2.6 Balaam Master, *St. Eloy in his Workshop*, engraving, 1440–60. Rijksmuseum, Amsterdam.

basic tools of the engraver, for we should not forget that the art of engraving was born in the workshops of goldsmith's.

Thanks to the development of the printed book, illustrated with woodcuts, broader layers of the populations became acquainted with the abundance of different crafts in a city. The book of Hartmann Schopper, *Panoplia omnium illiberalium mechanicarum aut sedentariarum artium genera continens* (Frankfurt am Main, 1568) was of singular importance. It contained 133 woodcuts of professions and trades by the Nuremberg artist Jost Amman. Amman depicted a very broad range of activities, among which were intellectual professions like a lawyer, pharmacist, and astronomer. Most woodcuts depict the manual arts, however, and in a very detailed way: a draughtsman, type founder, block cutter, printer, glazier, gem cutter, embroiderer, paper maker, merchant, coin minter, coin striker, peddler, brewer, barber, bell founder, coppersmith, clock maker, armorer, scale maker, weaver, cloth shearer, dyer, shoe maker, hat maker (Figure 2.7), belt maker, bag maker, lantern maker, sieve maker, mirror maker, needle maker, nail maker, brushes maker, stonemason, brick maker, sailor, fisherman, and so on.

The book became even more famous in a German edition, *Beschreibung aller Stände auff Erden* (1568) by the same publisher, Feyerabend, who asked the poet Hans Sach to provide 116 of the woodcuts with explanatory poems.[10] In the foreword Sachs describes Amman's woodcuts as "true depictions and descriptions of all ranks on earth … of all arts, crafts and trades … depicted in illustrations never seen before." Although the attention for the lower ranks of society is new, the moral is still medieval, for Sachs concludes at the end of the booklet that all these workers can be seen as an example that "everyone should act in solidarity, assist each other and refrain from vices like selfishness and laziness, for God will reward us for our efforts and labour with our daily bread." That was a commonplace, of course, but the effect of the book was no cliché. It served as model book of trades on behalf of artists and craftsmen and after its publication numerous representations of professions became an independent genre in drawings, prints, and paintings.

The *Nova reperta* (New Inventions of Modern Times, c. 1591), nineteen large engravings after drawings by Johannes Stradanus (Jan van der Straet), is a kind of continuation of Amman's *Book of Trades*. Stradanus was a painter and designer from Bruges, who emigrated to Florence to work for the grand dukes of Tuscany. His print designs were engraved and published by Antwerp engravers and distributed among an international public. His *Nova reperta* has no typographical text and only engraved Latin inscriptions, but it was a great improvement in representation, because of the large and detailed engravings that give a much better picture of the activities around each trade and industry than Amman's small and rather simple woodcuts of a few decades before. The *auctor intellectualis* of Stradanus's series was the Florentine scholar Luigi Alamanni to whom the series is dedicated. It was his intention to extol the discovery of America that was believed to be the work of the Florentine Amerigo Vespucci, but also to contrast the primitive American culture with the highly developed technological culture of Europe.[11] The series includes a number of modern inventions that provide an excellent view of different employments. Well-known are the prints devoted to the invention of book printing (Figure 3.4), oil painting, and copper engraving. Other prints show the invention of the compass, wind mill, water mill, distillation, gunpowder, eyeglasses, the polishing of armor, the making of clockwork, and the discovery of guayaco wood as a cure for syphilis (Figure 2.8). This last item was not unimportant in view of the epidemic growth of venereal diseases

FIGURE 2.7 Jost Amman, *The Hat Maker*, from *Panoplia*, 1568. British Museum, London. Photo: Trustees of the British Museum.

FIGURE 2.8 Studio of Philips Galle after Johannes Stradanus, *The Preparation of Guayaco for Treating Syphilis*, engraving, c. 1591. Rijksmuseum, Amsterdam.

FIGURE 2.9 Studio of Philips Galle after Johannes Stradanus, *The Production of Refined Sugar from Sugarcane*, engraving, c. 1591. Rijksmuseum, Amsterdam.

during the sixteenth century, but it was, regrettably, the only invention that proved itself less successful. The prints, depicting the production of olive oil and refined sugar from sugarcane (Figure 2.9), represent industries developed on the domains of the grand dukes of Tuscany, who were the patrons of Stradanus. The artist presented all these inventions in the form of seemingly realistic scenes, displaying not only the production itself but also its social organization.

Another series of engravings after Stradanus is *Vermis Sericus* (c. 1595; The Silkworm); the six engravings are depicting the introduction of the silkworm in Europe and the production of silk.[12] All stages are shown: the incubation of the silkworm eggs, the eggs spread out on shelves, the gathering of mulberry leaves, the feeding of the silkworms, and the heating of the eggs and the reeling of silk (Figure 2.10). Conspicuously, nearly all the work is done by women, old and young together—some of them are carrying children on their arms. The production of silk was concentrated in Italy and France, and Stradanus seems to have been familiar with the process. He dedicated this series to Costanza Alamanni, the sister of the Florentine scholar.[13]

DEPICTIONS OF WORK IN THE CONTEXT OF GUILDS AND REGIONAL TRADES AND INDUSTRIES

Craftsmen, including painters and other artists, belonged to one of the numerous, different craft guilds that protected the interests of the workers and the quality of their products. Their trade was often visualized in small scenes in stone tablets on

FIGURE 2.10 Johannes Stradanus, *The Heating of the Silk Worm Eggs and the Reeling of Silk*, engraving, c. 1595. Rijksmuseum, Amsterdam.

the facade or in stained-glass windows in churches, donated by the guild.[14] With the rise of panel painting, guilds started to order altar paintings for their chapels in churches; most panels depict their patron saints. St. Crispinus and St. Crispianus, the patron saints of shoe makers and tanners, for example, are depicted in their workshop in an altarpiece from Fribourg by the Master of the Carnations from around 1500 to 1510 (Schweizerisches Landesmuseum, Zürich) and in a panel dated around 1520 by the Master of the legend of Crispinus (Belvedere, Wien). A realistic, three-dimensional representation is the large sixteenth-century sculpture in the Church of St. Panthaléon in Troyes, rendering the arrest of both brothers by two soldiers and displaying a large piece of leather naturalistically hanging from their working table. The Gouda Church of St. Jan housed the exceptional painting of two tanners at work, painted by an anonymous painter on the reverse of Pieter Pourbus's *The Baptism of Eustachius* (Figure 2.11). Mary's husband Joseph was the patron saint of the carpenters. The guild of the Gouda carpenters donated an altarpiece to the Church of St. Jan with *The Flight into Egypt* (1560–5) by the local artist Michiel Claesz; the predella shows four small scenes with exceptionally realistic renderings of the four kinds of crafts belonging to the guild: shipyard workers, carpenters, cabinet makers, and turners of chair legs (Figure 7.2).

A special place should be reserved for the guild to which the painters themselves belonged, the guild of Saint Luke. Most altarpieces of Saint Luke represent their patron

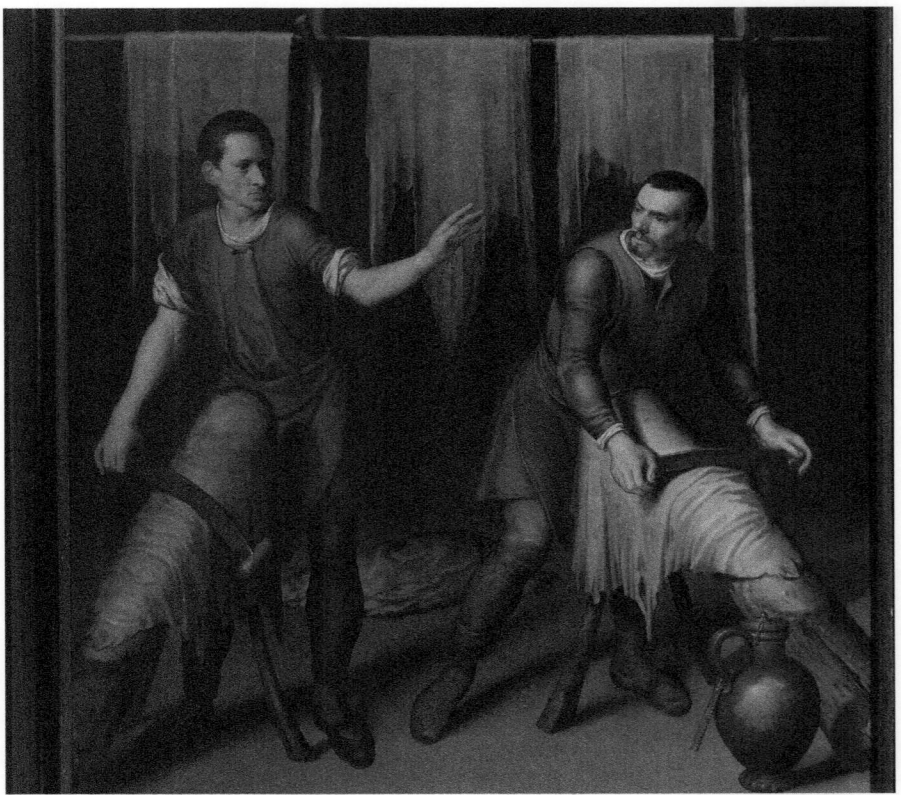

FIGURE 2.11 Anonymous, *Two Tanners*, oil on panel, c. 1580. Museum Gouda, Gouda. © Museum Gouda.

painting the legendary portrait of the Madonna; they often give a realistic picture of the painting process or the organization of the workshop and the activities of pupils and assistants. Giorgio Vasari's fresco in the chapel of St. Luke in the Santissima Annunziata in Florence is a famous Italian example, but the theme of St. Luke painting the Madonna was especially popular in the north. Moreover, the numerous self-portraits and portraits of painters in their studio or the portrayal of their pupils at work give useful visual information of their trade.[15] It is not surprising that painter's activities are visually so well documented.

Another genre is the depiction of activities of a special region or town. The Erzgebirge in present-day Germany and the Czech Republic were famous for their silver mines. These activities were depicted in the visual art of the region: in stained glass, miniatures, wall paintings, and altar paintings. The "Bergaltar" (1517) in the St. Annenkirche in Annaberg-Buchholz (Saxony) for instance shows all kind of mining activities.[16] Georgius Agricola spent many years of his life in Chemnitz (Saxony) and Joachimsthal (Czech Republic) and recorded the mining activities there in *De re metallica libri XII* (Basle, 1556). His book became the standard treatise on the technology of mining, refining, and smelting of metals, thanks not least to the many explanatory woodcuts with number-coded captions that served as illustrations of the text (Figure 2.12, 3.5, 3.6).

Images of regional trades were an important means to show success and strengthen the sense of community. That is also obvious in the case of Leiden's wool (serge) production and textile trade, which was an important source of income of the city. The production grew explosively after 1575 thanks to the immigration of many specialized workers from the southern Netherlands. To mark its success, the governors of the "saaihal" (the hall where the serge was assayed) ordered an exceptional series of seven larger-than-life paintings from the Leiden painter Isaac Claesz van Swanenburgh, to be placed in the governor's chamber. Swanenburgh worked on the commission from 1594 to 1596; he was not only an accomplished painter and a member of the city council (chosen as burgomaster three times), but also the son-in-law of a draper and well informed of the production process. Two of his paintings are allegories, a third one is lost, but the remaining four panels (Museum De Lakenhal, Leiden) give a complete picture of the technical process. One panel depicts the shearing and combing of the wool—the beating of wool is in the background. A second panel is devoted to the spinning, warping, and weaving (Figure 2.13).

The large figures of two women and the two large spinning wheels are eye-catching; to the left a woman is bringing them a bundle of wool, and in the right background corner a girl is winding the yarn on to a reel. The third panel portrays the dirty work of fulling and dyeing. This work is done by half-naked fullers, whereas a woman is holding the cloth. A later addition to the series is a 1607 panel that depicts an earlier stage of production: the washing of the fleeces, the unloading of a barge, and the grading of the wool. Thanks to the large size of the paintings, the painter was able to represent the many dealings of the production process in detail. That made the paintings a more informative source than texts.[17] In or before 1602 Swanenburgh got the commission for a series of representations in stained-glass panels in the dwelling house of Jan van Hout, Leiden's town clerk, who was the driving force behind the modernization of the textile production. The windows are lost, but the eleven preparatory drawings are preserved (Gemeente Archief, Leiden). Eight of them show the same constituent processes of the serge production as depicted in the panels.[18] Such representations might not only have contributed to the proud consciousness of a community, but also stimulated further productivity.

FIGURE 2.12 *Glass blowing*, woodcut in *De re metallica*, 1556. Wellcome Library, London. Wellcome Images images@wellcome.ac.uk.

FIGURE 2.13 Isaac Claesz van Swanenburg, *The Spinning, Warping and Weaving of Wool*, 1594–6. Museum De Lakenhal, Leiden. © Museum De Lakenhal, Leiden.

VOCATIONAL PORTRAITS AND SATIRES ON FINANCIAL PROFESSIONS

In the late Middle Ages, portraits by artists were the privilege of princes, noblemen, and the high-clergy. In the early modern period, they were more and more commissioned by citizens. Vocational portraits were an essential means of enhancing status and were provided with realistically rendered attributes denoting the profession concerned. One of the first professional groups that ordered portraits of themselves were the goldsmiths, who enjoyed a high social prestige and earned enough to be able to afford such commissions. A very early example is Jan van Eyck's portrait of the Bruges goldsmith Jan de Leeuw (1436; Kunsthistorisches Museum, Vienna); the man is holding a ring as a token of his craft. Another painting, dated 1449, is *A Goldsmith in his Workshop Visited by a Wealthy Couple* (Figure 2.14) by the Bruges painter Petrus Christus. This goldsmith was long identified as St. Eloy due to the presence of a halo. Technical research revealed that the halo was a later addition and that the underdrawing of the face of the goldsmith was more carefully modelled than the faces of his clients. Consequently, it was suggested that the panel portrays the Bruges goldsmith Willem van Vlueten.[19] Perhaps it is not accidental that Duke Philip the Good commissioned a wedding present for Mary of Guelders and James II, king of Scots, from the same Van Vleuten in exactly 1449, the date of the painting. That couple may well be depicted here as fictional clients; the goldsmith seems to weigh a wedding ring on a scale.

A second important vocational group that was portrayed in early times with all the attributes of their profession were the mighty merchant-bankers. An example is Maarten van Heemskerck's *Portrait of a Merchant* (1529; Rijksmuseum, Amsterdam); the man is counting coins and gives the viewer a self-confident look. The champion of the early

FIGURE 2.14 Petrus Christus, *A Portrait of a Goldsmith Visited by a Wealthy Couple,* oil on panel, 1449. Robert Lehman Collection, Metropolitan Museum of Art, New York.

sixteenth-century vocational portrait, though, is Hans Holbein, Jr., who spent most of his career in England and whose portraits underline the social rise of the upper middle-class court circles. His large *Portrait of the Merchant Georg Gisze* (1532; Figure 7.1) includes an assemblage of objects and attributes of the mercantile profession: money, seal, ink pots, keys, balance, boxes, and scissors. Obviously, Holbein intended to show his remarkable gifts not only in portraying people but also in rendering objects and textures according to reality. He and his European contemporaries portrayed clients from other respectable professions, such as scholars, sculptors, writers, musicians, and art collectors. It is remarkable that sixteenth-century art shows sitters in full regalia of their professions, but that the seventeenth century preferred sitters to be portrayed with fewer or no professional attributes.[20]

PICTURING WORK 49

But there was another side of the coin. While merchants and bankers were portrayed surrounded by the attributes belonging to their status and showing the self-image that they had of themselves, an antipodal genre became extremely popular in Antwerp from 1535 until 1550: the satirical portrayal of professions dealing with money. Several paintings by Jan Massijs and Marinus van Reymerswale show caricatures of ugly looking and corrupt tax collectors, money-brokers, lawyers, and money-changers (Figure 2.15).[21] Their offices are crammed with large account books, chaotically ordered heaps of slips of paper and

FIGURE 2.15 Circle of Marinus van Reymerswale, *The Tax Collector,* 1545. Fine Arts Museum, Bilbao.

coins, while the simple people who enter their offices look impressed but totally helpless. The genre might have been developed from the popular biblical story of "Christ Calling the Publican Matthew" from Matthew 9:9, the traditional example of Christ's power to bring sinners to repentance, a subject dear to the Antwerp painter Jan van Hemessen. A painting like *A Peasant Family Offering a Chicken to the Leaseholder* by Jan Massijs (1539; Gemäldegalerie, Dresden) demonstrates that satire extended to all professions that exploited common people. After all, in the eye of the general public, nearly any financial position was associated with avarice and dishonesty—avarice being one of the traditional vices in the late medieval system. The sudden rise of this subject in Antwerp panel painting might be seen in the light of the activities of the great banking houses and the money trade that had its center in the city, and thus might criticize contemporary situations and events.[22]

The distrust of merchants and lawyers is still to be observed later in the century. A print series by Hendrick Goltzius around 1576 deals with the abuses of law and criticizes profit-seeking. In one of the prints two merchants, assisted by the personifications of fraud and dishonesty, are negotiating on the price of their merchandise, while a blindfolded notary (meaning that he doesn't want to see the fraud) records the bargain. Other prints in the series demonstrate that the institution of legal proceedings costs only money and guarantees no success. In a later repetition of Goltzius's series by Adriaen Collaert in around 1595, the deceitful merchant is depicted as a Turk; the notary is still blindfolded and unaware of the fraud (Figure 2.16).[23]

FIGURE 2.16 Adriaen Collaert, *The Frauduleus Sale Agreement*, engraving, c. 1595. Rijksmuseum, Amsterdam.

THE REPRESENTATION OF WORK IN ALLEGORICAL THEMES

Next to the "Works of the Months", allegorical themes concerning the micro- and macrocosm were a helpful means of classifying society. These themes had also an antique origin and survived in the visual arts until the seventeenth century. The depictions had a tenacious pictorial tradition and are an interesting source for the visualization of work and professions. One of them is the representation of the "Children of the Planets." Traditionally, each planet was thought to favor characteristic qualities, social positions, and trades. In the visual arts, these qualities remained more or less unchanged during more than a century, from the miniatures in the astrological treatise *De sphaera* (c. 1470; Biblioteca Estense, Modena), late-fifteenth-century Italian prints and drawings by the Master of the Hausbuch, woodcuts by Georg Pencz (1531), and engravings after Maarten van Heemskerck (c. 1568) and Hendrick Goltzius (1596). The children born under Luna or the moon, considered cold and damp, were all supposed to have an occupation connected with water: they are sailors, fishermen, people cultivating fish in fish ponds, catching water birds, or just fond of swimming (Figure 2.17). Children born under the influence of the planet Mercury were believed to be learned and artistic (scholars, musicians, painters, sculptors, and other artisans), but also eloquent and good in dealing with money—in Heemskerck's print a merchant is counting coins at the table corner (Figure 2.18). Goltzius replaced the planet gods hovering in the heavens with more realistic looking classical statues. By putting emphasis on the liberal arts, he tried to promote both artistic and scholarly professions. The children of Jupiter were traditionally depicted as rulers and clerics of rank, but in Goltzius's version they represent wisdom and science and appear as geographers, astronomers, painters, musicians, and men of letters. Mercury presides over the visual and rhetoric arts. Goltzius depicted painters and a sculptor; two discoursing scholars represent rhetoric in the foreground (Figure 2.19).[24]

The concept of the four temperaments was also a suitable means to classify human characters and professions. The theory was based on the four kinds of fluid, or humors, secreted by the human body: blood (*sanguis*), choler (*cholos*), black bile (*melas cholos*), and phlegm (*phlegma*). Depending on the relative preponderance of these humors, one spoke of a person having a sanguine, a choleric, a melancholic, or a phlegmatic temperament, which determined a person's mental and physical constitution. In the visual arts the representation of the four temperaments followed a more or less established iconographical tradition, but around 1600 the depiction of the temperaments was reduced to immediately recognizable situations centering on everyday human actions and daily work.[25] In a print series engraved by Pieter de Jode after designs of de Vos the four types are represented by couples as the representatives of specific professions; the slow and cold Phlegmatic temperament as a fisherman and fisherwoman at the market, and the hot-tempered Choleric temperament as a soldier marching off sold to war accompanied by a female camp follower (Figure 2.20).

Camp followers were selling soldiers extra food and drink during periods of rest, but one of the rare independent depictions of a sutler, a painting by Jan van Bijlert (c. 1630–40; Centraal Museum, Utrecht) shows a different side of the profession. The woman's nude breasts, smile, beer mug, and the feather on her hat (a symbol of frivolity) denotes her as a woman of easy virtue, which is confirmed by the bird she is carrying. Apart from being a symbol of the food she is selling, the bird refers to the Dutch verb "vogelen," birding, one of the vulgar expressions for copulating.[26] De Vos's print *Cholerici* is also not without erotic associations. We observe the same development from an allegorical

FIGURE 2.17 Georg Pencz, *The Children of the Moon*, woodcut, 1531. Rijksmuseum, Amsterdam.

FIGURE 2.18 Herman Jansz. Muller after Maarten van Heemskerck, *The Children of Mercury*, engraving, c. 1568. Rijksmuseum, Amsterdam.

to a realistic design in the representation of the four elements; in this case allegories or classical deities were also replaced by trades and professions. Claes Jansz Clock represented earth as a peasant, water as a fisherman, air as a falconer, and fire as a blacksmith (Figure 2.21). Jacques de Gheyn the Younger saw earth as a hunter, air as a bird hunter, fire as a female cook, and, naturally, water as a fisherman. When Goltzius created a similar iconography, he represented his cook as a corpulent male. De Vos again made a choice for couples. Couples are a helpful motif for artists who like to include erotic overtones, as his fishmongers representing water demonstrate (Figure 2.22).

In another allegorical theme, the "Four Times of the Day" (c. 1594), Goltzius depicted a range of homely activities, like a mother preparing slices of bread for her children and making bobbing lace, and a father and son doing carpenter's work. Also, the five senses were a reason for depicting professions in the seventeenth century. Popular was the burlesque representation of touch (or feeling) in the form of a "dentist" hurting his patient—his victim being invariably a simple peasant.[27]

MARKET SCENES AND KITCHEN MAIDS

Around 1550 a new type of subject arose due to the creativity of the painters Pieter Aertsen and his cousin and pupil Joachim Beuckelaer: market and kitchen scenes. The market scenes display abundances of different foods offered by peasants or fishmongers.

FIGURE 2.19 Jan Saenredam after Hendrick Goltzius, *The Children of Jupiter*, engraving, 1596. Rijksmuseum, Amsterdam.

Sometimes these market stalls belong to an original series of four and represent the four elements, deduced from the supply of respectively vegetables (earth), fish (water), birds (air), and meat (fire). The popularity of this kind of painting was partly due to the growing importance of Antwerp as a trade and business center and the increased prosperity of its residents, but the scenes are no realistic snapshots. Often the painters—at least until

FIGURE 2.20 Pieter de Jode after Maarten de Vos, *A Soldier and Camp Follower as the Choleric Temperament*, engraving, c. 1600. Rijksmuseum, Amsterdam.

1566, the year of the Iconoclasm—included a small, appropriate biblical narrative in the background in order to fix the attention on the spiritual food as a contrast with the materialistic food they displayed in the foreground.[28] After 1566, Beuckelaer included erotic allusions in his market scenes, particularly in the case of the fish stalls (Figure 2.23), for not only birds could be interpreted as a sexual symbol but fish as well (cf. de Vos's depiction of the couple selling fish).

This kind of allusion seemed to have heightened the pleasure of the spectator and was often underlined by explicit looks and gestures. Not accidently it was "humble" scenes and "contemptable" occupations—at least in the eyes of the public that could afford to buy these large paintings—that were filled with an erotic content, for links between food and sexual pleasure were repeatedly made in moralizing literature, naturally accompanied by all kinds of warnings.[29] Seventeenth-century Dutch, Flemish, or German market scenes, however, do not have this erotic or moral tenor and could be considered just one of the many types of genre art. The sixteenth-century market scenes of the Italian Bassano family are an early example of genre art but are as little realistic in their visualization as their Flemish counterparts.

Another specialty of Aertsen and Beuckelaer was paintings of kitchens with a rich display of food in the foreground and in the background a small scene of Christ visiting Mary and Martha (Luke 10:38–42). A good example is Pieter Aertsen's *Christ in the House of Martha and Mary* (1553; Museum Boijmans van Beuningen, Rotterdam). These scenes were very popular, but should be understood as representations of the

FIGURE 2.21 Nicolaes Jansz Clock, *A Blacksmith as the Element Fire*, engraving, 1597. Rijksmuseum, Amsterdam.

FIGURE 2.22 Crispijn de Passe after Maarten de Vos, *Fish Mongers as the Element Water*, engraving, c. 1600. Rijksmuseum, Amsterdam.

active and the contemplative life: Martha was constantly busy with the household, while Mary was sitting and listening to Christ, choosing "the best part." Aertsen's conspicuous motif of the two kitchen maids prominently at work in front of the apostles St. Peter and St. John—one plucking a chicken, the other putting it on the spit—was repeated in paintings with a kitchen or a kitchen maid without any biblical context. Most of these representations are far from neutral and do not aim to represent the actual situation of a maid responsibly performing her daily work.[30] Beuckelaer's *Kitchen Maid* (1559; Musei di Strada Nuova, Genoa) is rather suggestive, for the superabundance of meat put on to her spit, the toppled pot, and the empty oyster shells (the oyster being a well-known aphrodisiac and sexual symbol) suggest a not too virtuous behavior. Beuckelaer's *Kitchen Scene* in Antwerp is still more explicit and telling (Figure 2.24). The kitchen has become a place for libidinous conduct, where not only the maids and male servants, but also the housewife, are enjoying alcohol, food, and physical pleasure, while the depressive owner of the house is banned to a deserted living room. This representation could have meant a moralistic lesson, but its detailed execution certainly contributed to the pleasure of the viewers. This principle is in line with the northern art theory of the period that recommends the pursuit of a combination of *utile* and *dulce*, profit and

FIGURE 2.23 Joachim Beuckelaer, *Fish Mongers at the Market*, 1568. Metropolitan Museum, New York. Lila Acheson Wallace gift and Bequest of George Blumenthal.

FIGURE 2.24 Joachim Beuckelaer, *Kitchen Scene*, oil on panel, 1565–70. Museum voor Schone Kunsten / MAS, Antwerp.

pleasure, as described in Horace's *Ars poetica,* a treatise that became very influential after its printed edition of 1541. This partly explains the suggestive tenor of so many images of daily life.[31]

Kitchen maids and female servants remained a favorite subject in Dutch art of the seventeenth century, the obscene allusions in the shape of fish and poultry included. It seems justified to conclude that a kitchen maid was not so much represented for herself but for the connotations her presence evoked, much like other "lower" occupations that served the appetites. However, in Dutch seventeenth-century painting, the allusions were not restricted to maidservants, but also appear in "pleasant" scenes, where their mistresses are the main subjects.[32]

Interesting is the fact that the Spanish painter Diego Velázquez in his young years was influenced by Flemish kitchen scenes with a biblical scene in the background, which circulated internationally in engraved reproductions. His *Kitchen Maid with Christ in the House of Martha and Mary* (1618; Figure 2.25) represents a young kitchen maid and an older woman with a finger pointed in warning. Also Velázquez depicted a choice between two ways of living, one according to the teachings of Christ (symbolized by the fish in the middle, which is not a phallic symbol in this case, but a symbol of the Greek "Ichthus," the name of Christ) and a life of worldly pleasures (symbolized by the garlic and red pepper, traditionally considered male aphrodisiacs, and the eggs as a symbol of female fertility and male sexual stimulant).[33] In a related composition, *The Kitchen Maid with the Supper of Emmaus* (c. 1617/18; National Gallery of Art, Dublin), Velázquez took as a model a print by Jacob Matham after a composition of Aertsen. The Spanish painter replaced the sumptuous fish still-life with a very simple one, and the well-fed Flemish maid with the figure of a pensive mulattin. Not long after the painting was finished, the owners decided to adapt it to their taste and robbed it of its meaning: the small biblical background scene was entirely overpainted and the original composition restored only in 1933.

FIGURE 2.25 Diego Velázquez, *Kitchen Maid with Christ in the House of Martha and Mary*, c. 1618. National Gallery, London.

VIRTUOUS WOMEN

In nearly all representations discussed so far, women play their parts as farmers, kitchen maids, sellers of fish and vegetables, workers in the wool and silk trade, care-givers of the sick, and even as assistants of St. Eloy. But there are other kinds of occupations that belong exclusively to the domain of women. In the visual arts, female virtue is mostly expressed by being industrious inside the domestic realm. As seen in the images of Adam and Eve after the Fall, spinning was the ideal occupation of a virtuous housewife, and middle-class ladies were often portrayed spinning as a model of industry. This activity was associated with the most respectable female role model, the Virgin Mary. According to the protogospel of St. James, Mary was among the eight virgins summoned by the high priests to sew a veil for the temple of the Lord and was the one chosen to spin the wool. Another helpful source was Proverbs 31:10–31 in praise of the virtuous housewife, a text visualized by Heemskerck and Coornhert in a series of six engravings (1555). The first print depicts the housewife spinning, sewing, and carding wool with her daughters and maids. In another print, she is serving dinner (Figure 4.1) and performing good deeds for the poor. She is also selling the clothes she produced to a pedlar (Figure 2.26) and is even buying a field with the profit of her work.[34]

A print series by Philips Galle after Goltzius depicts the story of Lucrecia. Goltzius depicts not only the rape scene but also the moment when Tarquin first sees Lucrecia and is struck by her diligence. That she and her servants are preparing the wool until late in the evening indeed corresponds to Livy's text. The spindle also became an attribute of a virtuous woman, when the original story did not mention that activity. The parable

FIGURE 2.26 Dirck Volkertsz Coornhert after Maarten van Heemskerck, *The Virtuous House Wife Selling her Wares to a Pedlar*, engraving, 1555. Rijksmuseum, Amsterdam.

of the wise and foolish virgins (Mt. 25:1–13) says nothing about the virtuous maidens' occupation, except of busying themselves with oil lamps, but in the engraving, *The Wise and Foolish Virgins*, by Galle after Pieter Bruegel, the wise maidens are seen industriously spinning, sewing, and doing the washing, whereas their foolish counterparts are dancing and making music. In Crispijn de Passe's prints of the same parable, after drawings by Maarten de Vos, two engravings are devoted to the activities of the wise maidens. In one print, they are performing traditional good works; in the other one they are spinning, sewing, and weaving, but also reading and writing, another visual proof of some unorthodox ideas about the role of women in the Low Countries (Figure 2.27).³⁵

FIGURE 2.27 Crispijn de Passe the Elder after Maarten de Vos, *The Wise Virgins at Work*, engraving, c. 1600. Rijksmuseum, Amsterdam.

While women spinning were a symbol of industry, a spinning instrument idly resting in a woman's lap meant the opposite. The pensive young woman in a painting by Pieter Pietersz (c. 1570; Figure 2.28) sits next to a spinning wheel while holding a spindle in one hand and a bobbin winder in the other. But she does not give much attention to her work and seems to be listening to the man next to her, who is grasping a tankard of beer and tries to distract her from her task.

WOMEN OF EASY VIRTUE

A book like this one should also pay attention to the visualization of "the world's oldest profession." Large quantities of Netherlandish prints and paintings in the

FIGURE 2.28 Pieter Pietersz, *Temptation to Idleness*, oil on panel, c. 1570. Rijksmuseum, Amsterdam.

period represent brothels and the activities of prostitutes and procuress's. A large part of the oeuvre of the Netherlandish "Master of Brunswick" (c. 1530) shows large and crowded taverns, where a lot of alcohol is served and harlots are seducing customers while robbing them of their purses; the openly sexual activity is enhanced by background scenes of couples going upstairs or mounting a bed. Sometimes a brawl between a bawd and one of her harlots, who seems to be drunk, is depicted; consider a Berlin "Brothel Scene" (1537; Figure 4.2). The actors are common people, so their actions could be watched from a distance and with laughter by the citizens of the middle class. The paintings of the Master were highly successful and were often replicated and copied.[36]

Another tradition of sixteenth-century brothel scenes is derived from representations of the biblical scene of the prodigal son among the harlots (Lk. 15:11–32).[37] The Bible only tells us that the prodigal son spent his inheritance on "a life of luxury," without any further details. But this short information aroused a lot of fantasy about the exact ways he was spending his money, with the consequence that the prodigal son in a brothel became one of the main subjects of sixteenth-century Netherlandish art. A painting by Jan van Hemessen (1536; Museum voor Schone Kunsten, Brussels) shows a brothel scene with references to the original story in the background: the prodigal son among the swine, his repentance, and the return at his father's home.

Although considered a great evil, prostitution was regulated in the Netherlands by the city and restricted to particular quarters or even confined to municipal brothels. That changed during the Reformation. One of the first acts of the Calvinists when taking over a city government, was to close the municipal brothels and declare all forms of illicit sex a criminal offense. As a result, prostitution retired to smaller, more secret places, owned by a bawd who lived there with one or two harlots. The bawd was the business woman; she administered the income and provided the girls with a proper outfit—on credit.[38] This change in the prostitution trade is also reflected in paintings from 1620 onwards. Instead of large taverns crowded with people, the painters concentrated on a few figures, often a close up of half figures, whose pleasure is enhanced by food and music making: a merry young courtesan dressed in a smart dress showing a half-nude bosom and a feather decoration in the hair (or a feather on her client's cap as a symbol of frivolity), one or two of her admirers, and the bawd, who is always represented as an old, ugly, turbaned woman, receiving or counting the money and revealing the mercenary nature of the love scene. This brothel type became popular among Utrecht artists around 1620 to 1640, as is to be seen in the work of Gerrit van Honthorst, Jan van Bijlert, and Dirck van Baburen. Although there were hardly any real courtesans in the Netherlands and whores were often neither young nor attractive, the so-called Utrecht Caravaggisti had no intention to represent reality but rather strove to imitate the modern painting style of Caravaggio, whose works they had admired during their trips to Italy, and whose fame partly explains the success they had with this genre. It was no problem for respectable persons to have these scenes at their walls. The famous and often copied composition *The Procuress* (1622: Museum of Fine Arts, Boston; Figure 2.29) by Van Baburen belonged to the mother-in-law of Johannes Vermeer; he included this painting in the background of two of his works with chaste subjects: *The Concert* (Museum of Fine Arts, Boston) and *A Young Woman Seated at the Virginal* (National Gallery, London).[39]

FIGURE 2.29 Contemporary copy after Dirck van Baburen's, *A Procuress, a Prostitute and a Client*, oil on panel, c. 1622–30. Rijksmuseum, Amsterdam.

Other painters, like Hendrik Pot, Pieter Quast, Jacob Duck, Jan Olis, and a bit later also Jan Steen, specialized in living rooms with merry and elegant companies, that appear to be smart brothels for the bourgeois. The genre was properly called "Bordellos," or more accurately "Little Bordellos" (*bordeeltjes*), in contemporary art literature.[40] There are no half-dressed or feathered ladies present, but well-dressed bourgeois ladies, often in the company of a bawd; they are making merry, drinking, sometimes smoking a pipe, and are uninhibitedly touched by their male visitors. While the sixteenth-century representations might have been meant as *exempla contraria*, an admonition to shun brothels, the later paintings just seem to have been produced for the pleasure of the spectator.

Although depictions of women who were selling their body were predominant in the Netherlands, the business was far from restricted to the north. Remarkably, though, there exists hardly a visual tradition of this genre in southern Europe, apart from the famous representations of Venetian courtesans. When we look, for example, for sixteenth-century depictions of Spanish prostitutes, we end up again with the work of a Dutchman: an etching of 1547 by Jan Vermeyen, made during his travels in Spain. The image includes the well-known motif of women robbing the purses of their clients (Figure 2.30).

FIGURE 2.30 Jan Vermeyen, *Spanish Prostitutes*, etching, 1545. Rijksmuseum, Amsterdam.

CONCLUSION

The representation of work generally belongs to a certain iconographical or conceptual tradition and is less often depicted as a subject in itself. But this tradition, as well as symbolism and allegory, is a useful source for notions and ideas about work and profession. When work is depicted as a theme for itself—like Jost Amman's *Book of Trades*, the print series of Stradanus of modern inventions and the silk industry, and Swanenburgh's paintings of the Leiden serge trade—the images appear to visualize the production processes in detail. So, these objects of art are really an essential visual source for our knowledge of work in the period under discussion.

CHAPTER THREE

Work and Workplaces

JOSEF EHMER

The "long" sixteenth century was characterized by remarkable public and intellectual interest in the world of work, which included, at least to some degree, workplaces and work practices. This interest had various roots.[1] One of them was part and parcel of what J. D. Bernal called the first two phases of the "scientific revolution" from 1440 to 1650. This revolution was characterized, in Bernal's view, by close—although historically rare—relationships between scholars and craftsmen as well as between theory and practice in general.[2] It was manifested by a book production boom throughout western and central Europe, based on the rapid expansion of the printing industry from the middle of the fifteenth century. Two kinds of books addressed the world of work: first, encyclopedic descriptions of all known human professions, from the top of the social ladder all the way down to its lowest ranks. Two especially successful publications of this kind should be mentioned: Tomaso Garzoni's *La piazza universale di tutte le professioni del mondo*, first published in Venice in 1585, and Jost Amman's *True description of all ranks on earth, high and low, spiritual and secular, of all arts, crafts and trades, from the greatest to the smallest, also their origin, invention and customs*, published in Frankfurt in 1568, usually known in German as *Ständebuch* and in English as the *Book of Trades*. Garzoni's text presented a total of 540 occupations. For many of those in the crafts and trades and agriculture, he described entire production processes, with emphasis on raw materials, tools, and finished products, and sometimes included a look at work practices and workplaces. Whereas the first edition of Garzoni's work lacked any illustrations, the merit of the book by Amman, a Nuremberg wood cutter, is its visual representation of work. His book contains woodcut illustrations of 132 professions, accompanied by short poems by the famous Nuremberg shoe maker and master singer Hans Sachs. Almost one hundred of them are devoted to crafts and trades. And all the protagonists of the artisanal occupations are depicted at work and within their respective workplaces, while the remaining "ranks"—from pope and king on top, through various military ranks, and all the way down to all kinds of "fools"—are identified by their appearance and attire, and not by a particular space. Both books were "veritable bestseller(s)" in their days, going through several editions and translations into other European languages.[3]

The second genre of books dealing with work was devoted to economic sectors or production branches which were considered, in the sixteenth century, as particularly important or innovative. There is a rich body of contemporary writings particularly focused on mining, metallurgy, chemistry, machineries, and fortification.[4] Even more widespread and popular was literature for landowners on agriculture and proper household management, such as "books of husbandry," "domestic conduct books," and the so-called *"Hausväterliteratur"* in the German-speaking world.[5] Most of these publications were richly illustrated, and they also came out in several editions as well as in translations into the vernacular (when originally written in Latin). Even when work practices were not at the very center of these publications, both texts and illustrations offer glimpses of workplaces in various economic branches.

Of course, such descriptions and visual representations do not automatically and necessarily represent realities of sixteenth-century work and labor. Most authors embedded their writings into moral reflections, and they took parts of their evidence from classical texts, as well as from the writings or drawings of their contemporary colleagues and competitors. They regularly offered idealized, normative, or schematic versions of work, or they endeavored to stimulate the imagination of their readers. However, they also claimed to provide practical knowledge or even applied science. And the professional habitus of Renaissance and humanist scholars included the readiness to learn from practitioners of the "mechanical arts." When Leon Battista Alberti wrote an autobiographical text in 1438, at age thirty-four, in order to construct an identity, he claimed that he used to learn from humble folks, too, particularly from the practical work experiences of artisans, and even of shoe makers.[6] However idealized this attitude was, it had a realistic substance as well. Publications from the first phases of the "scientific revolution" and, more generally, the spread of a new knowledge culture in the sixteenth century, certainly inspire the historical study of workplaces.

However, there are other historical sources as well. First, there is an enormously rich body of visual representations of workplaces of various kinds beyond the realm of book publications—for instance, paintings on altar panels or frescoes on church walls or other public buildings, which were usually related to the identity formation of specific social groups. Some historians believe that the sixteenth century was "The Golden Age" in the iconography of work.[7] Other sources stem, for instance, from the administrative remnants of trade associations such as guilds or of large enterprises such as mines, workhouses, state-run shipyards, and the like, which were recorded by their officials.[8] Medieval and early modern archaeology has helped to find out where in cities which workplaces were in operation.[9] Also of great importance are "traditional" serial qualitative sources such as court records, protocols and minutes, contracts, and the like, which provide—usually by chance—glimpses of work situations.[10] In light of the fact that writing autobiographical texts was highly esteemed by Renaissance scholars and artists, autobiographies and other ego-documents offer access to the workplaces of learned men.[11] Such sources are, in different ways, close to workplace realities, even if they, of course, call for careful interpretation.

All these historical sources have been used by historians, but in selective ways. The study of sixteenth-century workplaces is not a prominent topic within the historiography of work and labor, but rather situated at the interface of several historical (sub)disciplines. Historians of science and of technology are particularly interested in innovative changes in tools, machineries, and production processes.[12] Economic historians look at the major economic sectors such as agriculture, industry, and trade with a particular emphasis on large enterprises.[13] As a rule, historians of small-scale production in artisanal crafts and trades or in rural protoindustry focus much more intensely on workshops and work practices.[14] The same holds true for local or regional microstudies that emphasize all aspects of daily life, including work.[15] Most of these studies include the household and female reproductive activities.[16]

To sum up, the reconstruction of workplaces of the "long" sixteenth century is like putting together a puzzle by taking pieces from various sources. And, of course, presenting workplaces in the space of a single chapter requires selectivity. The aim of the chapter is twofold. First, it shows examples of the diversity of workplaces and of the changes in those sectors which were economically and culturally significant for the sixteenth century, which employed considerable parts of the population, and which are well-documented in sources and historiography. The emphasis is on agriculture, urban crafts and trades, and large enterprises. Second, it aims to discuss three basic features of sixteenth-century work and labor: the combination of various workplaces by individual men and women; the connections of outdoor and indoor work; and the fluid borders between the workplace and other spheres of life.

THE ECONOMIC BACKGROUND

Already in early modern times, the characteristics of workplaces depended on the structure and development of the economy. The period from 1450 to 1650 was a period of demographic and economic growth. In the two centuries between the "crisis of the late Middle Ages" and the "crisis of the seventeenth century" the European population grew by half, from about seventy million to at least one hundred and five million. All sectors experienced economic growth, agriculture as well as industry, commerce, and finance. Part and parcel of this process was increasing social differentiation, the rise of smallholders and of landless families on the countryside, and the rise of unpropertied classes in towns. However, these economic and social transformations did not take place in a linear manner throughout the period under observation, and not at all evenly in all European regions.

The economic and social changes of the long sixteenth century had an enormous impact on workplaces in two respects. First, new workplaces were created, existing ones changed, and others vanished. Second, the expanding but unstable markets for wage labor required a flexible labor force, which meant workers of both sexes had to be ready—or were forced by need—to work in one place for a couple of days or weeks, and in another for a different period of time, and to change their workplaces according to the demand of employers. Temporary or seasonal labor migration was an important element of this fluid labor market regime. But also, those peasants or master artisans in crafts and trades who managed to keep their workplace throughout their entire life course had to adapt to changing demands by consumers and, more generally, "markets."

However, markets in early modern times were still embedded in non-market-related activities much more than in the industrial age and much more strongly influenced by noneconomic factors. In most parts of Europe, agriculture was embedded in feudal power relations, which influenced or limited the scope of producers' activity, again across a broad spectrum. Since family and household were basic units of agriculture and, although to a lesser extent, of crafts and trades, there was a strong influence on the world of work of the respective culturally based family systems and household patterns. All these factors had severe consequences for the structure of workplaces in the whole economy.

WORKPLACES IN AGRICULTURE

Until the seventeenth century, the vast majority of the European population worked in agriculture and lived in the countryside. In his famous social survey conducted in 1688, English statistician Gregory King even estimated that 88 percent of his fellow countrymen and countrywomen were engaged in agriculture, although many of them not on a full-time basis but in combination with various other economic activities.[17] Highly urbanized regions did exist, such as Holland in the sixteenth and seventeenth centuries or parts of northern Italy since the Renaissance, but they were exceptions.

The weather and climate had a discernible influence on agricultural workplaces and processes. From the Middle Ages until the mid-sixteenth century, Europe enjoyed a favorable, warm and mild climate, but at about 1550 a remarkable decline in temperatures set in, which led to the "Little Ice Age" of the seventeenth century. The impact of this change, however, varied considerably depending on climate zones and ecological conditions. Agricultural workplaces also differed because of socioeconomic factors such as the size of farms or holdings; labor organization; family and household structures; the various degrees of peasants' independence versus feudal subordination; and regional-sepcific factors and produce. Everywhere, the world of sixteenth-century peasants included elements of subsistence economy as well as elements of market orientation, due to the pressure and the desire to make money to pay taxes or rents, to buy land or goods, or simply to have savings to draw on in years of bad harvest.

Moreover, in most parts of early modern Europe mixed farming dominated, albeit to varying degrees. That means that the work of peasants was not bound to one single workplace or a single work process only, but involved several workplaces, and each of them required a range of activities which changed over the course of the seasons. The predominant feature was diversity and variety of workplaces. This applied to an even greater extent to smallholders or landless villagers, who supplemented their income with various forms of wage labor, quite often as part-time workers in cottage industry or as seasonal migrant workers at a great distance from their own homes. When the French philosopher and politician Michel de Montaigne visited Rome in spring 1581, he made a day trip to Ostia on March 15 to see the famous harbor and salt works and, more generally, the region surrounding Rome. In a diary entry, he mentions a meeting with migrant workers: "On my journey hither I met diverse troops of villagers from the Grisons and Savoy on their way to seek work in the Roman vineyards and gardens, and they told me they gained this wage every year." Montaigne explained the need for migrant workers in terms of the lackadaisical work ethic in Rome. "The city is all for the court and the nobility, every one adapting himself to the ease and idleness of ecclesiastic surroundings."[18] More often, however, the destinations of migrant agricultural laborers were economically flourishing rural areas which specialized in market production and export. There was a considerable trend towards specialization in the sixteenth-century European rural economy, including the reemergence of great latifundia—for instance, rice cultivation on the northern Italian Po plain. Specialization made work and workplaces in agriculture more uniform and less varied in principle, but for the seasonal labor migrants, it created once more short-term workplaces among the many they experienced throughout the year.

The following paragraphs discuss some examples of sixteenth-century agricultural workplaces, based on regional and local studies. Italy, in particular, is blessed with microstudies on early modern peasantries and village life. A particularly inspiring example is Gregory Hanlon's "thick description" of Montefollonico in the late sixteenth and early seventeenth centuries, a small Tuscan village southwest of Siena, situated in the hilly area between the Val d'Orcia and the Val di Chiana. Here the peasants practiced a "carefully varied polyculture."[19] Their main workplaces consisted of enclosed plots of land lined with hedgerows in which they cultivated grapevines as well as olive and other fruit trees, interspersed with grain, mainly wheat, and various vegetables. In addition to producing their own food, they cultivated industrial plants such as hemp, flax, and mulberry trees, whose leaves were used to raise silkworms. Such a mixed agriculture required and offered a wide range of labor activities throughout the year. The most labor-intensive season was summer, when grain was harvested with a sickle, followed by the grape harvest and winemaking in early autumn. There followed plowing arable land and sowing the winter seed, and then picking olives. Rejuvenating the vineyards and fertilizing the soil were typical winter tasks, followed by mowing grass in the spring, and so on and so forth. Women participated in many of these activities, but their workplaces were more concentrated around the farmhouse. In addition to their household chores, they worked in the gardens, fed and milked the few animals, and were responsible for the poultry. In the house, they produced cheese, processed saffron, or raised silkworms and prepared their cocoons to sell in towns.

In a wider sense and far beyond their own fields, the workplaces of Montefollonico's peasants encompassed the whole village. The olives had to be carried to the press, animals that grazed on fallow land had to be monitored and kept off enclosed fields. The surrounding forests offered fodder for animals, as well as fuel for heating and cooking. And many villagers were economically active far beyond the village borders—performing seasonal work at one of the large estates in the Maremma for a few weeks, or engaging in transhumance migration towards the coast. The versatility of work and the variety of rural workplaces in such a setting is expressed in the words of a forty-year-old villager involved in a criminal case in 1662, who owned and cultivated his own land, but performed many other activities as well.

> I am a soldier and a sergeant, sometimes I'm a blacksmith and sometimes I work on my land … Ten days ago I went with my horse (a donkey) to Foiano with the father Provincial and his companion (as passengers), and then I returned home to Montefollonico to be paid for it … Sometimes I go to collect wood with my horse, which I pasture on my own land, sometimes I take on chores of my own and sometimes I help maestro Camillo, blacksmith, and for other business, I exercise my hoe.[20]

While Montefollonico serves as an example of workplace diversity in Mediterranean mixed farming, a look at the Dutch rural economy provides insights into an area of advanced agricultural specialization. In 1567, the Florentine noblemen Ludovico Guicciardini, who had lived in Antwerp since 1542 and travelled frequently throughout the Low Countries, published *Description of All the Low Countries* (*Descrittione di tutti i Paesi Bassi*). The book became a success and was translated into several languages and shaped how the Netherlands came to be imagined by generations of educated European readers. Guicciardini was impressed by Holland's agrarian landscape, where—according to his observation—"the fields have mainly a very favourable appearance … with rich green pastures full of all sorts of grazing cattle, which pastures, according to common opinion, are much greener and richer than in Italy; which is, I think, because of the plenteous dampness of the earth."[21] Illustrations in this book as well as contemporary paintings, such as the *The Polder Het Grootslag* by an anonymous artist about 1595 (Figure 3.1), show rows of farmsteads of similar appearance and size, consisting of narrow but rather long strips of land, separated from their neighbors by drainage canals.[22] Seen from the village road, a farmhouse was situated at the beginning of each of these rectangular plots, and they were followed by a series of meadows/pastures, divided by small tributary canals, where cattle grazed or hay was harvested. This is the image of

FIGURE 3.1 Anonymous, *The Polder Het Grootslag*, 1595. © City of Enkhuizen.

an extremely well-ordered rural economy, typical of recently drained polders in Holland and other parts of the Netherlands. In these areas in the sixteenth century, agriculture was interwoven with commercial capitalism and dominated by livestock farming and dairy production for Dutch urban markets and for export abroad.

Under these conditions the workplaces of the farmers, their families, and their servants had a clear magnitude, and their work a clear focus and a regular rhythm: raising and caring for cattle, milking about two dozen cows and processing the milk, providing fodder and keeping enough grass and hay in the barns, manuring the pastures, and last but not least keeping the drainage system working. Some amount of milk may have been sold in nearby towns, but more often it was used to produce butter and/or cheese. Farmers in southern parts of Holland specialized in butter and skimmed milk cheese, while in the northern parts of the province whole milk cheese prevailed. Livestock farming required throughout the whole year a stable workforce in which women got involved, particularly for milking—which required considerable experience and skill—and the making of butter and cheese. In the affluent Dutch farming regions, a trend emerged in the sixteenth century towards a new farmhouse architecture combining a dwelling, stables, and barns—and all related labor activities and workplaces—under one big roof.[23]

These images give an idealized picture, but it was not unrealistic one, in the long sixteenth century, for a large number of Dutch farmers in some regions. Besides dairy farming and cattle breeding, other specializations of agricultural production developed in a garden-like manner. Hemp was cultivated in small, heavily manured gardens, prepared during the winter months, and sold to urban ropeyards. Cash crops such as madder were planted and exported to England. Farmers in the vicinity of large towns specialized in horticulture, producing onions, horseradish, cabbage, carrots, and other vegetables. In the early seventeenth century, the cultivation of tulip bulbs expanded and culminated in the famous "tulipomania" boom in the 1630s.[24]

All these workplaces were integrated into regional, supraregional, and international markets and transportation networks. However, they coexisted with earlier patterns of mixed farming and with the manifold activities of poor rural folks, who "pieced together a livelihood by whatever means were at their disposal," such as reed collecting, peat digging, freshwater fishing, fowling, boat and wagon transport, seafaring, dike and ditch labor, and not to forget spinning. In the Dutch economy of the Golden Age, the well-ordered agrarian workplace for some was accompanied by varied combinations of highly diverse workplaces for many others.[25]

Specialization in agricultural production was not always related to good income and affluent peasantries. On the other end of the social scale, we find impoverished specialization in which poor people bound their hopes to economic niches. Let us have a look at the rural economy in southern France. As in other parts of Europe, quite different agricultural work situations coexisted here in small regions due to local variations in soils, climate, and altitude, but also in respect to market accessibility and economic specialization. The Languedoc in southern France, stretching from the Mediterranean coast to the mountainous areas of the Cévennes, is a fine example of variation within one province. Furthermore, the workplaces of peasants and agricultural laborers underwent continuous change throughout the sixteenth century, reflecting the varying local and transregional demand for and price of certain products. In climatically favored parts of the Languedoc there was a "renaissance" of the olive tree and of olive groves, and an expansion of wheat fields due to rising grain prices—both at the expense of vineyards. In the less favored Cévennes, however, a traditional food and cash crop gained new significance, the chestnut.[26]

In most Mediterranean regions chestnuts were an essential part of the diet, not only but particularly among the poor. In southern France, they also became an important market crop throughout the sixteenth century. In the mountainous plateau of the Cévennes, in its steep valley slopes and its southern and eastern fringes towards the Rhône valley and the coastal areas, trees were planted and harvested by large property owners as well as by small peasants, cottagers, and laborers. Therefore, forests of chestnut trees were workplaces for large parts of the rural population, at least in some periods of the year. Working there meant much more than simply collecting ripe chestnuts in the autumn. The work cycle started with creating terraces on the steep hills or repairing the walls of already existing ones. The next step included planting new young trees and cutting the soil around them. Mature trees required some care once a year, such as pruning and crafting, which were usually done in January. March was the time for cutting those young trees which had grown wild, and which were a valuable raw material, demanded by local and more distant coopers for the manufacture of barrels. In October, the ripe chestnuts were collected, sold to wholesale buyers, or processed—for instance, ground. The Cévennes were—in the words of Le Roy Ladurie—in the sixteenth century still "a land without bread," a region based on the chestnut.[27]

WORKPLACES IN URBAN CRAFTS AND TRADES

The long sixteenth century was a time of renewed dynamism of population growth and urbanization in most European regions, before it came to a halt with the crises of the seventeenth century. In the sixteenth century, however, most of the cities were small, consisting of several hundred or a few thousand people. Only about 10 percent of the European population lived in cities with more than five thousand inhabitants. By 1600 we find two or three dozen cities with more than thirty thousand inhabitants throughout Europe, and about a dozen with more than one hundred thousand.

However large or small, all towns and cities were centers of crafts and trades. Wealth usually stemmed, apart from real property, from trading and financial operations, and rich merchants—next to and overlapping with urban aristocrats—dominated the urban upper classes. The urban economy on the whole, however, was numerically dominated by artisans. In the German trading center of Frankfurt, which had about seven to eight thousand inhabitants in the second half of the fifteenth century, a census in 1440 listed about 1,800 "economically independent male persons." Almost 60 percent of them belonged to the various artisanal branches, 13 percent to trade, transport, and innkeeping, and 18 percent to various forms of agriculture. Moreover, the urban artisanal sector displayed strong economic and technological dynamism, which is most clearly expressed in the increasing division of labor by specialization of occupations. At about 1500, 340 individual occupations existed in Frankfurt, most of them in the crafts and trades. The medieval craft of the "smith"—to mention just one example—had split up into forty-five specific occupations.[28] The specialization of knowledge and skills, of tools and techniques, and altogether of workplaces was part and parcel of this development.

A particularly useful source of artisanal workplaces is—as already mentioned in the first paragraph of this chapter—Jost Amman's Nuremberg *Book of Trades* from 1568. Amman shows a wide range of workshops not only as sites where production takes place, but also as spaces where raw materials and finished products are stored or presented, and where tools are kept, ideally in good order. Amman's about one hundred woodcuts devoted to crafts and trades include very simple spaces with only a few furnishings and tools—for instance, a cobbler sitting on his stool with a shoe on his knees. Others are depicted as being more elaborately equipped—tailors' workshops, for instance. Tailors used to do their needlework sitting at a large table next to the window. This workplace ensured the best supply of daylight, and the pieces of clothing in progress were protected against dust and dirt on the floor. Tailors' workshops usually also contained another large table where clothes are cut (Figure 3.2). Weavers, in contrast, preferred cellars as cool and humid workplaces that made fibers flexible. Metalworkers such as a blacksmith or locksmith worked in forges, which were equipped with fireplace, bellow, and anvil, at which they worked standing upright, but there were also benches to sit on when polishing semifinished products with a file. But Amman's woodcuts also show spaces of higher complexity including large machineries, such as oil-mills, where oil fruits were cleaned, mashed, and pressed. Some crafts required caloric energy; therefore, fireplaces or ovens were in the very center of their workplaces, such as bakers and most of the metal trades. Others made use of water power including all kinds of millers and paper makers, who had to situate their workplaces along waterways.

Whenever possible, Amman also paid attention to the various steps of the work processes. The potter is shown while working in his shop at the pottery wheel, but in the background the view opens to the preceding and to the following work stages: a worker in the clay pit, producing the raw material, and another one who is firing the burning kiln. Indeed, both workplaces were quite often rather distant from the workshop. Suitable clay had to be extracted on the outskirts of a city or even further away, and as the potters' kilns were a fire hazard, they were often relegated to remote corners or even outside of the city walls. In one craft, however, the wider workplace required so much space that it did not fit into the frame of Amman's woodcut: rope makers needed lanes or trails up to several hundred meters long to twine threads into thicker and thicker ropes, which were required for offshore shipping. Hamburg's ropers, for instance, decided in the early seventeenth century to leave their traditional quarter within the city walls due to lack of space and adapted new workplaces in a suburb, which later took its name from the workplace: the famous "*Reeperbahn*" (rope makers' trail).

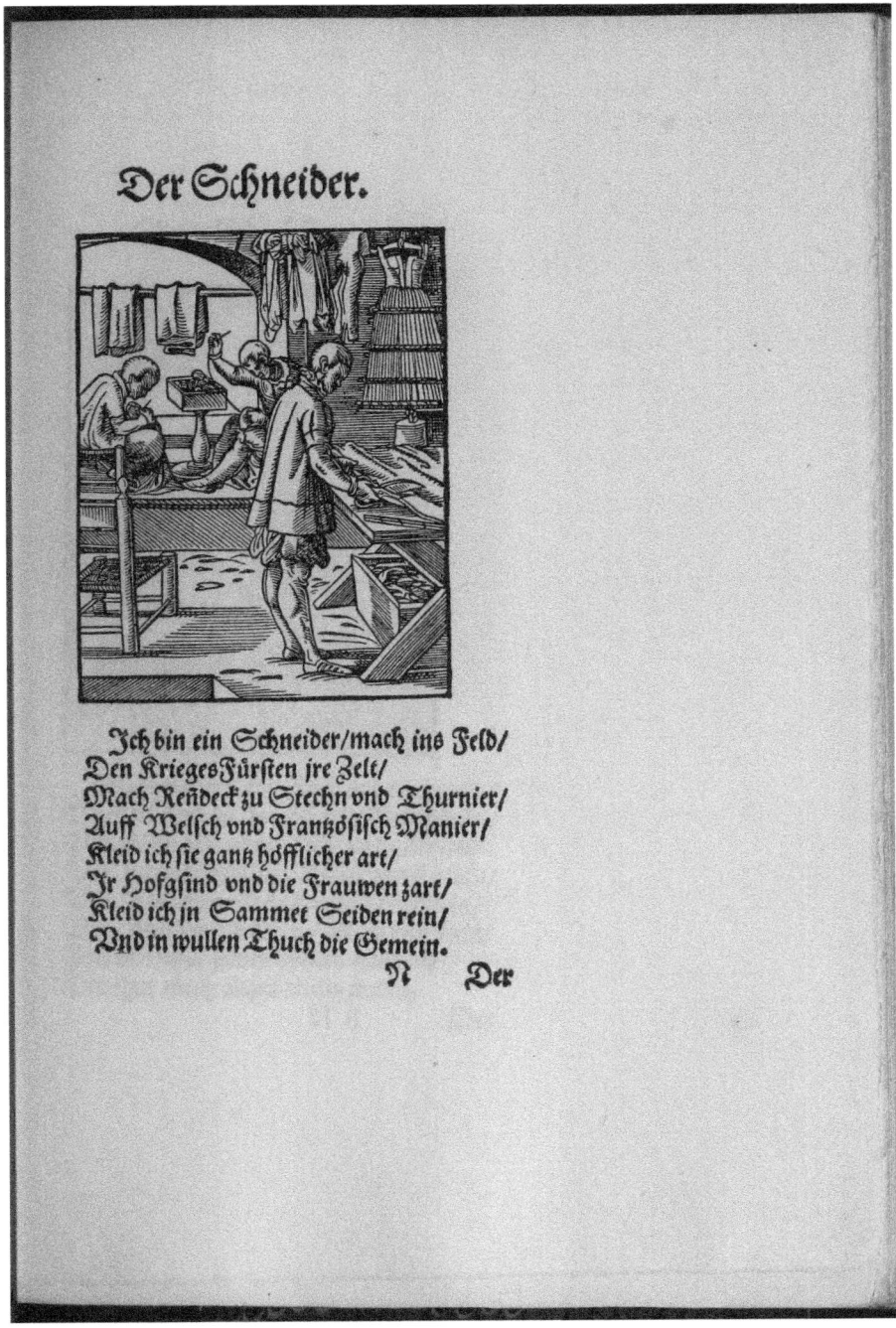

FIGURE 3.2 Jost Amman, Tailors' workshop, *Book of Trades*, 1568. Public domain.

Tanners are another good example to illustrate the complexity of some sixteenth-century artisanal workplaces (Figure 3.3). Tanners in towns such as Nuremberg, Strasbourg, and

FIGURE 3.3 Jost Amman, Tanners working in the water workshop, *Book of Trades*, 1568. Public domain.

Colmar owned multilevel houses, built right next to each other, between a street at the front and a body of running water—be it a river or a canal—to the rear. As the processing of animal hides with all their residual waste products emits a terrible stench, tanners' lanes were usually situated in remote corners of the cities. All these arrangements reflect the complex multilevel work process of tanning. The first step consisted in the preparation of hides after they had been bought on the market or directly from the butcher, and was performed in the so-called "water workshop" at the rear of the houses. The hides were washed and rinsed several times and subsequently scraped to remove all residual meat, fat, and hairs. This work was done standing in the running water, which washed away all the waste. The next step consisted in pushing the hides into tanning pits filled with fresh water and tanbark, where they remained between six months and three years, depending on the quality of the hides and of the intended leather. When the actual tanning process was completed, the hides were brought back to the water workshop for rinsing. After letting them drip off, they were carried into the upper storeys of the tanner's house, which contained special drying rooms providing permanent air circulation. Finally, the dry final product, the leather, was moved into another workshop within the tanner's house, where it was polished, cut, and folded.

Tanning was a complex and capital-intensive craft; thus, master tanners usually were among the wealthier artisans. As a rule, they owned the houses which included their workshops and households as well. There is increasing evidence throughout Europe, however, of spatial separation of workshop and dwelling among urban artisans, as well as of various forms of spatial combinations. The Florentine census of 1427 reveals that no more than 26 percent of master artisans had their workplace and dwelling in the same building, with the "*bottega*" at ground level and the family home on an upper level. This combination of working and living spaces diminished to 18 percent in 1480. Throughout the century, bakers and wine taverners practiced such an arrangement more often than masters of other crafts and trades, and most of them also owned these houses.[29] But in small Swedish towns, too, in the seventeenth century, artisanal workplaces and family homes were more often separated than has previously been assumed.[30]

Jost Amman's woodcuts provide an idealized but nevertheless detailed view of sixteenth-century artisanal workplaces. Though his interest focused on the master artisan—the male skilled workmen and guild member, who operated as employer or self-employed—in some cases his perspectives extend further to include depictions of the interactions and cooperation between small workgroups, and sometimes even auxiliary workers too: the needle maker is accompanied by a young woman who sticks the ready-made needles and pins into pieces of paper to allow it to be stored, transported, and sold. In the workshop of the paper maker we see a young boy who carries a stack of sheets. Such images may be topical attributions to particular crafts, or stereotypes. Nevertheless, they remind us to remain cognizant of the fluid borders between household and workshop. The women in the needle maker's workshop might be his wife, or his daughter, or a maid. The boy helping the paper maker could easily be his son, or an apprentice, or just a poor boy from down the street who occasionally earns a little money doing menial tasks. Natalie Zemon Davis, in her dense description of "Women in the Crafts in Sixteenth-century Lyon," shows how often and to what extent all family members participated in the master artisan's work, thus emphasizing that connection between household and workplace.[31] And she also demonstrates how often women were the principal workers in crafts and trades, running their own shops. Such female activities and positions were certainly beyond the scope of Amman's meritorious book, as it was dedicated to the "ranks" of society in that day and age—that is, to a male order.

WORKPLACES IN LARGE ENTERPRISES

From the fifteenth to the seventeenth centuries, various forms of large enterprises came into existence. These include, among others, charitable institutions which attempted to create workplaces for orphans, foundlings, or widows. In Venice, for instance, by about 1600 a considerable part of the city's lace production stemmed from such institutions. In the private sector, the printing industry was one of the booming urban trades from the late fifteenth to the seventeenth century. Since Gutenberg's technological revolution in the 1440s, printing with movable type, the printing industry spread throughout Europe. Among these workplaces were small, family-based workshops but, particularly in economically booming urban centers such as Seville, Antwerp, Lyon, Paris, Venice, Basel, and Nuremberg, there emerged large printing houses which employed several dozen workers—the largest of them, such as the Plantin–Moretus workshop in Antwerp, even more (Figure 3.4). Their workplaces were characterized by an elaborate division of labor as well as by cooperation among crews of skilled workmen: type founders, compositors, correctors or readers, and pressmen. The challenge for business owners was to establish an optimal number and ratio of these crews to each other in order to achieve a continuous production process.[32]

The mining industry is a further example of a booming economic sector in central Europe in the sixteenth century, particularly mining the ore of precious metals such as silver and copper in the central European Alps. At Falkenstein near Schwaz (Tyrol) in the early sixteenth century, about ten thousand miners worked in almost three hundred shafts. Another large Tyrolian mine was the Holy Ghost Shaft at Röhrer Bühel (Rerobichel) near

FIGURE 3.4 Jan Collaert after Jan van der Straet (Johannes Stradanus), Printers at work, *Impressio librorum*, c. 1590. Metropolitan Museum of Art, New York. Public domain.

Kitzbühel, where in the 1530s rich veins of silver ore were discovered and subsequently attracted the most important investors such as the Fuggers. By about 1600, up to two thousand miners were employed, and the shafts were as deep as 886 meters, which made it by far the deepest mine in early modern Europe. The complexity of the labor process in silver mining meant that only one out of eight workers was occupied with breaking ore below the surface. This was the skilled hewer, who used hammer and chisel while standing upright, kneeling, or sitting on a slanted wooden bench for hammering at the ceiling (Figure 3.5). When shafts were extended, carpenters went down and braced them with timber beams. Unskilled laborers were used for transporting the ore with small lorries on wooden rails in horizontal shafts or galleries, and for winching the ore from one horizontal level to the next and finally to the surface. On the ground, ores were rinsed and sorted and separated from dead rocks, and then transported to melting huts, all of which was usually done by women (Figure 3.6).[33] Melting and forging was then the task of skilled metalworkers. And important groups of workmen had to take care of the water supply management and disposal. Such workplaces represented "high-tech mining districts,"[34] which used complicated systems of machines and complex pipe systems to create effective mine-draining infrastructure.

Other forms of large enterprises in the sixteenth century were state-run naval dockyards. Shipyards constituted complex workplaces in which a wide range of raw materials or semi-finished products were processed by workmen of different occupations. In Europe at that time, shipbuilding was still mainly organized in a huge number of small private shipyards. As the global maritime trade and naval warfare became more important for European powers during the sixteenth century, governments became increasingly interested in the establishment of a standing navy and of state-run docks in which ships were built, based, or overhauled. In England, for instance, there was considerable growth in large-scale shipbuilding between about 1540 and 1640, in which royal dockyards played a major role, surpassing private docks in size, output, and complexity of organization of production. In Stuart England, they represented perhaps the country's "largest industry."[35]

Venice, however, had an even longer tradition of state-controlled shipbuilding, and in the sixteenth century its *Arsenale* constituted by far the largest and most productive and complex industrial site in this branch of production—and a very peculiar workplace. Foreign visitors in the sixteenth and seventeenth centuries praised the arsenal as a "Factory of Marvels" or as "the eighth miracle of the world."[36] Founded by the Venetian state in the thirteenth century at the latest as a state-run shipyard, it expanded continuously up to the late sixteenth century in both size and function. From the 1470s it consisted of three large basins, surrounded by dry and wet docks and by regular series of sheds. In each of these sheds two ships could be built at the same time. The docks and sheds were accompanied by other buildings used as storage sites or workshops for a wider range of activities. In the 1570s some particularly large buildings were added: the "*corderie*," a rope factory hall 315 meters in length and 21 meters wide, whose roof construction was supported by two rows of massive columns; and the "*gaggiandre*," two huge covered wet docks for the construction of especially large ships. While most shipbuilding in Europe in this period took place in the open air, the covered docks of the Venetian arsenal made workplaces less vulnerable to bad weather conditions (Figure 3.7).

In the sixteenth-century boom period, the Venetian arsenal was a multifunctional institution. Its main function was the building, outfitting, and repairing of merchant and naval vessels, which was performed by three occupational groups, each of them organized in a specific guild. The shipwrights constructed the keel, the frame, and the ribbing of

FIGURE 3.5 Georgius Agricola, Miners working in three shafts, *De re metallica*, 1556. Public domain.

292 BOOK VIII.

If the ore is rich in metal, the earth, the fine and coarse sand, and the pieces of rock which have been broken from the hanging-wall, are dug out of the dump with a spade or rake and, with a shovel, are thrown into a large sieve or basket, and washed in a tub nearly full of water. The sieve is generally a cubit broad and half a foot deep; its bottom has holes of such size that the larger pieces of broken rock cannot pass through them, for this material rests upon the straight and cross iron wires, which at their points of contact are bound by small iron clips. The sieve is held together by an iron band and by two cross-rods likewise of iron; the rest of the sieve is made of staves in the shape of a little tub, and is bound with two iron hoops; some, however, bind it with hoops of hazel or oak, but in that case they use three of them. On each side it has handles, which are held in the hands by whoever washes the metalliferous material. Into this sieve a boy throws the material to be washed, and a woman shakes it up and down, turning it alternately to the

A—SIEVE. B—ITS HANDLES. C—TUB. D—BOTTOM OF SIEVE MADE OF IRON WIRES. E—HOOP. F—RODS. G—HOOPS. H—WOMAN SHAKING THE SIEVE. I—BOY SUPPLYING IT WITH MATERIAL WHICH REQUIRES WASHING. K—MAN WITH SHOVEL REMOVING FROM THE TUB THE MATERIAL WHICH HAS PASSED THROUGH THE SIEVE.

FIGURE 3.6 Georgius Agricola, Women shaking the sieve, *De re metallica*, 1556. Public domain.

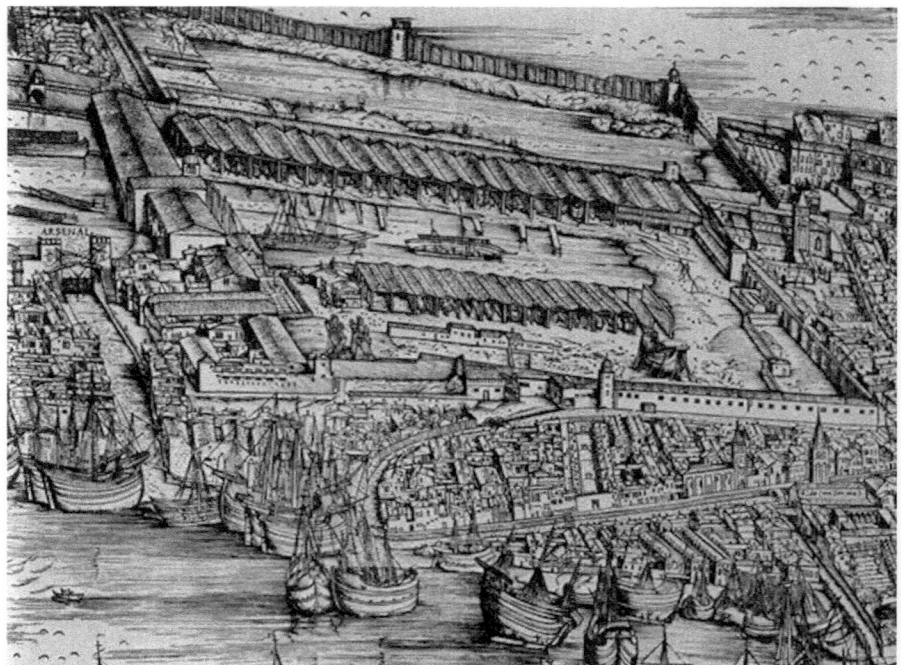

FIGURE 3.7 Jacopo de Barbari, The Venice arsenal, *Veduta di Venezia*, 1500. Detail: Arsenale, Museo Correr, Venice.

the ships; the caulkers were responsible for finishing the hull, adding the cabins, and for caulking; and the oar makers produced the large number of oars required for propelling galleys, the dominant Venetian ship type. The "masters" of these three groups and their apprentices, and a few smaller occupations such as mast makers, pulley makers, and woodcarvers, made up about 75 percent of the entire workforce. In addition, the arsenal was also a site for manufacturing arms and gunpowder and for the storage of weapons—in the sixteenth century mainly cannons and bullets—and it included a storehouse for hemp and a rope factory. And the workforce included hundreds of porters, bricklayers, blacksmiths, sawyers, and many others—altogether in the boom period of the 1540s and 50s perhaps four to five thousand men. They were accompanied by about two or three dozen seamstresses making sails, controlled by a "mistress of the sail room."[37] In the eyes of contemporary visitors and later historians this was "the biggest industrial establishment in all Christendom, perhaps the biggest of the world."[38] As most of the workers lived nearby, the *Arsenale* and the neighboring residential district formed a distinct city quarter of Venice.

During the fourteenth and fifteenth centuries, the arsenal appeared, some historians assume, as a "massive agglomeration of semi-independent workshops" rather than a centralized enterprise.[39] However, over the centuries there also developed, without any explicit plan, an organization of production which displayed, in the sixteenth century, some similarities to the "assembly lines" of the industrial age.[40] There were several peculiarities of the arsenal as a workplace. The first had to do with the concentration of all raw materials and the production of all the equipment, including weapons and munitions, in the same place. This made it possible to have a hundred or more galleys under construction at the same time, although at different stages of production and finishing. Therefore, all the workmen who were specialized in one particular step or stage were continuously participating in the production process. Contemporary visitors praised this system for its efficiency, and some sources indeed give impressive production figures. One hundred fully armed galleys are said to have left the arsenal "in less than two months" in 1571 before the naval Battle of Lepanto.[41] However, this might have been almost-finished vessels left in storage until needed. Nevertheless, the arsenal was equipped and prepared for mass production. This included the concentration on one particular type of vessel, the light galley, and the standardization of components such as masts, spars, benches, deck fixings, oars, and others. Moreover, the new large docks built in the mid-1500s allowed for an accelerated production process:

> as the galley neared completion, it moved down a kind of assembly line. Hulls were constructed in the New Arsenal or Newest Arsenal. They were then brought into the Old Arsenal where they moved past a series of warehouses' where they were outfitted with cordage, arms, and everything else that was required. The different parts of the arsenal "were located in a pattern that on the whole facilitated this assemblage".[42]

However, all these images of a "modern" industrial workplace must not be exaggerated. Labor relations and working conditions displayed many characteristics more typical of the fifteenth and sixteenth centuries than of later historical periods. By the early 1500s, being enrolled included the privilege of getting paid to work there whenever one wanted, and even old and sick workers unable to perform any activity received a daily pay when they managed to at least show up in the morning. A permanent problem the management faced was getting workers to spend the whole day at the worksite. Moreover, arsenal workers might choose to work in one of the small private docks, which still existed in Venice. They constituted a "fluid workforce accustomed to move freely" from workplace to workplace.[43]

WORKING AND LIVING: FLUID BORDERS OR SEPARATE SPHERES?

The spatial separation of working and living, of the workplace and the private sphere of family and home, has become self-evident in modern societies, even if there are also multifold entanglements in these societies. Can we speak, with regard to early modern Europe, of the workplace as a distinct place or a separate sphere apart from other dimensions of life? If we consider the predominant, prescriptive discourses of the time, at first glance the answer seems to be "no." From the fifteenth to the seventeenth century, political and economic thought was dominated by the concept of the "house" as a basic unit of society and economy, in which living and working were closely interconnected and inseparably combined. These ideas stemmed from classical Greek philosophers such as Aristotle and Xenophon, and were revived in the Renaissance and particularly in the period of humanism. They attained popularity in most European countries during the sixteenth century, when they were widely disseminated by "domestic conduct books" of various kinds. Owners of large farms or small rural manors were a particularly important target group, receiving guidance not only on practical issues of agriculture and the family economy, but also on various aspects of private life, on the principles of a well-ordered house, and on financially successful estate management.

We find comparable ideas of unity of work and life in early-sixteenth-century urban communities. A well-documented example is Augsburg, a southern German city with about thirty thousand inhabitants, booming artisanal production, a financial industry of global importance, and which was thus a major economic center of the time. The predominant vision of moral and social order, as expressed in discipline ordinances as well as in everyday policies of the city council, was based on the ideal of the "household workshop," as Lyndal Roper called it. The very center of this unit was the married couple of master and wife, who were expected to "work faithfully with each other" to secure their "sustenance," as it was phrased in the sources. This vision bridged "the divide between labour within the workshop and what we might term housework—the labour of cooking, cleaning, and caring for a workshop labour force."[44]

Reality, however, was much more complex, as the previous paragraphs of this chapter have shown, and strongly influenced by social position. An entanglement of household and workplace was particularly pronounced in the middling ranks of society, in family farming or in the households of small-scale merchants and master artisans—wherever a family mode of production persisted. But also in these cases borders were drawn. Lyndal Roper's study on Reformation Augsburg identified a second meaning of "work" restricted to occupational activities and gainful employment, which accentuated the difference between the sexes. Throughout the sixteenth century there were repeatedly struggles in Augsburg—as in many other European industrial centers of the time—by guilds and journeymen brotherhoods to prohibit the occupational activities of masters' wives or daughters or of female servants, thus banishing them from the workplace proper. And the custom that boarding apprentices were expected not only to work and to learn their trade, but also to perform household chores in their master's home became contested from the sixteenth century onwards.[45]

Families of the laboring poor showed a particularly clear separation of workplace and household.[46] As the only marginally stratified medieval peasantry became differentiated by an increasing number of land-poor and landless households, a new housing type spread across western and central Europe: the cottage. Cottagers had to work for wages at various and rapidly changing workplaces outside their homes. This experience was shared by large numbers of the laboring poor in towns, who had no house at all, however tiny, but instead rented a cheap chamber in a slum area or in a suburb, and worked wherever they found a job, usually short-term employment. Skilled workers experienced a clear separation of workplace and home when they were employed in large enterprises—for instance, in the building trades, in shipyards, in mining, and in the printing industry. And there was an increasing number of jobs—due to intensification of trade and transport, and new forms of warfare—which necessitated leaving one's home for longer time spans, such as with sailors or mercenaries, itinerant peddlers, and seasonal laborers in agriculture.

Also in the upper ranks of society, there emerged a trend towards spatial separation of work activities, which had quite a different character. If we start at the very top of the social ladder, we find the dissociation of government administration from the households of the ruling princes, most clearly expressed in Florence by the construction of the "*Uffizi*" in 1559 to 1581 as a special office building. A kind of separate office space also became fashionable in private upper-class houses. In Leon Battista Alberti's four *Books on the Family* (*I libri della famiglia*), written in Florence in the years

1432 to 1441, it is said that the *paterfamilias*, as the head of the house, should occupy a chamber of his own, the study ("*studiolo*"), where he keeps all relevant business and family records, valuables, and money as well as his library. In the houses of noblemen and rich merchants, as well as affluent intellectuals, the study was not only a privileged workplace but also a separate space for intellectual pleasures. Machiavelli, in a letter dated December 1513, describes the study of his country house in Sant'Andrea in Percussina, a few miles south of Florence, as a retreat to spend his evenings in virtual discourse with ancient poets and philosophers, after a day spent performing various tasks in managing his little estate.[47] When Sir Hamon Le Strange, a member of the English Parliament, justice of the peace and a wealthy member of the upper gentry, rebuilt and enlarged Hunstanton Hall, his Norfolk manor house, in the 1620s, it contained a study as his actual workplace.[48] In sharp contrast to them, scholars of more modest means, such as German schoolmasters at about 1500, complained about being incessantly disturbed in their aspired working-"life of solitude" by wives, children, and servants running around.[49]

In addition, remarkable changes in working and housing spaces took place. Late medieval peasant houses throughout Europe used to consist of only one large room for humans and animals. During the fifteenth century in northern Italy, a new house type began to emerge in the better off peasantry, "with more rooms, on two floors instead of one. This new type reached France during the early sixteenth century, and England ... by the last quarter of the century."[50] This trend is best documented for England, where between 1570 and 1640 what William Hoskins called a "revolution in housing" or a "Great Rebuilding" took place. Rural houses became larger and more comfortable, and contained more and more specialized rooms: a kitchen for cooking, a buttery, a dairy, a separate bedroom for master and mistress, a chamber for servants, a parlor for dining and for leisure activities, and in the case of rural artisans, such as weavers, a separate workshop. Jane Whittle observed that in sixteenth- and early-seventeenth-century England "well before productive work was commonly located away from the house, there was a trend of segregating working from nonworking areas within the home, particularly in middling and elite houses. However, this is qualified by the fact that women's and servants' work remained spread throughout the house."[51] The English "housing revolution" was triggered by the "price revolution" of the sixteenth century, which provided larger agricultural producers—the bigger husbandmen, the yeomen, the gentry—with a substantial rise in income. But it also signalled the beginnings of a cultural change that placed greater value on privacy. This observation is perhaps even more accurate for the Dutch urban upper classes in the "Golden Age," when cleanliness and homeliness became major cultural values, and when properly appreciated work within the home consisted of methodically performed housework including intensive scrubbing, scouring, or dusting.[52]

These trends towards segregation of work and life, of workplace and household, were counterbalanced, to some degree, by the spread of protoindustrial domestic production in a wide range of industrial branches, mainly in the countryside, but also in towns. Domestic production meant, for instance in the case of the textile industry, that spinners (usually women) and weavers (usually men) worked in their own homes, but in a supraregional market-oriented economic network organized and controlled by merchant capitalists. Often it was based on the cooperation of several family members, including children. All in all, sixteenth-century Europe was characterized by the coexistence of unity of work and life on the one hand, and segregation of the workplace on the other, and by a wide range of transitional forms.

COMBINATION OF WORKPLACES, INDOOR AND OUTDOOR

The strong emphasis on the "house" in sixteenth-century European discourse coexisted with the fact that most people worked predominantly or at least partially outdoors. Workplaces located in open-air settings displayed a particularly strong influence of weather and climate on the work process, resulting in irregular and discontinuous rhythms of work during the year or the day. They entailed specific hardships and health risks due to exposure of workers to extreme heat or cold, moisture and precipitation, or dust. But also, indoor workplaces had their specific problems. Late medieval houses with very small and unglazed windows, with one fireplace only and without a chimney, and without separated workrooms, were dark, cold, full of smoke, dust, and dirt. The advancement in housing in the sixteenth century improved not only living conditions but also workplaces, due to larger and more often glazed windows, chimneys, candles, or separation of storage spaces. Nevertheless, most artisans preferred to work outside their houses when the character of their activities and the weather made it possible, and enjoyed fresh air, daylight, and the conversation with diverse people strolling by.

Working inside or outside the house was also related to gender roles. Normative writings such as sixteenth-century "domestic conduct books" and particularly Protestant reformers' treatises on Christian matrimony were quite clear in that respect. "Whatever is to be done without the house, that belongeth to the man, and the women to study for things within to be done," wrote the Swiss reformer Heinrich Bullinger in his book *Der christliche Ehestand* published in Antwerp in 1541 and translated into English in 1575 as *The Christian State of Matrimonye*.[53] Even if these were hegemonic cultural values, in practice the bond of women's work to domestic locations was weak and not necessarily stronger than that of men.[54] First, the "house" had a rather symbolic meaning in these normative texts, including wider spaces for the family economy, be they the fields or gardens of farmers or the workshops or market stalls of artisans. Second, in the early modern period, outdoor work quite often had lower prestige than indoor work. Therefore, it was often practiced by men of low social status or by women and included, for instance, carrying heavy loads. In the salt mines of the Austrian Alps, as in Hallstatt, male miners worked in shafts beneath the surface, while one of the female labors was to carry on their backs large blocks of salt several hundred meters down from the portals to the village. When in the Black Forest of southwestern Germany an explosive growth of worsted weaving began in the 1580s as rural protoindustrial domestic manufacturing, the male weavers, skilled workmen organized in guilds, operated their looms at home, while their wives and daughters and female servants carried the raw materials from and the finished textiles to the export merchants in the next town. In addition, these women took care of the small agricultural holdings that were usually affiliated with the weavers' households.[55]

The relevance of outdoor work is enhanced by the fact that most working men and women had to combine several workplaces in order to perform their tasks. This applies not only to most forms of agricultural work, particularly to small family farms, and even more so to peasants or smallholders who combined agriculture with crafts and trades, but also to urban artisans whose work ranged from the extraction of raw materials to selling finished products at markets. Outdoor work certainly predominated in all historical periods before the Industrial Revolution. Some changes, however, can be identified during the long sixteenth century, albeit not in the same direction. Urbanization, the rise of urban crafts and protofactories, and the spread of rural domestic industries account for an expansion of indoor workplaces. The rise of the building trades as an upshot of urbanization, the intensification of transregional traffic and transportation, and generally high and growing geographical mobility contributed to the spread of outdoor workplaces. It is not clear which of these two opposing trends was of greater importance in the period under observation, or whether they remained in balance.

CONCLUSION

In sum, the diversity and variety of workplaces in the "long" sixteenth century certainly increased. Within this process, however, two opposing trends interacted: on one hand, there was a trend towards division of labor and professionalization, which means differentiation and specialization of workplaces; on the other hand, many of these specialized workplaces were not isolated from each other, but closely linked in different ways—as parts of production lines in single large enterprises, or in commodity chains connecting several businesses. In social terms, one observes an increasing combination of several workplaces by individual men and women of lower classes due to their need to earn an income from various sources during their daily, weekly, or seasonal work and during their life course.

Looking at sixteenth-century workplaces in a long-term historical perspective also yields ambivalent results. Some types of workplaces that emerged during the "long" sixteenth century continued to exist well into the onset of the industrial age at least—for example, most of the new, specialized crafts or agricultural branches. Others, however, disappeared or declined in importance. This fate was shared by most of the huge silver mines, but also by large state-run enterprises such as the highly admired arsenal in Venice where, beginning in the seventeenth century, the importation of ships overtook local production due to a regional timber shortage and, more generally, due to the declining economic and political position of Venice in the global economy. It turned out that the most modern-appearing workplaces in large enterprises were the ones whose future was regionally and temporally limited, whereas specialized workplaces in small-scale production were more likely to remain in existence.

CHAPTER FOUR

Workplace Cultures

ANNA BELLAVITIS

The term "culture" can refer to training and preparation for a specific job and, at the same time, all the expectations, codes of behavior, rituals and hierarchical relationships linked to it. Any workplace can be considered the expression of one or more, specific "cultures," at a specific time and place. Out of all the changes which characterized the period included in this chapter, we have chosen to concentrate on the following topics: state-building and the professionalization of state service; the process of professionalization that concerned midwifery; religious reforms, which included, among many other fundamental consequences, a reorganization of the gender divisions and the moral standards within workplaces; and the reshaping of guilds, which, in some cases, tended increasingly to reserve their "social capital" for members of the masters' families. Those specific evolutions that characterized the period under discussion had an impact on workplaces as different as houses and courts, brothels, and workshops, even if it would be inappropriate to see them as part of a process of "modernization." We shall present different examples of workplaces, to try to highlight the identities of the professional and working figures that populated them, with special attention to gender identities and to relations between generations.

THE EDUCATION OF CIVIL SERVANTS

The evolution of European states between the end of the Middle Ages and the first centuries of the early modern period involved a reorganization of aristocratic courts and, more generally, of administrative bureaucracies in dynastic as well as in republican states. This resulted in the creation of bodies of personnel with increasingly sharp identities, defined by their academic education, humanistic culture, and professional cohesion. Paternalism and deference in the "maison du roi"[1] and ambiguity between "voluntary servitude and political oppression"[2] characterized the culture of civil servants and of persons who were entrusted with the secrets of government, the "secretaries."[3]

Courts of Italian Renaissance states are a good example of increasing professionalization as well as of a persistent merging of ecclesiastical and lay personnel. The perfect courtier[4] was born in Urbino, "a city shaped like a palace," at the court of Elisabetta Gonzaga, in ideal harmony between those who governed and those who were governed. A vast humanistic culture and "savoir vivre" were translated, in the treatise *Il libro del cortegiano* (Florence, 1528) by Baldassarre Castiglione (1478–1529), into a "new word," "*sprezzatura*, concealing artifice and showing what is done and said without effort and almost without thinking about it."[5] A court was revealed only minimally, as shown in the frescoes of the *Camera picta,* painted by Andrea Mantegna in Mantua's Ducal Palace in 1475. The allegories of good government and its effects, in their settings both in the inner space of the court, where the prince's *"familia"* gathered, and in the outer space, where he carried out his diplomatic and military activities, appear on two adjacent walls of a small, frescoed room. On the other two walls of the small frescoed room a large curtain is painted, showing and concealing at the same time, while from the ceiling *oculus* putti and domestic staff are observing the scene.[6] Between the fifteenth and sixteenth centuries, from the palace-city built in Urbino by Laurana to the Vasari corridor that allowed Cosimo de' Medici to walk across Florence from Palazzo della Signoria to his family home in Palazzo Pitti without coming into contact with his subjects, the spaces devoted to government and daily life were becoming increasingly separate and specialized.

The choice of entering into a prince's service or of becoming one of his counsellors implied, for humanists such as Guillaume Budé in France (1467–1540), Thomas More in England (1478–1535), Niccolò Machiavelli (1469–1527) or Francesco Guicciardini in Italy (1483–1540), the resolution of a typically humanistic dilemma: the choice between committing to the world and engaging in politics (*vita activa*) or retreating from the world and devoting themselves entirely to study (*vita contemplativa*).[7] The early modern evolution of European bureaucracies was a complex process that did not follow a unidirectional path. While the secularization of the civil servant is often considered as a general process following, as has been written, a south–north trajectory, "from a more ancient to a younger Europe," members of the clergy had still an important role in many Italian states. Nevertheless, the evolution towards a better education and specialization of administrative elites can be considered a general process, in which not only the study of rhetoric or law, but also, and increasingly, the one of double-entry bookkeeping was important. Between the fifteenth and sixteenth centuries, the main economic and administrative centers of the Mediterranean area, the Hanseatic League and the northwest of Europe had in their services jurists trained in the main European universities. In universities and academies, the future elites acquired, in addition to their professional training, a social, moral, and political education befitting the norms and values of the society they would later guide. Since the final centuries of the Middle Ages, most civil servants had attended courses in universities which, in some cases, could be very far from their home towns: the *peregrinatio academica* was instrumental to the circulation of cultures and ideas, particularly in some European areas, such as the Holy Roman Empire. Italian and French universities were the destinations favored by northern European students between the sixteenth and the seventeenth centuries, becoming the obligatory stops in a sort of academic Grand Tour. In this respect, England was a different story, as universities did not provide a coherent education in customary law, a task that was taken over by the Inns of Court, where, for example, Thomas More received his legal education. After the abolition of the teaching of canon law in universities, Inns of Court acquired a status comparable to that of universities.[8]

The case of the Republic of Venice deserves our attention, because the formation of its administrative elite, at least at the central level, was never based on a juridical education. On the contrary, the Venetian government tried by all means to avoid the formation of an elite of jurists: a legal education was never the basis of the culture and training either of the patrician political leadership or of the bourgeois administrative staff. With the territorial expansion of the Venetian republic, between the fourteenth and fifteenth centuries, a class of bourgeois civil servants, defined by their social identity rather than by their university education, began to appear beneath the patrician political class and to shape the social identity and culture of the ducal chancery. The chancery, then, was the workplace in which two different relationships to "public service" coexisted. Patricians identified themselves with the state, supposedly since its origins, even if in fact they had seized power at a precise moment of the history of the Republic. Among the "ordinary citizens" who held offices in the ducal chancery, there were also members of families that had been excluded from this process. The potential conflict between the patriciate and those wealthy, skilled, and cultivated citizens could never find any political expression, but appears in the background of some Renaissance political treatises, such as the *De bene institute re publica* (*On the Well Managed Republic*, 1497/1509) by Domenico Morosini, or *La republica e i magistrati di Vinegia* (*The Republic and Magistracies of Venice*, 1544) by Gasparo Contarini, the last one being the most accomplished expression of the political myth of Venice, "as a flawlessly functioning republic embodying the perfection of justice."[9]

In ducal processions, which took place several times a year, the great chancellor, head of the ducal administration, and, thus, a Venetian commoner, processed immediately ahead of the doge, who was then followed by the most important state dignitaries, all patricians. In 1456 Venice's Council of Ten defined the chancery as the "heart of the state," an expression which was not simply rhetorical, but which bore witness to a very precise moment in the development of the Venetian administration. This had grown consistently between the fourteenth and fifteenth centuries and needed competent and above all trustworthy personnel in order to coordinate the republic's main executive bodies. Half way through the fifteenth century, when Venice was consolidating its power over the mainland, trusted personnel meant above all people coming from the capital city, who shared its history and culture, and not from the subject cities of the growing state. Relationships with members of the patriciate were useful, particularly for career advancement and, by the end of the fifteenth century, there were various patronage networks within the chancery linking influential patricians to notaries and secretaries who, in the course of their careers, were able to "serve" various members of the patriciate, working in close contact with them during their diplomatic missions abroad.[10]

In 1446, the School of Saint Mark was founded, for the purpose of training the "*cives populares*" prior to their entry in the ducal chancery. In this way, from the fifteenth century, the foundations had been laid of that chancery culture, based on the teaching of grammar and rhetoric, but not on the teaching of law, which in the case of Venice always remained substantially absent from the training both of the patrician ruling elite and of the bourgeois bureaucratic elite.[11]

STATES' CONTROL AND PROFESSIONALIZATION: THE CASE OF MIDWIVES

In early modern Europe, the process of constructing a professional identity more and more closely linked to university education can be found in health-care, where it sometimes gave rise to conflicts related to the practitioner's gender. At that time, particular attention was paid to the training of midwives, one of the few female professional figures imbued with a public role and with powers to certify the religious and personal identity of the population. Their tasks expanded in the course of our period but, at the same time, the competition represented by university-educated doctors also increased.

The reasons for this change are manifold. It was important to ensure that the events surrounding the reproduction of the population happened in the best possible conditions, but equally abortions and infanticides had to be avoided, by placing ever tighter controls over traditional female practices and knowledge. The first treatises on obstetrics written by doctors in the sixteenth century insisted upon the midwives' witchcraft, which, in some cases, could bring charges of heresy upon them. This is particularly true where different religious cultures coexisted: in sixteenth-century Spain, midwives from the Moorish community, that is, Muslims who had converted to Christianity, were particularly suspect, despite the fact that their community's medical culture was highly developed and of recognized effectiveness, even among the Christian population. In practice, however, the number of midwives brought to trial in European courts of law, whether for carrying out abortions or for practices bordering on witchcraft, was never very great, contrary to what has been thought on the basis of treatises on Satanism, rather than the legal sources.[12]

The question of the public role given to those persons who dealt with childbirth is particularly important. During the early modern period, their tasks became ever more complex, following the development of institutions and practices to control the population, but also as a consequence of changes in the relationship between lay and religious institutions in early modern Europe. A 1468 Munich ordinance ruled that, if a midwife feared for the life of the baby, she had to baptize him, or else "she will have to answer before God for her laziness and irresponsible behaviour." A century later, in 1585, a Württemberg ordinance specified that midwives had to go to the pastor of their local church to learn the correct way to administer a baptism.[13] Even in Catholic territories, midwives had to baptize infants if their lives were in danger and, after the Council of Trent (1545–63), the Catholic Church took a close interest in their activity: on various occasions it reiterated that the parish priest had to carefully instruct midwives on baptism rites; and in 1614 bishops were ordered to check the actions of midwives during pastoral visitations.[14] In Catholic areas it was possible, if the rite had not been conducted correctly, to ask a priest to baptize the child again. This raised more complicated issues in Protestant communities, where repeating a baptism was considered close to the Anabaptist heresy. A midwife's role was therefore even more important and invested with public significance. Between the sixteenth and seventeenth centuries, growing moral concerns caused a new task to be given to midwives: reporting illegitimate births in every possible way. According to an ordinance passed in 1605 in Strasbourg, a midwife assisting an unmarried woman had to report to the authorities "the name of the man called out by the woman during her labour." Similar norms can be found in England, where midwives were subject to the control of Anglican ecclesiastic authorities. They were responsible for gathering the mothers' statements about the identity of their babies' fathers and could be called as witnesses in court in cases where couples were accused of premarital sex. Their testimony that the new-born showed all signs of being premature could save a mother's honor, even when she was lawfully married. In non-Anglican communities (Catholics, Presbyterians, Quakers), it was necessary for all these reasons to be able to rely upon a tolerant midwife, when one from the same religious confession was not available.[15]

As early as the fifteenth century, many towns in Flanders, southern Germany, and northern Italy had established the office of a town midwife, paid by the community to serve the needs of women regardless of their social class. The establishment of town midwives required governing bodies to impose a series of rules, the main purpose of which was to set clear boundaries between the activities of the midwife and those of doctors or surgeons.[16] The midwife's training was mainly based upon practical experience. At this time a contradiction began to arise between the acknowledgment by governing authorities of the value of experience and the desire to control the midwives' activities, even by imposing a more theoretical training to them; this process reached its conclusion during the seventeenth and eighteenth centuries. In Burgundy, as in Alsace and Lorraine, local authorities hired women as midwives who had already attended some childbirths, and who up until then had practiced freely, probably receiving no payment or only a small fee or gift. In Lille, the town aldermen hired such women as midwives during a public ceremony, following an inquiry into their competence in matters of childbirth; in Swiss towns, the town council chose among the women who had served for some time as apprentices with one of the town midwives. From the sixteenth century, in the towns of southern Germany, the examination of midwives was entrusted to "honorable women" who belonged to the local patriciate, assisted by town doctors, despite the fact that pregnancy and labor figured very little in their training of medicine doctors. During the examination, doctors would ask technical questions, whereas the "honorable women" would test the candidate's moral standards. In 1549, in Nuremberg, the midwives complained that the "honorable women" would not help them assist the poor and asked that they be replaced by women from the artisanal class, that is, their own social class.[17]

Since the fifteenth century, the competition represented by university-educated doctors increased and the workplace—in this case, the homes of the women in labor or the hospitals where poor or sick women gave birth—became the place of a clash of cultures and powers. In some cases, such as in Spain, doctors imposed their control upon this ancient female activity very early on;[18] in other contexts, such as the Netherlands, where public midwives were organized much later than in the rest of Europe, they kept the control of childbirth until the end of the early modern period.[19] In France the intensification of state control over childbirth during the eighteenth century gave to an exceptional woman, Madame Du Coudray, the opportunity to build one of the most interesting careers of any woman in early modern France.[20]

HOUSEHOLD CULTURE AS WORKPLACE CULTURE

Houses have always been places for many work activities, from reproductive tasks to different kinds of craft activities carried out by members of the family or by apprentices and servants, who shared not only the working, but also the living spaces, with the master's family, in a characteristic confusion of living and working roles (Figure 4.1).

In Mediterranean Europe, domestic slavery was still quite common, especially for women, but the difference between a slave and a servant was clear, in contemporaries' eyes, as appears from the testimonies presented in Venice at a 1594 trial of a master accused of abusing her servant and of treating her "as a slave."[21] Sexual abuse of female slaves and servants by their masters was common reality, but young women could invoke the protection of the law even in these cases. A pregnant servant, particularly if she was assisted by her family, could sue her master in court, sullying his reputation, or, more frequently, she could threaten to do so and eventually obtain a dowry or some kind of compensation.[22] This was of course almost impossible for a female slave, even if such cases existed, as, for example, in eighteenth-century Spain.[23]

In the case of domestic service, the working relations between masters and workers could be very intimate, as is apparent from last wills of servants leaving their goods to their masters or of masters making bequests to their servants.[24] In Spain, where the word for

FIGURE 4.1 Dirck Volkertsz Coornhert after Maarten van Heemskerck, *The Virtuous House Wife Serving a Meal to her Family*, engraving, 1555. Rijksmuseum, Amsterdam.

servants was *criados,* meaning "raised," the creation of an artificial kinship between servants and masters was also a strategy to evade taxes on servants.[25] The family-type relationship that could exist between masters and servants could also be a double-edged sword, however, when it became a pretext not to pay the salary due to the workers, who nevertheless could pursue a legal action against their masters. If they were also accused of bad treatment, servants could win the case and also be allowed to leave the household, before the end of their contract. Violation of the duration of a contract by workers was one of the main reasons for judicial conflicts between masters and servants in the European courts.[26] The "sanctity" of contracts had to be respected, and municipal authorities, who fixed limits to the salaries of domestic servants, were also concerned with the possibility of their flight.[27]

Confusion between service and apprenticeship was quite common, especially in the case of girls. Apprentices worked in the workshop, but most of the time they lived with the master, who had the role of *paterfamilias*. In consequence, the time of apprenticeship was also the time during which very young boys and girls learned a professional and social culture, based on respect of rules, hierarchies, and a specific vision of the surrounding world.[28] The educational tasks implicit in their relationship with a master or a mistress, who contracted to deal with the apprentice as a good father or mother, could sometimes exceed its limits: the judicial archives of early modern Europe contain many cases of violence on apprentices.[29]

The family-type relationship between masters and apprentices or servants is particularly evident in the case of children who were recruited in foundling hospitals to become low-cost workers and in fact to become part of the master's family.[30] Contracts as well as other documentary sources, such as the last wills of masters and mistresses, show that the boundaries between adoption and apprenticeship could be porous.[31] Furthermore, apprenticeship contracts could be fosterage contracts between masters and young people, not necessarily orphans. In Renaissance Italy, some apprentices with painters took the name of their masters, as one can see in the *Lives of the Most Excellent Painters, Sculptors and Architects* (1550) by Giorgio Vasari (1511–74). It is for example, the case of Piero di Cosimo (1462–1522), the son of the goldsmith Lorenzo di Antonio Chimenti, who took as patronymic the first name of his master Cosimo Rosselli (1439–1507). Vasari commented that "in truth, when a man teaches us excellence and gives us the secret of living rightly (*virtù*), he deserves no less gratitude from us, and should be held no less as a true father, than he who begets us and gives us life and nothing more." According to the guilds' rules, a father who apprenticed his legitimate or natural son had no obligation to stipulate a contract, so the father–son relationship with one's apprentice could become an excuse not to pay him a salary. This was the case for the great Italian painter Andrea Mantegna (1431–1506) who, in 1456, won a court case against his master Andrea Squarcione (1394–1468), who refused to pay him for his work or release him from service.[32] "Charity" should inspire family relations, according to contemporary moralists, but the confusion between family and work relations could become an excuse not to pay those members of the family who worked in the family workshop.[33]

Apprenticeship was a common experience for young people in all European regions, but its characteristics could be very different from one region to another. Andrea Trevisan, the ambassador of the Republic of Venice in London, reported in 1498 that the English did not love their children because when the children were seven or eight years old, their fathers left them as "*apprendizii*" in someone else's house for seven or nine years. The reason, he wrote, was they preferred to be served by strangers than by their own offspring. His astonishment did not come from the existence of apprentices or servants, but from the fact that, as he wrote, "very few people were rich enough to be exempted from this fate."[34] In 1564, another member of the Venetian patriciate, Giovanni Maria Memmo, wrote that fathers should not be ashamed to leave their children in someone else's house, because they would be free from "the paternal shadow," and would not dare to be as arrogant as they could be in their own family. They then would become "much better masters." Fathers should leave their children to "humane men and not to cruel beasts," who would beat, hurt, or even kill them. Merchants should send their children abroad, living and learning with their fathers' clients and colleagues, according to Memmo, so they could learn to be more modest and respectful. Only members of the patriciate were supposed to stay at home and be educated in their early years by their mother, then by preceptors and, finally, by their own father.[35]

BECOMING A MASTER ... OR A MISTRESS

Work identities were much more complex than the idealized image that has been transmitted until now. Masters could be heads of workshops, having journeymen and apprentices under their authority, but they could themselves also be under someone else's authority. In the Venetian silk industry, two different words expressed this distinction:

"chief-masters" were the heads of workshops and "masters" had passed the masters' examination, but did not have workshops of their own.[36] In the wool manufactory of Padua, on the contrary, masters were not necessarily those who had passed the masters' examination, but rather those who were heads of a workshop or of a working team, but in wool weaving and knitting workshops the title of master could also apply to a salaried worker. The younger personnel called "*garzoni*" could be either apprentices or salaried workers; women were called "mistresses," a title which did not refer to status in a workshop or guild, but to the fact that they were hired to teach knitting to children in the workshop.[37]

In the Italian industrial cities of the Renaissance, such as Florence, Venice, or Milan, apprenticeship was reserved to artisans, in order to become "much better masters," but the theoretical career from apprentice to journeyman to master should not be taken for granted, in Italian as in any other European town, especially at a time of population growth. The fact that most of the time apprentices received a "salary" (*salario*) at the end of the contract, suggests that they were not considered only as "pupils," but that they were directly involved in the production process.[38] The duration of apprenticeship could vary according to the craft, but also according to the age of the apprentice or the stipulations of the contract, as we can see from some Venetian examples. In 1632, a twelve-year-old boy from Friuli, in the territory of the Venetian Republic, was recruited as apprentice by a manufacturer of rosaries made out of wood and bone, who engaged to host him, to keep him safe and clean, to "teach his art" to him and to pay for all the time a salary of eighteen ducats. Another one, aged twenty, coming from the same territory, agreed to a contract for four years with a manufacturer of mirrors, for a salary of thirty ducats. The clauses of the contracts were similar, but the master engaged himself to give to the young man also "one shirt, two pairs of shoes and a hat *Schiavona* style." The same year, a tailor accepted as apprentice a thirteen-year-old boy and engaged only to teach him "his art" and to give him his everyday lunch, for six years. A sixteen-year-old apprentice to a mercer was lodged and fed, but did not receive any salary at the end of a five-year contract; and a ten-year-old boy, apprentice to a diamond-cutter for eight years, received five ducats per year, without board and lodging.[39] The variety of clauses depended on the crafts but also on the relations that could exist between the master and the apprentice or his family. The stipulation of a work contract was not necessarily the beginning of a work relationship between two actors who did not have any previous social or economic relationship, but, as it was recently pointed out, "it often was the conclusion of a '*probationary period* with masters. It was only *after* such trial periods that employers and employees signed contracts and received fixed wages for apprenticeships. Masters regarded testing apprentices' abilities as a pre-requisite for contracts."[40]

It is often difficult to know exactly what apprentices learned in the workshops and what kinds of masterpiece were required to become a master. A recent study has shown that less than half of the—numerous—Italian guilds had specific rules on apprenticeship. This was the case in all kinds of crafts, not only of less skilled activities. The fact that guilds' rules and apprenticeship's contracts give little information on what was actually taught to an apprentice has certainly a lot to do with the "mysteries" and the secrets of the crafts, but also with the continuous evolution of standards and requirements that were necessary to deal with competition.[41]

The multidimensional meanings of the word "culture" could be the object of long discussions; in the history of work maybe one of its most widespread uses concerns the ceremonies, processions, and rituals more generally that were the expression of guilds' cultures and marked the time of masters' lives. Processions were indeed the opportunity to demonstrate craftsmanship but also to affirm status. The one that took place in Antwerp for the Feast of Assumption in 1521 was described by Albrecht Dürer, who noted "the sartorial splendour of the various guildsmen – goldsmiths, painters, weavers, masons, joiners, carpenters, butchers, bakers, and so on – as well as the emblems of their trade."[42] Similar examples can be found all over Europe, and were part of a set of rituals that strengthened the identities of urban craftsmen, often excluding craftswomen who, in many cases, were not part of the guilds' organization. Urban rituals were an expression of hierarchies and, in early modern cities, they could reveal deep social conflicts. In 1502, King Louis XII visited Genoa, which at that time was under French control, a dispute about orders of precedence arose between the "popular faction," represented by the artisan guilds, and the "noble faction": it was one of the manifestations of a long-lasting social conflict.[43] Gender hierarchies, too, were a fundamental aspect of work and workplace cultures, and, in early modern cities, the participation of women in public events was not at all self-evident. We can mention the case of Catania where women were not admitted to guilds, but followed the procession of the patron saint.[44] It is worth noting, however, that when they had access to urban rituals, working women considered them as important opportunities to build their group cohesion and professional identity as was declared, in 1584, by the Strasbourg midwives.[45]

European guilds were mostly, even if not exclusively, a male world. Some guilds were mixed and many guilds admitted the widows and sometimes also the daughters of the masters, but in two French cities, Paris and Rouen, there were, from the Middle Ages and until the end of the *ancien régime*, female guilds, and, in Cologne, female silk weavers' guilds existed until the fifteenth century. In the female guilds, like the one of the *lingères en neuf* (linen drapers of new clothes) in Rouen, women followed careers that were, in all respects, the same as those of men in any other guild: they were apprentices, produced a masterpiece, and became mistresses.[46] In many other cases, in the urban textile industry, craftswomen worked more or less in secret, producing manufactured goods that competed with those produced by men's guilds. In Barcelona's silk industry, the question of illegal female labor was for a long time at the heart of conflicts that engulfed the silk weavers' guild and the town government. The problem was that what women produced, independently of the guilds' structure, represented considerable competition for the weavers' workshops. Any potential action taken by the town government was compromised, however, not only by the substantial tax revenue the local authorities received from the women's work, but also by a sense of religious duty to allow the "poor women" the right to earn a living. In 1636, the city council issued a decree that allowed women to produce and sell taffeta and other silk fabrics which, until then, had been the exclusive monopoly of the guilds. The guilds that produced silk velvets and other silk fabrics opposed the ruling for years, accusing the women of manufacturing low-quality fabrics and undercutting the market by selling them at low prices, and asked the town authorities to limit the authorization exclusively to women who had no other means of supporting themselves. Opposing the monopoly of the guilds and implementing a partial liberalization of the labor market in certain strategic sectors were probably the reasons behind the 1636 rule. However, the official reason, and the only one that could be accepted by the members of the guilds, was that the decree was necessary in light of the poverty of the female workers, a stark reality in seventeenth-century Barcelona, where many women were the heads and main breadwinners of low-income households.[47]

MORALITY AND IMMORALITY

The influence of religious reforms on the organization of work, and on the professional opportunities available in different European regions, have been the subject of debate in recent years, especially regarding the imposition of strict moral codes and discipline in the family as well as in the workplace. In the case of Protestant reform, emphasis has been placed on the strengthening of the male role as the head of the family to the detriment of the autonomy of his wife and children. This is often held to be a consequence of the unification in one person of masculine authority figures that in the Catholic religion were previously separate: the religious role of the priest and the lay role of the *paterfamilias*, united in the figure of the Protestant pastor. On the other hand, the case has also been made that the appearance of a new feminine figure, the pastor's wife, with a role recognized by the community, paved the way to the professional emancipation of women.[48]

In some German cities, the rules of some guilds prevented master craftsmen from marrying women whose morality was considered doubtful, as well as from living with wives accused of adultery. A husband unable to control his own wife could not be considered a good master craftsman. Where guilds prohibited men from working with female apprentices and workers, the only women allowed in the workshop were the men's wives, who themselves were not allowed to undertake any work autonomously, other than spinning.[49] This newfound moralistic impetus is confirmed by the case of Calvinist Geneva, where, during the sixteenth century, the town council intervened repeatedly to prohibit men from working with women in weaving, silk-carding, and tailoring workshops. This made it difficult for a widowed craftsman to employ female apprentices, or for a craftsman's widow to take on male workers.[50] Where admission to guilds was limited to the children of master craftsmen or to men who had married either the daughter or the widow of a master, the workers marginalized by these conditions reacted by collectively resisting not only the presence of women in the guilds, but also marriage, which by then had become an essential requisite to joining a guild and becoming a master. Behind these relatively extremist expressions of religious moralism, however, were much more concrete actions. A particular example is the attempt by the authorities to keep women's salaries low and to force independent female workers in the textile industry either to continue living with their families, or to accept a position as a subordinate to a male master craftsman. In response to the repeated measures taken by the authorities in sixteenth-century Augsburg, female spinners retorted that they were not so stupid as to work for a master weaver, when they might have earned three times as much by spinning independently and then reselling their product to the weavers.[51]

The attitude of protection and assistance of poor women workers was commonplace in Catholic as well in Protestant Europe and in many other historical contexts prompted by the fear that the alternative, for them, would be to become prostitutes. The same argument was used by Parisian seamstresses to achieve official recognition of their guild in the last decades of the seventeenth century and, one century later, by the members of the seamstresses' guild to refuse the abolition of theirs.[52] These arguments were of course rhetorical. It is obvious that European cities offered women opportunities for many different legal and illegal activities, independent of guilds, but it is also true that women accused of prostitution often engaged in this illicit activity to supplement their insufficient earnings from a respectable artisan job.[53]

Religious reforms also had an impact on the regulation of prostitution. In the late Middle Ages, prostitution was regulated by public authorities and the only requisites for it were registering at specific municipal offices and paying taxes. It was still the case in early modern Italian cities, such as Florence, Venice and Bologna.[54] In Rome, the capital of the Catholic world, prostitution was widespread, given the high percentage of males in the population and the continuous influx of pilgrims. The popes of the Counter-Reformation sought to contain the phenomenon by ordering the expulsion of prostitutes from the city's center, as well as by establishing a neighborhood, in which prostitution could be practiced openly, based on the model of the Jewish ghettoes that were becoming commonplace in the Papal State. Each of these initiatives was met with opposition from the town authorities and general populations, however, whose protests were based on economic reasons: prostitution was a source of income for the city.[55]

Maritime cities with large ports have always been fertile ground for prostitution. The case of sixteenth-century Seville is particularly significant, as its social and economic fabric was, in very little time, radically altered due to the role that the city took in the transatlantic trade. The appearance of syphilis, in particular the 1568 epidemic, forced the municipal authorities to strengthen their control of the sex trade. Brothels were established in houses owned by the civil authorities or by the cathedral chapter. They were run by public officials, known as *padres*, who in their turn let them to prostitutes. The 1621 municipal ordinance limited the number of *padres* to two and forbade them from letting beds or clothes to the prostitutes, as well as from using the women as currency to settle unpaid debts. Medical visits to check the prostitutes' state of health alternated with visits from preachers attempting to redeem them. Ambiguity and hypocrisy reigned sovereign; the municipal authorities, under the pretext of protecting the women and their clients from syphilis, were in fact profiting from prostitution, a "business" whose success, in a lively maritime city like Seville, was never in doubt.[56]

In Augsburg, before the Protestant Reformation imposed a new, albeit ephemeral, moral order, brothels paid taxes to the local municipal authorities, and prostitutes underwent regular checks by the town midwives, who had to certify that they were of age and in good health. In Nuremberg, prostitution was also controlled by the city council; it is reported to have ruled that prostitutes had to accept all clients and not only those who were young and good-looking. In the rhetoric of urban authorities, there was no contradiction between religious practice and prostitution. On the contrary, brothels helped to increase the honor and piety of the city, insofar as they offered unmarried men an outlet for their sexual urges, ensuring they did not jeopardize the honor of young, unmarried or married, women. Indeed, as apprentices were, by definition, unmarried young men, brothels can be seen as being part of the workshop culture, insofar as they protected the honor of masters' wives and daughters and, therefore, the honor of the master himself (Figure 4.2).

As places of common pastimes, where people ate, drank, and danced, brothels were blatantly based upon a structural disparity between the freedom men found there and the constraints imposed upon the women working there. Subject to very long working hours, women who engaged in prostitution had to compensate the brothel for each working day they missed, supplementing their earnings from prostitution with other activities, such as spinning, undertaken during the day. As a consequence, these women regularly found themselves in a vicious cycle of debt, from which it was impossible to escape. They could then be used as tradable assets between one brothel and another, to the extent that either the city council or the religious authorities had to intervene in order to condemn and forbid this practice. The Protestant Reformation tried to impose a new moral code that included, among other things, the closure of brothels; it also led to the persecution of prostitutes, who found themselves practicing the same profession illegally on the streets.[57]

FIGURE 4.2 Brunswijkse Monogrammist, *Brothel Scene with a Brawl*, oil on panel, 1537. Gemälde Galerie, Berlin.

CONCLUSION

The choice of different and sometimes "extreme" workplaces points out the consequences for workplace cultures of specific historical events, such as state-building, demographic growth, and religious conflicts, that characterized the period between the second half of the fifteenth and the first half of seventeenth centuries. In some cases, these transformations can be considered the beginnings of long-lasting evolutions. It is the case for the processes of bureaucratization and professionalization of early modern administration that gave birth to new social groups, whose culture and economic behaviors nevertheless became increasingly like those of the old nobilities that they were originally supposed to replace. The extreme religious tensions that characterized the German Empire in the sixteenth century had also some effects on the moral codes of workplaces that accompanied a more general evolution of the role of women's work in urban workshops and in guilds across Europe. The long-lasting process of exclusion of women from guilds and skilled activities that is supposed to begin in this period—according to the so-called "decline thesis"— should be replaced in specific historical contexts, however. The further transformation of the labor market or of state organization led in many cases during the seventeenth and eighteenth centuries to the inclusion of women from guilds or even, as was the case in France, to the creation of new female guilds. The evolution of the European household and family is certainly not the topic of this book, but insofar as the household was a workplace, it was also the expression of specific workplace cultures. In England, the role of apprenticeship and service as a widespread strategy of education was to some extent unique in Europe, but apprenticeship and domestic service as work-training and as means of subsistence were common experiences for boys and girls all over Europe. How the transmission of skill worked in apprenticeship is still subject to debate among historians, especially at a time of technical and artistic innovation, such as the Renaissance.

CHAPTER FIVE

Work, Skill, and Technology

KAREL DAVIDS

Work commonly involves the use of skills—that much is clear. What often is less clear is which skills are involved in a particular kind of work and how these skills are learned. For the early modern period, these are especially intriguing questions because direct evidence on these matters is scarce, whereas other information suggests that both the array of skills and the manner of learning at the time were substantially changing. Pictures of artisan workshops from this period, for example, frequently show masters and apprentices working close to each other in the same place but they hardly give an idea of what skills their work exactly entailed and they rarely represent masters manifestly engaged in the act of teaching, or apprentices visibly engrossed in the act of learning.

Yet, we should not jump to the conclusion that skills were only transferred by silent observation, imitation, and repetition. Some pictorial and scriptural evidence seems to point in a different direction. A series of drawings attributed to the Florentine goldsmith and engraver Maso Finiguerra dating from around 1460, for example, depicted apprentices in the act of reading or drawing.[1] Florentine painter Cennino d'Andrea Cennini in the early fifteenth century insisted that one could never learn the art of painting without serving "in a shop under some master to learn how to work at all the branches which pertain to our profession," but he nonetheless put in writing a wealth of information on materials and techniques of the trade in a book, *Il libro* dell'arte.[2] Many artisans in northern Italy and southern Germany at that time likewise began to record their knowledge on architecture, gunnery, fortification, or siege-craft. Dutch paintings from the seventeenth century showed lecturers demonstrating to students by gestures the anatomy of the human body while simultaneously giving oral explanations.[3] A print by Crispijn van Passe dating from about 1650 depicted a hall where a teacher instructed a group of men in the art of navigation with the aid of books, maps, and instruments. Clearly, learning could take place in a variety of ways, which were partly related to progressive changes in the spectrum of skills.

Learning, skills, and knowledge, and the changes therein in the early modern period, today fall squarely within the sphere of interest of the history of technology. In the past few decades, the historiography of technology has changed in fundamental respects. Historians of technology nowadays are interested both in artifacts or materials and in the formal or tacit knowledge and the manual or mental skills that are brought to bear to master or manipulate nature. They have expanded their inquiries to include technology-in-practice in the broadest sense of the word.

Moreover, historians of technology, like historians of science, have increasingly moved away from a "center-periphery" or "top-down" approach to their research object and towards a more balanced, symmetrical view, which is more sensitive to the variety of ways and directions in which knowledge and skills can flow between different places and groups. "Circulation" rather than "diffusion" or "transfer" has become the focus of investigation. The concept of circulation does not presuppose a kind of hierarchy among the places between which flows of knowledge and skills take place, although in historical reality hierarchical relationships sometimes nevertheless may be imposed. Circulation has both spatial and social dimensions and it can occur in many forms and ways and through many different carriers: people, goods, images, sounds, or texts. In the course of circulation, historians argue, knowledge and its carriers themselves can change, too; both can be seen as mutable in nature.

Thirdly, the conventional distinction between "mental" and "manual" work is also being questioned. The relation is now increasingly viewed as being fluid and hybrid rather than clear-cut. The activities of the "mind" and the "hand" in the generation of knowledge and skills were apparently much more intertwined than historians traditionally thought. Finally, the old idea that technological change was more or less absent before the Industrial Revolution no longer holds. Although no one would dispute that transformations in technology in Europe since the late eighteenth century have been more rapid and pervasive than before, research in the past few decades has abundantly demonstrated that technology advanced in many ways during the Middle Ages and the early modern period as well. The discontinuity between the preindustrial and industrial periods has been less radical than previously thought.

Learning, skills, and knowledge, and the changes therein between about 1450 and the middle of the seventeenth century, are the subject of this chapter. The first three sections of this chapter discuss developments of skills and modes of learning among craftsmen and other groups of workers. The final two sections examine how these developments were related to economic transformations and changes in technology and to variations in the broader institutional and political environment. The chapter concludes with a brief epilogue.

APPRENTICESHIP AND TRAMPING

Cennini's statement remained true for the world of urban crafts throughout the early modern period. The ordinary way for men to learn a craft—whether painting, shoemaking, dyeing, bricklaying, cooperage, or baking bread—was by serving an apprenticeship with a master. In the past few decades, historians have examined apprenticeship particularly in the framework of debates on the supposedly beneficial, or harmful, impact of guilds on economic and technological development. Apprenticeship and guilds were after all connected in various ways. Guild statutes often stipulated that only master artisans could train apprentices and many masters during their working life did so.[4] Guilds could also be involved in apprenticeship contracts, which, when a boy became apprenticed to a master, were drawn up to register the rights and duties of the parties concerned. In England, for example, masters in incorporated towns, such as London, Bristol, or Norwich, had to register apprenticeship contracts with their guilds and the urban authorities. Yet recent studies have shown that guilds were by no means everywhere involved in such contractual arrangements. In France, for example, a royal edict requiring apprentices to get a contract drawn up in presence of a notary and signed by guild officers was not issued until 1691.[5] Moreover, although guilds usually tried to keep a check on admissions to mastership, and not without some measure of success, their supervisory role in the training of apprenticeship was quite limited. Guild control of apprenticeship was not very extensive or tight.

What further emerges from recent historical research is the sheer variety in the practice of apprenticeship according to craft, place, time, and gender. The length of apprenticeship differed between crafts and between cities and could increase, or decrease, in the same craft in the course of time. Generally, an apprenticeship lasted anywhere between two and twelve years, with the shortest and longest terms recorded on the continent.[6] For England, the Statute of Artificers of 1563 stated that the term of service for apprentices would be at least seven years, regardless of the craft in which they would be trained. In practice, many apprentices in English towns left their masters before the end of their term. The City of London in the seventeenth century actually facilitated the dissolution of apprenticeship contracts by decisions of the Lord Mayor's court. If an apprentice pleaded with the court to cancel his indenture to a master, there was every chance that his petition would be granted.[7] In German cities, the duration of apprenticeship in some crafts could be reduced by paying an additional fee. Conversely, apprentices who could not afford to do so, usually served a year longer.[8] In seventeenth-century Amsterdam, the length of apprenticeship often exceeded the two to five years prescribed in the by-laws of guilds.[9] Considering this abundance of variations, it is hard to escape the conclusion that there was no direct relationship between the length of apprenticeship and the level of skills required for a particular craft.

Women were less often apprenticed than men, but in a number of crafts, such as spinning, knitting, and sewing, it was not unusual at all. Aside from an in-house training in an orphanage, girls could also be apprenticed to a male, or female, master to learn the tricks of the trades. The Heilige Geest Weeshuis (the Holy Ghost Orphanage) in Leiden, for example, between 1607 and 1623 boarded out nearly 400 girls, most of them to be trained in spinning.[10] A few craft guilds, notably tailors, admitted women to mastership and occasionally women formed their own guilds in textile-related trades. Amsterdam and Paris had guilds of seamstresses for many years. However, the general pattern in this period was that women were progressively excluded from the corporate system.[11]

Training of apprentices seems to have been an intermittent, messy process rather than a continuous, well-organized affair. Instruction normally did not follow a definite, regular program. The quality and content of training varied from master to master, dependent upon their skill and diligence. Guilds offered little or no effective regulation of apprenticeship. Apprenticeship contracts rarely spelled out in detail what an apprentice would learn during his period of training. The contents of instruction were at best described in the most general sort of terms, such as learning the "customs" or "secrets" of a trade, "to become a master" or "to be capable of making a masterpiece." The final test for admission to mastership did not offer any clear guidance either, even though the making of a masterpiece was, in principle, the instrument *par excellence* to assess an apprentice's competence. In many crafts and trades, the requirement to produce a masterpiece was not introduced until long after these occupations had been organized in guilds and apprenticeship had become mandatory. In most cities in the southern Netherlands master trials did not become a widespread practice until the sixteenth century. The urban authorities in Ghent, for example, first obliged craft guilds to give a detailed description of the requirements for masterpieces in 1599.[12] In the northern Netherlands, too, master trials appeared at a rather late date and never became universal. The shoe makers' guild of Arnhem, for example, which was founded in the fifteenth century, did not introduce a proof requirement for the mastership until 1674.[13]

Apprenticeship could be followed by tramping. Tramping, or *Wanderschaft*, meant that journeymen—trained workmen who had completed an apprenticeship but not yet attained the status of master—were required by custom, or by statute, to spend some time travelling between cities outside their home region. In the course of their *Wanderschaft* journeymen could acquire new knowledge and skills. Thus, this form of artisan mobility could contribute to the circulation of knowledge, although this was not necessarily the purpose of the practice. In the Holy Roman Empire, tramping by the end of the sixteenth century was made compulsory wherever crafts were organized into guilds. Tramping also became a regular practice in France and, to a lesser extent, in England. In the southern Netherlands and the Dutch Republic, many journeymen in the seventeenth century regularly travelled from one city to another, too, even though an organized system of *Wanderschaft* as in central Europe never came into existence.

LEARNING BY SCHOOLING

As Finiguerra's picture of a reading apprentice suggests, artisans also acquired skills in other places than a workshop's floor. A craftsman's body of knowledge consisted of not only a proficiency in selecting and handling materials, but also a competency in reading, writing, or counting. Historians, philosophers, and social scientists have made a distinction between "tacit," or not explicated knowledge, and "codified" or "explicit" knowledge, namely knowledge that can be explicated or explained. While the former is mostly learned by doing and trial and error, the latter can be obtained by schooling or by perusing "storage devices" such as images, manuscripts, or printed books.

Education in schools expanded throughout Europe in the early modern period.[14] Classroom schooling could precede, follow, or be combined with a term of apprenticeship. Paul Grendler has shown that in Florence, Genoa, Rome, Lucca, and other Italian cities, many sons (and some daughters) from artisan backgrounds attended a vernacular school. The education of these children, aged between five and twelve, was sometimes paid by their families, sometimes provided for free by communal or church schools, or independent teachers.[15] In France, parishes and religious organizations, such as the Christian Brothers from the middle of the seventeenth century onwards, founded charity schools, which offered free education for poor children before they entered apprenticeship.[16] In the northern Netherlands, provisions for education spread from the sixteenth century onwards, too. The high degree of literacy among artisans in the Dutch Republic suggests that they must have enjoyed a substantial amount of schooling indeed. For the seventeenth century, literacy rates have been found ranging from about 50 percent among bricklayers and textile workers to 70 and 80 percent among coopers and shipwrights, and 80 percent or more among bakers and tailors.[17] Literacy rates among urban artisans (especially males) in other parts of Europe appear to have been rather high as well. Inventories and autobiographies of artisans not seldom show some familiarity with the world of books.[18]

In addition to, or instead of, schooling in an institutional setting for a specific period, tuition could take place on a more private basis as well. Artisan autobiographies sometimes make mention of instruction in reading or writing by family members, neighbors or fellow-workers. Apprenticeship contracts sometimes expressly stipulated that a master should teach an apprentice to read or write.[19] Particular skills could also be acquired through training "by the piece." These individualized forms of training often concerned operations that were outside the domain of guild regulation, such as soap boiling or borax refining, but they could also relate to skills that might be useful for masters in guild-controlled occupations, such as keeping accounts. The son of master-cooper Pieter Fiool in Rotterdam, for example, in the 1670s received instruction in double-entry bookkeeping from a private teacher.[20]

As more and more artisans became skilled in reading, writing, or counting, the circulation of knowledge on trades and crafts in manuscript or print also increased between 1450 and 1650, although still on a modest scale. Two opposite tendencies can be observed in this period. On the one hand, craftsmen were often keen to protect the "mysteries" of their trade. From the High Middle Ages onwards, cities in western Europe experienced, concomitant with the expansion of guilds, the development of a more "proprietary" attitude towards craft knowledge.[21] While evidence of secretive attitudes in antiquity and the early Middle Ages is rare, secrecy in this period came to be viewed as an essential instrument to ensure that artisan knowledge would not spread beyond certain well-defined circles of insiders—or more specifically, people who according to guild regulations had been admitted to mastership in a particular craft. Bernard Palissy, a potter and glassmaker from Agen, France, argued in his *Admirable discourses* of 1580 that disclosure of craft secrets would lead to mass-production and thus eventually cause the downfall of the small, independent producer.[22] Glassmakers from Altare (Montferrat) and Murano (Venice), who spread to many countries in Europe from the late Middle Ages onwards, protected the secrets of their trade, even when privileges granted by princes or cities outside Italy required them to teach their art to local apprentices.[23]

On the other hand, the number of technical writings authored by artisans increased markedly from the early fifteenth century onwards.[24] Dyers, masons, goldsmiths, and silversmiths began to transmit some of their knowledge in the form of recipes, tracts, and manuals, both in manuscript and in print.[25] Tacit knowledge in the world of crafts thus slowly and partly was more explicated and codified. For occupations that largely remained outside the orbit of craft guilds, secretive attitudes were less common, or they were even overtly condemned. In the fifteenth and sixteenth centuries, a growing number of books appeared in the German states and Italy on mining, ore processing, assaying, and gunpowder artillery. The authors of these writings aimed to present a full, detailed overview of the techniques and devices employed in such areas of production. They wished to reveal rather than conceal the mysteries of the trade. In contrast with Palissy, authors such as Vannoccio Biringuccio in *De la pyrotechnica* (1540) and Georgius Agricola in *Bermannus* (1530) and *De re metallica* (1556) loudly proclaimed the value of openness of knowledge against the petty, deceptive practice of secrecy.[26] Moreover, Marco Belfanti has demonstrated that trade "secrets" also circulated more widely due to the movements of skilled artisans between cities. This mobility was stimulated by the enactment of patent laws by princes and urban governments, which offered various benefits to craftsmen and other entrepreneurs who would set up new manufactures or introduce other sorts of innovations.[27] Pioneered in Italy in the fifteenth century, the practice of patenting spread to many areas of Europe in the sixteenth and seventeenth centuries.[28]

In arts and professions in the service sector, such as bookkeeping, surveying, surgery, and medicine, knowledge likewise became accessible to a wider audience thanks to the printing press and to private or public schooling. Vernacular schools in Italy, for example, began to teach the art of double-entry bookkeeping in the late Middle Ages. In cities in south Germany, instruction in this new art of bookkeeping by *Rechenmeister* (counting masters) started in the 1520s and 1930s. By the middle of the sixteenth century, the subject was also taught in the southern Netherlands. Formal schooling in bookkeeping in cities in Holland, including in Leiden and Amsterdam, is in evidence from the 1570s. The basic text on the subject was written by an itinerant teacher in Italy, Luca Pacioli. Pacioli's tract, first printed in Venice in 1494, directly or indirectly influenced many of the manuals on bookkeeping that appeared in Italian and other European languages in the early modern period. Although the diffusion of knowledge about a new technique does not necessarily imply that it is adopted, there is evidence that the practice of bookkeeping in this manner *did* spread in larger firms, trading organizations and government administrations in Italy, the southern Netherlands, the Dutch Republic and England in the early modern period.[29]

Governments, next to private teachers, at some places made an important contribution to the growth of an educational infrastructure for surveying, surgery, and medicine. In the Dutch Republic, public institutes of higher learning such as the universities of Leiden and Franeker from the late sixteenth century offered vernacular courses in surveying. Prospective surveyors could obtain a certificate of competence from provincial authorities after passing a formal exam. Nineteen cities, including five university towns and the city of Amsterdam, established a permanent *theatrum anatomicum* (anatomical theater) where doctors and master surgeons, together with journeymen, apprentices, and other interested persons, could learn about human anatomy by witnessing the public dissection of bodies (Figure 5.1). Public lectureships in anatomy or surgery were created by municipal governments as well.

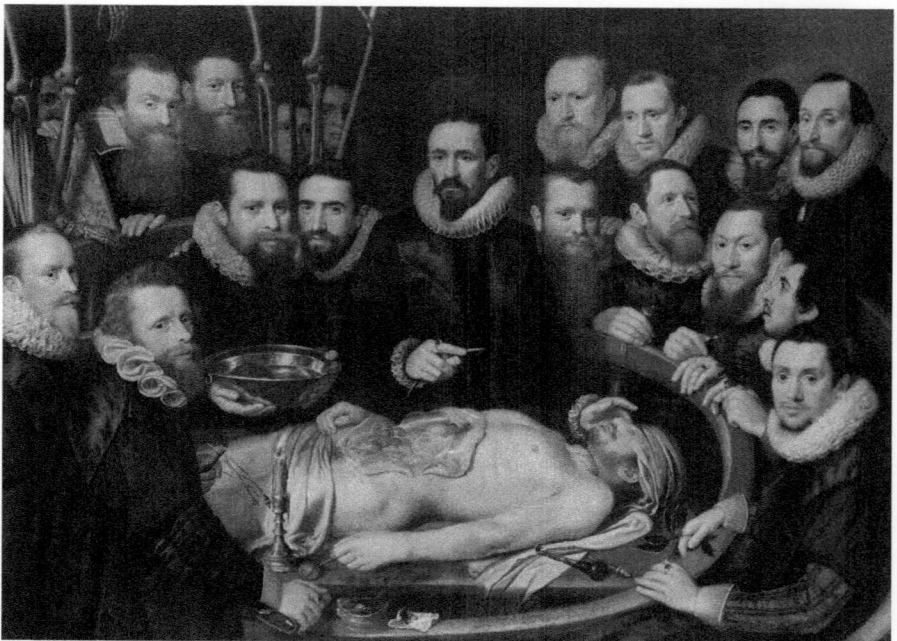

FIGURE 5.1 *The Anatomy Lesson of Doctor Willem van der Meer in Delft*, oil on canvas, 1617. Municipal Hospital, Delft, the Netherlands. Image courtesy of Getty Images.

OUTSIDE THE WORLD OF URBAN CRAFTS

The vast majority of Europeans in the early modern period did not live in cities, however, and most of them were not involved full-time in trades, crafts, or professions or engaged in some branch of industrial production. They earned a living as farmers, shepherds, fishermen, boatmen, drivers, peddlers, miners, or seafarers.

In some parts of rural Europe, where protoindustries arose in the early modern period, people could combine work in agriculture with employment in industrial production. Like urban craftsmen, protoindustrial workers in the countryside sometimes formed their own guilds. This occurred for instance in the worsted and linen industries in rural Württemberg and in the textile industries around Augsburg and Ulm.[30] A few examples of rural guilds outside protoindustry can be found as well. Glassmakers in Altare, northern Italy, which never enjoyed the status of a city, formed a guild before the end of the fifteenth century.[31]

Rural guilds were the exception rather than the rule. Most Europeans living outside towns and cities did not enroll in guilds, did not enter apprenticeship contracts, and did not complete masterpieces. They seldom attended schools or lectures and they rarely sat for exams. They usually acquired knowledge and skills by learning by doing or learning by using rather than by learning by schooling.[32] Know-how appears to have been mostly transmitted through families or small communities, with fathers teaching sons, mothers teaching daughters, the elderly teaching the young, without any formal rules or institutions regulating the process at all. Compared to the world of urban crafts, however, this subject has been much less studied by historians.

A common way to learn skills in husbandry was to find employment as a farm servant in a rural household. Many young people in rural Europe moved from farm to farm to work as servants. For early modern England, it has been estimated that at any time about 60 percent of the population between fifteen and twenty-four years of age were employed as farm servants. Farm servants were usually hired on a one-year contract basis and lived with the farmer's family. While working on a farm, they also had the opportunity to acquire and improve new skills. Female servants aided in dairying, took care of small animals, and helped in the preparation of food. Male servants looked after draught animals and cattle, tended sheep, drove carts, and helped to harrow and plow the fields. All servants assisted in bringing in the harvest.[33]

Modes of learning were not fixed, however, and workers outside the world of urban crafts could get access to literate culture, too. Take seafaring, for example. Dutch engraver, painter, and cartographer Cornelis Anthonisz wrote in his brief manual on navigation in the 1540s:

> In former times, old seamen used to teach young hands how to predict the tides, what Moon phase made the water in these lands and ports rise or fall, what courses had to be steered, how currents changed, how one could probe the depths and the nature of the seabed, what the coastal profiles of this land and other lands looked like and how these lands were situated with respect to each other.

But young people aspiring to become pilots were now discarding this mode of learning, Anthonisz observed. Instruments, charts, and written instructions became more and more important.[34] This change was the very reason why he composed his book. It also helped to effect that in the art of navigation, as in bookkeeping or surveying, circulation of knowledge and skills from the sixteenth century increasingly took place through print and formal schooling. Crispijn de Passe's picture of a classroom about 1650 gives a perfect illustration of this new setting (Figure 5.2).

FIGURE 5.2 Crispijn van de Passe, possibly, *Instructie van zeevaarders*, (II), 1652. Image courtesy of Rijksmuseum, Amsterdam. Public domain.

Portugal and Spain were in the vanguard of this change. State-sponsored institutions for the teaching of nautical knowledge were created in these countries in the early decades of overseas expansion. In Portugal, a *cosmografo-mor* (an official cosmographer) was charged with teaching navigation to mariners from the 1550s onwards. At the Casa de la Contratación (House of Trade) in Seville, which was responsible for organizing Spanish trade with the Indies, a pilot-major was appointed in 1508 to examine and license pilots. A separate professorship in the art of navigation and cosmography was established in 1552. Spanish manuals on navigation became the model for navigational textbooks published in other countries in Europe.[35]

LEARNING, ECONOMIC TRANSFORMATIONS, AND CHANGES IN TECHNOLOGY

The changes in skills and modes of learning discussed in the previous sections were partly related to economic transformations and developments in technology. Urbanization grew, merchant capitalism expanded, new industries arose and spread, long-distance commerce and ocean shipping increased, and technology advanced through a multitude of, mostly incremental, innovations. These larger economic and technological changes did not equally affect all parts of Europe, however. The period between 1450 and 1650 saw increasing variations between regions in more than one respect.

While the European economy remained overwhelmingly rural, the weight of cities slowly grew. The overall percentage of people living in cities grew from about 4 percent in 1400 to more than 8 percent by 1700. In some regions, however, urbanization rates rose more rapidly than in others. England and the northern Netherlands saw the level of urbanization increase from a few percent to 13 and 32 percent, respectively, by the end of the seventeenth century. In Portugal and in the European part of the Ottoman Empire urbanization rates almost tripled to 9.5 and 14 percent. The southern Netherlands, where already about 18 percent of the population lived in cities in the late Middle Ages, witnessed a further rise to slightly over 21 percent by 1700, while Germany and France in the same period saw a steady growth from 4 to 5 percent and from 5 to nearly 9 percent in 1700, respectively. In central and north Italy, by contrast, where urbanization levels once had been as high as in the southern Netherlands, far fewer people lived in cities in 1700 than in the late Middle Ages: only 13 percent.[36]

Urbanization implied that a growing number of people worked in urban crafts, trades, and other services and got involved in urban institutional structures for the transmission of knowledge and skills such as craft guilds and vernacular schools. In some regions, the shift in economic structure was corroborated by increased specialization and occupational differentiation in the countryside. In the countryside of Holland, the extent of nonagricultural activities probably already exceeded agricultural activities before the end of the fifteenth century.

The expansion of merchant capitalism, too, had an impact on skills and modes of learning. For one thing, the spread of capitalist practices and new forms of business organization in long-distance trade in northern Italian and southern German cities brought along new methods of bookkeeping and new legal arrangements, which put different demands on the training of merchants and clerks.[37] Moreover, merchant capitalists in the early modern period also entered into the sphere of production in cities and rural areas, assuming an organizing role in traditional industries as well as in new consumer goods industries and new processing industries. This may have had a negative impact on the array of skills which masters acquired. Masters perhaps no longer commanded the skills to design their products themselves. Artisans who worked as subcontractors in this way may have experienced a certain degree of "deskilling."[38]

Traditional industries were industries such as brewing, linen weaving, and cloth production, which already existed well before the sixteenth century. New consumer goods industries such as silk weaving, glassmaking, ceramics, paper making, and tobacco pipe manufacture comprised the making of specific new consumer goods for domestic or foreign markets with the aid of raw materials, which were expressly ordered for the purpose of production. New processing industries, such as oil-pressing, sawmilling, sugar refining, distilling, and tobacco processing consisted of the "working up" of a specific raw material into a set of standardized commodities that were sold as consumer goods or semi-manufactured products on domestic or foreign markets.[39] New consumer goods industries and new processing industries arose in the wake of the growth of long-distance commerce and the expansion of ocean shipping. They were mostly concentrated in, or near, centers of long-distance trade in northern Italy and the Low Countries such as Venice, Antwerp, and Amsterdam. The sheer range of these new industries in regions in Europe was greater than in any region in China, India, or the Ottoman Empire, of which we have knowledge. Work in new industries often required skills that were not offered by training programs in existing corporate structures. The rural district of the Zaanstreek (Zaan area) near Amsterdam, which in the seventeenth century was in the forefront of the development of several of these industries, had a system of apprenticeship but hardly knew any guilds at all.[40]

Technological change in the period between 1450 and 1650 may look minor in hindsight, compared with the changes that revolutionized industry in the later eighteenth and nineteenth centuries. Yet, the early modern period was in fact an era of significant technological advance. Contemporary observers were impressed by the measure of change. Many literati thought that theirs was truly an age of unparalleled technical achievement. The list of inventions or discoveries composed by papal librarian Giovanni Tortelli in 1449, published in 1471, was the first of many such catalogues appearing up to the eighteenth century. The most famous one is of course the set of three included in Francis Bacon's *Novum Organum* of 1620: gunpowder, the compass, and the printing press. Bacon's French contemporary Nicolas Briot claimed in 1617 that Europeans were different from non-Europeans in that they were "more ingenious and subtle in all things since the greatest part of the arts ... have been either invented or brought to their perfection here."[41]

Historians today no longer identify technological change with great breakthroughs or game-changing "macroinventions." Technological change is conceived to be complex and multifaceted in nature. Macroinventions are supplemented by "microinventions," or in Joel Mokyr's words "small, incremental steps that improve, adapt, and streamline existing techniques already in use." Process innovations are supplemented by product innovations, improvements leading to a growth in physical productivity of labor are supplemented by improvements leading to a rise in qualitative value per item produced.[42]

Much of the technological change taking place in the early modern period was incremental in nature, leaning towards product innovations rather than process innovations, towards improvements in quality rather than improvements in physical productivity. This holds true for developments in agriculture, fishing, mining, and inland transport as well as for those in crafts, trades, and traditional industries and even to a large extent for advances in new consumer goods industries and new processing industries.

In some respects, however, technological change showed a more radical or fundamental character. The early modern period saw a growing shift in energy sources. Nonanimate sources of energy became of increasing importance next to human and animal power. The use of water power in industry and mining was on the rise at many places in western and central Europe, and so was the application of wind power, peat, and coal in industrial production, particularly in the Low Countries and England.[43] Some technological changes were truly groundbreaking. The advance of astronomical navigation and the development of the gun-carrying, highly maneuverable oceangoing sailing ship made possible a huge expansion in European long-distance trade from the fifteenth century onwards, which contributed significantly to the innovations in industrial production and consumption discussed above. And the third great invention singled out by Bacon, the printing press, had far-reaching consequences, too. Even if the precise effects of the spread of printing by movable type since the middle of the fifteenth century continue to be a matter of debate,[44] there is no doubt that this macroinnovation had a profound cultural, social, and economic impact. The nature of skills, the scope and speed of the circulation of knowledge, and the relative weight of different modes of learning were thoroughly changed.

Meanwhile, the center of gravity of technological change between 1450 and 1650 gradually shifted from southern and central Europe to northwestern Europe. While Portugal, Spain, northern Italy, and south Germany were in the forefront of advances in the fifteenth and early sixteenth centuries, leadership in technological development then moved to the southern Netherlands and from there to the Dutch Republic, where it remained until the early eighteenth century. These were the regions in Europe that successively played an initiating role in the development of new technologies in a broad variety of fields, including new industries as well as ocean navigation, printing, and publishing. And these were also the regions that led the way in the rise of new modes of learning.

VARIATIONS IN INSTITUTIONAL AND POLITICAL CONTEXTS

Changes in skills and shifts in modes of learning were also related to variations in institutional and political contexts. A crucial variable was not the presence of a corporate system in a particular city or region per se, but the nature of power relations within guilds and of power relations between guilds and other actors such as urban governments, princes, or state bureaucracies. Guilds were usually better able to influence policies concerning the adoption of innovations in independent city-states, where they often exercised political power, than in larger territorial states, where they carried less weight.[45]

Moreover, guilds were in themselves neither inveterate opponents nor dedicated supporters of technological innovation and changes in ways of learning. Generalizing from a case study of the introduction of the engine loom (a Dutch invention) in the European silk ribbon industry in the seventeenth and eighteenth centuries, Ulrich Pfister has argued that labor-saving and capital-intensive process innovations, such as the engine loom, encountered resistance wherever a craft guild primarily represented the interests of small independent producers, who first and foremost wanted to protect the value of their skills and thus had a preference for labor-intensive, capital-saving product innovations. By contrast, big master-entrepreneurs or merchant-entrepreneurs involved in industrial production, who were more interested in enhancing profits, were as a rule in favor of labor-saving technology and forced through the adoption of new machines whenever they predominated in guilds and/or urban governments.

Although Pfister's thesis does not invariably hold at all times and places (witness the late adoption of the engine loom in seventeenth-century Amsterdam, where merchant-entrepreneurs *did* rule supreme), it does give a fairly adequate account of the sheer variety in relations between technological innovations and power relations in early modern Europe. A few examples from early modern Italy may illustrate the point. The record of the glassmakers' guilds of Altare and Venice shows that innovations sometimes could easily be carried out within guilds. The case of the silk industry in Vicenza attests, by contrast, that innovations also could *precede* the formation of guilds. The history of cloth manufacture in Padua illustrates that innovations could be adopted in a guild dominated by merchant-entrepreneurs in a small city, while the case of ribbon weaving in the territory of Venice demonstrates that innovations could be blocked by a guild dominated by small producers in a large city, supported by a powerful urban government, Finally, the example of the *Arte della Lana* in Florence shows that a princely bureaucracy, too, could be instrumental in hampering innovations.[46]

Changes in learning also could be influenced by administrative practices of guilds or by requirements imposed by urban governments or by state, company, or church bureaucracies. James Amelang has pointed out that the demand for literacy and numeracy among craftsmen increased when guilds became keener on record-keeping or when they more frequently engaged in litigation. In early modern Barcelona, municipal accounting practice in building projects necessitated local masons to become more literate and numerate.[47] State agencies in Portugal and Spain from the early sixteenth century onwards encouraged literacy and numeracy among seafarers by requiring navigators in the trade to the Indies to prove their competence in a formal examination. The Dutch East India Company likewise introduced compulsory exams for masters and mates in the seventeenth century. The Catholic Church after the Council of Trent (1545–63) started a prolonged campaign to raise the educational level of the parish clergy by issuing the directive that every diocese should at least establish one seminary for the training of future clerics. In France, this policy resulted in a first wave of foundations of seminaries between the 1560s and the 1610s and another, much greater one, between 1640 and 1720. All these forces added to the growth of explicit knowledge, next to tacit knowledge, and to the development of learning by schooling next to learning by doing or learning by using.

From the sixteenth century, some European states moreover became aiders and abettors of technological innovation themselves. The government in Tudor and early Stuart England supported all sorts of projects proposed by private entrepreneurs aimed at spreading the cultivation of new crops such as flax, hemp, madder, woad, and rape seed, or at stimulating the growth of new domestic industries, such as glassmaking, stocking knitting, soap making, alum mining, linen weaving, tobacco-pipe making, and knife and tool making.[48] Under the last Valois kings and Henry IV, the French state actively backed the establishment of new industries and the introduction of new technologies. French kings for example promoted the development of textile manufactures, took initiatives to improve the navigability of rivers, and encouraged the application of water power in a variety of industries. The much-vilified king of Spain Philip II beat them all by initiating a comprehensive set of grand projects meant to improve shipbuilding and navigation as well as warfare, mining, and medicine. The fact that the results of these projects often fell short of expectations, as David Goodman points out, tells us more about the limits of Habsburg power than about the ability of Spanish scholars, artisans, and engineers.[49]

CONCLUSION

Skills and modes of learning in Europe thus showed considerable changes in the period between 1450 and 1650, both inside and outside the world of urban crafts. Work, skill, and technology were by the middle of the seventeenth in many respects different from what they consisted of two centuries before. These changes in skills and modes of learning were related to economic transformations and technological developments as well as to political and institutional processes, notably to shifts in power relations within guilds and between guilds, urban governments, princes, and state bureaucracies.

Within the overall changes there were many variations by craft, trade, profession, and industry, by gender, by regions, and by urban or rural environment. The extent, nature, and timing of the changes and variations deserve further historical study, as does the role of individual actors—craftsmen, engineers, writers, entrepreneurs, bureaucrats, and others—in bringing these changes about. However creative these actors may have been, they still operated within a larger context that exceeded the grasp of individuals or small groups of people. As the introduction of this chapter made clear, these questions fit perfectly within the present research agenda of the historiography of technology.

CHAPTER SIX

Work and Mobility

JASON P. COY

In his tragic chronicle of his experiences during the Thirty Years' War, Hans Heberle described being chased from his home by marauding soldiers. Heberle, a cobbler from the village of Neenstetten in southern Germany, recorded the traumatic experience of becoming a refugee amid the chaos of war:

> When the Imperial army occupied the district, the people of Neenstetten fled into the forests. But no one could stay in the forests and woods because of the great hunger, for we had no bread, salt, fat, or anything else with which to nourish ourselves, and I could get none of these things, of which we formerly had plenty, to guard my wife and children from dying of hunger. We sought only peace and quiet. Then, my wife and I, with the little children and a whole crowd of others, were driven from the forest. We thought to take refuge in Württemberg and fled to Heuchlingen, but, dear God, there we got no peace. Two days later we had to leave the place, because the cavalry came in great numbers, plundered everything, and took whatever they could find.[1]

During the war, Heberle and his family were forced to flee their home village, a small hamlet near Ulm, thirty times. Ironically, their last flight came on November 12, 1648, the day before Ulm's town council announced a thanksgiving festival to celebrate the signing of the Peace of Westphalia that ended the war.[2] The experiences of the Heberle family were unfortunately quite typical amid the religious upheavals of the early modern period, as civilians were driven from their homes by the misfortunes of war. However, this was only one form of migration during a period marked by high levels of mobility.

Having debunked the myth of preindustrial Europe as static and sedentary, historians now recognize that migration and labor mobility were prominent features of early modern European society. Recent studies have demonstrated that a substantial proportion of European men and women relocated temporarily or permanently to earn their wages during this era.[3] According to an impressive attempt by Jan and Leo Lucassen to quantify migration in early modern Europe, at least forty-two million Europeans migrated between 1501 and 1650, with an increasing migration rate that likely topped 20 percent of the total population by the years 1601 to 1650.[4] In the German-speaking lands, for example, at least one-third of the population migrated at some point in their lives during this period.[5] These high levels of mobility were prompted by both push and pull factors. Many migrants took to the roads by choice, seeking economic opportunity, to acquire training or education, or to find a spouse. Others fled their homelands in the face of war, famine, disease, or religious persecution.

The dramatic changes that marked the early modern period—the beginnings of European overseas expansion, the development of the transatlantic slave trade, and the start of the Protestant Reformation and the destructive religious wars it spawned—accelerated rates of labor mobility and prompted shifts in attitudes towards itinerate labor. Labor mobility took many forms during the early modern era, as traditional forms of migration intensified in response to widespread economic change and new modes of overseas migration appeared. Men and women migrated seasonally, for a set term, or permanently in search of economic opportunity. Labor mobility was prominent across the entire economic spectrum: rural and urban, agrarian and artisanal, skilled and unskilled. Rural workers migrated to cities, and urban workers moved from town to town in response to economic conditions. Many rural migrants remained in the countryside, moving seasonally or taking jobs as farmhands or servants. The mobile poor, stigmatized as vagrants, also moved along Europe's roads seeking sustenance, their ranks swollen by economic downturns and religious unrest. The growth of European militaries prompted young men to sign on as soldiers and sailors. Others migrated to Europe's overseas colonies, either willingly as colonists or under coercion as convicts or slaves. Physical labor migration was not the only form of mobility that affected workers during the period, however; they also experienced marked socioeconomic mobility in an era of striking change.

While migration was a marked feature of early modern society, labor mobility patterns fluctuated, dependent on large-scale economic and demographic shifts. A period of steady population growth began around 1450, finally allowing Europe to recover from the demographic collapse of the Black Death. The population of the northern Low Countries, for example, nearly doubled during the 1500s and sustained growth occurred throughout most of Europe during the period. It was most pronounced in Europe's great capitals, thriving ports, and major trading cities, where the urban population swelled as waves of migrants from the countryside arrived. Rising population levels caused steep inflation, so that the purchasing power of wages declined, causing impoverishment among vulnerable urban wage earners. By 1630, this dramatic demographic expansion had ground to a halt, as famine, warfare, and epidemic disease led to a general downturn.[6] In many areas of Germany, the population losses associated with the Thirty Years' War largely erased the gains made in the 1500s.[7]

The demographic expansion of the sixteenth century and the contraction that followed in the seventeenth each contributed to labor mobility but did so in divergent ways. Motivated by economic opportunity in good times and seeking relief from poverty and hunger in bad, a steady stream of migrants took to the roads in early modern Europe. Population pressures caused by the expansion of the long sixteenth century fostered labor mobility by prompting landless peasants to find work as servants or farm hands away from their home villages or to seek their fortunes in nearby cities or towns. Likewise, when this expansion ground to a halt—as the Little Ice Age descended upon Europe in the mid-1600s and warfare gripped much of the continent—hungry migrants and refugees looking for work thronged Europe's roads.

RURAL LABOR MOBILITY

In early modern Europe, the bulk of the population lived in rural areas. Peasant landholding was the backbone of the rural economy, and most agricultural output was for local consumption. Even in this localized agrarian society, however, labor mobility was quite common. Most of this labor migration was temporary and rural, as the land-poor sought wages as farm laborers at harvest time or youths hired on as farmhands or servants. The agricultural cycle relied on seasonal labor for the harvest, and young men often left their villages each year to pursue these opportunities before returning home to help tend their own families' holdings. Transhumance also depended on seasonal migration, and tens of thousands of shepherds travelled over long distances with their flocks. A recent estimate suggests that around thirty to forty thousand shepherds migrated seasonally in sixteenth-century Spain alone. Thousands more worked as drovers, driving herds of cattle from east-central and northern Europe to the bustling population centers of central and western Europe.[8]

Seasonal migration for agricultural work not only attracted individuals, but in some areas, it also engaged entire villages. Large teams of itinerant agricultural workers, organized in the hinterlands, travelled at harvest time to the fields outside great cities like London and Paris. At the end of the season, after providing this essential labor, the harvesters usually returned home with the wages they had earned. One prominent example of this sort of labor migration is provided by the large numbers of Westphalians, known as *Hollandsgänger*, who helped provide the seasonal labor necessary to maintain Holland's growing commercial empire in the seventeenth century. By 1700 as many as fifteen thousand of these laborers travelled to Holland each year.[9] A recent estimate of the number of seasonal migrant laborers in Europe in the period 1601 to 1650 suggests that at least 1,175,000 people engaged in this sort of temporary agricultural labor in that half-century alone.[10]

Not all migration in rural areas was seasonal, and some rural inhabitants left home for longer periods. The marriage pattern prevalent in northwestern Europe, marked by relatively late marriage, made for a large pool of rural single people who left their parents' homes to find work as farmhands in neighboring villages. In early modern England, for example, most rural men and women left the parish of their birth. Few of these migrants travelled very far, with most remaining in their home county.[11] Most of these young agricultural laborers came from poor families that did not have enough land for them to work; they were the children of cottagers, day laborers, and sharecroppers. Changing employers every year, these migrants left little trace in tax rolls or account books, but they made up a substantial part of the rural population. In many areas of Europe, they comprised over a third of the rural labor force, providing labor that was essential for keeping the agricultural system going.[12] In many areas this sort of temporary migrant labor was an essential part of the lifecycle, a phase that paved the way towards establishing an independent household. The experience of serving as a migrant farmhand for a number of years gave poor rural youths valuable work experience and allowed them to make connections that often proved valuable when they sought to establish their own households.

Recent work on the European family has shed new light on the age at which young people left their family home to seek work. The best evidence comes from England, where the nuclear family predominated and the labor market for domestic servants was robust. There, most young people left their parents' homes in their mid to late teenage years. In regions where young people left home in their teens, men and women set out of their own at roughly the same age and generally went into domestic service as single people. This pattern held for most of northwestern Europe, but in certain areas, including Spain, Italy, France, and various parts of Germany, it seems that young people stayed under their parents' roof until their twenties. In regions where they delayed their departure into their twenties, however, and especially in eastern Europe, they generally left their parents' home upon marriage in order to establish their own households.[13]

FIGURE 6.1 Pieter Bruegel the Younger, *The Harvester's meal*, 1565. Private Collection. Image courtesy of Getty Images.

Labor was gendered in early modern Europe, and in rural areas it affected the ways in which men and women experienced labor mobility. Where seasonal migration was common, women often stayed behind to manage the village household in the absence of their men. Gender also determined the sort of work young farmhands performed. While men and women made up almost equal proportions of migrant farm workers, the sorts of work they did differed. Women worked as milkmaids, cared for barnyard livestock, and helped prepare meals. Men drove draught animals, herded sheep, and handled plowing. Only at harvest time, when everyone's labor was needed, did men and women work together to bring in the crops (Figure 6.1).[14]

URBAN MIGRATION AND LABOR

The rural and urban labor markets were closely tied in premodern Europe, fostering labor mobility as workers from the countryside sought opportunity in nearby cities and city dwellers ventured into the countryside to help work the harvest.[15] Rapid urbanization was a major feature of early modern European society, and cities provided a steady pull on migrants looking for work. In early modern Europe, cities relied on constant in-migration from the countryside to maintain their populations. Demographics sinks, cities had mortality rates that could not be offset by reproduction, especially given repeated waves of famine and disease. Given these high levels of mortality, caused by poor sanitation and frequent outbreaks of epidemic disease, surviving records probably underestimate the pace of urban migration, since many migrants likely died before appearing on tax rolls or employment records.[16] The pace of urban migration was impressive. The best recent estimate suggests that 1,067,000 people migrated to European cities between 1500 and 1550. Between 1551 and 1600 the figure climbed to 1,662,000 before returning to 1,052,000 in the period 1601–50.[17]

Most migrants to early modern cities came from their immediate hinterlands, areas with the most extensive trading relations between the urban core and rural periphery.[18] In northern Europe, delayed marriage prompted many young men and women to migrate to cities for a time in order to earn the money necessary to marry. Young women from the countryside usually found work as domestic servants, while men often provided casual labor. After a time in the city, many of these rural migrants returned to their home villages to establish a household, only to be replaced by another wave of newcomers from the countryside seeking opportunity. Given the intense labor requirements of early modern workshops, cities relied upon large numbers of these migrant laborers. A single bakery in seventeenth-century London, for example, might call upon the labor of thirteen people.[19]

Not every migrant came from the countryside, however, and levels of migration between urban communities also remained high throughout the period. These interurban migrants often travelled farther than rural migrants to reestablish themselves in another city, with practitioners of more skilled trades and more educated professions usually migrating the longest distances. Clerics, scholars, lawyers, and officials were particularly likely to move frequently in the course of their careers. While relatively few, these educated professionals had a significant impact on the communities they entered, bringing new skills and sparking innovation. Likewise, skilled craftsmen often brought new manufacturing techniques when they migrated or learned new methods abroad and then brought them back home. In fact, it has even been suggested that in the early modern period technological "innovation spread chiefly through the migration of skilled craftsmen who settled in foreign countries."[20] These highly valued migrants often came to cities from other, often distant urban centers, while unskilled laborers arrived from the surrounding countryside.[21]

By the end of our period, around 1650, the spread of rural protoindustrial textile production had changed traditional patterns of labor mobility in many parts of Europe, intensifying the movement of goods and people between city and countryside. Amid the volatile economic changes of the era, workers' prospects waxed and waned, as wages and prices fluctuated, but rural textile production and the artisanal production of goods for local consumption could augment the income of land-poor cultivators. Until factory-produced goods undercut this traditional market for homespun clothing and handcrafted tools and furnishings in the nineteenth century, this income often allowed marginal members of village society to stay on their land.[22] While protoindustrial manufacturing sometimes allowed poor peasants to scrape out a living in their home villages, the merchants who traded in these textiles often travelled great distances in search of customers, their economic activities taking them to far-flung annual fairs or important market towns.

Merchants often travelled throughout Europe and beyond to buy raw materials and sell their wares, a type of labor mobility accelerated by the rise of protocapitalism at the start of our period, which fostered increasing levels of long-distance trade. For example, between 1490 and 1492 Hanseatic merchants sailing out of Danzig shipped 20,000 tons of grain to ports scattered throughout western Europe. Nearby Bremen and Hamburg shipped beer to Frisia, Holland, and Flanders.[23] A few decades later, merchants from Cologne were buying cloth made from English wool in Antwerp and selling it in Frankfurt,

Italy, and in Europe's overseas colonies. The scale of Cologne's trade with Antwerp required the city's merchant firms to keep factors there to represent their interests. These factors, living far from their home city, also travelled extensively in the course of their duties, buying textiles from nearby towns and villages.[24] The scions of merchant dynasties often cut their teeth by living abroad managing their family's activities. Jan van Eyck's famous painting of the so-called "Arnolfini Betrothal" depicts just such a young man, the merchant Giovanni di Nicolao Arnolfini, a wealthy Luccan conducting business in Bruges at the time of the composition in 1434.[25]

Urban craft production also contributed to labor mobility in early modern Europe. Most manufacturing in the period centered on the urban workshop, where a master craftsman and his wife lived and worked alongside apprentices, journeymen, and servants. Most of these craft households served their town or its environs, selling a small range of artisanal products—textiles, furniture, bread, leather goods, metalwork—from the shop window or a market stall. As James Farr reminds us, however, this picture of small-scale, localized craft production, although largely accurate, can obscure the prevalence of long-distance trade and complex economic ties between urban communities in early modern Europe.[26] Certain trades, including construction and shipbuilding, often relied on a completely transient workforce of laborers who travelled to new work sites as soon as they finished a project and a new job became available. While labor mobility was especially pronounced in these trades, all urban manufacturing relied on high levels of migration among its workforce.

The guilds dominated urban manufacturing in preindustrial Europe, and their regulations also helped to spur labor mobility. While the economic contraction of the crisis period precluded many artisans from ever reaching the coveted position of master, in theory the training and socialization that constituted the "mysteries" of the craft began when boys left their families to become apprentices. Some local guild masters purchased apprenticeships for their sons, who went on to practice their trade in their own hometowns, especially as the economic situation worsened in Europe after 1550. Throughout the period, however, most apprentices travelled to learn their trade. In London in 1650, for example, 85 percent of the city's twenty thousand apprentices were migrants.[27] Thus, for most apprentices, mobility was part and parcel of their entry into the trade.

After four to ten years as apprentices, young men working in the guilds graduated to the rank of journeyman. As their name suggests, labor mobility was the norm for journeymen. In theory, they were supposed to travel for several years learning the mysteries of the craft at the elbow of various masters before attaining the coveted rank of master, settling down to get married and opening their own shops.[28] In Germany, guild regulations fostered this sort of temporary mobility by mandating a period of transience, the *Wanderjahr*, for journeymen. By the sixteenth century, hostels for wandering journeymen, known as *Herbergen* or *Trinkstuben*, began appearing throughout Germany. As journeymen arrived in a new town, they could find lodging in these houses, and guild masters could negotiate contracts with trained workers there.

As the European economy began to contract in the mid-sixteenth century many journeymen found themselves excluded from becoming masters as the guilds closed ranks. Precluded from establishing their own workshops, many journeymen were forced to migrate from town to town, earning their living as itinerant skilled laborers on the fringes of the guild system.[29] Some journeymen worked as skilled wage laborers in the shop of a guild master for years. Most journeymen, however, failed to find such stable employment and passed through a succession of short-term positions as they passed from city to city. As a result, over the course of the early modern period, the European workforce gradually segmented into a core of highly skilled craftsmen with relatively stable employment, a few of whom might eventually attain the rank of master, and a large and growing periphery of semiskilled or partially trained workers who stayed on in a given position for a short time before being discharged and moving on to another. In seventeenth-century Chester, for example, 50 percent of the journeymen joiners stayed in the city less than a year.[30]

Although by the seventeenth century many migrant apprentices and journeymen encountered roadblocks and never rose to the rank of master, others were more fortunate. In Vienna during the Thirty Years' War, for instance, 70 percent of the joiners and corset-makers who reached the rank of master were immigrants.[31] It is difficult to ascertain the number of apprentices and journeymen working in Europe's cities, since many of them moved each year and do not appear on tax rolls. However, where we can come up with a picture, it becomes clear that their numbers could be considerable. For instance, in 1600 there were around fifteen thousand apprentices and twelve thousand journeymen working in London.[32]

DOMESTIC SERVICE

Life-cycle service, meaning paid domestic labor performed by unmarried individuals living away from home, was quite common in early modern Europe and helped foster high levels of labor mobility. Much like working as a farmhand, moving away from home to work as a servant was part of becoming an adult in many parts of northern Europe, where delayed marriage and distinctive patterns of economic activity, property devolution and household formation encouraged young men and women to leave home in search of work before settling down to marry. Such life-cycle service was the norm in preindustrial Austria, Denmark, England, Flanders, western Germany, Iceland, and the Netherlands. Scholars estimate that in the seventeenth century servants made up at least 10 percent of the population in most western European countries, with as much as one-half to two-thirds of the population having worked as servants at some point in their lives. The situation was usually quite different in southern and eastern Europe, where few young people worked as servants before marriage. In Russia, for example, servants generally made up a distinct social class and remained in service for their whole lives, even after getting married.[33]

For many in early modern Europe, domestic service was an important part of the transition to adulthood, allowing young people of modest means to save enough money to marry. Given the relatively late marriage ages common in northern Europe, this period of domestic service could sometimes last as long as twenty years. Youths entering service often travelled from their home parish to find employment. These positions usually were not governed by a formal contract, but rather adhered to customary terms. In addition to annual wages, which they often received only when they left their master's employ, servants were provided with food, shelter, and clothing. Servants' labor was essential to running the preindustrial household, and every substantial household in both town and country included not only parents and children, but also as many servants as it could afford.[34]

In guild households, female servants might be employed in low-skilled aspects of the trade to help speed up production, packing up finished goods or cleaning up the workshop. These wage earners, excluded from the ranks of skilled laborers by guild regulations and notions of craftsmen's honor, worked alongside apprentices and journeymen as well as the domestic servants who assisted the master's wife in running the household.[35]

MARGINAL MIGRANTS

Constant mobility marked the lives of the truly itinerant in early modern Europe, the panhandlers, peddlers, and prostitutes who wandered as they sought to survive on the margins of society. The endemic warfare of the period, and the disease and famine they caused, pushed waves of refugees onto the roads and added discharged soldiers to the swelling vagrant population. This floating population of rootless vagabonds made up a substantial part of the population, and urban authorities and territorial rulers continually sought to regulate their movements. With the monumental religious changes of the era, and the parallel disciplinary initiatives of the Protestant and Catholic Reformations, the activities of beggars and prostitutes came under greater scrutiny. Likewise, new attitudes towards labor and community fostered by these religious upheavals brought the itinerate trades under suspicion.

The Protestant Reformation built upon late medieval efforts to curtail begging by the able-bodied poor. Undermining the spiritual benefits of almsgiving and emphasizing the sanctity of work, the Reformation at once reflected and amplified traditional hostilities towards vagrants. Informed by these theological currents, early evangelical church ordinances in Germany outlawed begging by foreign vagrants or able-bodied locals. The city of Wittenberg, for example, issued a poor law in 1521 that outlawed all begging and ordered that the "worthy" poor should be supported from a community chest instead. Throughout Germany, authorities embraced similar policies, restricting poor relief to local paupers and calling for the summary expulsion of foreign vagrants. Viewing the unemployed as shiftless idlers, authorities across Europe sought to distinguish between the "deserving" (aged or infirm local indigents eligible for poor relief) and the "undeserving" (able-bodied and foreign migrants without steady employment). While the former might draw support from the community chest, the latter, labelled "sturdy beggars," faced expulsion. Meanwhile, as rural impoverishment spread after 1550, paupers who could not secure a livelihood in their home parish were often forced to practice "subsistence migration," relegated to the ranks of the hungry beggars on Europe's roads (Figure 6.2).[36]

FIGURE 6.2 Pieter Bruegel the Elder, *The Parable of the Blind*, 1568. H. Armstrong / ClassicStock. Image courtesy of Getty Images.

The emphasis on banishing foreign beggars and unemployed migrants served to increase the number of rootless wanderers on Germany's roads, and local authorities increasingly resorted to violence in dealing with vagrancy. Early modern magistrates linked vagrancy with disease, disorder, and dissolution, and these attitudes shaped migration policies throughout Europe. The vagrancy problem intensified in the troubled decades of the seventeenth century, as impoverished villagers displaced by the era's chronic military conflicts, subsistence crises, and disease outbreaks took to the roads in a desperate search for stability and sustenance. In England, for example, around twenty-five thousand vagrants were arrested in the 1630s alone.[37] In response to the perceived threat posed by the wandering poor, magistrates fostered policies that centered on exclusion and expulsion.[38] By the late sixteenth century, authorities had even begun shipping convicts to far-flung overseas colonies. After 1597, English vagrancy laws called for banishing "rogues" to the colonies, mostly in the New World.[39]

Prostitutes were also part of the mobile population of rootless poor subject to increased regulation in the wake of the Reformation. With the closing of civic brothels in Protestant areas, and the increased regulation of prostitution in Catholic areas after Trent, prostitutes were often forced to wander from town to town in search of a living. In France, for example, prostitutes working in Paris often hailed from Alsace or Lorraine, those in Lyon from Bresse, Bugey, and Forez.[40] Driven to the sex trade out of desperation, prostitutes faced expulsion during round-ups of vagrants and undesirables and were forced to move on to a new locale. Thus, prostitutes, who had enjoyed a stable, if somewhat dishonorable social position within medieval society, suffered increasing prosecution in the wake of the Protestant Reformation.[41]

Not every member of Europe's rootless population resorted to begging or prostitution to make a living. Members of various itinerate trades, known in Germany as *fahrende Leute*, also frequented the roads. Not stigmatized to the same degree as beggars, wandering tinkers, day laborers, students, peddlers, and entertainers still faced considerable suspicion from the settled communities they entered and were forced by official sanctions against ambulatory trade to operate on the fringes of legality.[42] As the religious changes of the period intensified traditional animosities aimed at the wandering poor, and the confessional state redoubled its efforts to provide order, even these itinerant members of society faced intensified regulation.

CONFESSIONAL EXILES

The expulsion of religious outsiders by European rulers began before the Reformation. The most striking example is the expulsion of Jews and Muslims from Spain at the end of the *Reconquista* in 1492. Amid the confessional upheavals of the Reformation and the Wars of Religion, the migration of religious nonconformists intensified throughout Europe. Whether they were pushed out through expulsion or prompted to move to find safety among their coreligionists, thousands of religious refugees left their homelands in the wake of the Reformation. These changes caused Protestants and Catholics alike to migrate. In the wake of the Peace of Augsburg in 1555, for example, the principle of *Cuius regio, eius religio* authorized territorial princes in the Holy Roman Empire to enforce confessional conformity within their realms and permitted nonconformists to relocate. In response, Protestants and Catholics living under a prince who adhered to a rival confession often faced the prospect of rebuilding their lives in another territory.

Calvinists, excluded from the religious compromise reached in the Peace of Augsburg and particularly threatening to Catholic authorities, are the era's most famous religious refugees. English and Scottish Presbyterians fled to the continent when Mary Tudor took the throne in 1553.[43] During the Dutch Revolt against Spain, large numbers of Calvinists fled the Netherlands. Likewise, French Huguenots migrated during the French Wars of Religion. After the St. Bartholomew's Day Massacre in 1572, waves of French Huguenots settled in Germany, the Netherlands, and England. The scale of Huguenot emigration was striking: in the course of the seventeenth century, around one hundred thousand Huguenots left France.[44] Huguenot entrepreneurs and skilled craftsmen were so highly valued for their economic potential that agents from various German principalities recruited potential migrants in areas where the French refugees collected like Frankfurt and Rotterdam.[45] After the start of the Thirty Years' War in 1618, many thousands of Protestants from Bohemia and Austria, many of them Calvinists, were forced to relocate to friendly refuges in Germany. A recent estimate suggests that as many as one hundred thousand refugees left the Habsburg crownlands for central and southern Germany in the 1600s alone.[46]

MILITARY AND COLONIAL LABOR

The competition between Europe's dynastic states and the concomitant growth in military power also prompted increased labor mobility in the early modern period.[47] The increasing size of armies and navies was most apparent during the troubled seventeenth century, as ever more young men answered the call of recruiters or found themselves pressed into service. As the Wars of Religion and colonial conflicts pushed rulers to augment their military forces, recruiters combed Europe for manpower. Sent to garrison fortresses or to serve on ships far from home, recruits were often foreign mercenaries forced into military service by poverty and landlessness. Many did not live to see the end of their terms of enlistment.[48] The rapid growth of armies and fleets had ripple effects that also amplified labor mobility, as sutlers and shipbuilders flowed into garrison towns and port cities to make a living fashioning the sinews of war. Likewise, long trains of camp followers—the wives and children of soldiers, prostitutes, peddlers, and washerwomen—invariably accompanied premodern armies on the move. It has been estimated that during the crisis years in the first half of the seventeenth century a staggering 7.13 million men served as soldiers in Europe, earning pay as military migrants.[49]

Just like the growth of armies and navies, colonization was prompted by early modern state formation and the competition between the various European powers of the era, and it likewise affected mobility levels. Much of this migration took place within Europe, as Prussian, Polish, Habsburg, Russian, and Ottoman officials sent some four million peasants to colonize sparsely populated areas in central and eastern Europe.[50] While these colonization efforts entailed significant movements of European peoples, overseas expansion probably changed labor mobility in more profound ways. With the European discovery of the Americas, and European intrusion into Asia and Africa, millions of European mariners, settlers, soldiers, missionaries, and officials ventured overseas. By 1600, Portugal had established outposts in Africa, India, China, Southeast Asia, and the Americas, and had sent thousands of soldiers, sailors, and officials abroad to man forts and factories.[51] They soon faced stiff competition from a number of European rivals. According to the best recent estimates, just under a million migrants emigrated from Europe between 1500 and 1550. Approximately 1.5 million more emigrated in the period

1550–1600, and around 1.7 million did so between 1600 and 1650.[52] Some of these colonists went involuntarily, particularly those from sparsely populated Portugal, whose magistrates sentenced beggars, orphans, and petty criminals to settle their sprawling empire.[53]

Europeans ultimately remade the so-called "New World" demographically, ecologically, and biologically, a process fostered by the migration of European colonists, massive die-offs among the indigenous populations of the Americas, and the forced relocation of millions of African slaves. On the heels of their unlikely conquest of the mighty Aztec and Inca empires, the Spaniards established a sprawling empire in the Americas, one they peopled through waves of migration. The plains of Mexico and the Andean highlands never developed intensive slave-based cultivation of cash crops; instead, the Spanish imposed the hacienda system to harness the indigenous peoples to the work of building settlements and supporting agriculture. A steady stream of settlers, soldiers, and administrators came from Spain to run these new imperial possessions. Massive gold and silver strikes in New Spain (Mexico), New Grenada (Colombia and Venezuela), and Peru helped draw Spanish settlers to the interior, hoping to carve out land claims or to make their fortune in mining. Spain's massive overseas empire not only drew migrant workers from among its own subjects, but also attracted other Europeans to emigrate. The Nuremberg patrician Hans Tetzel, for example, set up a copper works in Cuba in the 1540s.[54]

In Spain's American colonies, the growth of towns testifies to the pace of overseas migration from Europe. The provincial capital known as Mexico City, erected on the ruins of Aztec Tenochtítlan in 1521, for example, numbered one hundred thousand inhabitants by 1580. The Spanish founded other important colonial cities overseas after Mexico City, including Lima in 1535, Buenos Aires in 1536, Bogota in 1538, and Caracas in 1567. Potosí, in modern-day Bolivia, where great silver mines were discovered in 1545, had grown to 120,000 inhabitants by 1580. By the end of our period, in 1650, it was the largest city in the Spanish-speaking world, with at least half of its population made up of African slaves or their descendants.[55]

The Spaniards and Portuguese could not maintain their exclusive claims to colonial possessions and soon faced competition from other European rivals. Europe's overseas expansion into Africa, Asia, and the Americas, beginning with Portuguese voyages in the fifteenth century and continuing throughout the early modern period, encouraged seafaring explorers and soldiers to leave home in search of riches. The English established the East India Company in 1600, to vie with the Portuguese on the Indian subcontinent, and the Dutch, the French, the Danes, and the Swedes soon followed.[56] The subsequent establishment of European colonies in the Americas and less populous outposts elsewhere, encouraged millions of settlers, men and women alike, to leave their homes in Iberia, the British Isles, the Low Countries, and France in search of a new life.

The Dutch built their own sprawling overseas empire in Asia and the Americas, which also served to intensify long-distance migration. In order to maintain their trading posts in Africa in the face of rampant mortality caused by tropical diseases, the Dutch West India Company actively recruited soldiers, sailors, and factors. In the fifty years after 1624, for example, the Company hired seventeen thousand men to serve in Africa.[57] By the end of the 1640s, the Dutch had emerged victorious from their war with Spain and had established the richest overseas trading empire of any nation. By the middle of the seventeenth century, some ten thousand Dutch ships were sailing the world's oceans. The Dutch East India Company, chartered in 1602, which encroached on Portuguese possessions in Africa and Asia and founded a lucrative colony in today's Indonesia, drove Dutch overseas expansion. The Dutch West India Company, founded in 1621, did the same in the Americas, establishing a colony in Curaçao, a colony based on sugar cultivation using slave labor.[58] To conduct their lucrative African trade and to protect their foothold in West Africa, the Dutch recruited thousands of merchants, sailors, and soldiers each year. With an average of thirty voyages to Africa each year and an average crew size of twenty men, it has been estimated that the Dutch recruited as many as fifteen thousand men between 1599 and 1623 to service the African trade alone. The need for men escalated after 1623, as the war against Spain recommenced, and the Dutch West India Company hired sixty-seven thousand men in the years 1623 to 1636 alone.[59]

The English also proved eager to migrate abroad. At least one hundred thousand people migrated from England alone to the Americas in the decades between 1660 and 1700, mostly young men without means looking to improve their lot overseas. In the earliest English colonies of North America, slaves were also present, but European migrants comprised most the population. In 1606, a joint stock company called the London Company obtained a royal charter granting rights to the Atlantic coast between Quebec and Florida. A year later, the first English settlement was established in Virginia. Within a decade, the English were cultivating tobacco in Virginia, and the labor-intensive native product helped prompt the importation of the first African slaves to the colony. By the 1630s, the English had founded colonies in Massachusetts and Maryland. By this time, they were also competing against their French and Dutch rivals in snatching up Caribbean islands as potential sites for lucrative sugar plantations: Bermuda in 1620, St. Kitts and Nevis in 1623, and Barbados in 1627. Just after the end of our period, in 1655, the English seized Jamaica from Spain.[60]

In 1663, a new English colony called Carolina was chartered. Within a century, rice, cultivated by African slaves, would become a major cash crop in South Carolina. Initially, indentured servants, contract laborers who worked for several years (often under exceedingly harsh conditions) in exchange for transport to the New World and perhaps a plot of land once they had fulfilled their contracts, provided much of the labor that sustained these English colonies in the Americas. Given the insalubrious climate in the Americas, however, it was not the preferred destination for English migrants, and more went to Ireland than to the Chesapeake region in the 1600s.[61] Indentured servitude was intended as a solution to this labor problem, but at its height in the mid-seventeenth century indentured servants only made up about a quarter of migrants to the British colonies in the Americas.[62] As the European appetite for sugar grew, however, the labor needs of the cane fields outstripped the number of indentured servants willing to toil in such deadly conditions, and the English increasingly turned to African slaves in their American colonies.

TRANSATLANTIC SLAVE TRADE AND SLAVE LABOR IN THE AMERICAS

The rise of the transatlantic slave trade represented perhaps the most dramatic change to patterns of labor mobility of the early modern period. It also caused an ominous shift in conceptions of work as forced labor came to be associated with race. By 1650, well over half a million slaves experienced forced migration from Africa to the Americas. The European slave trade had begun in the 1420s, when Portuguese mariners started trading for slaves on the African coast between Senegambia and Angola, exploiting existing slave-trading networks. The first slaves the Portuguese acquired made their way to Lisbon, destined for domestic servitude. By the 1440s, however, slaves were toiling on plantations in the Atlantic Islands, which had been settled by the Iberians. By the end of the fifteenth century, the Portuguese had established sugar plantations on the Azores, Madeira, and Cape Verde, exploiting methods of slave-based cultivation prevalent in Muslim areas of the eastern Mediterranean. The Spaniards quickly followed suit in the Canary Islands.

Soon after Columbus made landfall in Hispaniola, the Iberians introduced slave-based sugar cultivation to the New World, with staggering implications for global migration patterns. As early as 1518, African slaves were working on the Caribbean's first sugar plantations. The Portuguese established a permanent colony in Brazil in 1535. Amid the catastrophic mortality that the region's indigenous populations suffered after conquest, the Portuguese recognized that a new labor force was needed for the intensive and deadly work of sugar cultivation. By the 1550s, settlers in Brazil had established sugar plantations, and the first African slaves were brought to South America. Within decades, tons of sugar were being shipped from Brazil to Europe each year. In 1585, 120 Brazilian sugar mills were producing several thousand metric tons of sugar per year. By 1630, there were over 350 sugar mills in operation, producing around 20,000 metric tons each year.[63]

As European settlements expanded in the New World, areas suitable for slave-based cultivation of cash crops like sugar and tobacco, including Brazil, Cuba, Jamaica, and Virginia imported large shipments of African slaves, quickly becoming "slave societies" with the institution of slavery dominating the local economy. Most of the slaves transported to the Americas came from west-central Africa, mainly from the Fulani, Mandingo, Asante, Yoruba, Hausa, and Ibo peoples. Rarely penetrating the African interior, European powers followed the Portuguese in establishing forts on the coast and exploiting political strife in the region to acquire slaves taken in battle or that local warlords had captured in raids. Almost thirty thousand Africans were brought to Brazil as slaves in the thirty years between 1570 and 1600. By 1650, some 668,500 slaves had been shipped to the Americas, just over 5 percent of the 12.5 million souls eventually transported by 1867 (Figure 6.3).[64]

After 1580, the proportion of African slaves in European colonies in the Americas increased sharply. Between 1500 and 1580, 139,000 Europeans migrated to Spain's New World possessions, along with 45,000 African slaves. In the Portuguese colonies, 93,000 Europeans migrated, compared with just 13,000 Africans. The situation changed dramatically after 1580, however. In the period 1580–1640, 289,000 Africans migrated to the Spanish colonies in the New World, compared with just 188,000 Europeans. In Portugal, it was 181,000 Africans and 110,000 Europeans. In the Dutch New World colonies, it was 8,000 Africans compared with only 2,000 Europeans. In the British colonies, the proportion reversed, with 126,000 Europeans and 4,000 Africans.[65]

The forced migration of African slaves and the establishment of plantation societies in the European colonies in the Americas fostered racist ideas about labor. As Europeans turned to slave labor on their plantations in the New World, they gradually employed racial ideologies that associated servitude with race in order to justify the enslavement of Africans. The legal codification of slavery in the English colonies can be traced back to the Barbados Slave Code of 1661, which served as the basis of later slave codes in Jamaica (1664), South Carolina (1696), and Antigua (1702). These codes declared that African slaves, and children born to enslaved mothers, were chattel property belonging to their masters.[66] By condemning African slaves and their children to lifelong bondage, the codes restricted wage labor to whites and differentiated European indentured servants from African slaves on the basis of race.[67]

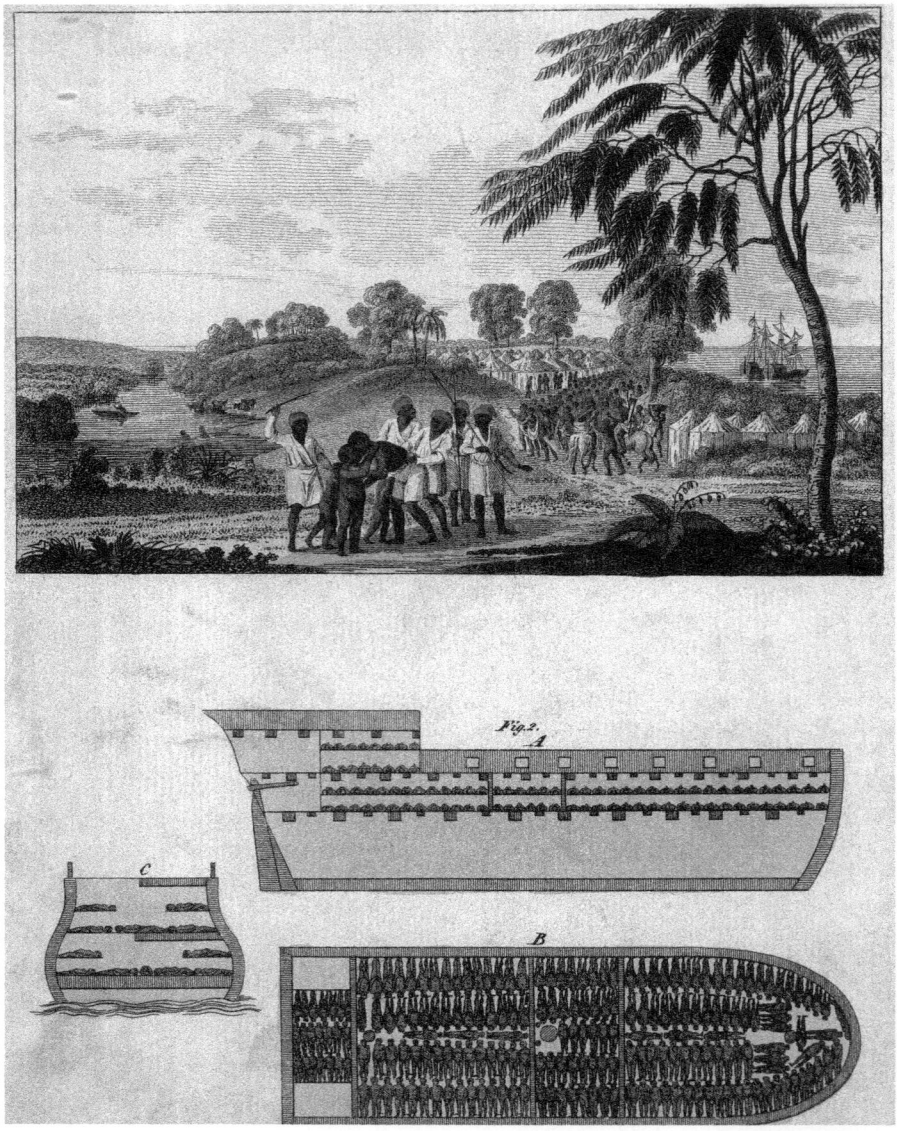

FIGURE 6.3 The slave trade and a slave ship, eighteenth century. DEA / M. Seemuller. Image courtesy of Getty Images.

CONCLUSION

During the early modern period, traditional patterns of labor mobility established in the Middle Ages continued in Europe. Young women and men left their home villages to work as agricultural laborers or domestic servants, to pursue training in a craft guild, or to earn an education. Particular professions, ranging from merchant and artisan to humble peddler, required extensive mobility. The landless poor forced onto the roads during this period sought to survive as soldiers, day laborers, beggars, or prostitutes.

While these traditional migration practices continued, a series of dramatic developments in the period 1450–1650 intensified the movement of European workers. These developments included the military revolution and the growth of European armies and navies, the European reformations and the Wars of Religion they spawned, and European overseas expansion and discovery of the Americas. Together, they introduced new forms of labor mobility that had profound global implications. As European powers competed in building their military and naval capacities, ever-greater numbers of young men were recruited or conscripted and sent to distant garrison towns or ports of call. The religious turmoil of the age also affected mobility, as attempts to enforce confessional conformity and to inculcate new attitudes towards labor created refugees and vagabonds. The establishment of European outposts in Asia and Africa and colonies in the Americas prompted Europeans to emigrate overseas to seek their fortunes, but also sowed the seeds for the transatlantic slave trade.

Migration to the New World fostered the most dramatic changes in European labor mobility, as millions of migrants—voluntary and forced—made their way to the Americas. The Americas not only attracted colonial administrators, settlers, and merchants from Europe during the early modern period, but also condemned hundreds of thousands of African slaves to forced labor in the cane fields and tobacco farms. By the time the slave trade, which began at the start of our period, had come to an end the number of Africans shipped to the Americas numbered in the millions.

The European migrants who left their homes and took to the roads in search of economic opportunity during the early modern period faced the prospect of a different type of mobility than the geographic relocation we have discussed. Migrants also experienced socioeconomic mobility. In recent years, scholars interested in migration have focused on the cultural factors that prompted and sustained migration: individual agency and communal values, kinship and friendship networks, demographic conditions, and marital customs.[68] Historians increasingly view wealth and poverty in dynamic terms, recognizing that the economic fortunes of individuals rise and fall in the course of a lifetime. Many individuals improved their lot in life by migrating to nearby towns, performing temporary agricultural or domestic labor, or going abroad to the colonies, but others saw their fortunes sink. Poverty was widespread in early modern Europe, and it threatened not only laborers and cottagers, but also artisans and middling peasants. Anyone could experience impoverishment brought on by misfortune, illness, or old age. If they could not rely upon the charity of family or neighbors, they could even become destitute.

Of the many hopeful migrants who entered European cities, hoping to better their lot only a few arrived with the necessary money and connections to purchase citizenship and enter a guild or pursue trade. The rest, relegated to poorly paid wage labor, risked suffering downward mobility. According to Christian Pfister, only half to two-thirds of the modest migrants who lacked the means to enter the closed ranks of the established merchants and craftsmen were able to carve out a livelihood that allowed them to maintain the social position of their parents. The rest had to endure a slow—or even sudden—slide into poverty.[69]

The same was true of rural migrants, who also experienced significant socioeconomic mobility during a lifetime of hard work on the farm. Even villagers who never came to own their own farm, and spent their entire lives as hired hands, might still expect to climb the rural social ladder. In East Holstein, for example, hardworking farm laborers could rise through a series of promotions to climb finally to the rank of head farmworker (*Vollknecht*), enhancing their income and social standing.[70] In old age, however, or after serious illness or injury, rural migrants could lose it all if they lacked the support of neighbors or kinfolk.

Peter Welser, a member of one Augsburg's wealthiest banking families, provides a dramatic example of the rise and fall of economic fortunes in this volatile age. Welser migrated to Zwickau, where his economic activities propelled him to the top of the heap in his adoptive home. His descendants did not share his good fortune, however, and ultimately his great-grandson ended up earning his living as a lowly gravedigger.[71]

As increasing levels of mobility changed the nature of work in early modern Europe, the Welsers were not alone in leaving their homeland in search of opportunity or in experiencing economic pressures. Millions of European migrants ventured from their homes to earn a living in this troubled period, finding employment in neighboring villages, nearby cities, or overseas in Europe's sprawling colonial possessions. Hundreds of thousands of Africans experienced forced migration, put to work as slaves on plantations in the Americas and the Caribbean. The dramatic changes of the early modern period, including the origins of European overseas expansion and colonization, the beginnings of the transatlantic slave trade, and the upheavals of the Protestant Reformation, not only spurred increasing levels of migration but also reshaped traditional attitudes about work. European colonists adopted many of the foodstuffs and agricultural techniques of the indigenous peoples they encountered abroad, profiting off new commodities like tobacco, coffee, and sugar, stimulants that in turn changed European society and sociability. Meanwhile, the transatlantic slave trade fostered new racist work regimes that reserved wage labor for Europeans and relegated enslaved Africans and indigenous peoples to unpaid work. Finally, the religious changes prompted by the Protestant Reformation changed attitudes towards work by intensifying traditional animosities towards mendicancy, prostitution, and the itinerant trades. Many of these shifts in labor mobility patterns and the concomitant changes in notions of work they prompted still echo in contemporary society.

CHAPTER SEVEN

Work and Society

CATHARINA LIS AND HUGO SOLY

Few periods in history have elicited so much debate as the transition from the European Middle Ages to what is described in this volume as the early modern age. Unanimity is lacking as to the chronological and geographical boundaries, as well as with regard to the long-term consequences of all kinds of phenomena and processes. The definition, scope, and impact of the Renaissance, humanism, the Reformation, Counter-Reformation, secularization, commercial capitalism, rationalization, individualization, state formation, and modern science—to name but a few concepts held to be relevant for this period— are disputed to this day. Because sociocultural perceptions of work relate in some way to all these concepts, they are all the more problematic. This does not necessarily mean that changing socioeconomic, political, and cultural-ideological contexts coincided with fundamental changes in attitudes towards work. The central question in this chapter is: In what respects were perceptions of work continuous or discontinuous?

From classical antiquity onwards, the prevailing principle was that everybody was expected to help sustain the social edifice, implying an allocation of tasks that might be conceived of in very different ways but in every case implying that activity and effort were regarded as being diametrically opposed to idleness. Throughout the preindustrial period this view was an unchangeable substrate, a generally accepted social consensus that permeated all discourses about work. In this respect, Christianity brought nothing new. For centuries texts and images had proclaimed the message that everybody had to work, that is, to make efforts.[1] Another aspect of continuity related to two questions about work that were pivotal in the self-images of social groups and their relations with other groups.

First, a constantly recurring question was which activities could be regarded as forms of work, that is, as efforts that benefited society. The point was that idleness at a collective level might carry over to parasitism, referring both to groups at the bottom and to those at the top of the social hierarchy. All groups therefore proclaimed that the efforts they made benefited not only their own members but served the public interest as well. This explains why religious, intellectual, and military activities were often presented as forms of work. After all, the definition of work is a sociocultural construct: an activity qualifies as work only once it has been acknowledged as such *by others*, and its prerequisite is always the provision of goods or services that meet needs recognized by these others. Reflections to this effect are certainly identifiable in the Middle Ages, but in the period 1450–1650 definitions of work became hot issues, expressed in a broad range of different and contradictory discourses.

The second important question concerned the valorization criteria used by different groups. These were subjects of debate in every period. Which criteria could or should be applied, and was one more important than the others? How were efforts to be evaluated? Were they valuable, and why or why not? Did those who made these efforts merit appreciation? This problem was crucial, as appreciation of a certain activity was not automatically extended to those performing it. Consensus was rarely or never achieved on these issues, owing not only to the presence of different power centers and interest spheres but also to the fact that changing status positions might lead valorization criteria to shift as well.

The continuity/discontinuity problem should therefore be considered from two perspectives. On the one hand, the question is whether definitions of work underwent changes. On the other hand, we need to examine which activities and efforts and which capacities and skills were more, or less, appreciated. Definitions and valorization criteria are always situated in specific contexts structured largely by balances of power. During the long sixteenth century changes in the urbanized areas west of the Elbe River deeply influenced relations among the different population groups, as became clear in debates and polemics about work. New images and self-images of occupational groups were constructed, applying valorization criteria that upgraded the status of particular forms of work and threatened to impact that of others. Different discourses about work and workers continued to coexist in European society, but by 1650 the areas of emphasis had shifted, and in some respects new views were being expressed.

"EVERYONE, FROM THE HIGHEST TO THE LOWEST DEGREE, HAS TO WORK"[2]

Keeping in mind the admonitions of Saint Paul, members of the clergy had to consider whether they were performing their Christian duty to work, in other words: whether their activities were forms of work or would at least be recognized as such by others. The tripartite scheme, which had rapidly proliferated after 1000, placed *oratores* (the representatives of the Church of Rome) very high in the social hierarchy but did not exempt them from the duty to work. Would preaching satisfy the Pauline imperative? Were monks supposed to perform manual labor, as Saint Benedict and other monastic reformers had argued? Or could they regard prayer as a type of work? These questions continued to be asked and restated, gave rise to fierce controversies, and necessitated repeated repositioning. At the end of the Middle Ages, clerics who preached could in any case present themselves as religious service providers. Late-fifteenth- and sixteenth-century city accounts reveal that internal rivalry was widespread; no effort was spared to obtain the largest remuneration possible. French sources qualify the sermons by Franciscans and Dominicans as *travail* (work) or *labeur* (labor), for which they received a *salaire* (wage).[3] The mendicants risked being labelled as parasites, however, because many members of the secular clergy, especially in the cities, regarded them as competitors in their capacity as preachers and confessors. In addition to questions of influence and status, the hard struggle for income in a time of changing economic conditions was a factor.

Perceptions of work remained deeply influenced by Christian ideas in early modern Europe. Since both the Old and the New Testament lent itself to various interpretations, the duty to work might be defined in different ways, although two imperatives were beyond dispute: lay people had to perform their duty to work in the order decreed by God, and they always had to consider that their efforts should be dedicated to a higher spiritual cause. Martin Luther elaborated on this tradition. John Calvin also stressed that working in a calling meant participating in the work of God. Every activity therefore had to serve the true objective of human existence, that is, eternal life. But the Protestant reformers did not accept the status quo. They revived causes that had received little consideration within the Church of Rome during the Middle Ages, especially appreciation for work done by lay people. They emphasized that all occupations were equivalent in God's eyes, and that pursuit of spiritual enrichment was not restricted to purely religious actions but also related to applying oneself in daily life. In this sense, work in Protestant countries could be seen as sufficient for Christian life, as an objective in its own right. The clergy in Roman Catholic areas continuously objected to this view.

The aristocracy during this period was challenged to reassess its position. According to the tripartite model, noble warriors wielded the sword to protect the population and to ensure the rule of law and order. Writings intended for the elite stated explicitly that all members of the aristocracy had to meet these obligations. In *The Game and Playe of the Cheese*, published by William Caxton in Bruges in 1474 and again in Westminster in 1483, it was stated that the people were to provide for the subsistence of the knights, but also that these knights "shold laboure that [the Laws] shold be wel kepte."[4] In the course of the sixteenth century, the process of state formation, changes in warfare, and the growing importance of humanists reduced the emphasis on the military feats of noblemen; they were now being depicted rather as "laborers in the vocation of government." The popularity of works by Cicero, especially *De officiis*, among scholars and politicians alike enabled noblemen to present public office as a worthy effort, as a manifestation of a strong work ethic. Rulers advanced ever greater numbers of "new men" to the aristocracy for their political service, rather than for their military heroics. In all kinds of texts noblemen started to be depicted as "laboring public servants." At the same time, the elites emphasized more than ever that everything they did entailed strenuous efforts, even though they did not perform manual labor. In the "Homily against Idleness" published in 1562, the Church of England argued that "when it is said, all men should labour, it is not so straitly meant, that all men should use handy labour." When Paul's *Epistles to the Thessalonians* were explained in 1583, the message was that the mental work by secular elites was far more taxing than the physical effort of the ordinary man: "The toil which princes take, and the great cares wherewith they are occupied, pass all other cares in the world."[5]

Attempts to refute accusations of idleness and hedonism by manifesting as a hard-working elite, thanks to good governance and public services, did not prevent noblemen from being taken to task by members of the social middle strata, especially by humanists. Like mendicants, noblemen were depicted as loafers and even as parasites in satirical texts by many commentators in the sixteenth-century Netherlands and elsewhere in northwest and central Europe. Erasmus argued that while the lifestyles of the two groups differed, both were paragons of uselessness. He lashed out against the laziness of friars and monks, and in his *In Praise of Folly* he targeted the numerous noblemen who indulged in excesses and did nothing useful at all.[6]

Merchants were a category apart, at least as far as those who traded internationally, preferably overseas, were concerned. Since classical antiquity, broad groups of the population regarded retailers of any sort unfavorably and continued to do so throughout the long sixteenth century. Attitudes towards great merchants were far more complex. For centuries, they had often faced allegations that their activities had little or nothing to do with work and had been accused of exercising an occupation of questionable moral standards. The first reproach had all but disappeared by the late Middle Ages. The church and the business world had achieved a *modus vivendi*. Most ecclesiastical authors believed businessmen made efforts and were therefore entitled to "wages," just as farm workers or artisans were. In some descriptions of urban society, merchants were even given a separate and in some cases honorable role, in a context of reciprocity and interdependence with other estates. As for the second reproach, from the late Middle Ages onwards, engagement in business was generally regarded as not intrinsically sinful. What mattered were the intentions and actions of the individual merchant. As a group, however, merchants were often accused of lacking moral qualities. This explains why they continuously emphasized that they made serious and worthy efforts. Manuals circulating for the benefit of merchants consistently stressed that their occupation was very demanding. In his *Book on the Art of Trade*, written in 1458 but published only in 1573, the Italian Benedetto Cotrugli vividly portrayed how the life of a great merchant involved toiling day and night, undertaking physically dangerous journeys and suffering hunger and thirst; only the physically fit could tolerate

FIGURE 7.1 Hans Holbein, *Portrait of the Merchant Georg Gisze* (1532), oil on panel, Gemäldegalerie, Berlin.

this way of life.⁷ The self-images shared by merchants in the early modern age mention hard work as the primordial condition for commercial success. According to Lowys Porquin, a moneylender in Middelburg, Zeeland, who took such pride in his success that he had an internationally renowned Antwerp printer publish his autobiography in 1563, diligence was the main attribute of all those who were economically active. His radical message was that the disgrace of parasitism was a fate worse than death.⁸ This view was shared by Roman Catholic and Protestant merchants alike. They all regarded hard work as a *sine qua non* for making a fortune, as well as a way of legitimizing their wealth.

Businessmen related their success to specific competencies as well, not only knowledge of bookkeeping but also more generally expertise in material affairs, organizational skills, experience with evaluating and assessing situations, striking a balance between trust and circumspection, and endurance. In other words, they valorized their work by applying criteria that they related largely if not exclusively to themselves. The idea that they had been called by God, and that He had entrusted these talents to them further enhanced the favorable self-image that was gaining currency in commercial circles, regardless of religious conviction (Figure 7.1). Overt manifestations of self-glorification appeared mainly in cities where economic dominance coincided with political control. In Amsterdam around 1650, great merchants and their next of kin saw cause to have themselves portrayed as biblical figures, classical gods and heroes, or even as monarchs.

Two groups of businessmen remained frequent targets of criticism in the early modern age: financiers/bankers and "monopolists." Money changers risked being perceived as usurers, who were unproductive, did not trade commodities, and, above all, sold something that belonged to God, namely time. Usurers were held to be worse than thieves, who at least "worked," whereas usurers made their money without any effort whatsoever. Harlots were less despicable, because although they offered their bodies for scandalous services, "they undergo bodily labor" and were consequently entitled to keep what they received for their work. Acceptance of practices liable to be labelled as usury, therefore, needed first of all to be acknowledged as forms of work. That is precisely what Franciscan philosophers did in the late Middle Ages and what their followers continued to argue in the early modern age. This did not mean that usury was no longer a problem. It remained controversial, as discerning spirits continued to object to owners of capital receiving interest without working for it.

"Monopolist" was the most frequent and most serious criticism directed at great merchants in the sixteenth century. Like usury, monopoly was a fluid term, which had many connotations but was used mainly to deplore practices "directed at gaining maximum control over the market."⁹ In central Europe large trading firms tightened their grip on the mining and metal industries, while merchant-entrepreneurs in northwest Europe tried to gain control of the most profitable areas of textile manufacturing and trade. The two main sources of opposition to the "monopolists" were the lower aristocracy and the urban middle strata. Viewing commercial capitalists as dangerous rivals, moderately affluent merchants and substantial master artisans criticized big business out of enlightened self-interest, but substantial ideological and sociopolitical criticisms were offered by both Protestant reformers and humanists and *belle-letttrists* of different religious persuasions in the Low Countries and southern Germany. Humanists figured prominently in debates about monopolies, in an isolated instance defending the large trading firms,¹⁰ in most cases harshly condemning those they stigmatized as nonworking cheaters, swindlers, or robbers.

Humanists developed new discourses about work, highlighting their own position as intellectuals. They based their reflections on the conviction that lay existence was as worthy and as honorable as the contemplative life. Moreover, only in lay circles was it possible to perform work that was both meaningful *and useful*, and to radically reject idleness, the great evil that they condemned in many writings. While in Christian discourses *desidia* (sloth) was represented as the progenitor of myriad sins, humanists expressed similar associations with respect to *otium* (leisure). Like Cicero, Seneca, and Livy, they related *otium* to physical and moral degeneracy. Nobody was allowed to indulge in hedonism. Resting after work was acceptable only with a view to relaxation of the mind and restoration of the spirit. Such cases concerned *otium honestum*, dignified leisure. Influenced by these humanist views, Federigo II Gonzaga, duke of Mantua, saw cause to place a Latin inscription indicating that he had his summer residence the Palazzo del Te (completed in 1534) built "for honest leisure [*honesto ocio*] after work to restore strength in quiet."[11] All other forms of *otium* were equated with nonwork and led to a sense of guilt or at least embarrassment.

The urge of humanists to manifest their views and their disdain for the "parasitism" of members of the clergy and noblemen resounded in a great many texts focusing on the work ethic. Their ideal entailed choosing the right course, that of living an active and virtuous life, never sidestepping difficulties. The image of *Hercules at the Crossroads* was understandably very popular among intellectuals and in artistic circles. Key words were *diligentia* (diligence), *industria* (industriousness), *labour* (work), *experientia* (experience), and *usus* (drive). They applied these qualities to themselves as authors, implying that *otium honestum* should ideally be dedicated to literary and philosophical pursuits, both means towards and evidence of self-improvement. In northern Italy and in northwest and central Europe, the views of the humanists on work ethic and honest leisure deeply impacted on the self-images that elites and broad segments of the social middle strata aimed to convey, regardless of their religious affiliation. Artists depicted work and diligence as general principles in society, especially in urban society, as fundamental means for acquiring affluence and self-respect and for achieving distinction.[12]

Glorification of the *vita activa*, of effort as a way of life, coincided with a general revulsion for everything that referred to inactivity and immobility in other settings. The idea gained ground that the world could not be idle but had to embody an active principle. The famous French potter and garden designer Bernard Palissy maintained that the stars and planets could not be *oisifs* (idle). Francis Bacon, who regarded himself as a paragon of hard work, was filled with disdain for representatives of the occult arts, reproaching them for believing they could achieve great things without making any serious effort.

In a context where both religious thinkers and humanists emphasized the moral and disciplining force of work, and diverse social groups presented themselves as exponents of an active society, directly or indirectly coercing wage dependents to work and punishing those unwilling to do so were deemed necessary policies. Such views and measures were not intrinsically new. The fourteenth-century crisis had paved the way for labor legislations that over the course of subsequent centuries became inextricably linked with both the prohibition of begging and prosecution of vagrancy, as well as highly restrictive poor relief. Between 1522 and 1545 a coordinated social policy was introduced in some sixty cities: in twenty to thirty in Germany, in fourteen in the Low Countries, in eight in France, in six in Switzerland, and in two in northern Italy. Everywhere, the system was based on three principles: begging was strictly prohibited, all able-bodied men and women without means of subsistence were required to work, and the existing relief funds were pooled in a "common box." In the Netherlands, France, England, Scotland, and Spain, the central governments proclaimed ordinances that aligned with these principles and were applicable throughout the realm. Curtailing geographical mobility, keeping wages low, and incarcerating "beggars" and "vagrants" in bridewells or workhouses— such policies were aimed at controlling persons labelled as "masterless men."[13]

In several countries, Roman Catholic and Protestant alike, the legislative objectives during the early modern age extended beyond forcing the able-bodied unemployed to accept any type of work. In humanist circles, where the idea of an active society was widely supported, even the deserving poor became targets. In *De subventione pauperum* (On Relief of the Poor), published in Bruges in 1526 and subsequently translated into Dutch, French, and English, the Spanish humanist Juan Luis Vives argued that the authorities should not allow the disabled, the elderly, and the blind "to sit around or wander about idly," going on to explain in detail how these groups could be made to do useful work. After all, he concluded, they lack not the capacity to work but the will to do it.[14]

The idea of universal activity flourished within a political economy that systematically reflected on the "useless bodies," that is, all those who did not conform to the ideal of the productive worker. The principle was that the power of the state depended on the maximum use of available labor. The preclassical political economists labelled as mercantilists often differed in their opinions but agreed that wealth was primarily the fruit of human labor and the exploitation of natural resources. In 1615, Antoine de Montchrestien made overwhelmingly clear that economics was in fact the science that studied the activities of the Third Estate. "Three kinds of men" constituted *le peuple*, the people: farmers, merchants and *gens du métier*, and artisans. The wealth of a country was entirely the result of interactions between these three groups, "destined to perfectly elaborate the soil of profit, which in any case is born as if from two live sources that never run dry—spirit and hand—working separately or together on natural subjects."[15] Montchrestien was especially interested in those whom he described as the itinerant able-bodied unemployed, without any occupation or fixed abode. In his view their circumstances were the result of choices they had made reflecting a deviation from human nature, as, he explained, "mankind is born to be permanently active." These individuals were to be tamed to bring them from the state of wild animals to that of domestic animals for the benefit of collective well-being. Idleness was a dangerous, contagious disease. Work was the only cure for a sick body: "Several places and parts of the body are like avenues, through which vice may penetrate and nestle in the soul. Nearly all may be closed off, however, by remaining continuously active."[16]

Both the conviction that inactivity and stagnation would seriously harm individuals and society alike and economic considerations gave rise to initiatives to put the children of paupers to work. In the first half of the sixteenth century, humanists and religious reformers had urged that such children learn a trade as early as possible, but they had envisaged mainly moral (re)education. While mercantilists also discussed educational objectives in their writings, these authors focused mainly on the economic importance of child labor. Poverty among jobless adults who were hale and hardy was consistently attributed to laziness or unwillingness that underlay their "deviance" as well. Unemployment, poverty, and a criminal disposition went hand in hand, according to most commentators. All kinds of megalomaniac employment projects were attributable to this context, especially in the manufacturing sector, which was considered to be the most productive and the most profitable. By the mid-seventeenth century, it had become appropriate "to look no more upon the poor as a burden but as the richest treasure of a nation, if orderly and well-employed," as Peter Chamberlen noted in *The Poor Man's Advocate* (1649). "Well-employed" implied, for example, that work by the poor would be acknowledged as such, only when their social superiors regarded this employment as economically useful and productive. Other employments were labelled as forms of idleness, even when they figured within survival strategies.

SHIFTS IN VALORIZATION

The economic, political, and religiously inspired discourses and measures addressing all those suspected of not making worthy efforts inspired self-reflection among various groups. They felt pressured by authorities and "right-thinking" citizens and spared no effort to demonstrate that they worked hard and, moreover, did useful work. The theater was a frequent target of criticism, as in all churches there were critics who reproached actors for not working and even accused them of preventing others from doing so. The pursuit of acting was therefore depicted as a worthy effort in several plays. Playwrights, poets, satirists, and other, nonaristocratic authors felt compelled not only to define their writings as "material work" but also to emphasize that their efforts related to a vocation and should therefore be regarded as a type of virtue. Thanks to printing technology, some could address a fairly broad audience. Authorial labor was the core of self-representation, with writing being perceived as an exclusive "mystery," a special gift, an art, reserved for those with "learning." Fencing masters also aimed to relate their activity to hard work, professionalism, and social utility. Professionalism was to be manifested by the capacity to formalize and disclose to the public personal knowledge, preferably through manuals featuring text and images demonstrating that this was an art. Throughout the sixteenth century, fencing masters in France, Italy, Germany, and England endeavored to establish their professional activity as an art, more specifically, as a "fine mathematical science," capable of reducing the chaos of fighting to an interplay of perfectly calculated gestures. They hoped this would upgrade their profession and raise their social standing. Dancing teachers aimed to do the same.

These examples indicate changes in how efforts were valorized in early modern Europe. During the Middle Ages, there had been many opinions, a "polyphony," about this. Aside from the central criterion of serving God, however, the concept of honor had been decisive. The *bellatores* defined their position in society by referring to a specific code of honor intended to distinguish them from the rest of society, and noblemen continued to do so during the early modern period. Consequently, engaging in non-agrarian activities, especially in the retail trade, came to be regarded as incompatible with their status. In France and some other countries, rulers started to proclaim *dérogeance* legislation after 1550, prohibiting noblemen from trading, although overseas trade was generally tolerated in practice. Such legislation often arose at the initiative of members of the Third Estate, who perceived the merchant noblemen as competitors.

Members of guild-based organizations regarded honor as a central concept that determined who belonged to a structured community and who did not (Figure 7.2).[17]

FIGURE 7.2 Michiel Claesz, *The Predella of the Altarpiece of the Carpenter's Guild for the Church of St. Jan in Gouda*, oil on panel, c. 1560–5. Museum Gouda, Gouda. © Museum Gouda.

Master artisans sought to distinguish themselves from those they held to be "inferior," including all craftsmen who did not organize in guilds and for precisely that reason were not entitled to claim "privileged status." In several cities in central Europe, specific manual trades came to be designated as *unehrlich* (dishonorable), but they were few and varied from one city to the next. In some cities, linen weavers would be labelled as dishonorable, whereas in many others they established their own guild and were even represented on the city council.[18]

In the Middle Ages, criteria such as knowledge and utility had been of secondary importance, relating to the relativizing or even disdainful attitude of most clerics towards technology and luxury commodities: in their view both phenomena indicated that people were not satisfied with what God had provided. In the period 1450–1650, however, these criteria gained increasing currency. As the Italian agronomist and translator of the works of Tacitus, Bernardo Davanzati, tersely stated, "Nature offers rough matter," highlighting the creative role of human labor. His view corresponded with the growing interest in mankind and nature alike; both were to be closely observed and understood on their own terms in the hope of finding solutions to secular problems. Efforts to fathom and transform nature increased interest in the concrete actions performed by those in specific occupational groups. In 1647 William Petty, aged twenty-four and the founding father of political economics, was regarded as the ideal author of a history of arts not only thanks to his thorough knowledge of mechanical processes but also because his favorite pastime since early childhood was "to be looking on the artificers."[19]

The interest in "practice" was inextricably linked with processes of state formation, commercialization, urbanization, ideological renovation, and increasing conspicuous consumption. The ambition to manifest and distinguish oneself as a powerful ruler, aristocratic family, city, or expert paved the way for a culture of technology, to a greater appreciation of "productive knowledge," and therefore also to the rise of a social type defined by master status: the expert, the engineer, the inventor, driving forces behind the new fortifications, firearms, hydraulic installations, bridges, cranes, precious materials, jewels, ornaments, and the like. These enhanced appreciation for technical creativity. Individuals and groups able to ride the resulting wave of opportunities encompassed a very broad spectrum and had a wide variety of backgrounds and skills. Rival states and enterprising investors relied increasingly on "expert mediators,"[20] who had the know-how to coordinate operations and could serve as knowledge brokers between the public or private principal and those carrying out the project. This development had sweeping consequences. In several industries, hands-on experience was insufficient to claim one was an expert, especially when the proliferation of technical books and images enabled people to claim knowledge without ever actually doing the work. Figures emerged who presented themselves as superior minds by asserting that they *understood* why things worked the way they did. Some principals among the political elites embraced the messages of these self-styled experts, who spoke in the same terms that they used, because they had little faith in people they regarded as unlearned practitioners. They were influenced by humanist ideas about education and believed that practical knowledge needed to be "elevated." They did not believe that the experience of manual artisans could hold a candle to an abstracted, text-based, theoretical version of expertise.

Humanist-trained authors published treatises describing the skills and knowledge involved in all kinds of practical arts. Their texts were written not for manual artisans but were aimed at convincing a cultured audience that the skills proposed and explained could also be practiced without pursuing profit and consequently with no loss of status.

Learned readers interested in improving their knowledge of practical arts helped increase appreciation for the crafts concerned and simultaneously advanced the social promotion of expert mediators. The latter manifested themselves as ideal mentors of experienced but subordinate artisans. They substantiated their added value by sharing insights based on mathematical knowledge, thereby presenting old problems in a new light. In this context, mathematics was pivotal, not only by bringing about new domains of expertise but also and especially by enabling a higher level of abstraction. This way, even highly skilled labor was attributed less value than the erudition of the expert mediator.

Conversely, however, a very different ideal of work underlined the connection between theory and practice, between reason and hands-on practice. The Florentine architect and sculptor Antonio Averlino, more commonly known as Filarete, who had several friends who were humanists, completed a treatise in the vernacular around 1464, in which he presented the plan for the ideal city of Sforzinda. He harshly condemned anybody who did not understand measurements and proportions but at the same time argued that the ideal architect had to be a skilled practitioner. He did not regard himself as purely a coordinator of construction workers but as somebody able to carry out all the tasks himself. In Sforzinda, in addition to liberal arts, "all crafts or trades that exist" would be taught, and the central House of Virtue located there was to be run by "three equals – a man of letters, one skilled in arms, and an artisan."[21] He was not alone in advocating that artisanal practice was equivalent to theoretical knowledge. In his commentary to the first Italian translation of Vitruvius' *De architectura*, published in 1521, Cesare Cesarione explained that every art consisted of "fabrication and reasoning," and that "reasoning" meant "speaking with reason about the handmade thing." While both aspects were inextricably linked, the work aspect (doing) was "almost of greater necessity" than the rational aspect (reasoning).[22] When the versatile Flemish artist Pieter Coecke of Aalst published a booklet in Dutch at Antwerp in 1539 for "anyone who takes pleasure in antique buildings," he expressed appreciation for the input of master artisans but regarded them as subordinates: designing a building was to be distinguished from constructing it, theory from practice, and the first aspect was by far the most important. The divergent views of the relationship between the—learned—architect and the master artisan led to disputes and court cases. In 1542, a carpenter in Antwerp was accused of violating guild regulations by designing buildings without being a master mason. In court, he argued that he was by no means the only one doing this (that is acting as an architect), and that masons should accept this; the court ruled in his favor. A few decades later a sculptor whose sketches and plans proved impossible to carry out argued in his defense that architects were "the schoolmasters of the masons" and therefore need not concern themselves with whether their plans could be realized in practice. Masons "brought the designs to life," but "would not be able to lay one single stone without the oversight of architects."[23]

In medicine the relationship between theory and practice received consideration as well. The Swiss physician Theophrastus von Hohenheim, commonly known as Paracelsus, regarded experience-based artisanal methods and manual labor as ideal for acquiring knowledge. In one of his works about surgery, written in German and translated into Dutch and French, he stated bluntly "that one does not become a master or surgeon by speculating but through hands-on experience."[24] Andreas Vesalius radically criticized dichotomy between medical training at a university and surgical training within a guild in a social hierarchy: physicians tended to look down on surgeons as practitioners of mechanical arts. In his great work about modern anatomy, *De humani corporis fabrica*, published in 1543, he stressed the unity of medical science. He urged his fellow professionals to desist from the "unfortunate division of the means of [medical] treatment" and "that detestable ritual whereby one group performs the actual dissection of a human body and another gives an account of the parts."[25] Evidence that surgeons might contribute fundamentally to medical science was provided by Ambroise Paré, the French pioneer in treating injuries sustained on the battlefield, by developing new methods and techniques, as well as by correcting and improving several points in Vesalius' *Fabrica*. By then, another physician, Georgicus Agricola, had published the first systematic treatise about geology, mineralogy, and mining. In *De re metallica* (1556), he demonstrated that skill was not identical to pure manual labor: economically independent miners needed to examine the origin and nature of the substratum to identify the veins, acquire expertise about ores and minerals and different methods for processing them, understand medicine to treat specific diseases, and master mathematics and drafting to construct complex machinery.

Interest in direct observation and research also gave rise to "vernacular science," which involved an approach to nature and matter that was incompatible with what came to be regarded as science in later periods. It was "an assemblage of knowing and making, and a means for struggling with matter," applied by artisans whose practices "were tied to a kind of lived theory," and based on "an underlying set of principles."[26] Exponents of this approach included Benvenuto Cellini and Bernard Palissy, who both tried to fathom the secrets of nature, focusing especially on the generative and transformative forces active there. Such efforts often derived from religious inspiration or were justified by the argument that studying God's book of nature complemented studying the book of God's word. The "hybrid expert" gained acceptance. He reconciled contradictions between theory and practice, between making and knowing, hand and spirit, and lived in a world that combined artisanal and learned practices. For the first time since classical antiquity, individuals of humble origins and without a university education started to claim a higher social and intellectual status. One notable example was Adriaen Coenen, the son of a fisherman who became a fish wholesaler in Scheveningen in the province of South Holland. During the second half of the sixteenth century he produced lengthy manuscripts describing everything he knew about the sea and the creatures that lived there and adding hundreds of colorful illustrations. His *savoir prolétaire*, "proletarian knowledge,"[27] derived from printed works; information obtained through conversations with fishermen, sailors, merchants, and collectors of material from nature; personal observations and reasoning; and what was considered to be common knowledge. Rather than simply copying what learned contemporaries presented to him, he formulated critical reservations about their texts, when his own observations justified such expressions, thereby establishing himself as an expert.

University-educated researchers realized in this period that a vast body of knowledge existed among occupational groups with little social appreciation: farmers, fishermen, woodcutters, gardeners, hunters, sailors. Though willing to acknowledge this, they realized that contacts with groups that received little appreciation or were even scorned might jeopardize the status of their field of knowledge. The Flemish physician and botanist Rembert Dodoens stated in the foreword to his *Cruydtboeck* (1554) that physicians wrongly scorned knowledge of herbs, because pharmacists and other "unlearned" people gathered and examined them, which was labelled as demeaning manual labor. Gaspar Gabrieli, the first professor of natural history at the University of Ferrara, urged that his knowledge "was suitable not only for humble persons low in the social hierarchy but also for those from social echelons known for their political power, wealth, aristocracy and knowledge."[28] Those who studied nature in its original settings were especially likely to jeopardize their social standing. This did not hold true for those engaging in astronomy, physics, mathematics, or mechanics, as these fields of knowledge were indisputably associated with the liberal arts and were the most conducive to numerical approaches, measurement, and experiments with costly equipment. Valorization criteria, such as quantifiability, verifiability, and predictability, therefore increasingly determined the status of scientific fields and their practitioners.

Towards the end of the long sixteenth century, university-educated scholars became progressively less inclined to regard those practising mechanical arts as their scientific equals. Francis Bacon explained why practice and theory were two different worlds. He praised mechanical arts, not only because they made many useful applications possible, but also because they revealed nature's hidden secrets and were thus a solid foundation for developing an accurate natural philosophy. Experience should never be scorned. Manual workers, however, should not be interpreting knowledge obtained by applying mechanical arts. Construction of an inductive natural philosophy based on countless experiments and observations required their involvement, but they were to follow the instructions from learned philosophers meticulously. In *New Atlantis* (1627), Bacon's posthumously published Utopia, a small group with fit and selected minds had to order and classify the obscure mass of data gathered by a great many researchers. Wherever the knowledge of manual workers was supposed to be common, the "greater observations, axioms and aphorisms" realized by a tiny minority, comprising philosopher interpreters, were not automatically considered suitable for disclosure.

At first sight, these developments might seem not to have been very significant for broad groups of the urban population. Such an impression is incorrect. Around 1500, literacy rates in Flemish, south German, and Swiss cities could be as high as 30 or even 40 percent and wealthy master artisans presented themselves increasingly as *literati*. In the Low Countries, they figured prominently in the *Rederijkerskamers*, Chambers of Rhetoric, and in many German cities they were very active as *Meistersinger*. Their plays reveal the reflections about various types of work within a vernacular humanism and a lay ethic. The topics proposed by the organizers of the *Landjuweel*, the great drama competition held in Antwerp in 1561, show how deeply the chambers were involved in the sociocultural problems of their day. Two titles referred directly to debates about the relationship between theory and practice, which was immensely important for a definition of worthy efforts: "Does experience or erudition contribute the most to wisdom?" and "What brings people the most to *Conste*?"[29] Cornelis Kiliaan, author of the first Dutch dictionary (1574), translated *Conste* into Latin as *ars* (art), *scientia* (science), and *artificium* (handicraft), and into Greek as *techne* (craftsmanship). One of the chambers considered the concept to be a comprehensive designation for liberal arts and mechanical arts and argued explicitly that the objective was always to manage both theory and practice. All chambers at the *Landjuweel* demonstrated that manual labor reflected the natural urge of mankind to realize his potential, which was entrusted to him by God. This did not concern just craftsmanship but related to *Conste* as well, that is the result of relentless toil, extended experience, continuous study and knowledge acquisition. They agreed with Vives, who had written in his treatise on education (1531), "This, then, is the fruit of all studies; this is the goal. Having acquired our knowledge, we must turn it to usefulness, and employ it for the common good,"[30] on the understanding that they too wished to demonstrate the knowledge that they had acquired with such effort. They were perfectly willing to serve the public interest but hoped to benefit personally as well. Being in control of one's fate was also immensely satisfying. Featuring *Hercules at the Crossroads* so prominently at the *Landjuweel* was not purely coincidental: each person had to take a decision. For rhetoricians, this meant pursuing their own predisposition and talent. They conveyed this idea of human perfectibility and the conviction that work was conducive to individual happiness and would benefit society. God was not absent from this event. Some chambers presented Him as the "supreme *constenaer*," the first and exemplary creator, who enabled mankind to come closer to Him by using His celestial gifts to understand creation. From this perspective, work retained a strong spiritual finality. Still, humanist influences were identifiable in nearly all texts. A secular concept such as "utility" appeared frequently, and a far more ambivalent concept such as "knowledge" acquired nonreligious connotations as well. The *Landjuweel* of 1561 revealed how urban middle strata appropriated learned knowledge. They aimed to prove that countless artisanal and commercial occupations involved arithmetic and geometry and readily devised their own classifications of the *artes*. The message was consistently that even the simplest manual work required *conste*.

Each chamber was instructed to address the question "which craft is the most useful and the most honest but receives very little appreciation?" The topic helped bring to mind a great many occupations, highlighting their attributes relating to manual labor, and demonstrating that they served the common benefit. Many trades were considered, all were highly praised, but the preferred manual labor was not supposed to be socially prestigious, leading the chambers to conclude unanimously that agrarian work belonged at the top of the list. In this way, they did not stigmatize an urban occupational group and confirmed a long-standing stereotype, that is, that farming was an exceptionally useful activity, but that farmers received little or no respect.[31]

In cities where craft guilds were run by the actual producers, and where they participated in local politics, belonging to such organizations conferred prestige and respectability, which might be expressed in public rituals and manifestations. Still, many individual master artisans aimed at establishing a reputation for themselves outside the guilds as more than producers who were skilled craftsmen, as more than representatives of the working arts. Some derived status from the political influence they wielded as the dean of a guild. Others described their occupation in terms that accommodated the views of intellectuals on liberal arts. Relating political to cultural capital was the best way for the most prominent in artisanal circles to elicit appreciation among superior social circles and was consequently deemed far more important than appearing as a craftsman. Work in whatever form was very rarely a theme in the personal writings of early modern master artisans.

According to the famous *Ständebuch*, (*Book of Trades;* 1568), which contained more than one hundred woodcuts of workshops and manual occupations by the Nuremberg artist Jost Amman,[32] the world of artisans was exclusively a male purview. This depiction was accurate, in that only a handful of women's guilds existed, and that very few craft guilds admitted female apprentices. In practice, however, wives and daughters of many master artisans were active in the workshop, where their role might be as crucial as in the household.[33] Whenever artists portrayed women working in an urban setting, they depicted them in retail occupations (which carried little social prestige), doing work that was hardly ever guild-based (such as spinning), or performing household chores.

Journeymen who had a strong position on the shop floor but were unable to attain master status for financial reasons, emphasized their "property in labor" and made clear what this meant through collective action. Labor disputes, in which subaltern groups defended their interests and made firm demands, were not a new phenomenon. All relevant tactics that might enhance the positions of urban wage workers had already been tried in the late Middle Ages: collective exoduses from the city; declaring an employer *foul* (which banned all journeymen from his workshop); targeted and selective strikes; destroying tools; intimidating and expelling "outsiders" and "scabs" and the like. This also applied to strategies such as forming leagues to enforce collective wage increases and to conclude carefully circumscribed employment contracts. The tactics and strategies used were certainly not representative of the great majority of urban wage workers, and the frequency and results varied greatly, depending on the place and time. Still, they reveal the views of the journeymen concerned about work and the criteria on which they based their collective identities. In the ideal they envisaged, their work comprised three closely related qualities: autonomy, independence, and self-sufficiency. Autonomy entailed the capacity to determine where, when, for whom, with whom, how, and for what rate they would work, which required both "property of labor" and "property of skill." Independence denoted the nature of the labor relationship, with employees assuming they were entering a partnership with employers and thus operating in a context of reciprocity and specific rules. Self-sufficiency related to the extent of subsistence security one might obtain through work, which in turn related to the degree of autonomy and independence. These criteria led to distinction and respectability. Distinction with respect to broad layers of the working population, for whom such an ideal was unattainable, respectability compared with all those higher up in the social hierarchy.

That skilled wage workers in trades such as book printing, cloth shearing, hat making, building, or mining tended to be well-organized and succeeded in taking a collective stand on the valorization of their work did not erase individual distinctions. In large companies or workshops remuneration varied not only depending on the specific task performed (implying that that same worker would receive a higher or lower wage from one day or week to the next, because he was assigned different tasks) but was also based on individual attributes. Often, at a construction site where about fifty masons worked, there would be fifteen or twenty different rates of pay. In the early seventeenth century at the *Officina Plantiniana* in Antwerp vast discrepancies existed in the wages of both the composers and the printers, who together had formed a powerful association (the "Chapel"). These differences related in part to years of experience. Systematic comparison reveals, however, that in some cases differences in technical competence are the only explanation possible. This suggests that both the journeymen and their employers acknowledged that individual attributes merited valorization.

Nowhere was talent and consequently individual distinction as decisive as in the visual arts. If the elites believed that a painter or sculptor excelled in his craft, he would attain immense prestige. In both northern Italy and in northwest and central Europe, such occupational groups organized in guilds in the late Middle Ages. Those who were appreciated by religious dignitaries, secular rulers, city councils, and/or aristocrats started to gain public notoriety in the fifteenth century. Since the themes in paintings were predominantly religious, they appeared as "cultural mediators," who could convey the mysteries of the Christian faith to those unable to read. Accordingly, they felt justified in presenting themselves as men with special talents. Rogier van der Weyden in Brussels and Sandro Botticelli and Domenico Ghirlandaio in Florence added their own likenesses to scenes depicting respected dignitaries. The pride of the craftsman-artist was, however, associated with Christian humility, for example by appropriating a specific saint to portray themselves as proclaiming the divine message. The growing need of territorial rulers for representations of power, especially propaganda media, and the rising demand from clerical and secular elites for luxury commodities similarly enabled skilled manual artisans manufacturing valuable objects to acquire prestige. Gold-and silversmiths in particular were highly respected.

Leon Battista Alberti and other fifteenth-century Italian humanists paved the way for claims that painting qualified as a liberal art. Their discourses virtually obliterated any view of the body of the artisan, which was completely overshadowed by the intellect of the scholar-painter. While around 1400 the crucial role of manual work had been stressed, and thorough knowledge of materials and technique was regarded as an absolute necessity, a century later abstract knowledge fields relating to the liberal arts that artists needed to master had become the main focus. Rivalry between painters and sculptors, each insisting that their respective arts were superior, led to a quest for suitable valorization criteria, in which greater or lesser physical efforts were often invoked as an argument. When the humanist Benedetto Varchi presented the problem of the relative merits and ranking of the arts, giving special consideration to painting and sculpture (the *paragone*), to eight leading artists in 1546, each one offered arguments to demonstrate that his own art was superior. Some years later, Giorgio Vasari offered a solution in his renowned *Lives*, arguing that both painting and sculpting were based on *disegno*, the interdependence of plan, design, and drawing, "the father of our three arts of architecture, sculpture and painting," proceeding from intellect. This concept made it possible to distinguish visual arts from artisanal pursuits and was the foundation for the *Accademia del Disegno*, established in Florence in 1563. Young painters and sculptors could pursue formal training here outside the *bottega* system and therefore outside the guild-based apprentice system. Several artists presented themselves not only as intellectual artists, but also as divinely inspired creators, who were equal or even superior to members of the elites. Cellini's *Vita* is an extraordinary statement of such a self-perception.

The image of the intellectual artist, inspired by creative genius, was not universally accepted in sixteenth-century Italy but nonetheless became the dominant paradigm. While several factors led to this outcome, the impression that rulers and aristocrats deeply influenced by humanist ideals left on cultural life was decisive. In the absence of a social and political counterforce, urban corporatism came to be regarded as a straitjacket, from which true artists needed to be liberated. In the Low Countries and southern Germany matters were different. New elites and segments of the social middle strata there often had a say in politics, in some cases wielded substantial purchasing power as a group, and had their own cultural channels. There were humanists who proclaimed the paradigm of the learned artist and artists who presented themselves as such, but they did not set the tone. In 1547 the influential writing master Johann Neudörffer the Elder composed a biographical lexicon, in which he listed seventy-nine men who had been distinguished artists in Nuremberg in the past century. He saw no reason to rank Albrecht Dürer above craftsmen-artists, including stonemasons, bronze casters, and printers. In the early seventeenth century, the Delft City Council stipulated explicitly that the Saint Luke's guild encompassed "all those earning their living ... by the art of painting, be it with fine brushes or otherwise, in oil or watercolours," like the sculptors, the engravers and an entire series of craftsmen who were regarded as practitioners of mechanical arts throughout Europe.[34]

CONCLUSION

As in other parts of the world and in other periods, different perceptions and definitions of work coexisted in early modern Europe, demonstrating that variable manifestations of human activity are always valorized within changing balances of power. Since classical antiquity, however, broad consensus existed on the principle that every person had to make efforts regardless of his or her status, and that idleness was both ethically and socially unacceptable. In the period 1450–1650 socioeconomic, political, and cultural-ideological changes led various groups to accuse the aristocracy and the clergy, or at least fractions of the traditional elites, of idleness and parasitism. Intellectuals, civil servants, merchants, and skilled master artisans simultaneously sought and found arguments to qualify their professional activities as worthy efforts. Even though scholars, businessmen, and artists applied different valorization criteria, depending on their status-elevating ambitions, they shared the conviction that they—like Hercules at the crossroads—had chosen the right path, that is, the course of relentless exertion. The poor laws adopted by city councils and central governments, the moral commandments of ecclesiastical authorities in both Roman Catholic and Protestant areas, the arguments presented by humanists and political economists concerning useful/productive work, and, last but not least, the ambitions of employers seeking access to cheap labor—all this was conducive to bringing about a material, intellectual, and conceptual space, in which the ideal of the active society took shape. Its negation comprised all those labelled as undeserving poor, as useless bodies. Both the elites and the social middle groups believed that such persons, regardless of their age and gender, had to be disciplined and had a duty to work.

The period 1450–1650 was immensely significant for perceptions of work over the centuries that followed—not only because the imperative of universal activation remained fundamental to all forms of coerced labor, but also because the valorization criteria that gained ground in the early modern age, especially knowledge and utility, became increasingly important in qualifying professional activities and structuring them hierarchically. Both criteria enabled various groups to present their activities as worthy efforts, taking special care to demonstrate knowledge. This held true for merchants and guild members alike. The new image of the "intellectual artist" also gained credence and even became the dominant paradigm in some cases, but it was certainly not accepted everywhere. Knowledge was an ambivalent concept in several respects. In the sixteenth century, the differences between theory and practice could be reconciled in certain contexts, as manual work was considered to be a source of knowledge, both by university scholars and by skilled tradesmen. This was, however, a passing stage. The adherents of Francis Bacon were immensely interested in artisanal practices but considered those practicing mechanical arts to be incapable of producing "true" knowledge. The contrast between "knowledge workers" and "manual workers" was irreversible from that point onwards.

CHAPTER EIGHT

The Political Culture of Work

BERT DE MUNCK AND JAN DUMOLYN

In both late medieval and early modern historiography, the history of labor and the history of popular resistance remain, to a large extent, two different strands of research. To overcome this, we propose to define the "political culture of work" during this period in terms of power relations centered around the position of labor within specific communities. The political (*le politique*) is thereby to be distinguished from politics (*la politique*) or the daily interplay of power between conflicting groups. We see the political rather as the symbolic space in which authority and legitimacy are constructed, and upon which political claims and communities are based. Given that work is a key variable in the provision, wealth, and well-being of any political community, it is by necessity at stake in the discursive strategies underneath political claims and arguments and, ultimately, the formation of communities. To understand the political culture of work during the preindustrial period, work should therefore be considered central to not only the material but also the ideological reproduction of local communities.

Whether explicitly or implicitly formulated in the sources, issues of labor and its control were often at stake in popular politics and they deserve focused historiographical attention. In the work of both liberal and Marxist historians between the end of the nineteenth century and the 1970s, some sort of socioeconomic class struggle was often present in explanations of political conflict in preindustrial towns, and revolts were considered to have been somewhat mechanistically caused by hunger or periods of economic crisis.[1] Starting with historians such as Henri Pirenne in the early twentieth century, guild revolts were not only seen as crucial steps in the emergence of more "democratic" institutions and practices, but they were also considered a class struggle of sorts. Artisans stood up against an oligarchy of merchants who not only denied them access to the political realm, but exploited them economically as well. In a similar vein, Boris Porchnev saw revolts in France between 1640 and 1670 as a class struggle of plebeians against the feudo-absolutist ruling class into which the urban bourgeoisie had been integrated because of state formation and the sale of offices. In contrast, Roland Mousnier emphasized vertical solidarities and the "society of orders," but he at least agreed on the causes of revolts: misery and burdensome taxes.[2]

During the 1970s and 1980s, historical sociology integrated Weberianism and Marxism and early modern revolts and rebellion were primarily approached from the point of view of state formation, as forms of resistance against Charles Tilly's expanding fiscal state. Revolts in early modern France in particular were overwhelmingly framed as "tax revolts against increasing royal fiscality," although local socioeconomic conditions varied across cities and rural regions, giving rise to specific "vertical" and "horizontal" solidarities and coalitions.[3] At the same time, within British Marxist history, the socioeconomic and political dimensions soon crystallized around the notion of a "moral economy," understood as a set of customs and laws to be defended against the intrusion of market forces.[4] While this concept somewhat saved the political dimension of revolts, it also reinforced the perception of the goals of subaltern social groups as conservative and anachronistic.

This is especially the case for rural revolts. While they have traditionally been explained in terms of outbreaks of collective anger against lords, whether in Marxist terms of class struggle against the extraeconomic appropriation of surplus or as a more irrational and conservative reaction to political change, they are now mostly studied in terms of local village communities defending rights to commons, most notably in the work of Yves-Marie Bercé and Peter Blickle.[5] Economic issues continued to form some of the main causes of political tension in the early modern city, notably the moral duty of governments to provide subsistence for its inhabitants, a notion inherited from the medieval commune, but since the 1980s, structural factors—including political ones—have faded further into the background. Attention largely turned towards cultural norms, values, and systems of meaning. At first, the emphasis shifted to the festive and carnavalesque aspects of peasant revolts, while class hatred, living conditions, and, above all, work were reduced to background at best. Today, early modern urban and rural communities are seen as often divided along religious or political lines, determined by local parties or factional politics, and the subaltern's goals are revealed to have often been symbolic—geared towards such notions as "honor" and the recognition of rights and autonomy, which are seen as unconnected to notions of work. Thus, while resistance is no longer seen as genuinely political, work is no longer seen as central to political strife. Even William Beik, who often set artisans and wage workers at the forefront of urban protest, considered labor disputes as stimulating rather than determining broader political movements.[6]

This is not to say of course that the focus on the discourses and performances of subaltern groups lacks merit. As James Scott's notions of "hidden transcripts" and the "weapons of the weak" suggest, they can be very important and effective even when they remain hidden.[7] Yet the time has come to reintegrate the more traditional perspectives of social structure and politics and the history of work into the history of popular politics—provided that the notion of politics is expanded to include the discursive strategies and claims upon which politics in the narrows sense rests. Already in 1990 Rudolf Dekker regretted the neglect of the study of early modern labor relations and deplored that riots and revolts were predominantly framed as "food riots" and "tax revolts."[8] One recent cultural historian who joins the study of rebellious ritual with social analysis is Peter Arnade, who saw "the language of masculine labor" at work during the 1566 iconoclasm in the southern Low Countries. It was craftsmen, mostly weavers, who had started it, and their forms of social organization and cultural expression shaped their rebellious and heretical actions and their working men's tools were their weapons.[9] Although the notion of work often remained hidden in their actions too, we will argue below that work was part of the agenda—even when implicit.

Building on and confronting the history of resistance and popular revolt and the history of work, we will try to reveal the political dimension in the experience and perception of work while at the same time understanding the role of labor, including labor relations, in resistance and revolt. Specifically, we will connect the issue of "common resources" to that of work. In late medieval Europe, as elsewhere, work was not simply understood as an individual activity undertaken for individual gain. Although artisans and workers could be very calculative, work was experienced as fundamentally embedded in communal structures. At least on the ideological level, it was not seen as separate from the broader issue of providing for and sustaining a larger community. As a result, the issue of wage and surplus extraction are questions to be understood from the perspective of conflicting views on the body politic concerned and the role of artisans and workers in it. Our focus will mostly be on corporately organized work and wage labor relations in an urban context, with rural work only serving as a point of comparison. Geographically, most of our examples will come from northwestern Europe because most historical research on our topic has been carried out for this part of the world.

In the first section, we will show that in resistance and revolts the "economic" and the "political" dimensions cannot be disentangled—especially not for this period. Nor can one dimension be seen as more fundamental, or as a cause of transformation in the other. Rather, a proper analysis should start from the intricate connection between economic productivity, on the one hand, and the political status and power of working groups within a community on the other. As we will see, what was often at stake in these conflicts was the connection between workers and the body politic. Nowhere is this more obvious than among the urban artisans and their organizations, which will be the subject of the second section. Artisans, often in large numbers and with the potential to engage in mass protest and even violence, were omnipresent in early modern urban revolts and in the urban landscape in general, and whether they were organized in guilds with some degree of political power or not, they often obtained a specific identity from their specific type of work.

POPULAR PROTEST AND THE EVACUATION OF LABOR FROM POLITICS

Riots are no longer reduced to irrational outbursts of a "mob" or a "crowd." George Rudé identified "faces in the crowd," while Eric Hobsbawm coined the phrase "bargaining by riot," suggesting that the individuals involved consciously pursued well-articulated interests.[10] However, on the rebound it became more difficult to examine labor-related protest and action without adopting a teleological perspective. Patrick Lantschner recently pointed out that such famous historical events as the Ciompi Revolt were all too easily seen by Marxist historians as "a veritable social and workers' revolution," while others, even up to the present day, have understood communal revolts as "harbingers of a modern state-centred political order."[11] Something similar applies to the organizations involved in these revolts. Under the strong influence of Robert Putnam, guilds are now even seen as the harbingers of a modern civil society. In a different but just as well teleological light, they are considered to have generated social capital and mutual trust and to have served as a breeding ground for democratic principles. Likewise, Catherine Lynch understands guilds and brotherhoods in a somewhat instrumental manner, as responses to the absence of social capital created by extensive kinship networks in urban contexts.[12] In a similar vein, economic historians influenced by the so-called new institutional economics consider guilds a response to an essentially modern problem, namely high transaction costs in an underdeveloped market.[13]

Even when the political dimension takes center stage, a narrative of modernity is often implied. In his recent synthesis on medieval social revolts, Samuel Cohn not only stressed demands for political inclusion and citizenship rights, he pointed to a shift in fourteenth-century Italy (due to the Black Death and its related demographic transformations) from a so-called "conservative" focus on privileges to a more "progressive" focus on political freedom and equality.[14] However, privileges and liberties were nearly synonymous in this period, as receiving a privilege amounted to becoming entitled to certain political or economic activities. For artisans, these economic and political dimensions were fundamentally entangled. Perhaps the most rewarding type of conflict for revealing this connection is to be found in the urban communal revolts from the thirteenth to the fifteenth centuries. The demands of the commoners, who often organized in guilds, were simultaneously economic and political. They requested privileges, which gave them well-defined rights to make certain products at the expense of outsiders, and at the same time, they fought for political participation and representatives in the urban councils alongside the mercantile magnates and patrician families.

This entanglement has often been obscured by discussions about the causes of revolts. In this debate, social and economic triggers of discontent and rebellion have often been seen as different from political motivations, with historians stressing either wages and prices or customs and privilege as causes. Focusing on revolts in southwestern France in the seventeenth century, Yves-Marie Bercé argued that the incidence of popular uprising did not overlap with economic distress, famine, or plague. These factors would have caused piety and apathy. A more important trigger of revolt would have been warfare and, relatedly taxation.[15] Most historians now agree that rebellions and revolts are triggered by an amalgamation of contextual factors, some more structural than others. Examining rural riots in the west of England in the late sixteenth and the first half of the seventeenth century, Buchanan Sharp identified food shortages and rising grain prices as contributing factors, alongside slumps in the sectors of broadcloth weaving, enclosures, and deforestations of crown woods.[16]

Collective action against enclosure may seem far removed from labor issues, but when seeing work as part of the broader issue of providing for and sustaining a community, it is one of the crucial fields where the political and economic intertwine. In England's western forests, the crown faced communities of miners and other industrial workers for whom the woods and waste lands were crucial to their struggle for survival, given that their wages were supplemented by livestock, which needed grazing space. In the absence of a modern market economy, being politically independent implies having access to resources and control of the use value of both land and labor. This is often what customs were all about. In the words of Andy Wood, guarding customs related to access to commons and wasteland not only revolved around food, fuel, and pasture, but, "the economics of custom were intimately bound up with senses of community and self."[17] Nor was this limited to commons. Socioeconomic demands connected to surplus extraction were nearly always inseparable from grievances related to the autonomy of a certain community or the political position of a group of individuals or families within it. This becomes clear once we overcome our present-day distinction between politics and the economy. In the late medieval context, the "political" or "judicial" realm was hardly distinguished from the "economic realm." And labor—or at least access to resources and use value—was a crucial hinge between the two.

In this vein, it might be appropriate to return to the older debates about the rise of capitalism and proletarianization, where the stakes are not exhausted by the fact that scarcity may have given way to unemployment as a cause of discontent and food riots. Labor was still scattered between individual artisan workshops during that period, but urban labor relations took various forms, typically involving vertical relations between petty commodity producers and merchant capital, including through subcontracting and "putting-out." Rural work could be free or unfree, but was always characterized by a variety of power relations between landlords, peasants, and their communities. Therefore, any shift in these power relations was simultaneously economic and political. In cities, increasing numbers of journeymen no longer had the prospect of becoming masters themselves and were bound to sell their labor power their entire active life. The status of masters as well often deteriorated, as part of them became either dependent on merchants and merchant capital or were subsumed by other masters' putting-out networks. To the extent that this process implied losing control over the means of production (that is, losing the ownership of tools and raw materials), this could be a process of proletarianization, although these masters mostly continued to work on their own premises. In the countryside, an increasing number of farmers lost land access, either because large leasehold farms started to dominate (as has traditionally been described for parts of England) or land ownership fragmented due to demographic pressure (as was the case for parts of the Low Countries). In both cases, protoindustrial activities in the countryside could replace or complement subsistence or income reaped from land, but growing dependence on merchant capital was imminent here as well—as the debate on protoindustry has shown.

The debate on protoindustry has typically concentrated on ownership of the means of production, distinguishing between a purchasing (or *Kauf*) system and a putting-out (*Verlag*) system—with only the latter implying a process of proletarianization because in the former the producers still owned their tools (such as, their looms) and or the raw material they worked with (such as, linen, wool, or purchased yarn). However, all these artisans were simultaneously deprived of access to the political sphere. The intrusion of market forces went hand in glove with both oligarchization and the growing encroachment of central states on the communal level. This has been noted for most if not all parts of Europe and in both the countryside and urban contexts, although of course the precise speed and shape of this process could differ substantially. In this respect, early modern developments were to a large degree determined by a path dependency established during the period c. 1280 – to c. 1380, when in different regions of medieval Europe, "political guilds" obtained strong positions in town governments. In cities guild-based artisans often succeeded in becoming a member of the body politic through their guilds, which were then integrated as a member in the urban body politic (while the individual artisans were in turn members of the guilds). Typically, a portion of the seats was reserved for them in the urban inner and outer councils. In certain cities and at certain moments in time, they completely overturned the existing order in that they ousted the oligarchic elites and appropriated all seats.

However, this was usually not long-lasting. Typically, a compromise was eventually reached in which a specific share of seats was reserved for specific groups of both patricians and guilds. This was notably the case in the southern Low Countries, the Rhineland, and (for short periods) various towns of northern and central Italy. Craft guilds had far less institutional autonomy and political power in most French, Iberian, Hanseatic, or southern-Italian towns, and even less so in England. In these cities, merchant oligarchies mostly ruled unchallenged throughout the medieval period and up to the eighteenth century. Even in the more exceptional cities and regions where guilds had obtained participation in government there was a general tendency towards losing those positions. This happened first in Italy where artisans were excluded almost everywhere from communal politics after 1400. In regions controlled by the Habsburg dynasty such as the Netherlands, Spain, and various German cities there was a systematic offensive against guild participation in government, especially during the period 1525–40, as a reaction to a wave of revolts. Henceforth, guilds were more rigidly controlled by urban and princely governments, less autonomous in their internal procedures and elections, and subject to more labor legislation imposed from above. In addition, they generally became more internally oligarchic after 1500, with the gap between richer and poorer masters and between masters and journeymen widening. The latter were soon entirely excluded from any position that they previously had within guild leadership.

In short, processes of economic marginalization were nearly always accompanied by processes of oligarchization and loss of political clout—as exemplified by guild-based (urban) artisans. Nevertheless, we should again be wary of reducing the political to something instrumental in the preservation of economic privileges. Once we see economic mechanisms and practices as ways of providing for or producing wealth in a specific political community, the economic is political by nature. And depending on how one understands the production and distribution of wealth in a certain community, specific economic functions will be valued or not. In a case study comparing Dutch and central European cameralism in the seventeenth century, Thomas Buchner has clearly shown that the perception of labor was contingent upon the way the political community was shaped and imagined. While the utility of labor as a means to mobilize and produce resources was recognized in both contexts, Dutch mercantilists valued commercial activities in particular. For the mercantile magnates in control in the Dutch Republic, the wealth of the country derived from the activities of their own social group. In comparison, German mercantilism had a broader view of the meaning of work, one in which peasants and artisans were valued higher—with peasants, artisans, and merchants ultimately dependent upon each other.[18]

It should come as no surprise, then, that the struggles of guild-based artisans for economic privileges and a larger share of the surplus can simultaneously be seen as a struggle to be recognized as political actors. In the medieval and late medieval context, political thought was heavily influenced by the writings of Aristotle and Plato, for whom being a political subject was at odds with having to work with one's hands. Handworkers and farmers were considered slaves to necessity, because of which they could not act in a disinterested way and, thus, develop a rational attitude in the service of the common good. This was reversed during the later medieval revolts, which resulted not only in economic privileges and access to urban councils, but also in the connection between guild membership (and thus economic privileges) and citizenship rights. After the revolts, access to the guilds as a master was often conditional upon being a burgher of the city, as was typically the case in the Low Countries and a range of cities in the German lands. Or else becoming burgher of the city either required being member of a guild or guild-like organization, as was the case in Liège at one point, or was conditional upon finishing an apprenticeship, as applied across England according to the Statute of Artificers in 1563. As in England, the crown was more powerful in France, but here as well, guilds and their members were recognized as political actors in the fifteenth century, albeit without any link to urban citizenship.

The most interesting long-term evolution of all, then, may be the one in which labor was eventually perceived as something separate from politics. As shown in Volume 4 in this series, a utilitarian view emerged after the mid-seventeenth century. Both mercantilist and enlightenment thinking, while stressing the importance of labor and productive activity, eventually reduced labor to no more than a factor in a production process. While a small part of the workforce was singled out as creative and valuable for the invention of new products and techniques, the largest part of the workers was reduced to a type of automaton in the writings of intellectual elites, who considered them devoid of ingenuity and, indeed, rationality. By implication, their privileges and customs were gradually framed by the elites as mere justifications on the part of insubordinate commoners and working people. This process peaked in the eighteenth century, but its seeds were sown before the mid-seventeenth century. A proper understanding of this process requires a closer look at the political dimension of labor conflicts, which is the subject of the following section.

POLITICS IN LABOR CONFLICTS: ARTISANS AND GUILDS IN DEFENSE OF SKILLS

How can we identify labor issues in popular protests, "ceremonies," and "rituals," or the daily bargaining of working people over their rights and standards of living? Work-related issues are of course clearly at stake in the case of strikes. From the seventeenth century onwards, with the expanding manufactory system, strikes seem to have become larger and frequenter. Appearing first in the textile towns of Flanders and northern France, strike movements were often known as *takehans*—a mysterious word of probable Middle Dutch origin—or *uutganck* ("walkouts").[19] Strikes, as well as boycotts and defamation campaigns against individual guild masters by journeymen or of merchants by artisans in general are also attested in fourteenth-century Germany. At stake were such issues and customs related to wages, leisure days, or sometimes demands by journeymen to restrict the number of apprentices working for lower than agreed-on wages. Other strikes could have more "political" motives, demanding measures from the urban government against, for instance, rural industries or protesting monetary reforms.

Strikes generally remained a regular feature of larger industrial towns during the early modern period. Yet many more labor conflicts took place on a micro level, within one workplace, or stopped after demands were formulated in a petition or legal action was taken. Such actions are of course less visible in the source material. On the other hand, various other types of power relations could be at stake in the artisan economy of a town apart from wage labor conflicts. In the cloth industry, some masters developed into "drapers" and acted as genuine entrepreneurs, using poorer masters as subcontractors. An endemic conflict also existed between guild masters and merchants, who had opposing interests despite being mutually dependent. While merchants obviously needed masters to produce finished and semifinished products, artisans often depended on merchants for access to raw materials, capital, and markets. Yet while merchants pressured for high quality but low prices or wages, masters typically negotiated for the opposite. They were also commonly accused of embezzlement of raw materials, or delivering products below standard quality. Such conflicts often translated into conflicts within guilds and between guilds and city governments, both resulting in petitions and regulations on not only working conditions and wages, but also product quality, political participation and representation, the power to control labor and product quality, and so on.

The bargaining power of the parties involved depended upon myriad of factors. In many towns, merchant elites had a very strong grip on labor regulations and guild organization. Urban governments dominated by mercantile elites could often issue labor regulations without interference from manufacturing guilds and use the latter to bring their regulations into effect and sanction offenders. In other towns, crafts guilds could act more autonomously and weigh on regulations related to work. This was typically the case when they had seats in the local councils which decided on economic and labor regulations. As to protoindustrial activities in the countryside the distinction between a *Kauf* (artisanal purchase) and a *Verlag* (putting-out) system is still relevant. In the former, the producers controlled the means of production because they owned their looms and/or provided for their own raw materials, for instance by growing flax or buying yarn. In the latter, this was no longer the case, given that the merchants supplied the raw materials and bought the looms or provided credit for buying them. The difference between the two in terms of labor relations is clear: in *the Kauf* system the masters had a minimum of control over prices and profits, which they had lost in the *Verlag* system.

Both in the cities and in the countryside, territorial state authorities could play a part too. On the one hand, they could issue labor regulations applicable in the country as a whole. This was notoriously the case in England, where the so-called Statute of Artificers, which in 1563 empowered local magistrates to fix wages, restricted workers' freedom of movement (as they needed permission to switch from one employer to another), and regulated training (with a minimum of seven years' compulsory training across a broad range of trades), was only the most conspicuous and most comprehensive of a series dating back to the fourteenth century. On the other hand, central state authorities could be appealed to by a local party and interfere in local disputes and policy making. Because manufacturing masters often relied on local monopolies and tried to oust competition from outsiders, their interests were mostly not defended by territorial states. The latter were more likely to be called upon by mercantile elites who tried to circumvent local (guild) monopolies, for instance by asking permission to trade in foreign products or establish production activities on the countryside (outside the reach of guilds). As argued above, territorial princes and administrations typically tried to roll back the power of guilds (and cities) altogether.

In any perspective, we should refrain from distinguishing features that supposedly heralded modern types of conflict. The linen weavers' revolts in the towns of Upper Swabia between 1580 and 1660 studied by Thomas Max Safley, pitched groups of small independent producers against a dominant merchant class. As such, they display continuity with more traditional "medieval" or "corporatist" relations of production rather than signs of "protocapitalist" tendencies. The smaller masters, supported by their dependent workers, wanted to limit the actions of entrepreneurs who imported foreign unfinished linen and bleached it.[20] Likewise, the journeymen who, in the work of Catharina Lis and Hugo Soly, sought to control the supply of labor only succeeded in pressuring masters and influencing wages and labor conditions with the help of corporative structures. Their strategies were based upon the distinction between free and unfree work, the difference being that a free journeyman had finished an apprenticeship and—if applicable—had made a trial piece for journeyman status, while the latter had not. This distinction enabled the free journeymen to prevent unfree journeymen from entering the labor market and working at below-minimum wages.[21]

The extent to which journeymen succeeded would appear to have been determined by their organizational capacity, which depended, in turn, on a range of factors, including numbers, geographic mobility and the need to cooperate on the shop floor. Yet the conflicts cannot be reduced to a conflict between labor and capital because cultural and political goals were also involved. As to journeymen strikes, Andreas Grießinger has argued that the incidence of labor conflicts did not simply follow changing socioeconomic conditions. Conflicts often revolved around notions of standing and honor, and in form resembled a type of purification ritual.[22] Grießinger wrote about the eighteenth century, but, if anything, the political importance of standing and honor must have been even more important between the fifteenth and seventeenth centuries. In that period, journeymen often had a liminal position in urban society. Ideally, becoming a master and entering a guild coincided with becoming married and the head of a household. Journeymen, like apprentices, often lived in their masters' households. Yet, between 1450 and 1650, it gradually became more difficult to become a master, as a result of which journeymen were often married adults and household heads themselves, thus claiming a standing and privileges similar to those of masters while lacking the protection of a guild. This explains why journeymen increasingly started to organize and establish journeymen associations, especially from the seventeenth century on.

Independent journeymen associations existed in the fourteenth century and probably earlier but they remain rather exceptional before 1450. At first, they are mostly attested to in the towns of the Holy Roman Empire but they also became more frequent and more durably organized in France, England, and the Low Countries during the sixteenth and seventeenth centuries—Alfons Thijs listed dozens of them for the Low Countries only.[23] More importantly for our purpose here, they often adopted the collective rituals of guild-based masters. They could organize strikes and work stoppages, or blacklist masters, but on a far more regular basis they also organized collective activities like masses, processions, and meals on their patron saints' day (Figure 8.1). In fact, as shown by Natalie Zemon Davis in her case study of the book printing trade in sixteenth-century Lyons, the journeymen's claims and discourses were not very different from those of their masters. The journeymen printers, who had organized in the so-called Company of the Griffarins above all refused to be treated like subordinates. Simultaneously, they stressed the importance both of a good relationship with their masters and of their skills.[24] Even when focusing on questions of wage and work, the ideological discourse in petitions and civil and criminal case files typically expressed the issues in terms of fraternity and other typical values of the guild ethos, including the respectability of independence and skills.[25]

FIGURE 8.1 Johan Meyer, *Procession of the guild of Butchers in Zurich*, seventeenth century. Cabinet des Éstampes et des Dessins, De Agostini / DEA / M. Seemuller. Image courtesy of Getty Images.

The same applies to the Antwerp journeymen printers of the large Plantin-Moretus company who were excluded from the masters' guild of Saint Luke and organized their own "chapel": they combined a "modern" insight into the nature of wage relations within this sector with a very religious and charitable attitude.[26] Such a combination was crucial on a more general level too—which is why artisans were often involved in insubordination and violence during the Reformation. While religious issues were profoundly entangled with political issues during the civil wars caused by religious conflict, artisans typically participated with their own economic and political demands; they were especially present in more radical movements such as the Anabaptists. Nor should this be surprising. What was at stake, after all, was often the very definition of the community that artisans shared with others. While the political context in a city would seem to have determined the way different religious strands took root or not, the Reformation has often been understood to be about the commitment of the clergy to the community. Commitment to the community was also part of the guild-based master's political self-image, which is perhaps why Protestant ideas about salvation and the related stress on brotherly love and unity and on the duty of government to care for the spiritual well-being of its subjects in the teachings of Ulrich Zwingli and Martin Bucer would have found more adherents in cities with a strong tradition of political participation.

More generally, the guilds' preoccupations often revolved around a "moral economy" of sorts, for instance when they argued that as heads of households they should be able to earn a decent living and provide for their family properly. This can easily be connected to what Werner Sombart has called *Nahrung* (sustenance), that is, the idea that providing for the local community should be privileged at the expense of both exclusion and competition. As such, *Nahrung* means a great deal more than material sustenance, at least in early modern Europe. It implies the ability and competence to live successfully and appropriately in society, because of which this term also entails a view in which political and economic and social aspects are integrated.[27] Up to a degree at least, this would seem to have been important for both municipalities and guilds. As their regulations betray, guilds mostly tried to instill a minimum of equality in their ranks, and hence capped the number of journeymen or machines a master was allowed to employ. In addition, the political dimension of skills would appear to have been important. For sixteenth-century Antwerp, it has been shown that master tinsmiths whose independency was threatened worried more about their guild-based standing and its connection to product quality than about ownership of the means of production. Some of them worked at piece rates for large merchants while being partly paid with raw materials, but this was not what they objected to. Rather, they complained about the fact that they were no longer recognized as the producers and the warrantor of the product's quality.[28] The broader issue was access to the guild (and, hence, the urban body politic), which they guarded formally, at least from the fifteenth and sixteenth centuries on, with an obligatory apprenticeship and master piece. A guild could only be entered once the craft was properly learned, while the guild privilege and monopoly were justified by the fact that guild-based masters made superior products or could in any case be trusted more than "false" or "unfree" masters. At least to the extent that the craft guilds had been integrated in the urban corporation, and as understood by the guild-based masters themselves, the legitimacy and value of skills was thus intimately connected to membership of the urban political community.

The artisans' goals did not include completely overturning the society of orders, but rather to become part of it and to become incorporated in the urban body politic. For an adequate understanding, it is important to bear in mind that late medieval and

Renaissance political society was imagined in a fundamentally corporative way. Both late medieval and humanist political thinkers, whether they sided with territorial princes, oligarchic republics, or the commoners, saw a "body politic" as an organic whole, rather than as a concatenation of individuals and groups, or as the institutional expression of the wills and ideas of individuals and interest groups. Within the older medieval tradition of John of Salisbury, a free republic was described by civic humanists as "one body with many heads, hands, and feet," and an individual's connection to the city like a body part's connection to the whole body.[29] The artisanal views, or at least the views of political thinkers pleading in their favor, differed only in that they had a more pluralistic conception of the urban body politic. While the oligarchic elites of most cities implied that the body politic entirely overlapped with their own group, the *Defensor Pacis* of Marsiglio of Padua, sometimes considered "the first systematic statement of the popular basis of authority," favored the inclusion of guilds in the body politic.[30]

Nevertheless, we should simultaneously refrain from reducing the urban revolts to something merely political. The official recognition of guilds amounted to receiving a privilege, through which they became part of the urban "liberties." Henceforth only members of the guild in question could make the products concerned within the city walls, although part of the hinterland was sometimes included. Consequently, guilds could also determine to a certain extent who could take part in the privilege and benefit from it. Provided that manufacturing masters continued to hold the reins in the guilds and have a say in urban politics, manufacturing was often reserved for the manufacturing masters, excluding merchants from production. Merchant-entrepreneurs, if they had not finished an apprenticeship term and made a masterpiece, could not hire journeymen, apprentices, or, for that matter, impoverished masters to produce the products on their own account rather than purchasing them from guild-based masters.

To be sure, the masters only succeeded in establishing this distinction in a range of cities, typically those with strong guilds like those in the Low Countries and the German lands. As argued above, the situation was entirely different in most Italian cities, and in greater parts of England, France, and the northern Netherlands. Most large and important guilds in these regions were controlled by a mercantile and oligarchic elite that had succeeded in denying manufacturing masters access to political office. In Venice, this process was already completed by the end of the thirteenth century; in Florence and most other large Italian city-states it took place in the fourteenth and fifteenth centuries. In most cities in the northern Netherlands, the guilds never gained a great deal of political power because urbanization took place later there and guilds were only erected after their momentum had passed. And even in cities where the manufacturing masters had formally succeeded in guarding their monopolies, merchants often found ways to act around such regulations—as was often the case in the free imperial cities of the Empire.

Nor can all this be reduced to political economy. Being recognized as a political actor involved a more fundamental shift than gaining a larger share of the economic surplus or gaining more control of economic regulation. The exclusion of artisans from politics in the Middle Ages, was based upon the idea that they were part of the realm of Nature. The idea that they were "slaves of necessity" and therefore incapable of acting in a disinterested and rational way in the service of the common good was grounded in a reading of Aristotle's work, which also made a strong distinction between Nature and Politics or Nature and Artifice. However, perhaps not coincidentally, the gap between Nature and Artifice narrowed more or less simultaneously when the guild-based masters became accepted as political subjects.[31] So there may have been a connection between epistemological transformations—in which the artisans were themselves involved in this period—and the political standing and privileges of artisans.[32] The granting of privileges and political rights to artisans also overlaps, in any case, with an economic shift in the cities towards the production of more expensive products in which the value added by skills had increased. So, the political goals and aims of artisans were in any case fundamentally entangled with the value attached to their skills.

A proper understanding thereof requires taking into account differences between cities and the countryside. Once they had gained political clout, urban economic actors, including manufacturing artisans, frequently tried to eradicate countryside production. Cities often enforced bans on producing crucial products outside a certain perimeter around the city, as was notoriously the case with Ghent. Urban manufacturers from this city are even recorded to have raided the countryside and to have destroyed production capacities in the urban hinterland, including in smaller cities.[33] In our period, Italian city-states unsurprisingly had better, progressive success in cornering the manufacturing of products with the highest added-value and reserving their production or the finishing stages for the capital of the state. Thus, a specialization typically materialized in which urban manufacturers produced the more sophisticated and more highly valued products, while countryside producers were only allowed to make the cheaper or semifinished products. And the idea that cities could dominate and politically represent the countryside was in this way intertwined with the idea that the products of urban manufacturers were superior to those manufactured in the countryside.[34]

All this was clearly reflected in the guilds' discursive and visual repertoires, which were inscribed in social and religious tradition. As a brotherhood, guilds typically organized masses and collective meals while forcing their members to attend not only processions and parades, but also the burial of fellow members. This is clearly attributable to their Christian (and perhaps also Germanic) origin, but it had a social and political dimension as well. According to Antony Black, guilds cultivated such values as friendship, brotherhood, and mutual aid, which translated into such rules as maximum numbers of apprentices and journeymen per master.[35] While such values had a political dimension in themselves, guilds moreover took part in the urban processions and parades, as a group or corporation, at least once they were incorporated. At these occasions, they also referred to their work. For instance, guilds are shown to have carried along their coats of arms, which mostly featured either one of their products or one of their typical tools. The products or tools in these weapons were embedded in a system of meaning which clearly referenced aristocratic cultural repertoires (Figure 8.2). Not only did these coats of arms have a similar shape and colors, but emblems such as crowns, lions, and garlands were also used.

Clearly, then, politics and labor were mutually entangled. The guilds' blazons were conspicuously visible in the public sphere, and they often still are, as they were typically used to adorn the facades of guild halls. And more often than not, their hallmarks not only referred to a certain product standard, but were simultaneously marks of origin. They often contained emblems referring to the city or its coat of arms. Consequently, these hallmarks are perhaps the best illustration that the perception and value of labor were inseparable from politics. Where guilds had the power to do so, they connected their skills to the body politic, suggesting that these skills were superior due to their political standing. Alternatively, their political standing and privileges were justified by the alleged superiority of their skills.

FIGURE 8.2 Signboard of the Guild of Cooperage, Italy, seventeenth century. De Agostini / DEA / A Dagli Orti. Image courtesy of Getty Images.

CONCLUSION

To be sure, only a small portion of guild-based artisans succeeded in justifying their political privileges and standing with reference to their skills and talents. In addition, from at least the sixteenth century on, this became increasingly untenable, as both commercial capitalism and the expanding territorial states encroached upon the guilds' privileges. This process could easily be described as one in which the levers of power simply shifted from the local level and the guilds and communities to the central level and mercantile elites. However, these processes were obviously connected, if only because they both resulted in renewed and intensified processes of oligarchization. While many of the protests and revolts were no doubt instigated by exploitation and surplus extraction upon the part of the oligarchic caste of merchants dominating textile production, merchants most often regained political power as the fiscal state expanded. Moreover, while fiscal measures have been identified as one of the principal triggers of the communal revolts, one of the most important requests of the artisans had been to have a say in the financial policy of the city—which, they argued, the mercantile or aristocratic elites did not do virtuously, neutrally, or in a way geared towards the common good.

Our synthesis suggests that a proper understanding requires taking into account transformations related to the value attached to certain types of work. What labor historians focusing on cultural systems of meaning have missed is that the rituals and repertoires of workers were often rife with references to labor and skills. One of the most prominent historians to plea for a cultural and symbolic understanding of the guilds' practices and repertoires is James Farr, who stressed that guilds prioritized honor and respect next to communality and solidarity. Moreover, Farr assumed that the guilds' rituals and discourses should be understood as a means to create community feelings and distinguish between insiders and outsiders.[36] Although Farr also focused on resistance and revolts, he did not record the link between the artisans' attitude to work, on the one hand, and their political actions and cultural discourses, on the other.

To be sure, ours is not a plea for a simple return to the old structuralist understanding of resistance and revolts. Rather than ignoring the merits of cultural analysis, we reintroduce a labor dimension to them. What fiscal revolts, foot riots, and strikes geared towards wages had in common is that they all revolved around surplus extraction and the distribution of economic fruits. This can be analyzed in a Marxist way and with a focus on the labor–capital conflict, but a proper understanding requires considering different views on the value of labor, which are in turn contingent upon different views of the body politic and the role of specific economic functions in it. Guild-based artisans had very specific views, in which their productive activity was key in the sustenance of the city in which they worked.

This link was often precisely what was at stake in the conflicts and bargaining processes involving workers and artisans in this period. While urban manufacturers had often gained recognition as political actors in the later Middle Ages—between the thirteenth to the fifteenth centuries, depending on the region—they typically lost that position again due to processes of oligarchization and state formation. This was accompanied by a process in which a great many independent masters became increasingly dependent on merchant capital, while journeymen—who had been part, to an extent, of the corporative world before—proletarianized. Moreover, both the political and the economic processes were in all likelihood connected to different perceptions of labor and skills, which also transformed substantially in this period. While a great deal of these transformations become visible only after the mid-seventeenth century, the reduction of artisanal work to a factor in a production process on the level of the state has its origins between 1450 and 1650.

CHAPTER NINE

Work and Leisure

ALESSANDRO ARCANGELI

In the final chapter of the present volume, as in the others of the same series, the cultural history of work in the early modern age will be examined in relation to what is ordinarily recognized as its opposite: leisure. However, definitions are not an easy matter, and precisely the nature and boundaries of leisure and the assessment of its relationship to work has been the subject of significant scholarly controversy. The reader will find, therefore, an initial brief survey of such debate, with the suggestion of the key concepts and interpretations one may find most useful in approaching our period and issues. This will include a sketched chronology of the main developments that are believed to have occurred over the two hundred years under consideration. We will subsequently regroup historical data under a cluster of focal points: attitudes towards leisure and work in their traditions and developments, also considered by taking into account the level of self-perception and awareness we may legitimately attribute to early modern agents; spaces and times of leisure practices; social hierarchy, gender, and age groups; cultural and regional variation; the variety of forms of leisure in its interaction with work; the trend towards a commercialization of leisure; and the relationship between leisure and political power including legislation and the judiciary.

DEFINING LEISURE VERSUS WORK

Considering the amount of scholarly reflection and debate that, in recent times, has been devoted to the definition of "leisure," it would be inappropriate to start this chapter without making some reference to the problematic status of such notion, and justifying the nature and limits of its use over the following pages. Since this volume is part of a series that covers a much more comprehensive chronology, the reader will find an assessment of the question in relation to previous and subsequent periods within the other volumes. Nevertheless, it would not be possible to discuss what may be specific to the early modern leisure culture, or to the attitudes towards leisure and work, without at least some reference to a tradition the epoch inherited and reinterpreted; nor by ignoring the fact that much historiography and leisure studies have emphasized the later periods as key theaters of change, thus implying or, more often, openly stating that the early modern age witnessed hardly any development on this front. Having said this, the principal scope of the present publication is neither theoretical nor historiographical; consequently, reference to questions of methodology will be limited to a general survey of the most useful critical interpretations, as a support to an analysis of actual historical material.

Leisure studies have significantly developed over the past few decades partly reflecting—one hardly needs to point it out—the growing importance, including economic, of today's leisure industry, as well as the changing nature of the relations between people, work, and personal and group identities that has come to characterize the postmodern society. Theoretical contributions have repeatedly attempted to provide a working definition of what we may fruitfully mean by leisure, and what is precisely its relationship with work. While a connection between the two tends to be included in all definitions, this is now understood as complicated: "work is the economic means for achieving the things that we aspire to in our leisure and without work our leisure is likely to be circumscribed"; on the other hand, "leisure can be described as free time but this tells us little about how we experience it," considering the importance played by the context.[1]

Among the best-known descriptions of spare-time activities is a list of forms of human practice provided by Norbert Elias and Eric Dunning in two versions.[2] For our purpose, they have the advantage of having been proposed by leading sociologists who considered the reality of the modern world but also had research interests in the early modern period, so that their application to the past will not represent per se a form of anachronism. We will need to return regularly, though, to the difference between our own categories of interpretation and those held by men and women who lived half a millennium ago, as it is far from irrelevant. A first list included private work and family management, rest, catering for biological needs, sociability, and the class of mimetic or play activities. In a more developed depiction of what Elias and Dunning defined as the "spectrum of leisure activities," they distinguished between routines on one hand, leisure activities one the other, and, in the middle, intermediary activities "serving recurrent needs for orientation and/or self-fulfilment and self-expansion."[3] Should we take into consideration, for instance, attendance to church service as a leisure activity, and what are the consequences in our appreciation of its cultural meaning for contemporaries of including or excluding it from the list? Private study, news reading, and voluntary work were other such intermediary spare-time activities enlisted by the two authors.

As for the more specific leisure category, Elias and Dunning further split it between strictly playing, generic socializing, and a complex variety of deroutinizing activities. On the basis of their classification, therefore, we should choose between a more inclusive consideration of leisure habits, which for instance may comprise travelling and sociable eating; or else opt for a narrower one, consisting of more specialized activities, pursued with the deliberate scope of entertainment, pastime, and recreation. Needless to say, within a volume devoted to the theme of work one should always take into account the mutual exclusion and interaction between these two concepts, and avoid both excessive overlapping with the other chapters and the opposite risk of leaving too much territory unchartered. There is always a third option, however: that of exercising some flexibility, and precisely the debated nature of leisure itself may rather suggest that, in considering this sphere in its historical relationship with work, we abstain from defining it by too rigid borders. Change over time provides a further reason for casting the net wide, or else one may miss the trade by which historical agents in different contexts may come to include or exclude from the given category some varieties of action (or inaction) that were at some other times assessed differently: with changing social structures and value systems, some forms of practice may have slipped in or out of lists of acceptable, esteemed, or prescribed behavior that, in their cultural context, appeared or not as someone's duty or available choice.

This variety of forms of social practice was performed to different degrees by different agents, and also held in varying esteem. No generalization would be really informative. However, the period witnessed conflicts over the legitimacy of given forms of human occupation, but also some cultural constants. Among the latter, we could safely enlist the justification of a need for rest and recreation, which even the strictest moralist had to concede.[4]

A WORKING CHRONOLOGY

More recently Peter Borsay, has provided, for the case of Great Britain, an assessment of its leisure experience in a historical perspective that begins from 1500.[5] Considering the important role which that particular national case has played both in history and in history-writing, his contribution may offer us a useful point of departure, particularly since it attempts to provide a working chronology, which could also be tested to examine other cultural areas. Although Borsay's book is arranged thematically, his introduction, drawing on the extant scholarship, suggests distinguishing between six subsequent periods over the five hundred years he examines. The author is aware that specific leisure practices and specific cultural contexts witnessed different rhythms and developments. Nevertheless, some general trends seem to him to be recognizable. The first two of Borsay's phases fall within the chronology of the present volume. Truly, there are religious and political circumstances suggesting the identification and timing of these phases that are specific to the British Isles; they will be worth examining all the same. The initial one is inspired by the work of Ron Hutton, a scholar who has systematically revisited the English traditional ritual year, and identified the period between 1350 and 1520 as that of the late medieval making of "merry England"—an accumulation of communal customs significantly enriching the nation's recreational culture.[6] The relevance of this frame to a discussion of leisure may appear more evident once we come to the topic of the feast. About a century ago, under the influence of the early anthropological writings of Edward Tylor and James Frazer, among others, a shared narrative emerged: the idea that seasonal customs represented a specific heritage of the countryside as opposed to urban culture, that they dated back to pre-Christian times and had remained virtually unchanged over centuries, as well as being performed by people unaware of their true meanings. As Hutton has convincingly argued, however, such standard tenet has vanished under more recent, closer scrutiny, concluding in the reversal of each of those statements.[7]

Next comes, in Borsay's reckoning, a period arching from the 1530s to the 1650s. This is strongly characterized by the advent of the Reformation, a development that marked it—in Scotland even more deeply than in England—by the Protestant concerns for the recreational culture inherited from late medieval Christianity. As Borsay puts it, this brought to a "process of attrition by which England was deprived of some of its traditional merry-making, such as mumming, maypoles, church-ales and summer games."[8] At the roots of the changes was a reevaluation of the importance of hard labor, which obliged people to reassess the interaction between work, leisure, and religion. The subsequent phase, a return to a more relaxed attitude towards pastimes after the Stuart Restoration, goes beyond our chronology. However, Borsay mentions that one of the features ordinarily attached to it, namely a shift towards a commercialization of leisure, had in fact been partially anticipated during the previous period: he singles out "the rise of the spa town and horse races and the flowering of the Elizabethan and Jacobean commercial theatre in London" as significant Tudor and early Stuart anticipations of the leisure world to come.[9] These specific historical examples, as well as the whole assessment of the general cultural development, will be worth remembering within our historical sketch.

If we try to generalize from Borsay's chronology and evaluate to what extent, and by what adjustments, it may be extended beyond Britain and applied to the rest of Europe, we must consider the scholarship on festive culture and the time shifts this has suggested in reconstructing the European experience; and assess how the early modern religious developments may have affected the culture and practice of leisure activities elsewhere.

The first point will be explored in the next section with specific reference to the work of Mikhail Bakhtin and Peter Burke, considering that it concerns the contemporary perception and organization of time. What must be weighed is the role festive culture—both in urban contexts and in villages—may have played as a fulcrum of sociability on weekends and special occasions, for whom, and with what developments through time. If compared with Borsay's British case, a generally accepted interpretation would perhaps postpone the crisis of a "European ritual year" by about fifty years, witnessing an intensification of social critique and pressure towards a reform of mores emerging closer to the end of the sixteenth century.

To the second point—religion as a significant variable—we will also return below. When considering it throughout Europe, one misses clear-cut turning points such as the loss of influence of the English Puritans after the Interregnum (1649–60). It is rather at the "crisis of the European consciousness" that one tends to attach a perceivable, more generalized decline of the cultural impact of Christianity in its various denominations on people's minds and choices.[10] But that, again, is a matter for the next volume in the present series.

SPACE AND TIME

Next in our outline comes a delineation of the spaces and times that were perceived and used as appropriate for leisure activities. Part of the argument in favor of the theory of a birth of leisure consubstantial with the Industrial Revolution is the idea that before the eighteenth century neither the time nor the space for leisure were distinguished from those for work. The promiscuity of diverse activities within the same times and spaces has indeed been considered, although not unanimously among scholars, as a characteristic of preindustrial societies. It has been noted that "the recreational activities of the Middle Ages ... recall the old primitive confusion as to where work ended and leisure began."[11] This said, multifunctional times and spaces should not be simply discarded as uninteresting with a teleological preference for developments to come, but rather appreciated in their own terms as typical of past/different cultures. Also, the period under consideration witnessed a tendency towards the separation and specialization of times and spaces due to a variety of factors, including the religious and political pressures on festive culture.

One social context and phenomenon that exemplifies such developments is the *villeggiatura*, the habit, for upper-class Renaissance Italians, of spending leisurely summer vacations in purpose-built countryside villas.[12] That some spaces (and times) are perceived as designated for leisure may occasionally be the result of a socio-economic shift by which they have lost a previous different meaning and purpose. From this perspective, based on the North Sea experience, it has been suggested that, in the early modern period, "the seaside was becoming a destination, not a harbour on the way to somewhere else over the water; and it was a playground, not a place of work and war."[13] While this development became more noticeable in the eighteenth century, its roots have been recognized as already perceivable in the seventeenth-century Netherlands. "Visitors to Holland who were interested in the struggle of the Dutch with the sea showed their countrymen the road to the sea as a spectacle." Literary sources suggest that "taking a ride or stroll along the seaside, drinking in a tavern or buying fresh fish on the beach was common practice in Holland even for the upper class."[14] Dutch landscape painting played a particular role in this story. During the first quarter of the seventeenth century sandy shores bordered with dunes had been depicted under the pretext of giving account of exceptional events. From the 1620s, the beach and the strand became the backdrop of an independent genre, whose aim was celebrating fishermen and other laborers: a painter like Jan van Goyen could hire a boat specially to draw such scenes and fill several sketch-books (Figure 9.1).

> Towards the middle of the seventeenth century, the meaning and the content of the beach scene began to change. … Admittedly, the beach remained the site of the fishermen's labour and an extension of the public space of the village; but it also showed the culmination of the ritual which was the urban outing. The shore was scattered with elegant bourgeois walkers engaged in flirtatious conversations or dashing horsemen, while other visitors came to gaze at the open sea.[15]

Commercial spaces, and particularly some primarily devoted to sell a variety of refreshments, played a fundamental role in shaping people's spare time and the forms of sociability that it contributed to define. "For the vast majority of our period the alehouse or pub, for the common people, and inn and tavern, for the better off, was the most important single commercial social institution for most the adult male population. Numbers on the ground were impressive."[16] They traditionally hosted also a series of games and forms of entertainment. Europe was (whereas it only partially still is) characterized by a geographical divide between a wine-drinking south and an ale- and beer-drinking north with a central zone where the two habits overlapped and a border for the cultivation of grapes and making of wine which went further north than today. This distinction brought different customs in production and consumption alike, highly relevant in discussing spaces and subject to developments through time. It has been

FIGURE 9.1 Jacob Esselens, *Coast Scene*, 1626–87. Metropolitan Museum of Art, New York. Public domain.

suggested that a significant shift occurred in England as an ironic effect of the Puritan pressure to reform manners and behavior. The parish church had been the center of the traditional community in a variety of senses, with the churchyard also providing the space for the meeting of guild and fraternity members and the holding of festive rituals, plays and performances, not religious in their contents and meaning. Church-ales—the selling of ale or beer in the churchyard after services to raise money for the parish—were a typical activity from this respect in their exemplifying a compromise between a secular pastime and the pious aim that could justify it. Protestant Reformers fiercely attacked these practices as ungodly; by doing so, however, they were instrumental in determining the transfer of similar communal activities to the alehouse:

> From the early seventeenth century, then, alehouses became for the poorer half of society the only alternative they had to the rituals of sociability that had formerly taken place on parish church property. We are speaking here of much more than a space for the buying and selling of beer (hopped ale), as various games, mummers, and other social activities that once took place in church now took place in the local alehouse.[17]

The early history of coffee consumption and coffeehouses also tells a very interesting story, one that acquires additional significance by offering a rich example of cultural transfer; it is in fact a story that originally develops in the Near East, in the urban Islamic coffeehouses of the fifteenth and sixteenth centuries, and is brought to Europe first in the form of the accounts of travellers, who encountered and experienced them abroad, later in a dramatic example of transcultural borrowing, with the import of, and familiarization with, a formerly exotic practice. As with the case of the venues devoted to the drinking of alcohol, it presents economic aspects, but ultimately represents a major development in social customs, by providing a fashionable and distinctive drinking habit and turning into a central space for urban sociability. Although the establishment of coffeehouses in the West occurred after the period considered in this volume, in London from the 1650s, in Paris from the 1670s, and Venice from the 1680s, the beans were already available in shops and Europeans could witness and share the habits of immigrant communities from the Levant as with the case of the Turks resident in Venice.[18]

The construction of dedicated places for the performance of music and drama offers another clear example of specialization of leisure places; it is ordinarily presented together with a development of professionalism, away from the home as well as court, or academy practice of *dilettanti* (amateurs), in the direction of performance before an increasingly paying audience. Examples are offered by Andrea Palladio's Teatro Olimpico in Vicenza (1580–5) and by the Teatro Farnese in Parma (1618)—though their two contexts, a Renaissance humanistic academy and a princely court, tell the specific story of their patronage and use. The trend towards commercialization is more visible in Elizabethan and Jacobean theaters in London, as well as in the birth of the business of the opera in seventeenth-century Venice—a scene particularly effective in the cultural construction of roles of femininity.[19] There are also examples of dedicated spaces built for one type of leisure activity, subsequently recycled to serve a different function due to a shift in habits and demand. The reuse may entail, as a side effect, an influence exercised on the new practice, as from some kind of inertia of the older structures and customs. This happened with a number of rooms especially designed, in Renaissance Italian palaces, for the game of real tennis; when, from the late sixteenth century, its fashion started declining, their spaces and organization, including a particular way of positioning stands for the viewers, were transformed into, and transmitted to, theatrical performances.[20]

As already hinted, festive culture, with a rich ritual calendar, traditionally represented, for a large portion of the population, the most visible legal opportunity to enjoy leisure activities. The story of carnival and laughter has become iconic in the critical tradition of interpreting power relations and social identities since the international circulation of the work of Mikhail Bakhtin.[21] Half a century later that reconstruction appears to have aged badly and to have little to offer to a postideological historical approach. It may be nevertheless worth remembering that, as the twentieth-century historical imagination had it, seasonal feasting was the stronghold of a widespread counterculture alternative to the dominant one, and inclined towards getting a full taste of earthly pleasures without betting on or postponing too much on the afterlife. Social change and the efforts of disciplining institutions would have put a substantial stop to that atmosphere somewhere between the sixteenth and seventeenth centuries.

Sundays and holidays in particular were the ground of a three-way conflict of destination: In a period in which they still took a significant amount of the year, should they be regarded as time appropriate for work, rest, or worship? The Sabbath day—as Puritans put it (though Christians of different denominations were not necessarily more lenient)—was time for neither work nor play; nevertheless, for the sake of work, in an environment characterized by a rising work ethic, it was necessary to find space for rest and recreation (not necessarily purely spiritual) at some point during the week and year.

Overall, leisure (play) entertains a special relation with space and time insomuch as it belongs into a sphere of its own. Also, time and space are experienced differently within the context of the ritual year. And some leisure activities—say, some forms of reading or theatrical performances—may allow people to travel through time and/or space with their imagination.

SOCIAL HIERARCHY, GENDER, AND AGE GROUPS

The obvious consideration that people belonging to different social groups may have different perceptions, evaluations, and experiences of work and leisure sometimes takes the form of the idea that leisure and work are, respectively, the monopoly (privilege or burden as each may be) of two distinct classes. In order to discuss this specific theory, and then move to a more general consideration of the social factor in the history of work and leisure, it will be appropriate to say a few words on the concepts we use to distinguish social strata in the early modern age, considering that both the categories in use at the time (the "emic" approach) and those adopted by later scholars looking back (the "etic" one) are various and controversial.

The key vocabulary is that of class. The notion has dominated the imagination and redefinition of social stratification since the Industrial Revolution. However, the Marxist practice of applying it to preindustrial societies as well has come under serious criticism at least since Max Weber pointed out the coexistence of status defined by legal rather than economic condition; it has therefore recently fallen out of use, in favor of more complex and situated models of describing social groups and their interaction.

The notion of a "leisure class" was introduced in the discourse of social theory by Thorstein Veblen. Veblen's interpretation is based on an evolutionary reconstruction of the emergence of conspicuous consumption in modern American society from earlier stages or economic cultures. His early critique of the moral and economic value of consumer culture is impressive: it uncovers the insincerity of the association of leisure with freedom and satisfaction and highlights the element of manipulative obligation. His perspective is, however, the result of a limited notion of leisure as per se nonproductive, as well as of a nostalgic view of the lost world of workmanship.[22]

One of the most influential works of sociology that played a comparable critical role during the twentieth century is Pierre Bourdieu's study of distinction.[23] Although the author presented it as some kind of ethnography of contemporary France, it may equally offer fruitful insights about taste as a dimension of cultural practices in the past: it would in fact be intriguing to try to explore in detail and in all their implications, *mutatis mutandis*, early modern equivalents of Bourdieu's monitoring and discussion of class preferences for, and evaluations of, different types of food, music, books, sports, or entertainments. His analysis thus emphasizes the importance of culture in producing social distinctions and hierarchies.

Catharina Lis and Hugo Soly have suggested that, far from being proud of not working and engaging in pastimes, members of the preindustrial elites were keen to emphasize the social importance of their daily duties, and only towards the end of the nineteenth century, once industrialization had thoroughly transformed the social landscape, they moved away from the need to play that role and justify their privileged status, thus acquiring a new liberty of pursuing pleasure and entertainment per se.[24] We may wonder to what extent and with what nuances the early modern elites perceived themselves as engaged in work and/or leisure activities. What value did they attach to their daily routines? To what extent did they themselves distinguish between work and leisure at all, and to what extent and how did they distinguish their activities from those of the hoi polloi?

Part of the question is, inevitably, what we—even more, what they—consider(ed) as work. Past and present groups have deliberately emphasized, on occasion, the importance of such service and duties as well exemplified by those traditionally associated with nobility and the clergy, clearly not to be confused with labor, nevertheless not ordinarily understood as leisure either. Elias and Dunning could include mass attendance into the wider notion of leisure activity, but would exclude from it the celebrating priest. As the reader of the medieval volume of this set will undoubtedly be aware, the tripartite model, according to which a community needed priests, knights, and laborers and each group served the whole, was an ideology that sustained the given social order and justified the privilege by which some men were exempt from the constrictions of labor. However, this was contested, and various professional groups struggled to defend the importance of their own occupation and the need to be recognized as a dignified rank.[25]

A subtheme within this issue is posed by the distinction between the physical and the mental, which applies to work and leisure likewise. Is there perhaps a certain proximity that couples non-manual service and intellectual recreations with one another, leaving physical jobs and lively sports to form an opposite group? Perhaps so to some extent, although one should never forget how much the Western medical tradition from antiquity, through Arabic medieval sources up to the European Renaissance emphasized the need of a significantly energetic physical exercise precisely for the preservation of the health of the sedentary *literati*.

Although ultimately the perception and attitudes held by historical agents would need searching and testing by comparing a variety of sources, including ego documents, there are bodies of prescriptive literature that, despite testifying to norms and expectations rather than practice and behavior, may offer us significant clues on the complex interplay between status and occupations, duties and off-duty alike. One of the most obvious among these genres is the influential series of sixteenth-century Italian texts on manners, the key

European reference books for elite lifestyle over the following two or three hundred years. Baldassarre Castiglione's *Il libro del cortegiano* ([1528] 1994) and Stefano Guazzo's *Civil conversatione* ([1574] 1738) offer two complementary accounts of such interplay. As published and widely circulated and translated texts, incidentally, they testify to the importance of the book and of practices of reading in contemporary society.

In Castiglione, a striking wealth of skills and practices we would easily recognize as leisure is introduced in the first two books as required from the ideal courtier: the latter should be both versed in sports and physical exercises and in languages and letters, a good musician, painter, sculptor able to excel in all these arts with nonchalance, that is, by turning art into a second nature and concealing the effort it takes. There are, however, limitations to the image of the Italian aristocrat as a full-time performer and art connoisseur that we should not overlook in Castiglione's text; in the end, when readers enter the fourth and last book, they surprisingly find out that all the courtly arts described at length over the previous sections are now described as futile per se, unless they serve the purpose of conquering the prince's trust and guiding him to perform his duties at best in the public interest. Such resemantization of the arts of courtly life as only worthwhile if they provide a means to higher ends defines Renaissance aesthetics and ethics as inseparable and should work as a caveat not to intend the aristocracy's daily occupations as mere idle pursuits.

Guazzo presents us with a partially different social context and personnel, his dialogue mostly consisting of a conversation between a physician and a knight, representing the world of the professions together with feudal nobility, an urban elite emerging with renewed self-consciousness. The literary form of fictional conversations staged one of the most common practices of everyday sociability. Itself situated in between work and leisure: Guazzo's text, in addition, presents the art of conversation itself as its specific subject, the social skill under debate. On the whole, the two Italian Renaissance classics seem to suggest that, if early modern aristocrats were self-consciously using time at their ease for the mere sake of it based on their position of power, they usually kept it for themselves rather than advertising it.

To what extent people belonging to different social echelons shared a festive culture and leisure activities has been a matter of discussion and can be reasonably assessed by combining prescriptive and descriptive source material. Peter Burke has provided the most authoritative of such assessments: although the very notion of popular culture is controversial, it is difficult to do without, and does not have to be understood as totally independent from that of the elites.[26] In fact, a tradition of studies during the last quarter of the twentieth century focused precisely on the interaction between different cultural levels. Inspired by Bakhtin, Burke suggested the turn from the sixteenth to the seventeenth century as the point of a significant shift, a withdrawal of the elites from previously shared culture and practice and a triumph of the spirit of Lent over Carnival, in the form of control and repression of popular revels. The Bakhtinian culture that supposedly underwent such transformation (ultimately falling into oblivion before its rediscovery by the Romantics) was a world dominated by the lower part of the body—the stomach, the bowels, and the sexual organs—in specular opposition to the elite value system and concern for the upper half.[27]

An important aspect in any consideration of the relationship between leisurely occupations and social structure is the question whether some habits were imitated along one or the other direction on the status ladder. According to a widespread interpretative model, "the commercialization of leisure is a function of expanding wealth, percolating through society, from the top downwards, in a series of chronological phases, each characterized by the absorption of a class or social group/s into the market place for leisure, until the whole society is encompassed."[28] The example given by the quoted historian is the British holiday resort: "Spas emerge, under a mixture of royal, aristocratic and gentry patronage, as places of fashionable health cure in the later sixteenth and early seventeenth century."[29]

Among entertainments popular with the working classes, those we have seen practiced near parish churches or at alehouses are well attested. A detail one should not underestimate is that they were traditionally held on such holidays as the feast of the local saint or the anniversary of the foundation of a church. Their relationship with the sacred, therefore, is ambiguous; hence the battle of moralists, particularly (though by no means solely) Protestants, who wanted to wash away all the sinful debauchery they saw embodied in such gatherings. Also, to the Protestant mind, popular revels and Catholic worship—with its materiality and performative nature, from the cult of relics to processions—tended to overlap and blend. One of the most interesting documents the period has left us is the northern iconography of the *kermis* (the abovementioned church or saint's feast). A series of German and Netherlandish artists invented the genre of the woodcut representation of peasant festivals—in its materiality, itself an object of leisure consumption; and although much scholarly controversy has debated the attitude the drawings convey, the fact that feasting and dancing are shown together with scenes of sexual promiscuity, vomiting, and defecating leaves little doubt that part at least of the message was of moral reproach (Figure 9.2).[30]

Another widespread activity in more than one European country was the medieval football (French *soule*) that was played in the fields between villages. It could be rough and aggressive and has been brought as clear example of the kind of popular sport

FIGURE 9.2 Pieter Bruegel the Younger, *The Return from the Kermis*, 1564–1637/8. Phillips, London.

that underwent a process of civilization, eventually tamed into modern team games.[31] A contemporary critic could easily depict it as "rather ... a friendly kinde of fight, then a play or recreation."[32] More literal fights were, on the other hand, another well-known form of popular entertainment, sometimes played on bridges, which have attracted anthropological reading as a form of ritual. In the case of the Venetian "war of the fists," patrician patronage has been observed, which offered the opportunity for betting.[33]

What has been said in the matter of social groups partly also applies to gender roles. Ironically entitled *Women's Work*, a recent volume on women and dance has suggested that the performing arts may have opened up to the European female population not just professional opportunities but also the potential for a skillful use of their body, at the same time socially expected from them and open to unexpected forms of display.[34] In general, occupations traditionally regarded as gender-specific, whether conceived as work or leisure, could play a prominent part in defining roles and represent challenging barriers to the questioning of gender attributes; previously less qualified, dance began to operate precisely as a feminine marker, in a way hunting did for men.[35]

In term of age groups, childhood and youth represent highly significant stages for a consideration of the leisure cultures of the past. The cases of early modern England and the Netherlands, among others, have been studied from this perspective and it has been convincingly argued that the historian's concerns should not be limited to give an account of adult opinions and prescriptions concerning youth. The historical investigation on childhood and youth has been in fact exceedingly dominated by one interpretation that fell into the abovementioned methodological trap—namely, Philippe Ariès' idea that the early stages of life did not represent a distinguished, recognized, and culturally elaborated phase in preindustrial Europe.[36] Despite some intriguing clues, such as the early modern infant dressed and physically depicted as a small adult, and with all its popularity with the general public, this thesis has long been discredited among specialists, and would prove heuristically unhelpful in our context. Similarly, the discovery of the youth cultures of the past induced by the experience of the 1960s has for a long time limited itself to dating their emergency to the eighteenth century, as if family structures and sentiments had suddenly changed under the influence of processes of modernization, and not even juvenile delinquency existed before that time.[37]

There is also a demographic side of this story, and for repeated periods over the sixteenth and seventeenth centuries in England it has been shown how visible the large and growing section of the population under fifteen (or generally young) was, a fact that was clearly noticed by contemporary observers. In a culture where processes of socialization of the youth were dominated by such institutions as apprenticeship and servitude, age relations were affected by a variety of factors, including poverty, immigration, and urban growth, as well as religious concerns in the age of Reformation.[38]

As for Holland's Golden Age, it has been argued that the group that led it to its outstanding international prominence was a generation of young men distinctively self-aware and rebellious in their attitudes towards tradition and social norm, as testified by their very appearances—wearing long hair and colorful clothing—and habits: heavy drinking, tobacco smoking, being promiscuous, and singing lewd songs; in sum, a comprehensive youth culture, which also gained a recognizable expression and circulation in print. During the 1610s and 1620s, a noticeable role was played by an increasing circulation of elaborate songbooks, at the same time a form of entertainment and a vehicle for the strengthening of group identity.[39]

At the opposite end of the spectrum, old age is a condition undoubtedly endowed with a leisure culture of its own. Regardless of the varying computations of the stages of aging, inevitably depending on the dominant health conditions and average life expectancy, the life span following ordinary working age is associated with notions and practices of retirement and rest, gentleness in physical activity, and compensatory spiritual satisfaction.

CULTURAL AND REGIONAL VARIATION

Throughout Europe, there is a significant sharing of leisure practices, sometimes in the form of a transnational success and circulation of cultural forms originating in some part of the continent.[40] Spatial variation includes traditional oppositions such as the one between urban and rural cultures. As is true for the distinction between higher and lower echelons of society, town and country were traditionally characterized by distinguished ways of setting the time, space, and meaning attached to work and other activities; at the same time, they never stopped influencing one another, the town usually acting as the agent of innovation, the country as a source of refreshing inspiration. Religion significantly intervened during the period, introducing a strong factor of cultural diversity as well as transnational affinities between coreligionists. The impact of the Reformation has already been mentioned, and similar points could be made about other cultural developments—including humanism and the Renaissance—whose chronology, geographical distribution, and depth of influence left varying marks in different territories and populations, which were added on top of preexisting elements of diversity. It is relatively easy to see how Renaissance developments in literature and the arts, including the performing arts, offered a growing public increasing opportunity for rather sophisticated leisure activities.

To describe the Reformation simply as a killjoy movement that channelled time and energies away from leisure and fun towards work and serious concerns would be a gross oversimplification. Contrasting views and practice can be seen throughout religious denominations. Also, similar patterns have been identified in the way Catholic and Protestant reformers alike moved towards a stricter disciplining of the body of the faithful, exemplifying the effects of a civilizing process.[41]

The extreme end of the spectrum of cultural diversity is represented by the stereotype of the lazy savage, attested in the classical tradition and renovated by the cultural encounters of the age of discoveries.[42] The other side of the coin is the idealization of the *selvaticus* in terms comparable to that traditional for the *rusticus*, which is showed for instance in some sixteenth-century French literature, where indigenous *otium* may testify of a (tropical) peace of mind, the privilege of a Golden Age.[43]

VARIETIES OF LEISURE

The period witnessed continuity and developments in vocabulary and perceptions, with overlapping and interaction between the connotations associated with notions of rest, leisure, and vacation or retreat.[44] A particular dimension of this cultural history of concepts and of clusters of words is offered by the timeless comparison between active versus contemplative life, which had found classical and Christian expressions and solutions, and by the end of the Middle Ages saw humanists, among other things, marking their distance from what they perceived as monastic idleness. The philosophical assessment of the matter in the writing of Plato and Aristotle remained most influential of all throughout the period; notwithstanding differentiating nuances, both identified intellectual reflection as the highest form of life, one only available to an elite endowed with leisure.[45] Despite the positive evaluation that Renaissance culture appears to have held of anything active and dynamic, a significant appreciation of the need for thoughtful rest and productive retreat was far from lacking. This cultural heritage underwent a series of adaptations, whose geography and chronology was strongly influenced by political and religious developments.[46]

Generally speaking, leisure tends to be perceived as the dominion of pleasure and of the disruption of the ordinary (although see above for Veblen's critique); the recreational consumption of food and drink (without forgetting sex) provides one of its most obvious manifestations.[47]

Throughout the period, historical developments affected the leisure experience to which many people had access; consider, for instance, new opportunities for travel, as well as the changes produced by processes of urbanization and by the advancement of literacy.

TOWARDS A LEISURE MARKET

Standard chronologies postponing the birth of leisure proper to the eighteenth century used the development of the commercial supply and demand of leisure goods and services as evidence that nothing quite comparable was available before that date. However, we have seen Borsay singling out, in the early modern English experience, spas, horse races, and theaters, as areas in which leisure was already moving in that direction. An example is offered by James Burbage, Elizabethan actor and impresario, who built one of the first London theaters since antiquity.

In relationship to what has been labelled an industrious revolution, an expression first coined to describe economic developments in East Asia, and dated back to the long sixteenth century, the birth of a consumer society has been dated very differently and nowadays is occasionally used with reference to the Italian Renaissance.[48] Material cultures, such as that of clothing, are the object of fascinating new enquiries, which discover the extent to which past agents were aware of its symbolic meaning and used it consciously.[49] Indeed, since at least the 1980s "materialism" had been identified as a distinctive early modern consumer development, with particular attention to the market of printed images, a type of object that surely served leisure as well as functional needs.[50]

If humanism and the Renaissance contributed in their own way to promote a new culture of leisure consumerism, the reverse is no less true—namely, that awareness of the worldly goods coveted by sections of the contemporary public helps us to shed more light on the exact nature and social implications of such cultural phenomena; take, for example, the profusion of precious objects depicted in Italian artworks, including such comparatively rare and exotic items as oriental rugs, and you will have some idea of the complex interplay that existed between the pleasure sought in sensual experience, the value attributed to luxury and refined taste, and the symbolic capital this would have represented for patrons and owners.[51]

LEISURE AND POWER

The interplay between the dialectics of work and leisure and relationships of power is an inevitable ingredient of what has already been said about social groups and uneven exposition to labor and rest. It is also attested by the interest paid by institutions and agencies (religious, political and administrative, judicial) towards the time, place, and any other way and circumstance in which individuals and groups were authorized or encouraged to participate in a variety of recreational activities. Legislation on playing games, including that issued by local authorities, abounded from the late Middle Ages, even if it may be regarded as evidence of concerns about the social troubles that tended to accompany their performance, rather than for the ludic sphere itself.[52] In an ambivalence between policies of "hands on" or "hands off" the world of leisure, political and religious institutions intervened and manipulated theater more often than other spheres. Censorship and the control of the companies of actors were introduced by acts of the English Parliament from the reign of Henry VIII, not to mention the stricter ordinances and army theater raids of the Interregnum.[53] The use of drama as an instrument of propaganda was widespread among religious authorities of different Christian denominations throughout Europe.

Legislation intervened with forms of regulation of popular recreation that have been also considered as an example of the rising role of the central state in the early modern period. The early Stuart *Book of Sport* offers an example of royal intervention to protect the legitimacy of recreations deemed as innocent versus the wholesale prohibition of Sunday pastimes advocated by evangelical Protestants. The attempt to abolish dance and theater on Sundays was not the monopoly of the Reformed side: however, it ultimately failed in Catholic lands too.[54]

Furthermore, "the importance of, say, royal patronage should not be underestimated. Early modern British monarchs, particularly the Tudors and Stuarts, operated courts that played, and were expected to play, a leading role in cultivating elite arts and pastimes such as music, theatre, masques, horse racing, golf, hunting, painting and architecture."[55] The establishment of Newmarket as the headquarters of horse racing, for instance, owed much to royal patronage. Gambling is another area in which governments' intervention was not limited to repression; in the late medieval Italian city, within a process of social disciplining aware of the need to fund the expenses of public authorities, exclusive rights for setting up gambling were granted to given individuals and sites, while prohibiting the activity elsewhere as illegal.[56]

Utopias and imaginary social orders present another side of the story, which a long tradition—in learned fiction and in popular culture alike (for all, consider *The Land of Cockaigne*)—fills with food, drink, all sorts of pleasure and lack of work or any other obligation, a paradoxical confirmation of the leisure preference culturally associated with the working classes. Ultimately, the implementation via legislation and law enforcement of a calendar in which holidays and opportunities for festive ritual behavior shrank, while working time expanded, must have played a key role, both symbolically and practically.[57]

In conclusion, while eighteenth- and nineteenth-century social and economic change undoubtedly produced a contrast and interplay between work and leisure that has since become established up to the point of appearing natural and self-explanatory, the early modern world experienced a leisure culture of its own, or rather a multiplicity of them, whose importance should not be underestimated in historical perspective. The variety of activities, as well as the forms of accepted rest and comparative inactivity, that it involved were not necessarily understood as undertaken purely for fun. However, this fact itself deserves historical inquiry and attention; in moving from one epoch and social context to another, we do not simply witness a given range of human activities shifting in their evaluation and dropping in or out of sets of categories by which they are given meaning and value—so that, for instance, coffee drinking, ball games, and theatergoing may gain or lose in their comparative social respectability accordingly. It is the categories themselves that alter: the notions of play, pastime, recreation, or entertainment, the measure in which they are provided by professionals to a public and the social acceptance of such professionalization, the need to justify a leisure preference according to one's status, are all socially determined and culturally specific variables that offer an intriguing perspective on the way of life of the past, one without which we would only consider the daily existence and anthropological experience of our ancestors from a very partial point of view.

NOTES

Introduction

1. See Ann Bermingham and John Brewer, eds., *The Consumption of Culture, 1600–1800: Image, Object, Text* (New York: Routledge, 1995); Neil McKendrick, John Brewer, and John H. Plumb, *The Birth of a Consumer Society: The Commercialization of Eighteenth-Century England* (Bloomington: Indiana University Press, 1982); John Brewer and Roy Porter, eds., *Consumption and the World of Goods* (London: Routledge, 1993).
2. For a recent state of the art, Stephan R. Epstein and Maarten Prak, eds., *Guilds, Innovation, and the European Economy, 1400–1800* (Cambridge: Cambridge University Press, 2008). See also the debate between Stephan R. Epstein and Sheilagh Ogilvie: Sheilagh Ogilvie, "'Whatever is, is right?' Economic Institutions in Pre-Industrial Europe," *Economic History Review* 60, no. 4 (2007): 649–84; Stephan R. Epstein, "Craft Guilds in the Pre-Modern Economy: A Discussion," *Economic History Review* 61, no. 1 (2008): 155–74; Sheilagh Ogilvie, "Rehabilitating the Guilds: A Reply," *Economic History Review* 61, no. 1 (2008): 175–82.
3. Elinor Ostrom, *Governing the Commons: The Evolution of Institutions for Collective Action* (Cambridge: Cambridge University Press, 1990); Elinor Ostrom, *Understanding Institutional Diversity* (Princeton, NJ: Princeton University Press, 2005). For recent historiography see Tine De Moor, "What Do We Have in Common? A Comparative Framework for Old and New Literature on the Commons," *International Review of Social History* 57, no. 2 (2012): 269–90; Tine De Moor, *The Dilemma of the Commoners – Understanding the Use of Common-Pool Resources in Long-Term Perspective* (Cambridge: Cambridge University Press, 2015).
4. See Harry Braverman, *Labor and Monopoly Capital: The Degradation of Work in the Twentieth Century* (New York: Monthly Review Press, 1974); Stephen Marglin, "What Do Bosses Do? The Origins and Functions of Hierarchy in Capitalist Production. Part I," *The Review of Radical Political Economics* 6, no. 2 (1974): 60–112.
5. Catharina Lis and Hugo Soly, *Worthy Efforts: Attitudes to Work and Workers in Pre-Industrial Europe* (Leiden: Brill, 2012).
6. Martin Luther, *Von Kauffshandlung und Wucher* (Wittenberg, 1524).
7. John Calvin, *Institutes of the Christian Religion*, trans. Henry Beveridge (Edinburgh: The Calvin Translation Society, 1845), esp. bk. III, chap. 24.
8. Amintori Fanfani, *Catholicism, Protestantism and Capitalism* (Norfolk, VA: IHS Press, 2002); Richard H. Tawney, *Religion and the Rise of Capitalism* (Hong Kong: Hesperides Press, 2006); Brad Gregory, *The Unintended Reformation: How a Religious Revolution Secularized Society* (Cambridge, MA: Harvard University Press, 2012).
9. Max Weber, *Die protestantische Ethik und der "Geist" des Kapitalismus*, reprint 1904/05 (Weinheim: Beltz Athenäum, 1996), 19.
10. Ibid., 19.
11. Ibid., 26.

12. Gordon Marshall, *In Search of the Spirit of Capitalism* (New York: Columbia University Press, 1982), 45.
13. George Ovitt, Jr., *The Restoration of Perfection: Labor and Technology in Medieval Culture* (New Brunswick, NJ: Rutgers University Press, 1989).
14. Lynn White, Jr., *Medieval Technology and Social Change* (Oxford: Oxford University Press, 1975).
15. Jeroen Deploige, "By the Labor of Whose Hands? Two Reflections on the Appreciation of Work in Medieval Christianity," *The Low Countries Journal of Social and Economic History* 11, no. 1 (2014): 89–104.
16. Jacques Le Goff, *Time, Work and Culture in the Middle Ages* (Chicago, IL: University of Chicago Press, 1982).
17. Thomas Max Safley, *Children of the Laboring Poor: Expectation and Experience among the Orphans of Early Modern Augsburg* (Leiden: Brill, 2005).
18. Bronislaw Geremek, *The Poor in Late Medieval France* (Cambridge: Cambridge University Press, 1989), passim.
19. Juan Luis Vives, *De subventione pauperum sive de humanis necessitatibus. Libri II*, ed. and trans. Constant Matheeussen and Charles Fantazzi (Leiden: Brill, 2002; *Selected Works of J. L. Vives*, vol. IV). See also the still relevant synthesis by Catharina Lis and Hugo Soly, *Poverty and Capitalism in Pre-Industrial Europe* (Brighton: The Harvester Press, 1979).
20. Pamela H. Smith, *The Body of the Artisan: Art and Experiment in the Scientific Revolution* (Chicago, IL: University of Chicago Press, 2004); Pamela O. Long, *Artisan/Practitioners and the Rise of the New Sciences, 1400–1600* (Corvallis: Oregon State University Press, 2011), chap. 2.
21. Pamela H. Smith, "Artists as Scientists: Nature and Realism in Early Modern Europe," *Endeavour* 24, no. 1 (2000): 13–21; and "Vital Spirits: Redemption, Artisanship, and the New Philosophy in Early Modern Europe," in *Rethinking the Scientific Revolution*, ed. Margaret J. Osler (Cambridge: Cambridge University Press, 2000), 119–36.
22. Richard J. Oosterhoff, "*Idiotae*, Mathematics, and Artisans: The Untutored Mind and the Discovery of Nature in the Fabrist Circle," *Intellectual History Review* 24, no. 3 (2014): 301–19.
23. Jean-François Gauvin, "Artisans, Machines, and Descartes's *Organon*," *History of Science* 44, no. 2 (2006): 187–216.
24. Oosterhoff, "*Idiotae*," 304.
25. Timothy J. Reiss, *Knowledge, Discovery and Imagination in Early Modern Europe* (Cambridge: Cambridge University Press, 1997).
26. Hélène Vérin, "La réduction en art et la science pratique au XVIe siècle," in *Institutions et conventions: La réflexivité de l´action économique*, eds. Robert Salais, Élisabeth Chatel, and Dorothée Rivaud-Danset (Paris: Éditions de l'EHESS, 1998), 119–45; Hélène Vérin, "Généalogie de la 'réduction en art': Aux sources de la rationalité moderne," in *Les nouvelles raisons du savoir: Vers une prospective de la connaissance*, eds. Thierry Gaudin and Armand Hatchuel (La Tour d'Aigues: Éditions de l'Aube, 2002), 29–41; Pascal Dubourg Glatigny and Hélène Vérin, eds., *Réduire en art: La technologie de la Renaissance aux Lumières* (Paris: Éditions de la Maison des sciences de l'homme, 2008).
27. Zirka Zaremba Filipczak, *Picturing Art in Antwerp, 1550–1700* (Princeton, NJ: Princeton University Press, 1987), 11–19, 40–45. For recent views and references, see Lis and Soly, *Worthy Efforts*, 365–99.
28. Bert De Munck, "Le produit du talent ou la production de talent? La formation des artistes à l'Académie des beaux-arts à Anvers aux XVIIe et XVIIIe siècles," *Paedagogica Historica*

37, no. 3 (2001): 569–607; and "Corpses, Live Models, and Nature: Assessing Skills and Knowledge before the Industrial Revolution (case: Antwerp)," *Technology and Culture* 51, no. 2 (2010): 332–56.
29. Filipczak, *Picturing Art in Antwerp*, 40–45. Also Luke Syson and Dora Thornton, *Objects of Virtue: Art in Renaissance Italy* (Los Angeles, CA: J. Paul Getty Museum, 2001), 135–6.
30. Knut Schulz, *Denn sie lieben die Freiheit so Sehr... Kommunale Aufstände und Entstehung des europäischen Bürgertums im Hochmittelalter* (Darmstadt: Wissenschaftliche Buchgesellschaft, 1992), 104–31; Jan Dumolyn and Jelle Haemers, "Patterns of Urban Rebellion in Medieval Flanders," *Journal of Medieval History* 31, no. 4 (2005): 369–93.
31. Steven L. Kaplan, *La fin des corporations* (Paris: Fayard, 2001); Heinz–Gerhard Haupt, ed., *Das Ende der Zünfte: Ein europäischer Vergleich* (Göttingen: Vandenhoeck & Ruprecht, 2002); Alberto Guenzi, Paola Massa, and F. Piola Caselli, eds., *Guilds, Markets and Work Regulations in Italy, 16th–19th Centuries* (Aldershot: Ashgate, 1998).
32. Marc Boone and Maarten Prak, "Rulers, Patricians and Burghers: The Great and Little Tradition of Urban Revolt in the Low Countries," in *A Miracle Mirrored: The Dutch Republic in European Perspective*, eds. Karel Davids and Jan Lucassen (Cambridge: Cambridge University Press, 1995), 99–134.
33. For example, Alfons K.L. Thijs, *Van "werkwinkel" tot "fabriek." De textielnijverheid te Antwerpen (einde 15de–begin 19de eeuw)* (Brussels: Gemeentekrediet, 1987), 219–57; Arnd Klüge, *Die Zünfte* (Stuttgart: Franz Steiner Verlag, 2009), 172–3; Bert De Munck, "One Counter and Your Own Account: Redefining Illicit Labour in Early Modern Antwerp," *Urban History* 37, no. 1 (2010): 26–44.
34. See James R. Farr, *Artisans in Europe, 1300–1914* (Cambridge: Cambridge University Press, 2000), 161–2, 176. See also Steven L. Kaplan, "The Character and Implications of Strife among the Masters inside the Guilds in Eighteenth-Century Paris," *Journal of Social History* 19, no. 4 (1986): 631–47.
35. James R. Farr, *Hands of Honor: Artisans and Their World in Dijon, 1550–1650* (Ithaca, NY: Cornell University Press, 1988); Mack Walker, *German Home Towns: Community, State, and General Estate, 1648–1871* (Ithaca, NY: Cornell University Press, 1971).
36. See Bert De Munck, "Fiscalizing Solidarity (from below). Poor Relief in Antwerp Guilds between Community Building and Public Service," in *Serving the Community: Public Facilities in Early Modern Towns of the Low Countries*, eds. Manon Van Der Heijden and Griet Vermeesch (Amsterdam: Aksant, 2009), 168–93; and "From Brotherhood Community to Civil Society? Apprentices Between Guild, Household and the Freedom of Contract in Early Modern Antwerp," *Social History* 35, no. 1 (2010): 1–20. Also, Gervase Rosser, "Going to the Fraternity Feast: Commensality and Social Relations in Late Medieval England," *Journal of British Studies* 33, no. 4 (1994): 430–46.
37. Eamon Duffy, *The Stripping of the Altars: Traditional Religion in England, 1400–1580* (New Haven, CT: Yale University Press, 1992), pt. II.
38. Philip J. Broadhead, "Guildsmen, Religious Reform and the Search for the Common Good: The Role of the Guilds in the Early Reformation in Augsburg," *The Historical Journal* 93, no. 3 (1996): 577–97; Heinz Schilling, "Reformation und Bürgerfreiheit: Emdens Weg zur Calvinistischen Stadtrepublik," in *Stadt und Kirche im 16. Jahrhundert*, ed. Bernd Moeller (Gütersloh: Gütersloher Verlagshaus Mohn, 1978), 128–61.
39. See Nicholas Terpstra, *Lay Confraternities and Civic Religion in Renaissance Bologna* (Cambridge: Cambridge University Press, 1995).
40. Charles Tilly, *European Revolutions, 1492–1992* (Oxford: Blackwell Publishers, 1993), 38–9.

41. Wiliam Beik, *Urban Protest in Seventeenth-Century France: The Culture of Retribution* (Cambridge: Cambridge University Press, 2008), 6.
42. Perez Zagorin, *Rebels and Rulers, 1500–1660* (Cambridge: Cambridge University Press, 1982).
43. Jan de Vries, "Luxury in the Dutch Golden Age," in *Luxury in the Eighteenth Century: Debates, Desires and Delectable Goods*, eds. Maxine Berg and Elizabeth Eger (Basingstoke: Palgrave Macmillan, 2002), 41–56; Richard A. Goldthwaite, *Wealth and the Demand for Art in Italy, 1300–1600* (Baltimore, MD: Johns Hopkins University Press, 1995).
44. Bert De Munck, "Skills, Trust and Changing Consumer Preferences: The Decline of Antwerp's Craft Guilds from the Perspective of the Product Market, ca. 1500 – ca. 1800," *International Review of Social History* 53, no. 2 (2008): 197–233; Barbara Bettoni, "Usefulness, Ornament and Novelty: The Debate on Quality in Button and Buckle Manufacturing in Northern Italy, XVIII–XIX Century," in *Concepts of Value in Material Culture, 1500–1900*, eds. Bert De Munck and Dries Lyna (Aldershot: Ashgate, 2015), 171–206.
45. Bert De Munck, "Artisans, Products and Gifts: Rethinking the History of Material Culture in Early Modern Europe," *Past and Present* 224 (August 2014): 39–74.

Chapter One

1. "economy, n.". OED Online. December 2015. Oxford University Press. http://proxy.library.upenn.edu:2526/view/Entry/59393?redirectedFrom=economy (accessed February 7, 2016).
2. "work, n.". OED Online. September 2015. Oxford University Press. http://www.oed.com/view/Entry/230216?rskey=V9ASMV&result=1&isAdvanced=false (accessed December 2, 2015).
3. Earnest H. Phelps Brown and Sheila V. Hopkins, "Seven Centuries of Building Wages," *Economica* 22, no. 87 (1955): 195–206.
4. Earnest H. Phelps Brown and Sheila V. Hopkins, "Seven Centuries of Prices of Consumables Compared with Builders' Wage-rates," *Economica* 23, no. 92 (1956): 296–314.
5. See James E. Thorold Rogers, *Six Centuries of Work and Wages* (London: Swan Sonnenschein & Co, 1884), chap. XIX. Cited in Earnest H. Phelps Brown and Sheila V. Hopkins, "Wage-Rates and Prices: Evidence for Population Pressure in the Sixteenth Century," *Economica* 24, no. 96 (1957): 289–306.
6. Earnest H. Phelps Brown and Sheila V. Hopkins, "Builders' Wage-Rates, Prices and Population: Some Further Evidence," *Economica* 26, no. 101 (1959): 18–38.
7. Gustav von Schmoller, "Le mouvement historique des salaires de 1300 à 1900 et ses causes," *Revue Internationale de Sociologie* 12 (1904): 3–21, here 14.
8. Adam Smith, *An Inquiry into the Nature and Causes of the Wealth of Nations* (New York: Random House, 1994), bk. 1, chap. 8, 89.
9. Donald Woodward, "Wage Rates and Living Standards in Pre-industrial England," *Past and Present* 91 (1981): 28–46, here 45.
10. Joel Mokyr, ed., *The British Industrial Revolution: An Economic Perspective* (Boulder, CO: Westview Press, 1993), esp. 118–30 and 123–26.
11. Donald Woodward, *Men at Work: Labourers and Building Craftsmen in the Towns of Northern England, 1450–1750* (Cambridge: Cambridge University Press, 1995), 207.
12. Ibid., 207–8.
13. Österreichisches Staatsarchiv Wien. IÖMuBw 134/1. Bericht der Commission zu Idrija vom 25. April 1536 zum 2. Februar 1537.
14. Wages at Idrija were paid in *Rhenish Gulden*, a common silver coin of exchange. There were multiple, smaller coins in circulation, all of which were subunits of the *Gulden*. One *Gulden*

was comprised of 60 *Kreuzer* or 210 *Pfennigs*, for example. Alternatively, 1 *Gulden* worth 60 *Kreuzer* also equalled 15 *Batzen*, 30 *Shilling* or 420 *Heller*. See Moritz I. Elsas, *Umriß einer Geschichte der Preise und Löhne in Deutschland vom ausgehenden Mittelalter bis zum Beginn des neunzehnten Jahrhunderts*, 2 vols. (Leiden: Brill, 1949), vol. I, 118.

15. See, for example, Leonard N. Rosenband, *Papermaking in Eighteenth-Century France: Management, Labor, and Revolution at the Montgolfier Mill, 1761–1805* (Baltimore, MD: Johns Hopkins University Press, 2000); Corinne Maitte and Didier Terrier, eds., *Les temps du travail: Normes, pratiques, évolutions (XIVᵉ–XIXᵉ siècle)* (Rennes: Presses universitaires de Rennes, 2014).
16. Eric Hobsbawm, *Labouring Men: Studies in the History of Labour* (London: Weidenfeld & Nicolson, 1968), 334–79.
17. Peter Scholliers and Leonard Schwarz, eds., *Experiencing Wages: Social and Cultural Aspects of Wage Forms in Europe since 1500* (New York: Berghahn Books, 2006), 3–24, here 5.
18. See also Harald Deceulaer, "Institutional and Cultural Change in Wage Formation: Port Labour in Antwerp (Sixteenth–Eighteenth Centuries)," in *Experiencing Wages*, eds. Scholliers and Schwarz, 27–52; Edward H. Hunt, *Regional Wage Variations in Britain, 1850–1914* (Oxford: Clarendon Press, 1973).
19. John Rule, *The Labouring Classes in Early Industrial England* (London: Longman, 1991).
20. Alfred O. Hirschman, *Exit, Voice and Loyalty: Responses to Decline in Firms, Organizations, and States* (Cambridge, MA: Harvard University Press, 1970), 19.
21. Peter Scholliers, "Wages," in *The Oxford Encyclopedia of Economic History* (Oxford: Oxford University Press, 2003).
22. "wage, n.". OED Online. March 2016. Oxford University Press. http://proxy.library.upenn.edu:2440/view/Entry/225018?rskey=sevlmE&result=1 (accessed May 30, 2016).
23. Natalie Zemon Davis, "City Women and Religious Change," in *Society and Culture in Early Modern France*, ed. Natalie Zemon Davis (Stanford, CA: Stanford University Press, 1975), 65–95, here 94.
24. John Hatcher, "Women's Work Reconsidered: Gender and Wage Differentiation in Late Medieval England," *Past and Present* 173 (2001): 191–8, here 194.
25. The problematic relationship between wages and productivity in the early modern age has become the focus of intense debate among scholars since the publication of Jan de Vries, *The Industrious Revolution: Consumer Behavior and the Household Economy, 1650 to the Present* (Cambridge: Cambridge University Press, 2008). This study focused on the question of development and industrialization, but it posed questions no less relevant to an earlier age.
26. James Oakes, "Capitalism and Slavery and the Civil War," *International Labor and Working Class History* 89 (2016): 195–220, here 203.

Chapter Two

1. Peter van der Coelen et al., *De ontdekking van het dagelijks leven: Van Bosch tot Bruegel* (Rotterdam: Museum Boijmans van Beuningen, 2015).
2. "Art and Reality," in *Art in History, History in Art: Studies in Seventeenth-Century Dutch Culture*, eds. David Freedberg and Jan de Vries (Santa Monica, CA: The Getty Center Publications, 1991), 29–248.
3. Bridget Ann Henisch, *The Medieval Calendar Year* (University Park: Pennsylvania State University Press, 1999).
4. For depictions of the Months and Seasons 1500–1750, see Yvette Bruijnen, *De Vier Jaargetijden in de kunst van de Nederlanden 1500–1750* (Zwolle: Waanders, 2003).

5. Hans-Joachim Raupp, *Bauernsatiren: Entstehung und Entwicklung des bäuerlichen Genres in der deutschen und niederländischen Kunst ca. 1470–1570* (Niederzier: Lukassen Verlag, 1986); Van der Coelen et al., *De ontdekking van het dagelijks leven*, 201–24.
6. Ilja M. Veldman, *Images for the Eye and Soul: Function and Meaning in Netherlandish Prints (1450–1650)* (Leiden: Primavera Pers, 2006), 174–8; Ilja M. Veldman, "Representations of Labour in Late Sixteenth-Century Netherlandish Prints: The Secularization of the Work Ethic," in *The Idea of Work in Europe from Antiquity to Modern Times*, eds. Josef Ehmer and Catharina Lis (London: Routledge, 2009), 152–4.
7. See also Chapter Seven in this volume.
8. Veldman, "Representations of Labour," 151–2.
9. Veldman, *Images for the Eye and Soul*, 178–88; Veldman, "Representations of Labour," 157–75.
10. Gero Seelig, *The New Hollstein German Etchings, Engravings and Woodcuts 1400–1700. Jost Amman* (Rotterdam: Sound and Vision Interactive, 2002), vol. III, nos. 50–1.
11. Alice Bonner McGinty, "Stradanus (Jan van de Straet): His Role in the Visual Communication of Renaissance Discoveries, Technologies, and Values" (unpublished diss., Tuft University, USA, 1974).
12. Marjolein Leesberg, *The New Hollstein Dutch and Flemish Etchings, Engravings and Woodcuts 1450–1700. Johannes Stradanus* (Rotterdam: Sound and Vision Interactive, 2008), vol. III, nos. 322–41.
13. Ibid., nos. 346–51.
14. Annette de Vries, *Ingelijst werk: De verbeelding van arbeid en beroep in de vroegmoderne Nederlanden* (Zwolle: Waanders, 2004), chaps. 5 and 6.
15. See also Chapter Five in this volume.
16. Gerhard Jaritz, "The Visual Representation of Late Medieval Work: Patterns of Context, People and Action," in *The Idea of Work in Europe*, eds. Ehmer and Lis, 128–35.
17. Kenneth G. Ponting, "Sculptures and Paintings of Textile Processes at Leiden," *Textile History* 5 (1974): 128–51; Frank van Deijk, "Een ooggetuige van belang? Isaac Claeszoon Swanenburg en zijn weergave van de Leidse saaiproductie," *Textielhistorische bijdragen* 33 (1993): 7–42.
18. Ibid., 10–11.
19. Hugo T. van der Velden, "Defrocking St Eloy: Petrus Christus's *Vocational Portrait of a Goldsmith*," *Simiolus* 26, no. 4 (1998): 242–76.
20. De Vries *Ingelijst werk.*, chaps. 2 and 4.
21. Van der Coelen et al., *De ontdekking van het dagelijks leven*, 103–12; Larry Silver, "Massys and Money: The Tax Collectors Rediscovered," *Journal of Historians of Netherlandish Art* 7, no. 2 (2015): 1–23. https://doi.org/10.5092/jhna.2015.7.2.2.
22. Burr Wallen, *Jan van Hemessen. An Antwerp Painter between Reform and Counter-Reform* (Ann Arbor, MI: Umi Research Press, 1983), 72–7; Silver, "Massys and Money."
23. Marjolein Leesberg, *The New Hollstein Dutch and Flemish Etchings, Hendrick Goltzius* (Ouderkerk aan den Ijssel: Sound and Vision Interactive, 2012), vol. II, nos. 186–93.
24. Ibid., vol. IV, nos. 657–71.
25. Gerlinde Lütke Notarp, *Von Heiterkeit, Zorn, Schwermut und Lethargie. Studien zur Ikonographie der vier Temperamente in der niederländischen Serien- und Genregraphik des 16. und 17. Jahrhunderts* (New York: Waxmann Münster, 1998).
26. E. de Jongh, *Questions of Meaning. Theme and Motif in Dutch Seventeenth-Century Painting* (Leiden: Primavera, 2000), 22–46.
27. Veldman, *Images for the Eye and Soul*, 193–222.

28. Elizabeth A. Honig, *Painting and the Market in Early Modern Antwerp* (New Haven, CT: Yale University Press, 1998).
29. Günter Irmscher, "Ministrae Voluptatum: Stoicizing Ethics in the Market and Kitchen Scenes of Pieter Aertsen and Joachim Beuckelaer," *Simiolus* 16, no. 4 (1986): 219–32; de Jongh, *Questions of Meaning*, 142.
30. Jochen Becker, "Are these Girls Really so Neat?," in *Art in History*, eds. Freedberg and de Vries, 139–73; Van der Coelen et al., *De ontdekking van het dagelijks leven*, 182–93.
31. Veldman, *Images for the Eye and Soul*, 259–70.
32. De Jongh, *Questions of Meaning*, 22–46.
33. For the symbolism of the objects, see Johan op de Beeck and Eric de Bruyn, *De zotte schilders. Moraalridders van het penseel rond Bosch, Bruegel en Brouwer* (Gent: Snoeck, 2003).
34. Veldman, *Images for the Eye and Soul*, 153–6.
35. Ilja M. Veldman, *Profit and Pleasure: Print Books by Crispijn de Passe* (Rotterdam: Sound and Vision Interactive, 2001), 250–1.
36. Matthias Ubl, *De Braunschweiger Monogrammist. Wegbereiter der niederländischen Genremalerei von Bruegel* (Amsterdam: Michael Imhoff Verlag, 2014).
37. Elmer Kolfin, *The Young Gentry at Play: Northern Netherlandish Scenes of Merry Companies 1610–1645* (Leiden: Primavera Pers, 2005), 20–33.
38. Lotte C. van de Pol, "The Whore, the Bawd, and the Artist: The Reality and Imagery of Seventeenth-Century Dutch Prostitution," *Journal of Historians of Netherlandish Art* 2, nos. 1–2 (2010): 1–20, here 15–20. https://doi.org/10.5092/jhna.2010.2.1.3.
39. Joaneath Spicer, ed., *Masters of Light: Dutch Painters in Utrecht during the Golden Age* (New Haven, CT: Yale University Press, 1997), 244–8, no. 38.
40. Nanette Salomon, *Shifting Priorities: Gender and Genre in Seventeenth-Century Dutch Painting* (Stanford, CA: Stanford University Press, 2004).

Chapter Three

1. On the subject of contested perceptions and evaluations of work at the time, see Chapter Seven in this volume.
2. John Desmond Bernal, *Sozialgeschichte der Wissenschaften: Science in History*, vol. 2 (Reinbek bei Hamburg: Rowohlt, 1970), 356, 362–3, 384.
3. Luca Mocarelli, "Attitudes to Work and Commerce in the Late Italian Renaissance: A Comparison between Tomaso Garzoni's La Piazza Universale and Leonardo Fioravanti's Dello Specchio Di Scienta Universale," *International Review of Social History* 56, no. S19 (2011): 89–106, here 91.
4. Important examples are Georgius Agricola, *De re metallica* (Basel, 1556); Vannoccio Biringuccio, *De la Pirotechnia* (Venice, 1549); Jacques Besson, *Theatrum instrumentarum et machinarum* (Lyon, 1578). For this genre in general, see Marcus Popplow, *Neu, nützlich und erfindungsreich: Die Idealisierung von Technik in der frühen Neuzeit* (Münster: Waxmann, 1998), esp. 65–97. See also Chapter Five in this volume.
5. Important examples are Anthony Fitzherbert, *The Book of Husbandry* (London, 1523); Charles Estienne, *Agriculture et Maison rustique* (Paris, 1554); Johannes Coler, *Oeconomia ruralis et domestica* (Mainz, 1595–9). See Stefan Brakensiek, "Landwirtschaftskunde" in *Enzyklopädie der Neuzeit*, vol. 7 (Stuttgart: Metzler, 2008).
6. This claim made him, in the eyes of generations of cultural historians, a prototype of the "Renaissance man." See Jacob Burckhardt, *Die Kultur der Renaissance in Italien* (1860; repr., Stuttgart: Kröner Verlag, 1985), 97; Bernal, *Sozialgeschichte der Wissenschaften*, 366. For a

critical view, see Anthony Grafton, *Leon Battista Alberti: Master Builder of the Renaissance* (Cambridge, MA: Harvard University Press, 2002).
7. Reinhold Reith, "Praxis der Arbeit. Überlegungen zur Rekonstruktion von Arbeitsprozessen in der handwerklichen Produktion," in *Praxis der Arbeit: Probleme und Perspektiven der handwerksgeschichtlichen Forschung*, ed. Reinhold Reith (Frankfurt/Main: Campus Verlag, 1998), 18. See Chapter Two in this volume. See also Gerhard Jaritz, "The Visual Representation of Late Medieval Work: Patterns of Context, People and Action," in *The Idea of Work in Europe from Antiquity to Modern Times*, eds. Josef Ehmer and Catharina Lis (Aldershot: Ashgate, 2009).
8. See Wolfgang Lefèvre, *Picturing the World of Mining in the Renaissance: The Schwazer Bergbuch (1556)* (Berlin: Max Planck Institute for the History of Science Preprint 407, 2010).
9. This is particularly important for eastern and northern parts of Europe, where towns were dominated by less durable wooden structures. See Dag Lindström and Göran Tagesson, "On Spatializing History—The Household as Spatial Unit in Early Modern Swedish Towns," *META Historiskarkeologisk tidskrift* (2015).
10. For a paradigmatic example, see Sheilagh Ogilvie, *A Bitter Living: Women, Markets, and Social Capital in Early Modern Germany* (Oxford: Oxford University Press, 2003).
11. See Gadi Algazi, "Food for Thought. Hieronymus Wolf grapples with the scholarly habitus," in *Egodocuments in history: Autobiographical Writing in its Social Context since the Middle Ages*, ed. Rudolf Dekker (Hilversum: Verloren, 2003), which offers a convincing strategy to look behind the construction of a "scholarly habitus" in autobiographical writings.
12. This is particularly true for Marxist scholars with emphasis on the development of "productive forces" ("*Produktivkräfte*"). See Bernal, *Sozialgeschichte der Wissenschaften*; Wolfgang Jonas, Valentine Linsbauer, and Helga Marx, *Die Produktivkräfte in der Geschichte*, vol. 1 (Berlin: Dietz Verlag, 1969).
13. See Edwin Ernest Rich and Charles Henry Wilson, eds., *The Economic Organization of Early Modern Europe* (Cambridge: Cambridge University Press, 1977).
14. See Reith, *Praxis der Arbeit*.
15. See Gregory Hanlon, *Human Nature in Rural Tuscany: An Early Modern History* (New York: Palgrave Macmillan, 2007).
16. Natalie Zemon Davis, "Women in the Crafts in Sixteenth-Century Lyon," *Feminist Studies* 8, no. 1 (1982): 46–80.
17. Christopher Hill, *Reformation to Industrial Revolution* (Harmondsworth: Penguin Books, 1969), 61.
18. Michel de Montaigne, *The Journal of Montaigne's Travels in Italy by Way of Switzerland and Germany in 1580 and 1581*, trans. and ed. William George Waters, vol. 2 (London: John Murray, 1903), 133.
19. Hanlon, *Human Nature in Rural Tuscany*, 53.
20. Ibid., 57.
21. Quoted from Jan de Vries, *The Dutch Rural Economy in the Golden Age, 1500–1700* (New Haven, CT: Yale University Press, 1974), 34.
22. Simon Schama, *The Embarrassment of Riches: An Interpretation of Dutch Culture in the Golden Age* (London: Fontana Press, 1991), 48–9.
23. Jan Bieleman, *Five Centuries of Farming: A Short History of Dutch Agriculture 1500–2000* (Wageningen: Academic Publishers, 2010), 43.
24. Jan Bieleman, "Dutch Agriculture in the Golden Age," in *The Dutch Economy in the Golden Age: Nine Studies*, eds. Karel Davids and Leo Noordegraaf (Amsterdam: Nederlandsch Economisch-Historisch Archief, 1993), 164–70.

25. De Vries, *The Dutch Rural Economy*, 68, 72.
26. Emmanuel Le Roy Ladurie, *Die Bauern des Languedoc* (Munich: Deutscher Taschenbuch Verlag, 1990), 69, 75. (*Les Paysans de Languedoc*, Paris: Flammarion, 1969).
27. Ibid., 78–82.
28. Karl Bücher, Die *Bevölkerung von Frankfurt am Main im XIV. und XV. Jahrhundert* (Tübingen: H. Laupp, 1886), 340.
29. Maria Luisa Bianchi and Maria Letizia Grossi, "Botteghe, economia e spazio urbano," in *La grande storia dell' Artigianato. Vol. II: Il Quattrocento*, eds. Franco Franceschi and Gloria Fossi (Florence: Giunti, 1999), 34.
30. See Lindström and Tagesson, "On Spatializing History."
31. Davis, "Women in the Crafts". For a deeper discussion, see the section in this chapter "Working and Living: Fluid Borders or Separate Spheres."
32. See Michael Clapham, "Printing," in *A History of Technology*, vol. III, eds. Charles Singer, et al. (Oxford: Clarendon Press, 1969), 386–90; Jan Materné, "Social Emancipation in European Printing Workshops before the Industrial Revolution," in *The Workplace before the Factory. Artisans and Proletarians, 1500–1800*, eds. Thomas Max Safley and Leonard N. Rosenband (Ithaca, NY: Cornell University Press, 1993), 204–24.
33. Christina Vanja, "Mining Women in Early Modern European Society," in ibid., 100–17; Susan C. Karant-Nunn, "From Adventurers to Drones: The Saxon Silver Miners as an Early Proletariat," in ibid., 79.
34. Lefèvre, *Picturing the World of Mining*, 11.
35. Donald Cuthbert Coleman, "Naval Dockyards under the Later Stuarts," *Economic History Review* 6, no. 2 (1953): 155.
36. Robert Charles Davis, *Shipbuilders of the Venetian Arsenal: Workers and Workplace in the Preindustrial City* (Baltimore, MD: Johns Hopkins University Press, 1991), 3.
37. Ibid., 199.
38. Frederic Chapin Lane, *Venice. A Maritime Republic* (Baltimore, MD: Johns Hopkins University Press, 1973), 362.
39. Davis, *Shipbuilders*, 180.
40. Lane, *Venice*, 363.
41. Davis, *Shipbuilders*, 80.
42. Lane, *Venice*, 363.
43. Davis, *Shipbuilders*, 11, 20.
44. Lyndal Roper, *The Holy Household: Women and Morals in Reformation Augsburg* (Oxford: Clarendon Press, 1989), 40–1.
45. Ibid.; Bert De Munck, "From Brotherhood Community to Civil Society? Apprentices between Guild, Household and the Freedom of Contract in Early Modern Antwerp," *Social History* 35, no. 1 (2010): 14–6.
46. See Valentin Groebner, *Ökonomie ohne Haus Working and living: Fluid borders or separate spheres Zum Wirtschaften armer Leute in Nürnberg am Ende des 15. Jahrhunderts* (Göttingen: Vandenhoeck & Ruprecht, 1993).
47. Quoted in Friederike Hausmann, *Machiavelli und Florenz Working and living: Fluid borders or separate spheres Eine Welt in Briefen* (Munich: dtv, 2001), 84–6.
48. Jane Whittle, "The House as a Place of Work in Early Modern Rural England," *Home Cultures* 8, no. 2 (2011): 141.
49. Algazi, "Food for Thought," 37.
50. William George Hoskins, "The Rebuilding of Rural England, 1570–1640," *Past and Present* 4 (1953): 54.

51. Whittle, "The House as a Place of Work," 134.
52. Schama, *Embarrassment of Riches,* 376 ff.
53. Quoted by Whittle, "The House as a Place of Work," 137.
54. Ogilvie, *Bitter Living,* 148. However, the sexual division of labor, particularly in agriculture, varied enormously across European regions (119).
55. See ibid., 119, 147, 225, 283, although her empirical evidence concerns mainly the period 1646–1800.

Chapter Four

1. Norbert Elias, *La société de cour* (Paris: Flammarion, 1985), 17.
2. Franco Gaeta, "Dal Comune alla corte rinascimentale," in *Letteratura italiana,* vol. I, *Il letterato e le istituzioni*, ed. Alberto Asor Rosa (Torino: Einaudi, 1982), 241.
3. Salvatore Nigro, "Il segretario," in *L'uomo barocco,* ed. Rosario Villari (Rome–Bari: Laterza, 1991), 91–108.
4. Peter Burke, "Il cortigiano," in *L'uomo del Rinascimento,* ed. Eugenio Garin (Rome–Bari: Laterza, 1988), 133–65.
5. Baldassarre Castiglione, *Il cortigiano*, ed. Amedeo Quondam (Milan: Garzanti, 2002), vol. I, 48; vol. I, 2.
6. Daniel Arasse, "L'art et l'illustration du pouvoir," in *Culture et idéologie dans la genèse de l'Etat moderne*, Actes de la table ronde organisée par le Centre national de la recherche scientifique et l'Ecole Française de Rome, 15–17 octobre 1985 (Rome: Ecole Française de Rome, 1985), 231–44.
7. Quentin Skinner, *The Foundations of Modern Political Thought* (Cambridge: Cambridge University Press, 1978).
8. Hilde De Ridder-Symoens, "Chapitre 8: Formation et professionnalisation," in *Les élites du pouvoir et la construction de l'Etat en Europe,* ed. Wolfgang Reinhard (Paris: Presses Universitaires de France, 1996), 203–35; and more generally the entire volume, part of the series *Les origins de l'Etat moderne en Europe, XIIIe–XVIIIe siècle*, eds. Wim Blockmans and Jean-Philippe Genet. On the role played by law in the early modern state, see Christopher W. Brooks, *Law, Politics and Society in Early Modern England* (Cambridge: Cambridge University Press, 2008).
9. Margaret L. King, "The Venetian Intellectual World," in *A Companion to Venetian History, 1400–1797,* ed. Eric R. Dursteler (Leiden: Brill, 2013), 582.
10. Andrea Zannini, "L'impiego pubblico," in *Storia di Venezia dalle origini alla caduta della Serenissima,* vol. IV, *Il Rinascimento: Politica e cultura,* eds. Alberto Tenenti and Ugo Tucci (Rome: Istituto della Enciclopedia Italiana, 1996), 415–63.
11. Andrea Zannini, *Burocrazia e burocrati a Venezia in età moderna: i cittadini originari (sec. XVI–XVIII)* (Venice: Istituto Veneto di Scienze, Lettere ed Arti, 1993); Gaetano Cozzi, *Repubblica di Venezia e Stati italiani: Politica e giustizia dal secolo XVI al secolo XVIII* (Torino: Einaudi, 1982).
12. Elisabeth Perry, *Gender and Disorder in Early Modern Seville* (Princeton, NJ: Princeton University Press, 1990).
13. Merry E. Wiesner, "Gender and the Worlds of Work," in *Germany: A New Social and Economic History,* vol. 1, *1450–1630,* ed. Robert Scribner (London: Arnold, 1996), 209–32.
14. Nadia Maria Filippini, "The Church, the State and Childbirth: The Midwife in Italy during the 18th Century," in *The Art of Midwifery: Early Modern Midwives in Europe,* ed. Hilary Marland (Abingdon: Routledge, 1993), 152–75.

15. Doreen Evenden, *The Midwives of Seventeenth Century London* (Cambridge: Cambridge University Press, 2000).
16. Jacques Gélis, *La sage femme et le médecin: Une nouvelle conception de la vie* (Paris: Fayard, 1988).
17. Merry E. Wiesner, "The Midwives of South Germany and the Public/Private Dichotomy," in *The Art of Midwifery*, ed. Marland, 77–94.
18. Teresa Ortiz, "From Hegemony to Subordination: Midwives in Early Modern Spain," in *The Art of Midwifery*, ed. Marland, 95–114.
19. Hilary Marland, "The 'burgerlijke' Midwife: The *stadsvroedvrouw* of Eighteenth-Century Holland," in *The Art of Midwifery*, ed. Marland, 192–213.
20. Gélis, *La sage femme et le médecin*; Nina Gelbart, "Midwife to a Nation: Mme du Coudray Serves France," in *The Art of Midwifery*, ed. Marland, 131–51.
21. Anna Bellavitis, "Apprentissages masculins, apprentissages féminins à Venise au XVIe siècle," *Histoire Urbaine* 15 (2006): 49–73.
22. Bernard Capp, "The Double Standard Revisited: Plebeian Women and Male Sexual Reputation in Early Modern England," *Past and Present* 162 (1999): 70–100.
23. Alessandro Stella, "Des esclaves pour la liberté sexuelle de leurs maîtres (Europe Occidentale, XIVe–XVIIIe siècles)," *Clio. Histoire, femmes et sociétés* 5 (1997): 191–209; Alessandro Stella, "Se soumettre pour se libérer. Une esclave turque face à son maître espagnol à Cadix en 1704," *Clio. Histoire, femmes et sociétés* 1 (2003): 163–74.
24. Anna Bellavitis, *Famille, genre, transmission à Venise au XVIe siècle* (Rome: Ecole Française de Rome, 2008).
25. Raffaella Sarti, "Criados, servi, domestiques, gesinde, servants: for a comparative history of domestic service in Europe (16th–19th centuries)," *Obradoiro de Historia Moderna* 16 (2007): 9–39.
26. Gayle K. Brunelle, "Contractual Kin: Servants and Their Mistresses in Sixteenth-Century Nantes," *Journal of Early Modern History* 2 (1998): 374–94.
27. Dennis Romano, "The Regulation of Domestic Service in Renaissance Venice," *The Sixteenth Century Journal* 22 (1991): 661–77.
28. Steven L. Kaplan, "L'apprentissage au XVIIIe siècle: le cas de Paris," *Revue d'histoire moderne et contemporaine* 40 (1993): 436–79; Luciano Marcello, "Andare a bottega. Adolescenza e apprendistato nelle arti (sec. XVI–XVII)," in *Infanzie*, ed. Ottavia Niccoli (Florence: Ponte alle Grazie, 1993), 231–51; Simona Laudani, "Apprenties ou jeunes salariées? Parcours de formation dans les métiers de Catane (XVIIIe–XIXe siècles)," *Histoire Urbaine* 15 (2006): 13–25; Bert De Munck, Steven L. Kaplan, and Hugo Soly, eds., *Learning on the Shop Floor: Historical Perspectives on Apprenticeship* (New York: Berghan Books, 2007); Monica Martinat, "L'apprendistato," in *Storia del lavoro in Italia*, ed. Renata Ago (Rome: Castelvecchi, forthcoming).
29. Andrea Caracausi, "Beaten Children and Women's Work in Early Modern Italy," *Past and Present* 222 (2014): 95–128.
30. See for example: Daniela Lombardi and Flores Reggiani, "Da assistita a serva. Circuiti di reclutamento delle serve attraverso le istituzioni assistenziali (Firenze, Milano, XVII–XVIII secolo)," in *La donna nell'economia, secc. XIII–XVIII*, Atti delle Settimane di studi dell'Istituto internazionale di storia economica F. Datini di Prato, ed. Simonetta Cavaciocchi (Florence: Le Monnier, 1990), 301–19; Giovanna Da Molin, "Family Forms and Domestic Service in Southern Italy from the Seventeenth to the Nineteenth centuries," *Journal of Family History* 15 (1990): 503–27; Anne E. C. McCants, *Civic Charity in a Golden Age* (Urbana: University of Illinois Press, 1997); Thomas Max Safley, *Charity and Economy*

in the *Orphanages of Early Modern Augsburg* (Boston, MA: Humanities Press, 1997); Thomas Max Safley, *Children of the Laboring Poor: Expectation and Experience among the Orphans of Early Modern Augsburg* (Leiden: Brill, 2005).
31. Bellavitis, "Apprentissages masculins"; Bellavitis, *Famille, genre, transmission*.
32. Christiane Klapisch-Zuber, "Les apprentis peintres et sculpteurs italiens aux XVe et XVIe siècles," *Mélanges de l'Ecole Française de Rome, Italie-Méditerranée* 128, no. 1 (2016), https://doi.org/10.4000/mefrim.2469. For the English translation of Vasari, see: http://members.efn.org/~acd/vite/VasariPierodiCosimo.html (accessed January 21, 2018).
33. Renata Ago, *Economia barocca. Mercato e istituzioni nella Roma del Seicento* (Rome: Donzelli, 1998), 184–5 and, more generally, on unpaid work within the family, in a historical perspective, see: Manuela Martini and Anna Bellavitis, eds., *Households, Family Workshops and Unpaid Market Work in Europe from the 16th Century to the Present*, special issue of *The History of the Family* 19, no. 3 (2014); Anna Bellavitis, Manuela Martini, and Raffaella Sarti, eds., *Familles laborieuses: Rémunération, transmission et apprentissage dans les ateliers familiaux de la fin du Moyen âge à l'époque contemporaine en Europe, Mélanges de l'Ecole Française de Rome, Italie-Méditerranée* 128, no. 1 (2016), https://doi.org/10.4000/mefrim.2433.
34. Andrea Trevisan, "Relazione d'Inghilterra (1498)," in *Ambasciatori veneti in Inghilterra*, ed. Luigi Firpo (Torino: Utet, 1978), 3–48.
35. Giovanni Maria Memmo, *Dialogo del magnifico cavaliere messer Gio. Maria Memmo, nel quale dopo alcune filosofiche dispute, si forma un perfetto prencipe & una perfetta Republica, e parimente un senatore, un cittadino, un soldato & un mercatante* (Venice: Gabriele Giolito de' Ferrari, 1563).
36. Luca Molà, *The Silk Industry of Renaissance Venice* (Baltimore, MD: Johns Hopkins University Press, 2000); Marcello Della Valentina, *Operai, mezzadi e mercanti: tessitori e industria della seta a Venezia tra '600 e '700* (Padova: Cluep, 2003).
37. Andrea Caracausi, *Dentro la bottega: Culture del lavoro in una città d'età moderna* (Venice: Marsilio, 2008), 45–9.
38. See for example: Roberto Greci, *Corporazioni e mondo del lavoro nell'Italia padana medievale* (Bologna: CLUEB, 1988); Donata Degrassi, *L'economia artigiana nell'Italia medievale* (Rome: Carocci, 1996); Centro Italiano di Studi di Storia e d'Arte Pistoia, *La trasmissione dei saperi nel Medioevo (secoli XII–XV)* (Pistoia: Centro Italiano di Studi di Storia e d'Arte, 2005); Maria Paola Zanoboni, *Salariati nel Medioevo (secoli XIII–XV)* (Ferrara: Nuove Carte, 2009); Franco Franceschi, "… e seremo tutti ricchi." *Lavoro, mobilità sociale e conflitti nelle città dell'Italia medievale* (Pisa: Pacini, 2012).
39. Venetian State Archives (ASVe), *Giustizia Vecchia, Accordi dei Garzoni*, busta 119, reg. 165, fol. 91v.; 91r.; 92r.; busta 120, reg. 168, fol. 229r.; fol. 160v.
40. Andrea Caracausi, "The Price of an Apprentice: Contracts and Trials in the Woollen Industry in Sixteenth-Century Italy," *Mélanges de l'École française de Rome - Italie et Méditerranée modernes et contemporaines* 128, no. 1 (2016), §22, https://doi.org/10.4000/mefrim.2476.
41. Martinat, "L'apprendistato."
42. James R. Farr, *Artisans in Europe, 1300–1914* (Cambridge: Cambridge University Press, 2000), 259.
43. Claudio Costantini, *La Repubblica di Genova* (Torino: Utet, 1986).
44. Simona Laudani, "Mestieri di donne, mestieri di uomini: le corporazioni in età moderna," in *Il lavoro delle donne*, ed. Angela Groppi (Rome: Laterza, 1996), 183–204.
45. Wiesner, "Gender and the Worlds of Work."
46. Anna Bellavitis, *Il lavoro delle donne nelle città dell'Europa moderna* (Rome: Viella, 2016).
47. Marta Vicente Valentin, "Mujeres artesanas en la Barcelona moderna," in *Las mujeres en*

el Antiguo Régimen: Imagen y realidad (s. XVI–XVIII), ed. Isabel Pérez Molina (Barcelona: Icaria, 1994), 57–90; Marta Vicente Valentin, "Images and Realities of Work: Women and Guilds in Early Modern Barcelona," in *Spanish Women in the Golden Age*, eds. Magdalena S. Sanchez and Alain Saint Saëns (Westport, CT: Greenwood Press, 1996), 127–39.

48. Lyndal Roper, *The Holy Household: Women and Morals in Reformation Augsburg* (Oxford: Clarendon Press, 1989); Sherrin Marshall, ed., *Women in Reformation and Counter-Reformation Europe* (Bloomington: Indiana University Press, 1989); Luise Schorn-Schütte, "Matrimony as Profession: The Clergyman's Wife," in *Time, Space and Women's Lives in Early Modern Europe*, eds. Silvana Seidel Menchi, Thomas Kuehn, and Anne Jacobson Schutte (Kirksville, MO: Truman State University Press, 2001), 255–77.
49. Sheilagh Ogilvie, "Married Women, Work and Law: Evidence from Early Modern Germany," in *Married Women and the Law in Premodern Western Europe*, eds. Cordelia Beattie and Matthew Frank Stevens (Woodbridge: Boydell Press, 2013), 213–39.
50. Liliane Mottu-Weber, "L'évolution des activités professionnelles des femmes à Genève du XVIe au XVIIIe siècle," in *La donna nell'economia*, ed. Cavaciocchi, 345–57.
51. Wiesner, "Gender and the Worlds of Work."
52. Clare Crowston, *Fabricating Women: The Seamstresses of Old Regime France, 1675–1791* (Durham, NC: Duke University Press, 2001).
53. Bellavitis, *Il lavoro delle donne*.
54. Lucia Ferrante, "Il valore del corpo ovvero la gestione economica della sessualità femminile," in *Il lavoro delle donne*, ed. Groppi, 206–28.
55. Tessa Storey, *Carnal Commerce in Counter-Reformation Rome* (Cambridge: Cambridge University Press, 2008).
56. Elisabeth Perry, "Lost Women in Early Modern Seville: The Politics of Prostitution," *Feminist Studies* 4 (1978): 195–214; Alexandra Parma Cook, "The Women of Early Modern Triana: Life, Death and Survival Strategies in Seville's Maritime District," in *Women in Port, Gendering Communities, Economics, and Social Networks in Atlantic Port Cities, 1500–1800*, eds. Douglas Catterall and Jodi Campbell (Leiden: Brill, 2012), 41–68.
57. Lyndal Roper, "Discipline and Respectability: Prostitution and Reformation in Augsburg," *History Workshop Journal* 19 (1985): 3–28.

Chapter Five

1. Lorenzo Melli, *Maso Finiguerra, I disegni* (Florence: Edifir, 1995).
2. Cennino d'Andrea Cennini, *The Craftsman's Handbook: The Italian "Il libro dell'arte,"* trans. Daniel V. Thompson, Jr. (New York: Dover Publications, 1933), 64–5.
3. Doede Hardeman, et al., *De anatomische les. Van Rembrandt tot Damien Hirst* (Bussum: Thoth, 2013).
4. James R. Farr, *Artisans in Europe, 1300–1914* (Cambridge: Cambridge University Press, 2000), 34.
5. Patrick Wallis, "Apprenticeship and Training in Premodern England," *The Journal of Economic History* 68, no. 3 (2008): 834–5; Bert De Munck, *Technologies of Learning: Apprenticeship in Antwerp Guilds from the 15th Century to the End of the Old Regime* (Turnhout: Brepols, 2007), 41; Steven L. Kaplan, "L'apprentissage au XVIIIe siècle: Le cas de Paris," *Revue d'Histoire Moderne et Contemporaine* 40, no. 3 (1993): 436–79; Clare Crowston, "From School to Workshop: Pre-training and Apprenticeship in Old Regime France," in *Learning on the Shop Floor: Historical Perspectives in Apprenticeship*, eds. Bert De Munck, Steven L. Kaplan, and Hugo Soly (New York: Berghahn Books, 2007), 46.

6. Farr, *Artisans in Europe*, 35.
7. Wallis, "Apprenticeship and Training," 834, 838–41.
8. De Munck, *Technologies of Learning*, 44.
9. Karel Davids, "Apprenticeship and Guild Control in the Netherlands, c.1450—1800," in *Learning on the Shop Floor*, eds. De Munck, Kaplan, and Soly, 68.
10. Wallis, "Apprenticeship and Training," 834; Deborah Simonton, "Apprenticeship, Training and Gender in Eighteenth-Century England," in *Markets and Manufacture in Early Industrial Europe*, ed. Maxine Berg (London: Routledge, 1991), 234, 244–5; Clare Crowston, "An Industrious Revolution in Seventeenth-Century Paris: New Vocational Training for Adolescent Girls," in *Secret Gardens, Satanic Mills. Placing Girls in European History, 1750–1960*, eds. Mary Jo Maynes, Birgitte Søland, and Christina Benninghaus (Bloomington: Indiana University Press, 2005), 76; Bibi Panhuysen, *Maatwerk. Kleermakers, naaisters, oudkleerkopers en de gilden (1500–1800)* (Amsterdam: Stichting Beheer IISG, 2000), 191–4; Elise van Nederveen Meerkerk, *De draad in eigen handen: Vrouwen en loonarbeid in de Nederlandse textielnijverheid, 1581–1810* (Amsterdam: Aksant, 2007), 261–8.
11. Panhuysen, *Maatwerk*, 197–8, 205–6, 209–13; Farr, *Artisans in Europe*, 37–41.
12. Johan Dambruyne, *Corporatieve middengroepen: Aspiraties, relaties en transformaties in de 16de-eeuwse Gentse ambachtswereld* (Gent: Academia Press, 2002), 196–7; De Munck, *Technologies of Learning*, 68.
13. Davids, "Apprenticeship and Guild Control," 68.
14. R. A. Houston, *Literacy in Early Modern Europe, Culture and Education 1500–1800* (London: Longman, 1988); James S. Amelang, *The Flight of Icarus: Artisan Autobiography in Early Modern Europe* (Stanford, CA: Stanford University Press, 1998), 55.
15. Paul F. Grendler, *Schooling in Renaissance Italy: Literacy and Learning, 1300–1600* (Baltimore, MD: Johns Hopkins University Press, 1989), 46–7, 102–8.
16. Crowston, "From School to Workshop," 50–4.
17. Janneke Tump, *Ambachtelijk geschoold: Haarlemse en Rotterdamse ambachtslieden en de circulatie van technische kennis, ca.1400–1720* (Amsterdam: Vrije Universiteit Amsterdam, 2012), 189–204; Ad Knotter and Jan Luiten van Zanden, "Immigratie en arbeidsmarkt in Amsterdam in de 17ᵉ eeuw," *Tijdschrift voor Sociale Geschiedenis* 13, no. 4 (1987): 407–8.
18. Amelang, *Flight of Icarus*, 53, 64, 110–12; Tump, *Ambachtelijk geschoold*, 179–208.
19. Amelang, *Flight of Icarus*, 55; Van Nederveen Meerkerk, *Draad in eigen handen*, 264.
20. Davids, "Apprenticeship and Guild Control," 75–6; Tump, *Ambachtelijk geschoold*, 190.
21. Pamela S. Long, *Openness, Secrecy, Authorship: Technical Arts and the Culture of Knowledge from Antiquity to the Renaissance* (Baltimore, MD: Johns Hopkins University Press, 2001), 88–9, 245.
22. Amelang, *Flight of Icarus*, 214–5; Long, *Openness, Secrecy, Authorship*, 73.
23. Corinne Maitte, "The Cities of Glass: Privileges and Innovations in Early Modern Europe," in *Innovation and Creativity in Late Medieval and Early Modern Cities*, eds. Karel Davids and Bert De Munck (Farnham: Ashgate, 2014), 49–53.
24. Smith, *Body of the Artisan*, 31–2.
25. As shown in Amelang, *Flight of Icarus*, 54, 369 n. 9; Long, *Openness, Secrecy, Authorship*, 175 ff.; Tump, *Ambachtelijk geschoold*, 208–20; William Eamon, *Science and the Secrets of Nature. Books of Secrets in Medieval and Early Modern Culture* (Princeton, NJ: Princeton University Press, 1994), 113–20.
26. Long, *Openness, Secrecy, Authorship*, 176–88.
27. Carlo Marco Belfanti, "Guilds, Patents and the Circulation of Technical Knowledge. Northern Italy during the Early Modern Age," *Technology and Culture* 45, no. 3 (2004): 569–89.

28. See for example the special issue on "Institutions and Technical Change in Early Modern Europe" of *History and Technology* 16, no. 3 (2000).
29. Karel Davids, "The Bookkeeper's Tale. Learning Merchant Skills in the Northern Netherlands in the Sixteenth Century," in *Education and Learning in the Netherlands, 1400–1600*, eds. Koen Goudriaan, Jaap van Moolenbroek, and Ad Tervoort (Leiden: Brill, 2004), 236, 244, 249; Grendler, *Schooling*, 306, 319–23; Jacob Soll, *The Reckoning: Financial Accountability and the Rise and Fall of Nations* (New York: Basic Books, 2014), 70–8, 118–19.
30. Josef Ehmer, "Rural Guilds and Urban-Rural Guild Relations in Early Modern Central Europe," in *The Return of the Guilds*, ed. Jan Lucassen et al., *International Review of Social History*, Supplement 16 (2008), 144–7; Sheilagh C. Ogilvie, "Social Institutions and Proto-industrialization," in *European Proto-Industrialization*, eds. Sheilagh C. Ogilvie and Markus Cerman (Cambridge: Cambridge University Press, 1996), 31–2.
31. Maitte, "Cities of Glass," 35.
32. Learning by doing refers to gains in knowledge and skills by regularly repeating the same type of action in the stage of making a product; learning by using refers to gains in knowledge and skills generated by the subsequent utilization of the product.
33. Mark Overton, *Agricultural Revolution in England: The Transformation of the Agrarian Economy 1500–1850* (Cambridge: Cambridge University Press, 1996), 41–2; Leslie Page Moch, *Moving Europeans: Migration in Western Europe since 1650* (Bloomington: Indiana University Press, 2003), 22, 34; Ann Kussmaul, *Servants in Husbandry in Early Modern England* (Cambridge: Cambridge University Press, 1981), 34.
34. Cornelisz Anthonisz, *Onderwijsinge vander zee om stuermanschap te leeren* (Amsterdam: Jan Ewoutsz, 1558), 6–7.
35. A. Teixeira De Mota, "Some Notes on the Organization of Hydrographical Services in Portugal before the Beginning of the Nineteenth Century," *Imago Mundi* 28, no. 1 (1976): 51–60; David C. Goodman, *Power and Penury: Government, Technology and Science in Philip II's Spain* (Cambridge: Cambridge University Press, 1988), 74–6.
36. Data from Paolo Malanima, *Pre-Modern European Economy: One Thousand Years (10th–19th Centuries)* (Leiden: Brill, 2009), 246.
37. Jürgen Kocka, *Capitalism. A Short History* (Princeton, NJ: Princeton University Press, 2016), 39–49.
38. Bert De Munck, "Corpses, Live Models, and Nature: Assessing Skills and Nature before the Industrial Revolution (Case Antwerp)," *Technology and Culture* 51, no. 2 (2010): 342.
39. As described in Karel Davids, *The Rise and Decline of Dutch Technological Leadership: Technology, Economy and Culture in the Netherlands, 1350–1800* (Leiden: Brill, 2008), 117.
40. Davids, "Apprenticeship and Guild Control," 69.
41. Davids, *Rise and Decline*, 12–3; Briot is quoted in Henry Heller, *Labour, Science and Technology in France 1500–1620* (Cambridge: Cambridge University Press, 1996), 180.
42. Joel Mokyr, *The Lever of Riches: Technological Creativity and Economic Progress* (New York: Oxford University Press, 1990), 12–13.
43. Malanima, *Pre-Modern European Economy*, 70–8, 94; Richard W. Unger, "Energy Sources for the Dutch Golden Age: Peat, Wind and Coal," *Research in Economic History* 33 (1984): 221–53.
44. See for example Elisabeth L. Eisenstein, *The Printing Press as an Agent of Change* (Cambridge: Cambridge University Press, 1979); Adrian Johns, *The Nature of the Book: Print and Knowledge in the Making* (Chicago, IL: University of Chicago Press, 1998).
45. Ulrich Pfister, "Craft Guilds and Technological Change: The Engine Loom in the European

Silk Ribbon Industry in the Seventeenth and Eighteenth Centuries," in *Guilds, Innovation and the European Economy, 1400–1800*, eds. Stephan R. Epstein and Maarten Prak (Cambridge: Cambridge University Press, 2008), 179, 196.

46. Maitte, "Cities of Glass"; Eduardo Demo, "New Products and Technological Innovation in the Silk Industry of Vicenza in the Fifteenth and Sixteenth Centuries," in *Innovation and Creativity*, eds. Davids and De Munck, 81–93; Andrea Caracausi, "Textiles Manufacturing, Product Innovations and Transfers of Technology in Padua and Venice between the Sixteenth and Eighteenth Centuries," in *Innovation and Creativity*, eds. Davids and De Munck, 131–60; Francesco Ammannati, "Craft Guild Legislation and Woolen Production: The Florentine *Arte della Lana* in the Fifteenth and Sixteenth Centuries," in *Innovation and Creativity*, eds. Davids and De Munck, 55–87.
47. Amelang, *Flight of Icarus*, 56, 112.
48. Joan Thirsk, *Economic Policy and Projects: The Development of a Consumer Society in Early Modern England* (Oxford: Oxford University Press, 1978), 3–10.
49. Heller, *Labour, Science and Technology*, 89–96, 123–6, 174–83; Goodman, *Power and Penury*, 260–4.

Chapter Six

1. Gerd Zillhardt, *Der Dreissigjährige Krieg in zeitgenössischer Darstellung: Hans Heberles "Zeytregister" (1618–1672), Aufzeichnungen aus dem Ulmer Territorium. Ein Beitrag zu Geschichtsschreibung und Geschichtsverständnis der Unterschichten. Forschungen zur Geschichte der Stadt Ulm, herausgegeben vom Stadtarchiv Ulm*, vol. 13 (Ulm: Stadtarchiv Ulm, 1975), 93–4.
2. Hans Medick, "The Thirty Years' War as Experience and Memory: Contemporary Perceptions of a Macro-Historical Event," in *Enduring Loss in Early Modern Germany: Cross Disciplinary Perspectives*, ed. Lynne Tatlock (Leiden: Brill, 2010), 36–9.
3. See Jan Lucassen, *Migrant Labour in Europe, 1600–1900* (London: Routledge and Kegan Paul, 1987); Leslie Page Moch, *Moving Europeans: Migration in Western Europe since 1650* (Bloomington: University of Indiana Press, 1992); Nicholas Canny, ed., *Europeans on the Move: Studies on European Migration, 1500–1800* (Oxford: Clarendon Press, 1994); Dirk Hoerder, *Cultures in Contact: World Migrations in the Second Millennium* (Durham, NC: Duke University Press, 2002); Jan Lucassen and Leo Lucassen, "The Mobility Transition Revisited, 1500–1900: What the Case of Europe Can Offer to Global History," *Journal of Global History* 4, no. 3 (2009): 347–77.
4. Jan Lucassen and Leo Lucassen, "Discussion—Global Migration," *Journal of Global History* 6, no. 2 (2011): 304.
5. Steve Hochstadt, "Migration in Preindustrial Germany," *Central European History* 16, no. 3 (1983): 195–224.
6. Robert Jütte, *Poverty and Deviance in Early Modern Europe* (Cambridge: Cambridge University Press, 1994), 2.
7. Anne McCants, "Historical Demography," in *Oxford History of Early Modern European History, 1350–1750*, vol. I, ed. Hamish M. Scott (Oxford: Oxford University Press, 2015), 126.
8. Josef Ehmer, "Quantifying Mobility in Early Modern Europe: The Challenge of Concepts and Data," *Journal of Global History* 6, no. 2 (2011): 330–1.
9. Moch, *Moving Europeans*, 29–31, 41–3.
10. Lucassen and Lucassen, "Mobility Transition Revisited," 363.

11. Moch, *Moving Europeans*, 31.
12. Ibid., 33.
13. For European family patterns and labor mobility, see Mikolaj Szoltysek, "Households and Family Systems," in *Oxford Handbook of Early Modern European History*, ed. Scott, 326.
14. Moch, *Moving Europeans*, 14–5, 34.
15. Merry Wiesner, "Gender and the Worlds of Work," in *Germany: A New Social and Economic History, Volume 1, 1450–1630*, ed. Bob Scribner (London: Arnold, 1996), 220.
16. Regina Grafe, "Economic and Social Trends," in *Oxford Handbook of Early Modern European History*, ed. Scott, 281.
17. Lucassen and Lucassen, "Mobility Transition Revisited," 361. Note that these figures exclude Russia, Poland, the Balkans, and the Ottoman Empire and that the Lucassens acknowledge that these figures are likely to be too low, as they miss the many short-term migrants who moved into cities during the period.
18. Christian Pfister, "The Population of Late-Medieval and Early Modern Germany," in *Germany: A New Social and Economic History*, ed. Scribner, 55.
19. Moch, *Moving Europeans*, 46.
20. Carlo M. Cipolla, *Before the Industrial Revolution: European Society and Economy, 1000–1700* (New York: W.W. Norton, 1994), 157.
21. Pfister, "Population," 55–6.
22. Moch, *Moving Europeans*, 7–8.
23. Rolf Kießling, "Markets and Marketing, Town and Country," in *Germany: A New Social and Economic History*, ed. Scribner, 153–6.
24. William Wright, "The Nature of Early Capitalism," in *Germany: A New Social and Economic History*, ed. Scribner, 182–4.
25. Edwin Hall, *The Arnolfini Betrothal: Medieval Marriage and the Enigma of Van Eyck's Double Portrait* (Berkeley: University of California Press, 1994).
26. James R. Farr, *Artisans in Europe, 1300–1914* (Cambridge: Cambridge University Press, 2000), 49.
27. Ibid., 147.
28. Wiesner, "Gender and the Worlds of Work," 221–2.
29. Ibid., 224.
30. Farr, *Artisans in Europe*, 147.
31. Ibid., 36.
32. Ibid., 106.
33. Szoltysek, "Households and Family Systems," 326–7.
34. Pfister, "Population," 46.
35. Wiesner, "Gender and the Worlds of Work," 222.
36. Jütte, *Poverty and Deviance*, 145–6.
37. Ibid., 148.
38. For repressive measures against vagrants, see Bert De Munck and Anne Winter, *Gated Communities? Regulating Migration in Early Modern Cities* (Farnham: Ashgate, 2012).
39. Jütte, *Poverty and Deviance*, 167.
40. Ibid., 157.
41. See Lyndal Roper, *The Holy Household: Women and Morals in Reformation Augsburg* (Oxford: Oxford University Press, 1990).
42. See Danielle van den Heuvel, "Selling in the Shadows: Peddlers and Hawkers in Early Modern Europe," in *Working on Labour: Essays in Honor of Jan Lucassen*, eds. Marcel van den Linden and Leo Lucassen (Leiden: Brill, 2012).

43. See Heiko A. Oberman, *John Calvin and the Reformation of the Refugees* (Geneva: Droz, 2009).
44. Olivier Pétré-Grenouilleau, "Maritime Powers, Colonial Powers: The Role of Migration (c. 1492–1792)," in *Migration, Trade, and Slavery in an Expanding World: Essays in Honor of Pieter Emmer*, ed. Wim Klooster (Leiden: Brill, 2009), 64.
45. Ulrich Niggemann, "Inventing Immigrant Traditions in Seventeenth- and Eighteenth-Century Germany: The Huguenots in Context," in *Migrations in the German Lands, 1500–2000*, eds. Jason Coy, Jared Poley, and Alexander Schunka (New York: Berghahn, 2016), 152.
46. Alexander Schunka, "Migration in the German Lands: An Introduction," in *Migration in the German Lands*, ed. Coy, Poley, and Schunka, 13.
47. For the activities of soldiers as a form of labor mobility, see Erik-Jan Zürcher, "Fighting for a Living in Europe and Asia," in *Working on Labour*, eds. Van Den Linden and Lucassen.
48. Margaret R. Hunt, "Social Roles and Individual Identities," in *Oxford History of Early Modern European History*, ed. Scott, 363. See also Geoffrey Parker, *The Military Revolution: Military Innovation and the Rise of the West, 1500–1800* (Cambridge: Cambridge University Press, 1988).
49. Lucassen and Lucassen, "Mobility Transition Revisited," 368.
50. Ibid., 352, 357.
51. Eric Nellis, *Shaping the New World: African Slavery in the Americas, 1500–1888* (North York: University of Toronto Press, 2013), 44.
52. Lucassen and Lucassen, "Mobility Transition Revisited," 355.
53. See Timothy J. Coates, *Convicts and Orphans: Forced and State-Sponsored Colonizers in the Portuguese Empire, 1550–1755* (Stanford, CA: Stanford University Press, 2001).
54. Wright, "The Nature of Early Capitalism," 202.
55. Nellis, *Shaping the New World*, 65.
56. Stanley Engerman, "War, Colonization, and Migration over Five Centuries," in *Migration, Trade, and Slavery*, ed. Klooster, 22.
57. Wim Klooster, "Introduction," in *Migration, Trade, and Slavery*, ed. Klooster, 2.
58. Nellis, *Shaping the New World*, 55–6.
59. Filipa Ribeiro Da Silva, "Dutch Labour Migration to West Africa (c. 1590–1674)," in *Migration, Trade, and Slavery*, ed. Klooster, 76, 81.
60. Nellis, *Shaping the New World*, 77.
61. Pétré-Grenouilleau, "Maritime Powers, Colonial Powers," 68.
62. David Eltis, "Free and Coerced Migrations from the Old World to the New," in *Coerced and Free Migration: Global Perspectives*, ed. David Eltis (Stanford, CA: Stanford University Press, 2002), 44–5.
63. Nellis, *Shaping the New World*, 2, 52.
64. Ibid., 29, 51.
65. Figures from David Eltis, "Slavery and Freedom in the Early Modern World," in *Terms of Labor: Slavery, Serfdom and Free Labour*, ed. Stanley L. Engerman (Stanford, CA: Stanford University Press, 1999), 28–30.
66. Daragh Grant, "'Civilizing' the Colonial Subject: The Co-Evolution of State and Slavery in South Carolina, 1670–1739," *Comparative Studies in Society and History* 57, no. 3 (2015): 606–36.
67. Jacqueline Jones, "Labour and the Idea of Race in the American South," *Journal of Southern History* LXXV, no. 3 (2009): 613–26.
68. Leslie Page Moch, "From Regional to Global Repertoires of Migration", *Journal of Global History* 6, no. 2 (2011): 322.

69. Pfister, "Population," 56.
70. Edgar Melton, "The Agrarian East," in *Oxford History of Early Modern European History*, ed. Scott, 439.
71. Christopher Friedrichs, "German Social Structure, 1300–1600," in *Germany: A New Social and Economic History*, ed. Scribner, 247.

Chapter Seven

1. As argued in Catharina Lis and Hugo Soly, *Worthy Efforts: Attitudes to Work and Workers in Pre-Industrial Europe* (Leiden: Brill, 2012), especially chaps. 1–3.
2. The eminent English judge and scholar Sir Anthony Fitzherbert in the Prologue to his famous *Boke of Husbandry* (1523/34), https://archive.org/stream/bookofhusbandry00fitzuoft/bookofhusbandry00fitzuoft_djvu.txt (accessed January 16, 2018).
3. Hervé Martin, "La prédication comme travail reconnu et rétribué à la fin du Moyen Âge," in *Le travail au Moyen Âge: Une approche interdisciplinaire. Actes du Colloque international à Louvain-la-Neuve, 21–23 mai 1987*, eds. Jacqueline Hamesse and Colette Muraille-Samaran (Louvain-la-Neuve: Institut d'Études médiévales, 1990), 400.
4. Quoted in Lisa H. Cooper, *Artisans and Narrative Craft in Late Medieval England* (Cambridge: Cambridge University Press, 2011), 176.
5. Quotations in Tom Rutter, *Work and Play on the Shakespearean Stage* (Cambridge: Cambridge University Press, 2008), 61–2.
6. Desiderius Erasmus Roterodamus, *The Praise of Folly*, trans. and ed. Clarence H. Miller (New Haven, CT: Yale University Press, 1979), 77.
7. Cotrugli, *Traité de la marchandise et du parfait marchand*, trans. and ed. Luc Marco and Robert Noumen (Paris: L'Harmattan, 2008), 22–3.
8. Myriam Greilsammer, *Een pand voor het paradijs: Leven en zelfbeeld van Lowys Porquin, Piëmontees zakenman in de zestiende-eeuwse Nederlanden* (Tielt: Lannoo, 1989), 119.
9. Philipp Robinson Rössner, "Critical Introduction" in Martin Luther, *On Commerce and Usury (1524)*, ed. Philipp Robinson Rössner (London: Anthem Press, 2014), 142.
10. Conrad Peutinger, scion of a prominent merchant family and a senior official who figured prominently in Augsburg politics, was the only humanist who openly defended the Fuggers and other major companies. See especially Clemens Bauer, "Conrad Peutingers Gutachten zur Monopolfrage," *Archich für Reformationsgeschichte* 45 (1954): 1–43, 145–96.
11. Quoted by Brian Vickers, "Leisure and Idleness in the Renaissance: The Ambivalence of Otium," *Renaissance Studies* 4 (1990): 130.
12. See Chapter Three in this volume.
13. Catharina Lis and Hugo Soly, *Poverty and Capitalism in Pre-Industrial Europe* (Brighton: The Harvester Press, 1982), 87–90.
14. Juan Luis Vives, *De subventione pauperum sive de humanis necessitatibus: Libri II* in *Selected Works of J.L. Vives*, vol. IV, trans. and ed. Constant Matheeussen and Charles Fantazzi (Leiden: Brill, 2002), 101, 105.
15. Quoted and trans. Germano Maifreda, *From Oikonomia to Political Economy: Constructing Economic Knowledge from the Renaissance to the Scientific Revolution* (Aldershot: Ashgate, 2012), 178.
16. Antoine De Montchrestien, *Traicté de l'oeconomie politique*, ed. François Billacois (Geneva: Droz, 1999), 123 (our translation).
17. On the meanings of honor, see James Farr, *Hands of Honor: Artisans and Their World in Dijon, 1550–1650* (Ithaca, NY: Cornell University Press, 1988); Arnold Kluge, *Die Zünfte* (Stuttgart: Franz Steiner, 2007), 107–15, 121–4.

18. See especially Richard Van Dülmen, *Der ehrlose Mensch: Unehrlichkeit und soziale Ausgrenzung in der frühen Neuzeit* (Cologne: Böhlau, 1999).
19. Robert Boyle quoted in William E. Houghton, Jr., "The History of Trades: Its Relation to Seventeenth-Century Thought: As Seen in Bacon, Petty, Evelyn, and Boyle," *Journal of the History of Ideas* 2 (1941): 41.
20. The expression comes from Eric H. Ash, *Power, Knowledge, and Expertise in Elizabethan England* (Baltimore, MD: Johns Hopkins University Press, 2004).
21. Antonio Averlino Filarete, *Filarete's Treatise on Architecture*, vol. I, trans. and ed. John R. Spencer (New Haven, CT: Yale University Press, 1965), 245–55.
22. Quoted by Pamela O. Long, *Artisan/Practitioners and the Rise of the New Sciences, 1400–1600* (Corvallis: Oregon State University Press, 2011), 88.
23. Quoted by Christopher P. Heuer, *The City Rehearsed: Object, Architecture, and Print in the Worlds of Hans Vredeman de Vries* (London: Routledge, 2009), 45.
24. Théophraste Paracelse, *La grande, vraye et parfaicte chirurgie*. French translation of the (first) German edition of 1536 (Antwerp: Silvius, 1567), 90.
25. Andreas Vesalius, *On the Fabric of the Human Body: A Translation of "De Humani Corporis Fabrica Libri Septem,"* Book I: *The Bones and Cartilages*, eds. William Frank Richardson and John Burd Carman (San Francisco, CA: Norman Publishing, 1998), li.
26. Pamela H. Smith, "Vermilion, Mercury, Blood, and Lizards: Matter and Meaning in Metalworking," in *Materials and Expertise in Early Modern Europe*, eds. Ursula Klein and E.C. Spary (Chicago, IL: University of Chicago Press, 2010), 48.
27. The expression comes from Frank Lestringant, *L'atelier du cosmographe, ou l'image du monde à la Renaissance* (Paris: Albin Michel, 1991), 34, who uses it to characterize the knowledge of self-taught individuals such as Palissy.
28. Quoted by Florike Egmont, "Natuurlijke historie en *savoir prolétaire*," in *Kometen, monsters en muilezels: het veranderende natuurbeeld en de natuurwetenschap in de zeventiende eeuw*, eds. Florike Egmond, Eric Jorink, and Rienk Vermij (Haarlem: Arcadia, 1999), 55.
29. Quoted in Jeroen Vandommele, *Als in een spiegel: Vrede, kennis en gemeenschap op het Antwerpse Landjuweel van 1561* (Hilversum: Verloren, 2011), 371.
30. Juan Luis Vives, *De tradendis disciplinis*, trans. Foster Watson (Cambridge: Cambridge University Press, 1913), 283.
31. For more detail see Lis and Soly, *Worthy Efforts*, chap. 4. See also Chapter Two in this volume.
32. Jost Amman and Hans Sachs, *The Book of Trades [Ständebuch]*, ed. Benjamin A. Rifkin (New York: Dover, 1973).
33. On women in artisanal trades, see Chapter Three in this volume.
34. The quotation comes from John Michael Montias, *Artists and Artisans in Delft: A Socio-Economic Study of the Seventeenth Century* (Princeton, NJ: Princeton University Press, 1982), 75.

Chapter Eight

1. Michel Mollat Du Jourdin and Philippe Wolff, *Ongles Bleus, Jacques et Ciompi: Les révolutions populaires en Europe aux XIVe et XVe siècles* (Paris: Calmann-Lévy, 1970).
2. Boris Fedorovich Porshnev, *Les soulèvements populaires en France de 1623 à 1647* (Paris: S.E.V.P.E.N., 1963); Roland Mousnier, *Fureurs paysannes: Les paysans dans les révoltes du XVIIe Siècle (France, Russie, Chine)* (Paris: Calmann-Lévy, 1967).
3. See for example, Mousnier, *Fureurs paysannes*; Yves-Marie Bercé, *Croquants et Nu-Pieds. Les soulèvements paysans en France du XVIe au XIXe Siècle* (Paris: Gallimard, 1974); Robin

Briggs, *Communities of Belief: Cultural and Social Tension in Early Modern France* (Oxford: Clarendon Press, 1989), 117–63.
4. See of course the founding essay of E. P. Thompson, "The Moral Economy of the English Crowd in the Eighteenth Century," *Past and Present* 50 (1971): 76–136.
5. Bercé, *Croquants et Nu-Pieds*; Peter Blickle, *Kommunalismus: Skizzen einer geselschaftlichen Organisationsform* (Munich: Oldenbourg, 2000); as well as Wayne P. Te Brake, *Shaping History: Ordinary People in European Politics, 1500–1700* (Berkeley: University of California Press, 1998).
6. William Beik, *Urban Protest in Seventeenth-Century France: The Culture of Retribution* (Cambridge: Cambridge University Press, 1997), 6.
7. See James C. Scott, *Domination and the Arts of Resistance: Hidden Transcripts* (New Haven, CT: Yale University Press, 1990); James C. Scott, *Weapons of the Weak: Everyday Forms of Peasant Resistance* (New Haven, CT: Yale University Press, 1985).
8. Rudolf Dekker, "Labour Conflicts and Working-Class Culture in Early Modern Holland," *International Review of Social History* 35, no. 3 (1990): 379, has not led to further research.
9. Peter Arnade, *Beggars, Iconoclasts and Civic Patriots: The Political Culture of the Dutch Revolt* (Ithaca, NY: Cornell University Press, 2008), 106–7.
10. John E. Archer, *Social Unrest and Popular Protest in England, 1780–1840* (Cambridge: Cambridge University Press, 2000), 1–2, quotes on 1.
11. Quotes in Patrick Lantschner, "Revolts and the Political Order of Cities in the Late Middle Ages," *Past and Present* 225 (2014): 3, 5.
12. Katherine A. Lynch, *Individuals, Families, and Communities in Europe, 1200–1800: The Urban Foundation of Western Society* (Cambridge: Cambridge University Press, 2003).
13. See for example, Stephan R. Epstein and Maarten Prak, eds., *Guilds, Innovation, and the European Economy, 1400–1800* (Cambridge: Cambridge University Press, 2008).
14. Samuel K. Cohn Jr., *Lust for Liberty: The Politics of Social Revolt in Medieval Europe, 1200–1425* (Cambridge, MA: Harvard University Press, 2009).
15. Yves-Marie Bercé, *History of Peasant Revolts: The Social Origins of Rebellion in Early Modern France*, trans. Amanda Whitmore (Ithaca, NY: Cornell University Press, 1990).
16. Buchanan Sharp, *In Contempt of All Authority: Rural Artisans and Riot in the West of England, 1586–1660* (Berkeley: University of California Press, 1980).
17. Andy Wood, "The Place of Custom in Plebeian Political Culture: England, 1550–1800," *Social History* 22, no. 1 (1997): 51–2.
18. Thomas Buchner, "Perceptions of Work in Early Modern Economic Thought: Dutch Mercantilism and Central European Cameralism in Comparative Perspective," in *The Idea of Work in Europe from Antiquity to Modern Times*, eds. Josef Ehmer and Catharina Lis (Farnham: Ashgate, 2009), 191–214.
19. Jan Dumolyn and Jelle Haemers. "Takehan, Cockerulle and Mutemaque: Naming Collective Action in the Later Medieval Low Countries," in *The Routledge History Handbook of Medieval Revolt*, eds. Justine Firnhaber-Baker and Dirk Schoenaers (Abingdon: Routledge, forthcoming).
20. Thomas Max Safley, "Production, Transaction, and Proletarianisation: The Textile Industry in Upper Swabia, 1580–1660," in *The Workplace before the Factory: Artisans and Proletarians, 1500–1800*, eds. Thomas Max Safley and Leonard N. Rosenband (Ithaca, NY: Cornell University Press, 1993), 118–45.
21. Catharina Lis and Hugo Soly, "De macht van 'vrije arbeiders': Collectieve acties van hoedenmakersgezellen in de Zuidelijke Nederlanden (Zestiende-Negentiende eeuw)," in *Werken volgens de regels: Ambachten in Brabant en Vlaanderen, 1500–1800*, eds. Catharina Lis and Hugo Soly (Brussels: VUB Press, 1994).

22. Andreas Grießinger, *Das symbolische Kapital der Ehre: Streikbewegungen und kollektives Bewußtsein deutscher Handwerksgesellen im 18 Jahrhundert* (Berlin: Ullstein, 1981).
23. Alfons K.L. Thijs, "Religion and Social Structure: Religious Rituals in Pre-Industrial Trade Associations," in *Craft Guilds in the Early Modern Low Countries: Work, Power and Representation*, eds. Maarten Prak, Catharina Lis, Jan Lucassen, and Hugo Soly (Aldershot: Ashgate, 2006), 157–73.
24. Natalie Zemon Davis, "A Trade Union in Sixteenth-Century France," *The Economic History Review* 19, no. 1 (1966): 48–69; Also, Lis and Soly, "De Macht van 'Vrije Arbeiders'," 18; Catharina Lis and Hugo Soly, *Worthy Efforts: Attitudes to Work and Workers in Pre-Industrial Europe* (Leiden: Brill, 2012), 533.
25. An exemplary study in this respect is Norah Carlin, "Liberty and Fraternities in the English Revolution: The Politics of London Artisans' Protests, 1635–1659," *International Review of Social History* 39, no. 2 (1994): 223–54.
26. Jan Materné, "Social Emancipation in European Printing Workshops before the Industrial Revolution," in *The Workplace before the Factory*, eds. Safley and Rosenband, 204–24.
27. See Thomas M. Safley, *Children of the Laboring Poor: Expectation and Experience Among the Orphans of Early Modern Augsburg* (Leiden: Brill, 2005) esp. chap. 8.
28. Bert De Munck, "La qualité du corporatisme. Stratégies économiques et symboliques des corporations anversoises du XVe siècle à leur abolition," *Revue d'Histoire Moderne et Contemporaine* 54, no. 1 (2007): 116–44; and "Skills, Trust and Changing Consumer Preferences: The Decline of Antwerp's Craft Guilds from the Perspective of the Product Market, ca. 1500–ca. 1800," *International Review of Social History* 53, no. 2 (2008): 197–233.
29. Jeannine Quillet, "Community, Counsel and Representation," in *The Cambridge History of Medieval Political Thought*, ed. James Henderson Burns (Cambridge: Cambridge University Press, 1988), 530; Nicolai Rubinstein, "Italian Political Thought, 1450–1530," in *The Cambridge History of Political Thought: 1450–1700*, ed. James Henderson Burns (Cambridge: Cambridge University Press, 1991), 30–65, quote on 39.
30. Cary J. Nederman, *Community and Consent: The Secular Political Theory of Marsiglio of Padua's Defensor Pacis* (London: Rowman & Littlefield Publishers, 1995), 61; Antony Black, *Guild and State: European Political Thought from the Twelfth Century to the Present*, 4th edn. (New Brunswick: Transaction Publishers, 2009), 86–95; quote in Francis Oakley, "Legitimation by Consent: The Question of Medieval Roots," *Viator* 14 (1983): 317.
31. Pamela O. Long, *Artisan/Practitioners and the Rise of the New Sciences, 1400–1600* (Corvallis: Oregon State University Press, 2011).
32. As argued in Bert De Munck, "Disassembling the City: A Historical and an Epistemological View on the Agency of Cities," *Journal of Urban History* 43, no. 5 (2017) 5: 11–829.
33. Hans Van Werveke, *Gent. Schets van een sociale geschiedenis* (Ghent: Rombaut-Fecheijr, 1947), 46–8; Walter Prevenier and Marc Boone, "De 'stadstaat'-droom," in *Gent. Apologie van een rebelse stad*, ed. Johan Decavele (Antwerp: Mercatorfonds, 1989), 84.
34. Bert De Munck and Anna Bellavitis, "The Urban Imaginary as a Social and Economic Factor: Renaissance Cities and the Fabrication of Quality, 15th–17th century," in *Cities and Creativity from the Renaissance to the Present*, eds. Ilja Van Damme, Bert De Munck, and Andrew Miles (London: Routledge, 2017), 45–64.
35. Black, *Guild and State*.
36. See, among other work. James Farr, *Hands of Honor: Artisans and their World in Dijon, 1550–1650* (Cambridge: Cambridge University Press, 1988).

Chapter Nine

1. Tony Blackshaw, *Leisure* (London: Routledge, 2010), 22.
2. Norbert Elias and Eric Dunning, *Quest for Excitement: Sport and Leisure in the Civilizing Process* (Oxford: Blackwell, 1986).
3. Ibid., 97.
4. Alessandro Arcangeli, *Recreation in the Renaissance: Attitudes towards Leisure and Pastimes in European Culture, 1425–1675* (Basingstoke: Palgrave Macmillan, 2003).
5. Peter Borsay, *A History of Leisure: The British Experience since 1500* (Basingstoke: Palgrave Macmillan, 2006).
6. Ronald Hutton, *The Rise and Fall of Merry England: The Ritual Year 1400–1700* (Oxford: Oxford University Press, 1994).
7. Ronald Hutton, *The Stations of the Sun: A History of the Ritual Year in Britain* (Oxford: Oxford University Press, 1996), VII.
8. Borsay, *History of Leisure*, 14.
9. Ibid.
10. Paul Hazard, *The European Mind, 1680–1715*, trans. J. L. May (Harmondsworth: Penguin, (1935) 1973).
11. Keith Thomas, "Work and Leisure in Pre-industrial Society," *Past and Present* 29 (1964): 53.
12. Peter Burke, "The Invention of Leisure in Early Modern Europe," *Past and Present* 146 (1995): 147.
13. Michael Pye, *The Edge of the World: How the North Sea Made Us Who We Are* (London: Penguin, 2014), 2.
14. Robun Dettingmeijer, "The Emergence of the Bathing Culture Marks the End of the North Sea as a Common Cultural Ground," in *The North Sea and Culture (1550–1800)*, eds. Juliette Roding and Lex Heerma Van Voss (Hilversum: Uitgeverij Verloren, 1996), 489.
15. Alain Corbin, *The Lure of the Sea: The Discovery of the Seaside in the Western World, 1750–1840*, trans. Jocelyn Phelps (Berkeley: University of California Press, 1994), 38–9.
16. Borsay, *History of Leisure*, 30–1; Peter Clark, *The English Alehouse: A Social History, 1200–1830* (London: Longman, 1983); Beat Kümin and B. Ann Tlusty eds. *The World of the Tavern: Public Houses in Early Modern Europe* (Aldershot: Ashgate, 2002).
17. Mack P. Holt, "Europe Divided: Wine, Beer, and the Reformation in Sixteenth-Century Europe," in *Alcohol: A Social and Cultural History*, ed. Mack P. Holt (Oxford: Berg, 2006), 35–6.
18. Ralph S. Hattox, *Coffee and Coffeehouses: The Origins of a Social Beverage in the Medieval Near East* (Seattle: University of Washington Press, 1988); Markman Ellis, *The Coffee House: A Cultural History* (London: Weidenfeld & Nicolson, 2004).
19. Beth L. Glixon, and Jonathan E. Glixon. *Inventing the Business of Opera: The Impresario and His World in Seventeenth-Century Venice* (Oxford: Oxford University Press, 2003); Wendy Heller, *Emblems of Eloquence: Opera and Women's Voices in Seventeenth-Century Venice* (Berkeley: University of California Press, 2003).
20. Cees De Bondt, *Royal Tennis in Renaissance Italy* (Turnhout: Brepols, 2006).
21. Mikhail Bakhtin, *Rabelais and His World*, trans. H. Iswolsky (Bloomington: Indiana University Press, (1965) 1984).
22. Thorstein Veblen, *The Theory of the Leisure Class* (London: Allen and Unwin, 1899); Chris Rojek, "Veblen, Leisure and Human Need," *Leisure Studies* 14, no. 2 (1995): 73–86.
23. Pierre Bourdieu, *Distinction*, trans. Richard Nice (Cambridge, MA: Harvard University Press, 1984).

24. Catharina Lis, and Hugo Soly, *Worthy Efforts: Attitudes to Work and Workers in Pre-Industrial Europe* (Leiden: Brill, 2012), 552–3. Their main bibliographical reference for the reconstruction of this late shift is David Cannadine's work on the changes the British aristocracy underwent between the late nineteenth and the mid-twentieth centuries (David Cannadine, *The Decline and Fall of the British Aristocracy* [New Haven, CT: Yale University Press, 1990], passim and 386–7).
25. See also Chapter Seven in this volume.
26. Peter Burke, *Popular Culture in Early Modern Europe* (Farnham: Ashgate, (1978) 2009).
27. Edward Muir, *Ritual in Early Modern Europe*, 2nd edn. (Cambridge: Cambridge University Press, 2005).
28. Borsay, *History of Leisure*, 25.
29. Ibid.
30. Alison G. Stewart, *Before Bruegel: Sebald Beham and the Origins of Peasant Festival Imagery* (Aldershot: Ashgate, 2008).
31. Elias and Dunning, *Quest for Excitement*.
32. Philippe Stubbes quoted in Thomas, "Work and Leisure," 54 n. 21.
33. Robert C. Davis, *The War of the Fists: Popular Culture and Public Violence in Late Renaissance Venice* (New York: Oxford University Press, 1994).
34. Lynn Malluck Brooks, ed., *Women's Work: Making Dance in Europe before 1800* (Madison: University of Wisconsin Press, 2007).
35. Arcangeli, *Recreation in the Renaissance*.
36. Phillipe Ariès, *Centuries of Childhood*, trans. Robert Baldick (New York: Vintage Books, 1962).
37. Paul Griffiths, *Youth and Authority: Formative Experiences in England 1560–1640* (Oxford: Oxford University Press, 1996), 2–4.
38. Ibid.
39. Benjamin B. Roberts, *Sex and Drugs Before Rock'n'Roll* (Amsterdam: Amsterdam University Press, 2012).
40. Herman Roodenburg, ed., *Cultural Exchange in Early Modern Europe*, vol. 4, *Forging European Identities, 1400–1700* (Cambridge: European Science Foundation and Cambridge University Press, 2006).
41. Norbert Elias, *The Civilizing Process*, trans. Edmund Jephcott, rev. edn. (Oxford: Blackwell, (1939) 1994).
42. Frank Lestringant, "L'oisiveté du sauvage," in *L'oisiveté au temps de la Renaissancen*, ed. Marie-Thérèse Jones-Davies (Paris: Presses de l'Université de Paris-Sorbonne, 2002), 209–32.
43. Aldo Gennaï, *L'Idéal du repos dans la littérature française du XVIe siècle* (Paris: Classiques Garnier, 2011), 321–63. For some remarks on the Western and Christian work ethic in comparative perspective, see Lis and Soly, *Worthy Efforts*, 553.
44. Gennaï, *L'Idéal du repos dans la littérature française*, provides an in-depth analysis of sixteenth-century French literature, which also includes such authors as Erasmus and Thomas More.
45. Keith Thomas, *The Ends of Life: Roads to Fulfilment in Early Modern England* (Oxford: Oxford University Press, 2009), 10.
46. Brian Vickers, "Leisure and Idleness in the Renaissance: The Ambivalence of *Otium*," *Renaissance Studies* 4, no. 1 (1990): 1–37; no. 2 (1990): 107–54. See also Chapter Seven in this volume.
47. On the functions of alcohol in traditional Europe, see A. Lynn Martin, *Alcohol, Sex, and Gender in Late Medieval and Early Modern Europe* (Basingstoke: Palgrave, 2001); for an analysis of religious variation, see Holt, "Europe Divided," 25–40.

48. In a historiographical appendix, de Vries lists five commercial revolutions as identified by various scholars: Jan de Vries, *The Industrious Revolution: Consumer Behavior and the Household Economy, 1650 to the Present* (Cambridge: Cambridge University Press, 2008), 37–9. The first two fall in the period under consideration here: the Renaissance, and the Baroque (on which, see Roman Sandgruber, "Leben und Lebensstandard im Zeitalter des Barock: Quellen und Ergebnisse," in *Methoden und Probleme der Alltagsforschung im Zeitalter des Barock*, ed. Othmar Pickl and Helmuth Feigl [Vienna: Verlag der Österreichischen Akademie der Wissenschaften, 1992], 171–89); the latter, a "new world of goods" that supposedly was put in place between the sixteenth and the eighteenth centuries, would have provided a lasting set of consumer practices, on top of which the subsequent industrialization process only needed to alter techniques of production; Evelyn S. Welch, *Shopping in the Renaissance* (New Haven, CT: Yale University Press, 2005).
49. Ulinka Rublack, *Dressing Up: Cultural Identity in Renaissance Europe* (Oxford: Oxford University Press, 2010), with reference to carnival and mummery, doll-houses, garden parties, and much else.
50. Chandra Mukerji, *From Graven Images: Patterns of Modern Materialism* (New York: Columbia University Press, 1983).
51. Lisa Jardine, *Worldly Goods: A New History of the Renaissance* (London: Macmillan, 1996).
52. Allessandra Rizzi, ed., *Statuta de ludo: Le leggi sul gioco nell'Italia di comune (secoli XIII–XVI)* (Rome–Treviso: Viella-Fondazione Benetton Studi Ricerche, 2012).
53. Borsay, *History of Leisure*, 46–7.
54. Arcangeli, *Recreation in the* Renaissance, 81–5.
55. Borsay, *History of Leisure*, 49.
56. Gherardo Ortalli, *Barattieri. Il gioco d'azzardo fra economia ed etica. Secoli XIII–XV* (Bologna: Il Mulino, 2012).
57. This narrative was, however, questioned in a *Past and Present* conference discussion; see Thomas, "Work and Leisure," 63–6.

FURTHER READINGS

Allen, Robert C. "Economic Structure and Agricultural Productivity in Europe, 1300–1800." *European Review of Economic History* 4, no. 1 (2000): 1–26.

Allen, Robert C. "The Great Divergence in European Wages and Prices from the Middle Ages to the First World War." *Explorations in Economic History* 38, no. 4 (2001): 411–47.

Amelang, James S. *The Flight of Icarus: Artisan Autobiography in Early Modern Europe*. Stanford: Stanford University Press, 1998.

Arasse, Daniel. " L'art et l'illustration du pouvoir." In *Culture et idéologie dans la genèse de l'etat moderne*, edited by Centre National de la Recherche Scientifique, 231–44. Rome: Ecole Française de Rome, 1985.

Arcangeli, Alessandro. "Freizeit." In *Enzyklopädie der Neuzeit*, edited by Friedrich Jaeger, vol. 3, 1215–21. Stuttgart-Weimar: Metzler, 2006 (English translation in progress).

Arcangeli, Alessandro. *Recreation in the Renaissance: Attitudes towards Leisure and Pastimes in European Culture, 1425–1675*. Basingstoke: Palgrave Macmillan, 2003.

Arnoux, Mathieu, and Pierre Monnet, eds. *Le technicien dans la cité en Europe occidentale, 1250–1650*. Rome: École française de Rome, 2004.

Ash, Eric H. *Power, Knowledge, and Expertise in Elizabethan England*. Baltimore, MD: Johns Hopkins University Press, 2004.

Aston, Trevor H., and Charles H.E. Philpin, eds. *The Brenner Debate: Agrarian Class Structure and Economic Development in Pre-Industrial Europe*. Cambridge: Cambridge University Press, 1976.

Beck, Patrice, Philippe Bernardi, and Laurent Feller, eds. *Rémunérer le travail au Moyen Âge: Pour une histoire sociale du salariat*. Paris: A. et J. Picard, 2014.

Belfanti, Carlo Marco. "Guilds, Patents and the Circulation of Technical Knowledge. Northern Italy during the Early Modern Age." *Technology and Culture* 45, no. 3 (2004): 569–89.

Bellavitis, Anna. "Apprentissages masculins, apprentissages féminins à Venise au XVIe siècle." *Histoire Urbaine* 15, no. 1 (2006): 49–73.

Bellavitis, Anna. *Famille, genre, transmission à Venise au XVIe siècle*. Rome: Ecole Française de Rome, 2008.

Bellavitis, Anna. *Il lavoro delle donne nelle città dell'Europa moderna*. Rome: Viella, 2016.

Bellavitis, Anna, Manuela Martini, and Raffaella Sarti, eds. *Familles laborieuses. Rémunération, transmission et apprentissage dans les ateliers familiaux de la fin du Moyen Âge à l'époque contemporaine en Europe*. Mélanges de l'Ecole Française de Rome, Italie-Méditerranée 128, no. 1 (2016), https://mefrim.revues.org/2366.

Bercé, Yves-Marie. *Révoltes et révolutions dans l'Europe moderne, XVIe–XVIIIe siècles*. Paris: Presses Universitaires de France, 1980.

Bergin, Joseph. *Church, Society and Religious Change in France 1580–1730*. New Haven, CT: Yale University Press, 2009.

Beveridge, William. *Prices and Wages in England from the Twelfth to the Nineteenth Century*. vol I. *Price Tables: Mercantile Era*. London: Longmans, 1939.

Blackshaw, Tony. *Leisure*. London: Routledge, 2010.

Borsay, Peter. *A History of Leisure: The British Experience since 1500*. Basingstoke: Palgrave Macmillan, 2006.

Borucki, Alex, David Eltis, and David Wheat. "Atlantic History and the Slave Trade to Spanish America." *American Historical Review* 120, no. 2 (2015): 433–61.

Boulton, Jeremy. "Wage Labour in Seventeenth-Century London." *Economic History Review* 49, no. 2 (1996): 268–90.

Bowley, Arthur L. *Wages and Income in the United Kingdom since 1860*. Cambridge: Cambridge University Press, 1937.

Brandt, Robert, and Thomas Buchner, eds. *Nahrung, Markt oder Gemeinnutz: Werner Sombart und das vorindustrielle Handwerk*. Bielefeld: Verlag für Regionalgeschichte, 2004.

Brenner, Robert. "Property and Progress: Where Adam Smith Went Wrong." In *Marxist History-Writing for the Twenty-First Century*, edited by Chris Wickham, 49–111. Oxford: Oxford University Press, 2007.

Broadhead, Philip J. "Guildsmen, Religious Reform and the Search for the Common Good: The Role of the Guilds in the Early Reformation in Augsburg." *The Historical Journal* 39, no. 3 (1996): 577–97.

Brooks, Christopher W. *Law, Politics and Society in Early Modern England*. Cambridge: Cambridge University Press, 2008.

Brooks, Lynn M., ed. *Women's Work: Making Dance in Europe before 1800*. Madison: University of Wisconsin Press, 2007.

Bruijnen, Yvette. *De Vier Jaargetijden in de kunst van de Nederlanden 1500–1750*. Zwolle: Waanders, 2003.

Brunelle, Gayle K. "Contractual Kin: Servants and their Mistresses in Sixteenth-Century Nantes." *Journal of Early Modern History* 2, no. 4 (1998): 374–94.

Burke, Peter. "The Invention of Leisure in Early Modern Europe." *Past and Present* 146 (1995): 136–50.

Cannadine, David. *The Decline and Fall of the British Aristocracy*. New Haven, CT: Yale University Press, 1990.

Canny, Nicholas, ed. *Europeans on the Move: Studies on European Migration, 1500–1800*. Oxford: Oxford University Press, 1994.

Capp, Bernard. "The Double Standard Revisited: Plebeian Women and Male Sexual Reputation in Early Modern England." *Past and Present* 162 (1999): 70–100.

Caracausi, Andrea. *Dentro la bottega. Culture del lavoro in una città d'età moderna*. Venice: Marsilio, 2008.

Caracausi, Andrea. "The Price of an Apprentice: Contracts and Trials in the Woollen Industry in Sixteenth-Century Italy." *Mélanges de l'École française de Rome—Italie et Méditerranée modernes et contemporaines* 128, no. 1 (2016), http://mefrim.revues.org/2476.

Castiglione, Baldassare. *The Book of the Courtier*, translated by T. Hoby. London: Everyman, (1528) 1994.

Cavaciocchi, Simonetta, ed. *Il tempo libero: Economia e società (loisirs, leisure, tiempo libre, Freizeit) secc. XIII–XVIII*. Prato: Istituto internazionale di storia economica "F. Datini"-Le Monnier, 1995.

Cerman, Markus, and Sheilagh Ogilvie, eds. *European Proto-Industrialization*. Cambridge: Cambridge University Press, 1996.

Cipolla, Carlo M. *Before the Industrial Revolution: European Society and Economy, 1000–1700*. New York: W.W. Norton, 1994.

Clark, Alice. *Working Life of Women in the Seventeenth Century*. London: Franck Cass & Co., 1919.

Clark, Peter. *The English Alehouse: A Social History, 1200–1830*. London: Longman, 1983.

Coates, Timothy J. *Convicts and Orphans: Forced and State-Sponsored Colonizers in the Portuguese Empire, 1550–1755*. Stanford, CA: Stanford University Press, 2001.

Coleman, Donald C. "Proto-Industrialization: A Concept Too Many." *Economic History Review* 36, no. 3 (1983): 435–48.

Collins, Harry. *Tacit and Explicit Knowledge*. Chicago, IL: University of Chicago Press, 2010.

Coy, Jason, Jared Poley, and Alexander Schunka, eds. *Migration in the German Lands, 1500–2000*. New York: Berghahn, 2016.

Crossick, Geoffrey, ed. *The Artisan and the European Town, 1500–1900*. Aldershot: Scolar Press, 1997.

Crowston, Clare. *Fabricating Women: The Seamstresses of Old Regime France, 1675–1791*. Durham, NC: Duke University Press, 2001.

Crowston, Clare. "An Industrious Revolution in Seventeenth-Century Paris: New Vocational Training for Adolescent Girls." In *Secret Gardens, Satanic Mills. Placing Girls in European History, 1750–1960*, edited by Mary Jo Maynes, Birgitte Søland, and Christina Benninghaus. Bloomington: Indiana University Press, 2005.

Dambruyne, Johan. *Corporatieve middengroepen: Aspiraties, relaties en transformaties in de 16de-eeuwse Gentse ambachtswereld*. Gent: Academia Press, 2002: 69–82.

Davids, Karel. "Great Transformations: Economic History and the History of Technology." *Tijdschrift voor Sociale en Economische Geschiedenis* 11, no. 2 (2014): 307–26.

Davids, Karel. "The Bookkeeper's Tale: Learning Merchant Skills in the Northern Netherlands in the Sixteenth Century." In *Education and Learning in the Netherlands, 1400–1600*, edited by Koen Goudriaan, Jaap van Moolenbroek, and Ad Tervoort, 235–52. Leiden: Brill, 2004.

Davids, Karel. *The Rise and Decline of Dutch Technological Leadership: Technology, Economy and Culture in the Netherlands, 1350–1800*. Leiden: Brill, 2008.

Davids, Karel, and Bert De Munck, eds. *Innovation and Creativity in Late Medieval and Early Modern European Cities*. Aldershot: Ashgate, 2014.

Davis, Natalie Zemon. "The Rites of Violence: Religious Riot in Sixteenth-Century France." *Past and Present* 59 (1973): 51–91.

Davis, Natalie Zemon. "The Sacred and the Body Social in Sixteenth-Century Lyon." *Past and Present* 90 (1981): 40–70.

Davis, Natalie Zemon. *Society and Culture in Early Modern France*. 4th edn. Stanford: Stanford University Press, 1977.

Davis, Ralph. *The Rise of the Atlantic Economies*. Ithaca: Cornell University Press, 1973.

Davis, Robert C. *Shipbuilders of the Venetian Arsenal: Workers and Workplace in the Preindustrial City*. Baltimore, MD: Johns Hopkins University Press, 1991.

Davis, Robert C. *The War of the Fists: Popular Culture and Public Violence in Late Renaissance Venice*. New York: Oxford University Press, 1994.

De Jongh, Eddy. *Questions of Meaning. Theme and Motif in Dutch Seventeenth-Century Painting*. New York: Brepols, 2004.

De Munck, Bert. "Corpses, Live Models, and Nature: Assessing Skills and Nature before the Industrial Revolution (Case Antwerp)." *Technology and Culture* 51, no. 2 (2010): 332–56.

De Munck, Bert. "Disassembling the City: A Historical and an Epistemological View on the Agency of Cities." *Journal of Urban History* 5 (2017): 811–829.

De Munck, Bert. "One Counter and Your Own Account: Redefining Illicit Labour in Early Modern Antwerp." *Urban History* 37, no. 1 (2010): 26–44.

De Munck, Bert. *Technologies of Learning: Apprenticeship in Antwerp Guilds from the 15th Century to the End of the Old Regime*. Turnhout: Brepols, 2007.

De Munck, Bert. "The Agency of Branding and the Location of Value. Hallmarks and Monograms in Early Modern Tableware Industries." *Business History* 54, no. 7 (2012): 1–22.

De Munck, Bert, and Anne Winter, eds. *Gated Communities? Regulating Migration in Early Modern Cities*. Aldershot: Ashgate, 2012.

De Munck, Bert, Steven L. Kaplan, and Soly Hugo, eds. *Learning on the Shop Floor: Historical Perspectives on Apprenticeship*. New York: Berghan Books, 2007.

De Ridder-Symoens, Hilde. "Chapitre 8: Formation et professionnalisation." In *Les élites du pouvoir et la construction de l'Etat en Europe*, edited by Wolfgang Reinhard, 203–35. Paris: Presses universitaires de France, 1996.

De Vries, Annette, ed. *Cultural Mediators: Artists and Writers at the Crossroads of Tradition, Innovation and Reception in the Low Countries and Italy, 1450–1650*. Leuven: Peeters, 2008.

De Vries, Annette. *Ingelijst werk: De verbeelding van arbeid en beroep in de vroegmoderne Nederlanden*. Zwolle: Waanders, 2004.

De Vries, Jan. *The Dutch Rural Economy in the Golden Age, 1500–1700*. New Haven, CT: Yale University Press, 1974.

De Vries, Jan. *The Industrious Revolution: Consumer Behavior and the Household Economy, 1650 to the Present*. Cambridge: Cambridge University Press, 2008.

De Vries, Jan, and Ad van der Woude. *The First Modern Economy: Success, Failure, and Perseverance of the Dutch Economy, 1500–1815*. Cambridge: Cambridge University Press, 1997.

Deijk, Frank van. "Een ooggetuige van belang? Isaac Claeszoon Swanenburg en zijn weergave van de Leidse saaiproductie." *Textielhistorische bijdragen* 33 (1993): 7–42.

Dekker, Rudolf. *Holland in beroering: Oproeren in de 17de en 18de eeuw*. Baarn: Ambo, 1982.

Dekker, Rudolf. "Labour Conflicts and Working-Class Culture in Early Modern Holland." *International Review of Social History* 35, no. 3 (1990): 377–420.

Donoghue, John, and Evelyn P. Jennings. *Building the Atlantic Empires: Unfree Labor and Imperial States in the Political Economy of Capitalism, ca. 1500–1914*. Leiden: Brill, 2015.

Dubourg Glatigny, Pascal, and Hélène Vérin, eds. *Réduire en art. La technologie de la Renaissance aux Lumières*. Paris: Maison des Sciences de l'Homme, 2008.

Dumolyn, Jan. "'Our Land is Only Founded on Trade and Industry'. Economic Discourses in Fifteenth-Century Bruges." *Journal of Medieval History* 36, no. 4 (2010): 374–89.

Dumolyn, Jan, and Jelle Haemers. "Patterns of Urban Rebellion in Medieval Flanders." *Journal of Medieval History* 31, no. 4 (2005): 369–93.

Dumolyn, Jan, et al., eds. *The Voices of the People in Late Medieval Europe: Communication and Popular Politics*. Turnhout: Brepols, 2014.

Duplessis, Robert S. *Transitions to Capitalism in Early Modern Europe*. Cambridge: Cambridge University Press, 1997.

Eamon, William. *Science and the Secrets of Nature. Books of Secrets in Medieval and Early Modern Culture*. Princeton, NJ: Princeton University Press, 1994.

Egmond, Florike. "Natuurlijke historie en *savoir prolétaire*." In *Kometen, monsters en muilezels: het veranderende natuurbeeld en de natuurwetenschap in de zeventiende eeuw*, edited by Florike Egmond, Eric Jorink, and Rienk Vermij, 53–71. Haarlem: Arcadia, 1999.

Ehmer, Josef. "Arbeitsdiskurse im deutschen Sprachraum des 15. und 16. Jahrhunderts." In *Semantiken von Arbeit: Diachrone und vergleichende Perspektiven*, edited by Jörn Leonhard and Willibald Steinmetz, 93–114. Cologne: Böhlau, 2016.

Ehmer, Josef. "Artisans, Journeymen, Guilds and Labor Markets: Thinking about European Comparative Perspectives." In *Dalla corporazione al mutuo soccorso: Organizazione e tutela del lavoro tra XVI e XX secolo*, edited by Paolo Massa and Angelo Moioli. Milan: Franco Angeli, 2006: 57–69.

Ehmer, Josef. "Quantifying Mobility in Early Modern Europe: The Challenge of Concepts and Data." *Journal of Global History* 6, no. 2 (2011): 327–38.

Ehmer, Josef, and Catharina Lis, eds. *The Idea of Work from Antiquity to Modern Times*. Aldershot: Ashgate, 2009.

Eisenstein, Elisabeth L. *The Printing Press as an Agent of Change*. Cambridge: Cambridge University Press, 1979.

Elias, Norbert. *La société de cour*. Paris: Flammarion, 1985.

Elias, Norbert. *The Civilizing Process*, translated by E. Jephcott, rev. edn. Oxford: Blackwell, (1939) 1994.

Elias, Norbert, and Eric Dunning. *Quest for Excitement: Sport and Leisure in the Civilizing Process*. Oxford: Blackwell, 1986.

Ellis, Markman. *The Coffee House: A Cultural History*. London: Weidenfeld & Nicolson, 2004.

Elsas, Moritz J. *Umriss einer Geschichte der Preise und Löhne in Deutschland vom ausgehenden Mittelalter bis zum Beginn des neunzehnten Jarhhunderts*, 2 vols. Leiden: A. W. Sijthoff, (1936) 1949.

Eltis, David, ed. *Coerced and Free Migration: Global Perspectives*. Stanford, CA: Stanford University Press, 2002.

Eltis, David. "Slavery and Freedom in the Early Modern World." In *Terms of Labor: Slavery, Serfdom and Free Labor*, edited by Stanley L. Engerman, 25–49. Stanford, CA: Stanford University Press, 1999.

Epstein, Stephan R. "Craft Guilds, Apprenticeship and Technological Change in Preindustrial Europe." *The Journal of Economic History* 58, no. 3 (1998): 684–713.

Epstein, Stephan R., and Maarten Prak, eds. *Guilds, Innovation, and the European Economy, 1400–1800*. Cambridge: Cambridge University Press, 2008.

Evenden, Doreen. *The Midwives of Seventeenth Century London*. Cambridge: Cambridge University Press, 2000.

Farr, James R. *Artisans in Europe, 1300–1914*. Cambridge: Cambridge University Press, 2000.

Farrago, Claire J. "The Classification of the Visual Arts in the Renaissance." In *Knowledge from the Renaissance to the Enlightenment*, edited by Donald R. Kelley and Richard H. Popkin, 23–48. Dordrecht: Kluwer, 1991.

Fogel, Robert William, and Stanley L. Engermann. *Time on the Cross: The Economics of American Negro Slavery*. Boston: Little, Brown and Company, 1974.

Fourquin, Guy. *Les soulèvements populaires au Moyen Âge*. Paris: Presses universitaires de France, 1972.

Franceschi, Franco. "… e saremo tutti ricchi." *Lavoro, mobilità sociale e conflitti nelle città dell'Italia medievale*. Pisa: Pacini, 2012.

Freedberg, David, and Jan de Vries, eds. *Art in History, History in Art. Studies in Seventeenth-Century Dutch Culture*. Santa Monica, CA: The Getty Center Publications, 1991.

Games, Alison. *Migration and the Origins of the English Atlantic World*. Cambridge, MA: Harvard University Press, 1999.

Gélis, Jacques. *La sage femme et le médecin: Une nouvelle conception de la vie*. Paris: Fayard, 1988.

Gennaï, Aldo. *L'idéal du repos dans la littérature française du XVIe siècle*. Paris: Classiques Garnier, 2011.

Grendler, Paul F. *Schooling in Renaissance Italy: Literacy and Learning, 1300–1600*. Baltimore, MD: Johns Hopkins University Press, 1989.

Guazzo, Stefano. *The Art of Conversation*, translation. London: J. Brett, (1574) 1738.

Hall, Bert S. "'Der Meister sol auch kennen schreiben und lesen': Writings about Technology ca.1400–1600." In *Early Technologies*, edited by Denise Schmandt-Besserat, 47–58. Malibu, CA: Undena Publications, 1979.

Hamilton, Earl J. *American Treasure and the Price Revolution in Spain, 1501–1650*. Cambridge, MA: Harvard University Press, 1934.

Hamilton, Earl J. *Money, Prices and Wages in Valencia, Aragon and Navarre, 1351–1500*. Cambridge, MA: Harvard University Press, 1936.

Hamilton, Earl J. *War and Prices in Spain, 1651–1800*. Cambridge, MA: Harvard University Press, 1947.

Haupt, Heinz-Gerhard, ed. *Das Ende der Zünfte: Ein europäischer Vergleich*. Göttingen: Vandenhoeck & Ruprecht, 2002.

Hauser, Henri. *Ouvriers du temps passé (XVe–XVIe siècles)*. Paris: Alcan, 1927.

Hauser, Henri. *Recherches et documents sur l'histoire des prix en France de 1500 à 1800*. Paris: Impr. Les Presses modernes, 1936.

Heller, Henry. *Labour, Science and Technology in France 1500–1620*. Cambridge: Cambridge University Press, 1996.

Hilaire-Pérez, Liliane, and Catherine Verna. "Dissemination of Technical Knowledge in the Middle Ages and the Early Modern Era: New Approaches and Methodological Issues." *Technology and Culture* 47, no. 3 (2006): 536–65.

Hilton, Rodney H. *Bond Men made Free: Medieval Peasant Movements and the English Rising of 1381*. London: Routledge, 2003.

Hilton, Rodney H., ed. *The Transition from Feudalism to Capitalism*. London: NLB, 1976.

Hobsbawm, Eric J. *Labouring Men: Studies in the History of Labour*. London: Weidenfeld and Nicolson, 1968.

Hoerder, Dirk. *Cultures in Contact: World Migrations in the Second Millennium*. Durham, NC: Duke University Press, 2002.

Hoffman, Philip. *Growth in a Traditional Society: The French Countryside, 1450–1815*. Princeton, NJ: Princeton University Press, 1996.

Hoffman, Philip, et al. "Real Inequality in Europe since 1500." *Journal of Economic History* 62, no. 2 (2002): 322–55.

Horell, Sara, and Jane Humphries. "Old Questions, New Data, and Alternative Perspectives: Families' Living Standards in the Industrial Revolution." *Journal of Economic History* 52, no. 4 (1992): 849–80.

Horell, Sara, and Jane Humphries. "The Exploitation of Little Children: Child Labor and the Family Economy in the Industrial Revolution." Explorations in Economic History 47, no. 32 (1995): 485–516.

Houston, Robert A. *Literacy in Early Modern Europe: Culture and Education 1500–1800*. London: Longman, 1988.

Hunt, Edward H. *Regional Wage Variations in Britain, 1850–1914*. Oxford: Clarendon Press, 1973.

Hutton, Ronald. *The Rise and Fall of Merry England: The Ritual Year 1400–1700*. Oxford: Oxford University Press, 1994.

Hutton, Ronald. *The Stations of the Sun: A History of the Ritual Year in Britain*. Oxford: Oxford University Press, 1996.

Johns, Adrian. *The Nature of the Book: Print and Knowledge in the Making*. Chicago, IL: University of Chicago Press, 1998.

Joyce, Patrick, ed. *The Historical Meanings of Work*. Cambridge: Cambridge University Press, 1987.

Joyce, Patrick. *Work, Society and Politics: The Culture of the Factory in Later Victorian England*. Brighton: The Harvester Press, 1980.

Jütte, Robert. *Poverty and Deviance in Early Modern Europe*. Cambridge: Cambridge University Press, 1994.

Klooster, Wim, ed. *Migration, Trade, and Slavery in an Expanding World: Essays in Honor of Pieter Emmer*. Leiden: Brill, 2009.

Klooster, Wim, and Alfred Padula, eds. *The Atlantic World: Essays on Slavery, Migration and Imagination*. Upper Saddle River, NJ: Routledge. 2005.

Knotter, Ad, and Jan Luiten van Zanden. "Immigratie en arbeidsmarkt in Amsterdam in de 17^e eeuw." *Tijdschrift voor Sociale Geschiedenis* 13 (1987): 403–31.

Kocka, Jürgen. *Capitalism. A Short History*. Princeton, NJ: Princeton University Press, 2016.

Krausman Ben-Amos, Ilona. *Adolescence and Youth in Early Modern England*. New Haven, CT: Yale University Press, 1994.

Kriedte, Peter, Hans Medick, and Jürgen Schlumbohm, eds. *Industrialization before Industrialization*. Cambridge: Cambridge University Press, 1981.

Kümin, Beat, and B. Ann Tlusty, eds. *The World of the Tavern: Public Houses in Early Modern Europe*. Aldershot: Ashgate, 2002.

Kussmaul, Ann. *Servants in Husbandry in Early Modern England*. Cambridge: Cambridge University Press, 1981.

La trasmissione dei saperi nel Medioevo (secoli XII–XV). Pistoia: Centro Italiano di Studi di Storia e d'Arte, 2005.

Levasseur, Émile. *Histoire des classes ouvrières et de l'industrie en France de 1789 à 1870*. Paris: A. Rousseau, 1903–1904.

Levasseur, Émile. *Le coût de la vie: Suite de l'enquête sur le prix des denrées alimentaires depuis un quart de siècle dans 70 lycées*. Brussels: Office de la revue économique internationale, 1910.

Levasseur, Émile. *Les prix: aperçu de l'histoire économique de la valeur et du revenu de la terre en France du commencement du XIIIe siècle à la fin du XVIIIe. Avec un appendice sur le prix du froment et sur les disettes depuis l'an 1200 jusqu'à l'an 1894*. Paris: Chamerot et Renouard, 1893.

Lis, Catharina, and Hugo Soly. "'An Irresistible Phalanx': Journeymen Associations in Western Europe, 1300–1800." In *Before the Unions. Wage Earners and Collective Action in Europe, 1300–1850*, edited by Catharina Lis, Jan Lucassen, and Hugo Soly, 11–52. Cambridge: Cambridge University Press, 1994.

Lis, Catharina, and Hugo Soly, eds. *Werken volgens de regels: Ambachten in Brabant en Vlaanderen, 1500–1800*. Brussels: VUB Press, 1994.

Lis, Catharina, and Hugo Soly. *Worthy Efforts: Attitudes to Work and Workers in Pre-Industrial Europe*. Leiden: Brill, 2012.

Lis, Catharina, et al., eds. *Guilds in the Early Modern Low Countries. Work, Power and Representation*. London: Routledge, 2006.

Long, Pamela O. *Artisan/Practitioners and the Rise of the New Sciences, 1400–1600*. Corvallis: Oregon State University Press, 2011.

Long, Pamela O. *Openness, Secrecy, Authorship: Technical Arts and the Culture of Knowledge from Antiquity to the Renaissance*. Baltimore, MD: Johns Hopkins University Press, 2001.

Lucassen, Jan. *Migrant Labour in Europe, 1600–1900*. London: Routledge and Kegan Paul, 1987.

Lucassen, Jan, and Leo Lucassen, eds. *Migration, Migration History, History: Old Paradigms and New Perspectives*. Berlin: Peter Lang, 1997.

Lucassen, Jan, and Leo Lucassen. "The Mobility Transition Revisited, 1500–1900: What the Case of Europe Can Offer to Global History." *Journal of Global History* 4, no. 3 (2009): 347–77.

Lucassen, Jan, Tine De Moor, and Jan Lluiten van Zanden, eds. *The Return of the Guilds*.

Cambridge: Cambridge University Press, 2008 (*International Review of Social History*, Supplement 16).

Mackenney, Richard. *Tradesmen and Traders: The World of the Guilds in Venice and Europe, c. 1250–c. 1650*. London: Croom Helm, 1987.

Maifreda, Germano. *From Oikonomia to Political Economy: Constructing Economic Knowledge from the Renaissance to the Scientific Revolution*. Aldershot: Ashgate, 2012.

Malanima, Paolo. *Pre-modern European Economy: One Thousand Years (10th–19th Centuries)*. Leiden: Brill, 2009.

Manning, Patrick. *Migration in World History*. New York: Routledge, 2005.

Marcello, Luciano. "Andare a bottega: Adolescenza e apprendistato nelle arti (sec. XVI–XVII)." In *Infanzie*, edited by Ottavia Niccoli, 231–51. Florence: Ponte alle Grazie, 1993.

Marland, Hilary, ed. *The Art of Midwifery: Early Modern Midwives in Europe*. London: Routledge, 1993.

Martinat, Monica. "L'apprendistato." In *Storia del lavoro in Italia*, edited by Renata Ago. Rome: Castelvecchi, forthcoming.

Martini, Manuela, and Anna Bellavitis, eds. *Households, Family Workshops and Unpaid Market Work in Europe from the 16th Century to the Present*, special issue of *The History of the Family* 19, no. 3 (2014).

McCants, Anne E. C. *Civic Charity in a Golden Age*. Urbana: University of Illinois Press, 1997.

McClure, George W. *The Culture of Profession in Late Renaissance Italy*. Toronto: University of Toronto Press, 2004.

McIntosh, Marjorie Keniston. *Working Women in English Society, 1300–1620*. Cambridge: Cambridge University Press, 2005.

Mendels, Franklin Ford. "Proto-Industrialization: The First Phase of the Industrialization Process." *Journal of Economic History* 32, no. 1 (1972): 241–61.

Moch, Leslie Page. "From Regional to Global Repertoires of Migration." *Journal of Global History* 6, no. 2 (2011): 321–25.

Moch, Leslie Page. *Moving Europeans: Migration in Western Europe since 1650*. Bloomington: University of Indiana Press, 2009.

Mokyr, Joel. *The Gifts of Athena: Historical Origins of the Knowledge Economy*. Princeton, NJ: Princeton University Press, 2004.

Mokyr, Joel. *The Lever of Riches: Technological Creativity and Economic Progress*. New York: Oxford University Press, 1990.

Molà, Luca. *The Silk Industry of Renaissance Venice*. Baltimore, MD: Johns Hopkins University Press, 2000.

Muir, Edward. *Ritual in Early Modern Europe*, 2nd edn. Cambridge: Cambridge University Press, 2005.

Nederveen Meerkerk, Elise van. *De draad in eigen handen: Vrouwen en loonarbeid in de Nederlandse textielnijverheid, 1581–1810*. Amsterdam: Aksant, 2007.

Oakes, James. "Capitalism and Slavery and the Civil War." *International Labor and Working Class History* 89 (2016): 195–220.

Ogilvie, Sheilagh C. *A Bitter Living: Women, Markets, and Social Capital in Early Modern Germany*. Oxford: Oxford University Press, 2003.

Ogilvie, Sheilagh C. "Married Women, Work and Law: Evidence from Early Modern Germany." In *Married Women and the Law in Premodern Western Europe*, edited by Cordelia Beattie and Matthew Frank Stevens, 213–39. Woodbridge: Boydell Press, 2013.

Overton, Mark. *Agricultural Revolution in England: The Transformation of the Agrarian Economy 1500–1850*. Cambridge: Cambridge University Press, 1996.

Ozment, Steven E. *The Reformation in the Cities: The Appeal of Protestantism to Sixteenth-Century Germany and Switzerland*. 2nd edn. New Haven, CT: Yale University Press, 1980.

Panhuysen, Bibi. *Maatwerk: Kleermakers, naaisters, oudkleerkopers en de gilden (1500–1800)*. Amsterdam: Stichting Beheer IISG, 2000.

Perry, Elisabeth. *Gender and Disorder in Early Modern Seville*. Princeton, NJ: Princeton University Press, 1990.

Persson, Karl Gunnar. *An Economic History of Europe: Knowledge, Institutions and Growth, 600 to the Present*. Cambridge: Cambridge University Press, 2010.

Popplow, Marcus. *Neu, nützlich und erfindungsreich: Die Idealisierung von Technik in der frühen Neuzeit*. Münster: Waxmann Verlag, 1998.

Posthumus, Nicolaas W. *Nederlandsche prijsgeschiedenis*. Leiden: Brill, 1943.

Prak, Maarten R., ed. *Early Modern Capitalism*. London: Routledge, 2000.

Prak, Maarten, et al., eds. *Craft Guilds in the Early Modern Low Countries: Work, Power and Representation*. Aldershot: Ashgate, 2006.

Putnam, Robert D. *Making Democracy Work: Civic Traditions in Modern Italy*. Princeton, NJ: Princeton University Press, 1993.

Reddy, William M. *The Rise of Market Culture: The Textile Trade and French Society, 1750–1900*. Cambridge: Cambridge University Press, 1984.

Reher, David S. *Town and Country in Pre-Industrial Spain, Cuenca, 1550–1870*. Cambridge: Cambridge University Press, 1990.

Reher, David, and Esmeralda Ballesteros. "Precios y salarios en Castilla La Nueva: La construcción de un índice de salarios reales, 1501–1991." *Revista de Historia Econòmica* 11, no. 1 (1993): 101–51.

Reith, Reinhold. *Lohn und Leistung: Lohnformen im Gewerbe, 1450–1900*. Stuttgart: Franz Steiner Verlag, 1999.

Reith, Reinhold, ed. *Praxis der Arbeit: Probleme und Perspektiven der handwerksgeschichtlichen Forschung*. Frankfurt/Main: Campus Verlag, 1998.

Rizzi, Alessandro, ed. *Statuta de ludo: Le leggi sul gioco nell'Italia di comune (secoli XIII–XVI)*. Rome–Treviso: Viella-Fondazione Benetton Studi Ricerche, 2012.

Roberts, Lissa. "The Circulation of Knowledge in Early Modern Europe: Embodiment, Mobility, Learning and Knowing." *History of Technology* 31 (2012): 47–68.

Roberts, Lissa, Simon Schaffer, and Peter Dear, eds. *The Mindful Hand: Inquiry and Invention from the Late Renaissance to Early Industrialization*. Amsterdam: Edita, 2007.

Robinson, David James, ed. *Migration in Colonial Spanish America*. Cambridge: Cambridge University Press, 1990.

Rojek, Chris. "Veblen, Leisure and Human Need." *Leisure Studies* 14, no. 2 (1995): 73–86.

Romano, Dennis. "The Regulation of Domestic Service in Renaissance Venice." *The Sixteenth Century Journal* 22, no. 4 (1991): 661–77.

Roodenburg, Herman, ed. *Cultural Exchange in Early Modern Europe*, vol. 4, *Forging European Identities, 1400–1700*. Cambridge: European Science Foundation and Cambridge University Press, 2006.

Roper, Lyndal, *The Holy Household: Women and Morals in Reformation Augsburg*. Oxford: Clarendon Press, 1989.

Rosenband, Leonard N. *Papermaking in Eighteenth-Century France: Management, Labor, and Revolution at the Montgolfier Mill, 1761–1805*. Baltimore, MD: Johns Hopkins University Press, 2000.

Rutter, Tom. *Work and Play on the Shakespearean Stage*. Cambridge: Cambridge University Press, 2008.

Safley, Thomas Max. *Charity and Economy in the Orphanages of Early Modern Augsburg.* Boston, MA: Humanities Press, 1997.

Safley, Thomas Max. *Children of the Laboring Poor: Expectation and Experience among the Orphans of Early Modern Augsburg.* Leiden: Brill, 2005.

Safley, Thomas Max, and Leonard N. Rosenband, eds. *The Workplace before the Factory. Artisans and Proletarians, 1500–1800.* Ithaca, NY: Cornell University Press, 1993.

Sarti, Raffaella. "Criados, Servi, Domestiques, Gesinde, Servants: For a Comparative History of Domestic Service in Europe (16th–19th centuries)." *Obradoiro de Historia Moderna* 16 (2007): 9–39.

Schmid, Wolfgang. "Der Renaissancekünstler als Handwerker." In *Wert und Bewertung von Arbeit im Mittelalter und in der frühen Neuzeit. Herwig Ebner zum 65. Geburtstag.* Graz: Institut für Geschichte der Karl-Franzens-Universität, 1995.

Scholliers, Peter. "Wages." In *The Oxford Encyclopedia of Economic History.* Oxford: Oxford University Press, 2003.

Scholliers, Peter, and Leonard Schwarz, eds. *Experiencing Wages: Social and Cultural Aspects of Wage Forms in Europe since 1500.* New York: Berghahn Books, 2006.

Schulz, Knut. *Denn sie lieben die Freiheit so Sehr ... : Kommunale Aufstände und Entstehung des europäischen Bürgertums im Hochmittelalter.* Darmstadt: Wissenschaftliche Buchgesellschaft, 1992.

Schulz, Knut. "Die Politische Zunft: Eine die spätmittelalterliche Stadt prägende Institution?" In *Verwaltung und Politik in Städten Mitteleuropas. Beiträge zu Verfassungsnorm und Verfassungswirklichkeit in altständischer Zeit*, edited by Wilfried Ehbrecht, 1–20. Cologne: Böhlau, 1994.

Schulz, Knut, ed. *Handwerk in Europa vom Spätmittelalter bis zur frühen Neuzeit.* Munich: Schriften des historischen Kollegs, Kolloquien 41, 1999.

Schulz, Knut. *Handwerk, Zünfte und Gewerbe: Mittelalter und Renaissance.* Darmstadt: Wissenschaftliche Buchgesellschaft, 2010.

Schulz, Knut. *Handwerkgesellen und Lohnarbeiter: Untersuchungen zur oberrheinischen und oberdeutschen Stadtgeschichte des 14. bis 17. Jahrhunderts.* Sigmaringen: Thorbecke, 1985.

Schwarz, Leonard. "Custom, Wages and Workload in England during Industrialization." *Past and Present* 197 (2007): 143–75.

Scott, Hamisch, ed. *Oxford History of Early Modern European History, 1350–1750*, vol. I. Oxford: Oxford University Press, 2015.

Scribner, Bob, ed. *Germany: A New Social and Economic History, Volume 1, 1450–1630.* London: Arnold, 1996.

Sewell, William H., Jr. *Logics of History: Social Theory and Social Transformation.* Chicago, IL: University of Chicago Press, 2005.

Sewell, William H., Jr. *Work and Revolution in France. The Language of Labor from the Old Regime to 1848.* Cambridge: Cambridge University Press, 1980.

Sherrin, Marshall, ed. *Women in Reformation and Counter-Reformation Europe.* Bloomington: Indiana University Press, 1989.

Silver, Larry. "Massys and Money: The Tax Collectors Rediscovered." *Journal of Historians of Netherlandish Art* 7 (Summer 2015). https://doi.org/10.5092/jhna.2015.7.2.2.

Simonton, Deborah. "Apprenticeship: Training and Gender in Eighteenth-Century England." In *Markets and Manufacture in Early Industrial Europe*, edited by Maxine Berg. London: Routledge, 1991.

Skinner, Quentin. *The Foundations of Modern Political Thought.* Cambridge: Cambridge University Press, 1978.

Smith, Pamela H. *The Body of the Artisan: Art and Experience in the Scientific Revolution.* Chicago, IL: University of Chicago Press, 2004.

Smith, Pamela H. "Why Write a Book? From Lived Experience to the Written Word in Early Modern Europe." *Bulletin of the German Historical Institute* 47 (2010): 25–50.

Soly, Hugo. "Political Economy of European Craft Guilds: Power Relations and Economic Strategies of Merchants and Master Artisans in the Medieval and Early Modern Textile Industries." *International Review of Social History, Supplement* 53, S16 (2008): 45–71.

Sonenscher, Michael. *Work and Wages: Natural Law, Politics and the Eighteenth-Century French Trades.* Cambridge: Cambridge University Press, 1989.

Stedman Jones, Gareth. *Languages of Class: Studies in English Working Class History 1832–1982.* Cambridge: Cambridge University Press, 1983.

Stella, Alessandro. "Des esclaves pour la liberté sexuelle de leurs maîtres (Europe Occidentale, XIV^c–XVIIIe siècles)." *Clio, Histoire, femmes et sociétés* 5 (1997): 191–209.

Stella, Alessandro. "Se soumettre pour se libérer: Une esclave turque face à son maître espagnol à Cadix en 1704." *Clio. Histoire, femmes et sociétés* 17 (2003): 163–74.

Te Brake, Wayne P. *Shaping History: Ordinary People in European Politics, 1500–1700.* Berkeley: University of California Press, 1998.

Thirsk, Joan, "Industries in the Countryside." In *Essays in the Economic and Social History of Tudor and Stuart England,* edited by Frederick J. Fisher, 70–88. Cambridge: Cambridge University Press, 1961.

Thomas, Keith. "Work and Leisure in Pre-industrial Society." *Past and Present* 29 (1964): 50–62.

Tilly, Louise A. "The Food Riot as a Form of Political Conflict in France." *The Journal of Interdisciplinary History* 2, no. 1 (1971): 23–57.

Todd, Margo. *Christian Humanism and the Puritan Social Order.* Cambridge: Cambridge University Press, 1987.

Unger, Richard W. "Energy Sources for the Dutch Golden Age: Peat, Wind and Coal." *Research in Economic History* 9 (1984): 221–53.

Valentín Vicente, Marta. "Images and Realities of Work/Women and Guilds in Early Modern Barcelona." In *Spanish Women in the Golden Age,* edited by Magdalena S. Sanchez and Alain Saint Saëns, 127–39. Westport, CT: Greenwood Press, 1996.

Van den Heuvel, Danielle. "Selling in the Shadows: Peddlers and Hawkers in Early Modern Europe." In *Working on Labor: Essays in Honor of Jan Lucassen,* edited by Marcel van den Linden and Leo Lucassen, 125–51. Leiden: Brill, 2012.

Van der Velden, Hugo T. "Defrocking St Eloy: Petrus Christus's *Vocational Portrait of a Goldsmith.*" *Simiolus* 26, no. 4 (1998): 242–76.

Van der Wee, Herman. "Prices and Wages as Development Variables: A Comparison between England and Belgium." In *The Low Countries in the Early Modern World,* edited by Hermann van der Wee, 223–41. Aldershot: Ashgate, 1993.

Vandommele, Jeroen. *Als in een spiegel: Vrede, kennis en gemeenschap op het Antwerpse Landjuweel van 1561.* Hilversum: Verloren, 2011.

Veblen, Thorstein. *The Theory of the Leisure Class.* London: Allen and Unwin, 1899.

Veldman, Ilja M. *Images for the Eye and Soul: Function and Meaning in Netherlandish Prints (1450–1650).* Leiden: Primavera Pers, 2006.

Veldman, Ilja M. *Profit and Pleasure: Print Books by Crispijn de Passe.* Rotterdam: Sound & Vision Interactive, 2001.

Vickers, Brian. "Leisure and Idleness in the Renaissance: The Ambivalence of Otium." *Renaissance Studies* 4 (1990): no. 1:1–37, no. 2:107–54.

Von Schmoller, Gustav. "Le mouvement historique des salaires de 1300 à 1900 et ses causes." *Revue Internationale de Sociologie* 12 (1904): 3–21.

Von Tyszka, Carl. *Löhne und Lebenskosten in Westeuropa im 19. Jahrhundert (Frankreich, England, Spanien, Belgien), nebst einem Anhang: Lebenskosten deutscher und westeuropäischer Arbeiter früher und jetzt.* Munich: Duncker and Humblot, 1914.

Wallis, Patrick. "Labor, Law and Training in Early Modern London: Apprenticeship and the City's Institutions." *Journal of British Studies* 51, no. 4 (2012): 791–819.

Whaley, Leigh. *Women and the Practice of Medical Care in Early Modern Europe, 1400–1800.* London: Palgrave Macmillan, 2011.

Whittle, Jane. "The House as a Place of Work in Early Modern Rural England." In *Home Cultures* 8, no. 2 (2011): 133–50.

Wiesner, Merry. *Working Women in Renaissance Germany.* New Brunswick, NJ: Rutgers University Press, 1986.

Woodward, Donald. *Men at Work: Labourers and Building Craftsmen in the Towns of Northern England, 1450–1750.* Cambridge: Cambridge University Press, 1995.

Zanden, Jan L. van, and Peter C. M. Hoppenbrouwers, eds. *Peasants into Farmers? The Transformation of Rural Economy and Society in the Low Countries (Middle ages-19th Century) in the Light of the Brenner Debate.* Turnhout: Brepols, 2001.

Zannini, Andrea. *Burocrazia e burocrati a Venezia in età moderna: i cittadini originari (sec. XVI–XVIII).* Venice: Istituto Veneto di Scienze, Lettere ed Arti, 1993.

Zannini, Andrea. "L'impiego pubblico." In *Storia di Venezia dalle origini alla caduta della Serenissima*, vol. IV, *Il Rinascimento. Politica e cultura*, edited by Alberto Tenenti and Ugo Tucci, 415–63. Rome: Istituto della Enciclopedia Italiana, 1996.

INDEX

Note: Page locators in italics refer to figures.

active society 133–4
actors 136, 172
Adam as prototype farmer 36–7, *36*
administrative elites, education of 89–91
age groups and leisure 169–70
ages of man 37, *38*
agrarian landscape, Low Countries 71–3, *72*
agricultural laborers 11, 21, 70, 73, 114–16
agriculture
    specialization 70, 71, 73
    women in 71, 72, 116, *116*
    worker mobility 114–16
    workplaces 69–73
alehouses 163, 164
allegorical themes, representation of work in 51–3, *52*, *53*, *54*
Amman, Jost 40, *41*, 67, 74, *75*, *76*, *77*, 141
anatomy lectures 106, *106*
Anthonisz, Cornelis 107
apprentices 29, 84, 99, 118, 119
apprenticeships 94–5, *96*, 118
    contracts 95, 96, 102, 103
    learning of skills 101–4
    length of 96, 103
    masterpieces 103
    women 103, 141
architects 138
aristocracy
    dérogeance legislation 136
    Italian texts on elite lifestyle of 166–7
    leisure 166
    work effort 131, 133, 166
Aristotle 83, 150, 155, 170
armies 122
art, commercialization of 33
artisans
    in defense of skills 151–7, 157–8
    deskilling of 3, 8, 109
    growing distance between artists and 8–9, 143
    inclusion in and exclusion from body politic 149–50, 155–6, 158
    inequalities within same trade 9–10
    numbers in Frankfurt 74
    role in emergence of experimental sciences 7–8
    urban protest 9, 10–11, 145, 147, 155
    urban workplaces 73–7
Asia 13–14
"assembly lines," Venice *Arsenale* 82–3
Augsburg, Germany
    female spinners 98
    fustian manufacturing 12–13
    household workshop ideal 84
    poverty line 22
    prostitution 99
    women's pay 98
Averlino, Antonia 138

Bacon, Francis 110, 134, 140
bankers 47, 133–4
baptisms 92
Barbados Slave Code 1661 125
Barcelona silk industry 97
beer 163, 164
begging 120, 134
Beuckelaer, Joachim 55, *57*, *58*
blacksmiths 53, *56*, 74
Book of Trades 40, *41*, 67, 74, *75*, *76*, *77*, 141
bookkeeping 105–6, 109
books 66–8, 105
    representations of work in prints and 39–43
Bourdieu, Pierre 166
brothels 62–5, *65*, 99, *100*
Bruegel the Elder, Pieter 34–5, *35*, *120*
Bruegel the Younger, Pieter *116*, *168*
Bullinger, Heinrich 86
businessmen 131–2

capital accumulation 5, 15, 19, 25–6
carnival 165
carpenters 44, *132*
Castiglione, Baldassarre 167

Catholic Church 92, 98–9, 112, 131, 168
chestnuts 73
child labor 30, 32, 95, 135
childbirth 91–3
"Children of the Planets" 51, *52*, *53*, *54*
Christian
    views on matrimony 86
    views on work 5, 6, 129, 130–1
    views on work in art 36–7, *36*
The Christian State of Matrimony 86
Christus, Petrus 47, *48*
churches
    as center of traditional community 164, 168
    work themes in art of 33, 44–5, 68
cities 73, 109, 116, 156
civil servants, education of 89–91
clergy 112, 130, 134, 166
Coenen, Adriaen 139
coerced labor 27, 30, 144
coffeehouses 164
colonial labor 121, 122–4
commodification 2
confessional exiles 121–2
construction workers 19–20, 118
consumer goods 13, 14, 19, 20, 109
consumer society, birth of 171
consumption, increases in 13, 14, 15
convict labor 30, 32
cottage industry. *See* proletarianization
cottages 84

dance 169, 172
Deploige, Jeroen 6
"Description of All the Low Countries" 71
domestic industry. *See* proletarianization
domestic service 93–4, 100, 115, 119
Dunning, Eric 160, 166
Dutch colonies 123–4, 125
duty to work 36–9, 130–5, 144

economic growth 13–15, 69
    differential 14–15
economic transformations and developments in technology 108–10
economy of work 17–32
    beyond the wage 27–31
    early history of wage studies 18–20
    and links with emergent nations and global trade 25–6, 27
    problem with wage studies 21–4
    revision of wage studies 24–7

Elias, Norbert 160, 166
energy sources 110
engine loom 111
English colonies 124, 125
engravings 40–3, *42*, *43*, *53*
expert mediators 137–8

family
    incomes 29–30
    participation in master artisan's work 77
farm servants 107
farmers
    Adam as prototype 36–7, *36*
    depictions in paintings of 33–6
    duty to work 37
    losing access to land 149
    respect for 141
Farr, James R. 10, 118, 158
fencing masters 136
festive culture 162, 165, 167
fights for entertainment 169
financial professions
    criticized for lack of work effort 132–4
    satires of 48–50, *49*, *50*
    vocational portraits 47
fishmongers *53*, *55*, *57*, *58*
food prices 20, 28
football, medieval 168–9
four elements, representation of *53*, *54*, *56*
four temperaments, concept of 51
fustian manufacturing 12–13

gambling 172
Garzoni, Tomaso 67
gender
    hierarchies in workplace culture 97
    labor mobility and 116, *116*
    leisure and 169
    rates of pay and 29
    roles and working inside or outside house 86
geo-political environment, changing 13–14
glassmakers *46*, 105, 107
global markets 12–13, 17, 32
    economy of work and links with 25–6, 27
    new consumer goods for 109
    production networks to produce goods for 27, 32
globalization 11–13, 32
goldsmiths 47, *48*, 142
Goltzius, Hendrick 50, 51, *53*, *54*, 60

INDEX

government administration, separation from ruling households 84
Guazzo, Stefano 167
Guicciardini, Ludovico 71
guilds 118, 119, 141, 147–8, 156, *157*
    concept of honor 136–7
    declining power of 12, 13, 150, 152
    in defense of skills 151–7, 157–8
    female 97, 103
    hall marks 156
    images of trades 43–5, *44*, *132*
    inclusion in and exclusion from body politic 149–50, 155–6, 157, 158
    member's wives in Germany 98
    oligarchization within 9–10, 150
    processions and rituals 96–7, 153, *153*, 156
    protection of trade secrets 105
    responses to technological innovations 111
    revolts 145, 147, 148
    and rules on permitting women 97, 98, 100, 141
    rural 107
    stipulations on training of apprentices 95, 96, 102

hall marks 156
hat makers 40, *41*
Hatcher, John 29
health-care 24
Heberle, Hans 113
Hobsbawm, Eric 24, 31
Holbein Jr., Hans 48, *132*
holidays 165, 168
Hollandsgänger 115
honour, concept of 136–7
Hopkins, Sheila V. 19–20, 21, 24, 26, 29
household
    connection with workplace 77
    culture as workplace culture 91–5
    incomes 29–30
    separation of workplace and 77, 83–5
    young people establishing own 115, 117
houses 84–5, 86
Huguenot emigration 122
humanism 7–8, 133, 134, 137

idleness 129, 133–4, 135
    aristocracy and accusations of 131
    depictions of 37, 62, *62*
illegitimate births 92
indentured servants 124

indoor and outdoor working 85–7
Industrial Revolution 3, 30, 162
inns 163, 164
intellectual artists 143, 144
Italian Renaissance
    apprenticeships of 95, 96
    increasing professionalization of state courts 89–90
    upper class leisure time 162, 166–7
itinerant workers 115, 118, 120, 121

Jode, Pieter de 51, *55*
journeymen 104, 141–2, 149
    associations 153–4
    attempts to control supply of labor 152–3
    migration 118–19
Joyce, Patrick 4

"The Kitchen Maid with the Supper of Emmaus" 59
kitchen maids 57, 58, 59, *59*
kitchens 55–9, *58*, *59*
knowledge. *See also* skills and technology
    circulation of skills and 102, 105, 107
    proletarian and unlearned 139–40
    secrecy surrounding trade 105
    technical writings and spreading of 105–6
    theory and practice 138–40, 144
    value of 137–8

labor as separate from politics 147–51
labor disputes 10–11, 141–2, 146
    politics in 151–7
labor mobility. *See* mobility and work
labor regulations 151–2
labor relations 12, 146–7, 149, 152
Landjuweel 140–1
large enterprises, workplaces in 78–83, 87
law education 90
lawyers, images of fraudulent 50, *50*
Le Nain, Louis 36
leaving parents' home, young people 115, 119
leisure 159–73
    age groups and 169–70
    class 165–6
    commercialization of 161, 167–8
    cultural and regional variation 170
    defining leisure versus work 159–61
    and gender 169
    humanist view of 134
    legislation 172
    market 171

and power 171–3
social hierarchy 165–9
space and time for 162–5
varieties of 170–1
working chronology 161–2
linen weavers 137, 152
literacy 104, 111–12, 140
Luther, Martin 5, 7

Machiavelli 85
manners, Italian texts on 166–7
Mantegna, Andrea 90, *95*
manual labor
    acquiring knowledge through 138, 140, 144
    distinction between mental labor and 102, 131, 144
    status of 37, 137, 139, 141
marginal migrants 120–1, *120*
market scenes 53–5, *57*, *58*
marriage 115, 117, 119
masons 138
masterpieces 103
master(s)
    becoming a 95–7
    conflicts between merchants and 151, 155
    decline in status of 149
    deskilling 109
    economic downturn and difficulties in becoming 118–19
    immigrants reaching rank of 119
    increasing reliance on merchant capital 149, 158
mathematics 8, 111–12, 138, 140
medicine 106, *106*, 138–9
mercantilism 135, 150
merchant capitalism 85, 109, 149, 158
merchants
    artisans standing up to oligarchy of 145
    conflicts between masters and 151, 155
    control of protoindustrial domestic production 12, 30, 85, 109
    long-distance trade 109, 117–18
    monopolist criticism directed at 133
    self-glorification 133
    vocational portraits 47–8, *136*
    work effort 131–2
mercury mine, Idrija, Slovenia 22–4
metalworkers 39–40, *39*, 74
midwives 91–3, 97
migration. *See also* mobility and work

rates 113, 117
seasonal 69, 70, 115
military labor 122
mining
    large enterprise 78–9, *80*, *81*, 87
    mercury mine, Idrija 22–4
    salt 86
    silver mines, Erzgebirge 45
mistress, becoming a master or 95–7
mobility and work 11, 113–28
    confessional exiles 121–2
    domestic servants 119
    gender and 116
    interurban migration 117
    marginal migrants 120–1
    migration rates 113, 117
    military and colonial labor 122–4
    rural 114–16
    slave trade and labor 124–6, 127, 128
    socioeconomic mobility 127–8
    steady streams of migration 11, 113–14
    urban 116–19
money lenders 133
monks 6, 130, 131
monopolists 133
Montaigne, Michel de 70
Montchrestien, Antoine de 135
Montefollonico, Italy 70–1
morality and immorality 98–100

Nahrung (sustenance) 154
natural history 139–40
naval dockyards 79–83, *82*
navigation skills 107–8, *108*
needle makers 77
New World
    colonial labor 122–4
    slave labor 124–6, 127, 128
Nova Reperta 40–3
numeracy, increased demand for 111–12

ocean shipping, expansion in 109, 110, 123–4
office space, separate 84–5
oil-mills 74
old age 127, 170
oligarchization and state formation processes 9–11, 149–50, 155–6, 157, 158
opera 164
Ottoman Empire 13–14
outdoor and indoor working 85–7
ownership of means of production 2, 30, 85, 149, 152

painters
    apprenticeships with 95, 101
    of Dutch seaside 162–3, *163*
    guild of Saint Luke 44–5
    producing commercial art 33
    valorization criteria 142–3
panel painting, rise of 33, 34, 44
parasitism 130, 131, 132, 133
patenting 105
patron saints, representations of 39–40, *39*, 44
payments in kind 21, 22, 25
peasants
    depictions in paintings of 35–6, *35*
    duty to work 37
    housing 84, 85
    separation of workplace and household 84
    workplaces in agriculture 69, 70–1
Pfennwert 22
Pfister, Ulrich 111
Phelps Brown, E. H. 19–20, 26
physical exercise 166
picturing work 33–65
    allegorical themes 51–3
    in books and prints 39–43
    duty to work 36–9
    guilds 43–5, 136
    market and kitchen scenes 53–9
    satires of financial professions 48–50
    special regions or towns 45–7
    virtuous women 60–2
    vocational portraits 47–8
    women of easy virtue 62–5
    "Works of the Twelve Months" 33–6
piece rates or time rates of pay 25, 29, 30
Plato 150, 170
Polanyi, Karl 2
political culture of work 145–58
    politics in labor conflicts 151–7
    popular protest and evacuation of labor from politics 147–51
    revolts and rebellions 145–7
poor relief 6, 7, 120, 134
population growth 11, 19, 69, 114
    driving prices up and real wages down 20, 114
    and protoindustrialization 12–13
portraits, vocational 47–8, *48*
potters 74
poverty
    attitudes to women in 97, 98
    patrimony of 6, 7
    poor relief 6, 7, 120, 134

    Reformation and new responses to 6–7, 120
    socioeconomic mobility and 127–8
    views on causes and cures for 135
printing industry 78, *78*, 153–4
processions and rituals 96–7, 153, *153*, 156
productivity rates 26–7, 31
professionalization 89–91, 91–3
proletarianization 1–2, 7, 26, 148–9, 158
prostitutes 62–5, *64*, *65*, 98–9, *100*, 121, 132–3
Protestant Reformation
    attitudes to work 128, 130–1
    concerns over leisure and recreation 161, 164, 168
    confessional exiles 121–2
    and counter-reformation 5–7
    and new responses to poverty 6–7, 120
    regulation of prostitution 121
protests. *See* revolts and rebellions
protoindustrialization 12, 30, 85, 86
    and changing patterns of labor mobility 117
    fustian manufacturing 12–13
    and growing reliance on merchant capital 149
    ownership of means of production 2, 30, 85, 149, 152
    purchasing *(Kauf)* and putting out *(Verlag)* systems 149, 152
    worker guilds 107
public lectures 106, *106*

racist ideas about labor 125, 128
reason and practice 138–40
regional trades, images of 45–7, *47*
religious exiles 121–2
revolts and rebellions 145–7, 158
    and evacuation of labor from politics 147–51
    politics in labor 151–7
    rural 146
    triggers for 148
    urban 9, 10–11, 145, 147, 155
ribbon industry 111
ropemakers 74
royal patronage 172
rural
    economic actors, urban attempts to eradicate production of 156
    guilds 107
    labor mobility 114–16, 127
    revolts 146

Sadeler, Raphael 37, *38*
St. Eloy in his Workshop 39–40, *39*
saints' feasts 168, *168*
salt mines, Austrian Alps 86
schooling, learning by 104–6, 112
Schopper, Hartmann 40
scientific revolution 7–9, 67–8
sculptors 138, 142, 143
seafaring, learning skills of 107–8, *108*
seamstresses, Parisian 98
seaside as a leisure destination 162–3, *163*
seasonal migration 69, 70, 115
secrecy 105
separation of workplace and household 77, 83–5
serfdom 28, 29, 30, 32
serge production 45, 47
servants
    domestic 93–4, 100, 115, 119
    farm 107
    indentured 124
Seville, prostitution in 99
Sewell, William 4
sexual abuse 93
shipbuilders 79–83, *82*, 118
silk industry 43, *43*, 96–7
silver mines 45, 78–9, *80*, *81*, 87
skills and technology 101–12
    apprenticeships 101–4
    beyond urban crafts 107–8
    circulation of knowledge 102, 105, 107
    economic transformations and developments in 108–10
    government contributions to teaching of 106
    guilds and artisans in defense of 151–7, 157–8
    learning by schooling 104–6, 112
    technological change 110–11
    tramping 104
    variations in institutional and political contexts 111–12
slavery 28–9, 30, 32, 93, 124–6, *126*, 127, 128
Smith, Adam 2, 21
social class 3–4, 165
    and leisure 165–9
society and work 129–44
    definitions of work 17–18, 129
    duty to work 130–5
    shifts in valorization 136–43
    valorization criteria for work 129–30

socioeconomic mobility 127–8
Spain, domestic servants in 93–4
Spanish colonies 123, 125
spas 168
specialization in occupations 70, 71, 73, 74, 87
spinning 60–1, *61*, *62*, 85, 98
sport 168–9, 172
Ständebuch 40, *41*, 67, 74, *75*, *76*, *77*, 141
state formation, oligarchization and processes of 9–11, 149–50, 155–6, 157, 158
Statute of Artificers, 1563 152
Stradanus, Johannes 40–3, *42*, *43*, 78
strikes 151
the study space 84–5
sugar 28–9, *42*, *43*, 124, 125
Sundays 165, 172
surgeons 106, *106*, 138–9
surveyors 106
sustenance (*Nahrung*) 154
sutlers 51, *55*
Swanenburgh, Isaac 45, *47*
syphilis cure 40, *42*

tailors 74, *75*
tanners 44, *44*, 76–7, *76*
tax collectors 49–50, *49*
technical writings 105
technological innovations 3, 110–11, 112, 117
technology, skills and. *See* skills and technology
temporary work 69, 70, 115
theater 136, 164, 171, 172
theory and practice 138–40
Thirty Years' War 113, 114, 119, 122
Thompson, Edward P. 3
Tilly, Charles 10, 146
time rates or piece rates of pay 25, 29, 30
tinsmiths of Antwerp 154
trade
    long-distance 13–15, 19, 109, 110, 117–18
    secrets 105
traditionalism 5–6
training by the piece 104–5
tramping 104
tripartite model 130, 131, 166

unemployed 120–1, 135
university-educated scholars 139–40
urban
    attempts to eradicate countryside production 156

migration and labor 116–19
protests 9, 10–11, 145, 147, 155
rituals 96–7
socioeconomic mobility 127–8
workplaces 73–7
urbanization 11, 73, 109, 116–17
usurers 133–4

vagrants 120–1, *120*, 134
valorization criteria for work 129–30
duty to work 130–5
shifts in valorization 136–43
Veblen, Thorstein 165–6
Velázques, Diego 36, 59, *59*
Venice
administrative elite 90–1
Arsenale 79–83, *82*, 87
Vermis Sericus 43, *43*
vernacular science 139
Virgin Mary 60
Vivès, Juan Louis 7

wage studies
beyond the wage 27–31
definition of wage 28
different forms and systems of wages 21–2, 24–5, 142
divergence between productivity and real wages 26–7, 31
early history 18–20
mercury mine, Idrija 22–4
nominal wages 19, 31
payments in kind 21, 22, 25
piece rates or time rates of pay 25, 29, 30
population growth driving real wages down 20, 114
problem with 21–4
real wages 19–20, 31–2
revision of 24–7
unwaged 28–9, 30, 32
wage conflict 25–6
women workers 29, 30, 32
Wanderschaft 104
Wars of Religion 121, 122
weavers 85, 86, 137, 152
Weber, Max 5–6, 165
Welser, Peter 128
wine 163
women
active in master artisan workshops 141

in agriculture 71, 72, 116, *116*
allegorical depictions of sutlers 51, *55*
apprenticeships 103, 141
as assistants of St Eloy 39, *39*
attempts at banishment from workplace proper 84, 97, 100
attitude of protection and assistance of poor 97, 98
of easy virtue, images depicting 51, *55*, 62–5, *64*, *65*, *100*
guilds and restrictions on 97, 98, 100, 141
images of virtuous 60–2, *60*, *61*, *94*
indoor and outdoor labor 86
and leisure 169
part-time labor in protoindustry 30
as principle workers in crafts and trades 77
serge production 45, *47*
sieving silver ore 79, *81*
silk industry 43, *43*, 97
spinning 60–1, *61*, *62*, 85, 98
wages 29, 30, 32, 98
woodcuts 40, *41*, *46*, *52*
Woodward, Donald 21
wool
overseas trade in 12, 14, 117
production 45, *47*, 96
workplace cultures 89–100
becoming a master or mistress 95–7
education of civil servants 89–91
gender hierarchies 97
household cultures as 91–5
midwives 91–3
morality and immorality 98–100
workplaces 67–87
in agriculture 69–73
combination of indoor and outdoor 85–7
economic background 69
historical sources 67–9
in large enterprises 78–83, 87
reconstructing 16th century 67–9
spatial separation of dwellings and 77, 83–5
specialization in occupations 70, 71, 73, 74, 87
in urban crafts and trades 73–7
"Works of the Twelve Months" 33–6, *34*, *35*
writers 135

youth culture 169